REDS

Also by Maurice Isserman

The Winter Army: The World War II Odyssey
of the 10th Mountain Division, America's Elite Alpine Warriors

Continental Divide: A History of American Mountaineering

Fallen Giants: A History of Himalayan Mountaineering
from the Age of Empire to the Age of Extremes

The Other American: The Life of Michael Harrington

America Divided: The Civil War of the 1960s

If I Had a Hammer: The Death of the Old Left
and the Birth of the New Left

California Red: A Life in the American Communist Party

Which Side Were You On? The American Communist Party
During the Second World War

REDS

THE TRAGEDY OF AMERICAN COMMUNISM

MAURICE ISSERMAN

BASIC BOOKS

NEW YORK

Basic Books
Hachette Book Group
1290 Avenue of the Americas, New York, NY 10104
www.basicbooks.com

Printed in the United States of America
First Edition: June 2024

Published by Basic Books, an imprint of Hachette Book Group, Inc. The Basic Books name and logo is a registered trademark of the Hachette Book Group.

The Hachette Speakers Bureau provides a wide range of authors for speaking events. To find out more, go to hachettespeakersbureau.com or email HachetteSpeakers@hbgusa.com.

Basic books may be purchased in bulk for business, educational, or promotional use. For more information, please contact your local bookseller or the Hachette Book Group Special Markets Department at special.markets@hbgusa.com.

The publisher is not responsible for websites (or their content) that are not owned by the publisher.

Print book interior design by Sheryl Kober.

Library of Congress Cataloging-in-Publication Data
Names: Isserman, Maurice, author.
Title: Reds : the tragedy of American communism / Maurice Isserman.
Description: First edition. | New York : Basic Books, 2024. | Includes
    bibliographical references and index.
Identifiers: LCCN 2023040318 | ISBN 9781541620032 (hardcover) | ISBN
    9781541620025 (ebook)
Subjects: LCSH: Communist Party of the United States of America |
    Communism—United States—History.
Classification: LCC HX86 .I85 2024 | DDC 335.430973—dc23/eng/20230926
LC record available at https://lccn.loc.gov/2023040318

ISBNs: 9781541620032 (hardcover), 9781541620025 (ebook)
LSC-H
Printing 1, 2024

To my granddaughter Flora,

*who made her entry into the world and my life
the same week I completed the final draft*

What is written in the old books is no longer good enough. For where faith has been enthroned for a thousand years doubt now sits. Everyone says: right, that's what it says in the books, but let's have a look for ourselves.

—Bertolt Brecht,
A Life of Galileo, 1938

Never must the church tire of reminding men that they have a moral responsibility to be intelligent.

—Dr. Martin Luther King Jr.
"Love in Action," 1960

CONTENTS

Prologue

The test of a first rate intelligence is the ability to hold two opposed ideas in the mind at the same time, and still retain the ability to function.

—F. Scott Fitzgerald,
"The Crack-Up," 1936

It is possible to say many true things about the American Communist movement and yet not the whole truth. It is possible to be right about a part and yet wrong about the whole. The most contradictory things can be true—at different times and different places.

—Theodore Draper,
The Roots of American Communism, 1957

When the Red Army invaded Czechoslovakia in August 1968, ending the attempt by that country's Communist leaders to loosen their own party's dictatorial rule and institute in its place a liberalized "socialism with a human face," American Communist Party leaders endorsed the Soviet action, calling it a just and prudent measure necessary to prevent "counter-revolution." Gil Green, a veteran Communist, was among the few exceptions. In an interview with a reporter from the *New York Times*, he denounced the invasion as "completely unwarranted."[1]

1

In a memorandum to Federal Bureau of Investigation director J. Edgar Hoover, dated August 28, 1968, a Chicago FBI agent took note of Green's dissent and suggested he be "approached," with the aim of recruiting him as an informer:

> During the period of GREEN's residence [in Chicago] he was a maverick type. Apparently in New York City he has lost none of his independence and continues to be one of the most princi-palled [*sic*] members of the Communist Party (CP) hierarchy. . . . He has always believed in an independent brand of communism for the United States. In this respect he is different from other CP leaders who prostituted themselves long ago in their obedience to the Soviet line.[2]

Whether or not the FBI followed through is unknown, and it is almost certain that Green would have refused the offer. What is notable here is the willingness of one FBI agent to set aside his loathing for the Communist cause and its adherents, and recognize Green as a principled individual capable of thinking for himself. And he wasn't troubled by any apparent contradiction.

Ten years earlier, J. Edgar Hoover had published a best-selling polemic under his own name (actually ghostwritten for him by FBI agents), enti-tled *Masters of Deceit: The Story of Communism in America and How to Fight It*.[3] Communists certainly were capable of lying when it suited their political aims, as Gus Hall, the Party's leader in 1968, proved when he described the Soviet invasion of Czechoslovakia as a measure that would strengthen that country's independence. And yet, those kinds of state-ments only undermined the movement's credibility in the eyes of most Americans. The only form of deceit Communists truly excelled at was, in the end, self-deceit. Gil Green, by the 1960s, was an exception to the rule, as he struggled for the next several decades to break the movement he had devoted his life to away from its subservience to Soviet control. He believed in the Party's egalitarian ideals; he remembered its genuine achievements, especially in the struggles against racism and for industrial unionism in the 1930s; he was, as his admirer in the Chicago FBI office noted, determined and principled. And he was not alone in his desire to change the Party in fundamental ways. Throughout its history, from its founding in 1919 to the collapse of the Soviet Union in 1991, the Communist Party USA generated a stream of doubters, dissenters, and rebels against orthodoxy (most of whom, unlike Green, would depart its ranks sooner rather than later, either of their own volition or because they were expelled).

The history of American Communism requires the ability to weigh complex and often ambiguous evidence and judgments. Arriving at the "whole truth," as onetime Communist and pathfinding historian of the movement Theodore Draper argued, challenges facile generalizations. And, as novelist F. Scott Fitzgerald suggested more generally, two seemingly incompatible things can be true simultaneously. Contradiction and tension are present in any historical situation, and the search for understanding requires that these be made visible. Following the example of the FBI agent back in 1968, readers of what is to come should be prepared to keep two opposed ideas in mind. Those unwilling to do so would be well advised to put this book down *right now*. It's only going to get worse.

A few principal contradictions shaped the rise and fall of American Communism.

The Communist cause attracted egalitarian idealists, and it bred authoritarian zealots. Communism, like the Socialist movement from which it broke in 1919, arose from democratic premises. As democratic socialists whose political involvement began in the 1930s, Irving Howe and Lewis Coser despised Communism's betrayal of their ideals. Nonetheless, in an early and influential history of American Communism, published in 1957, they acknowledged that in the first years of the movement's existence thousands of genuinely well-intentioned idealists were drawn to the cause, including "immigrant workers for whom the dream of America had not come true, young people who blazed with hopes for a better world, intellectuals who found in the Russian Revolution a symbol of aspiration." And yet, those dreams, hopes, and aspirations were distorted and subverted by the instrument that was supposed to lead to their realization, the democratic-centralist party organization, devised by Russian revolutionary leader Vladimir Lenin to overthrow the tsarist autocracy.[4]

The Communist movement helped win democratic reforms that benefited millions of ordinary American citizens, at the same time that the movement championed a brutal totalitarian state responsible for the imprisonment and deaths of millions of Soviet citizens. In the 1930s, in the period of its greatest influence, the Communist Party fought for causes like unemployment insurance, social security, and racial equality that in years to come helped make the United States a better, fairer society. In coalition with non-Communists, they helped pushed the Democratic Party leftward in outlook and policy. And yet, although they were sometimes referred to as "liberals in a hurry," Communists believed that the ends to which they were hurrying were embodied by the "workers' state" taking shape in the Soviet Union under Joseph Stalin, a decidedly illiberal dystopian experiment. That they were, for the most part, genuinely ignorant of the brutality at the core of the Soviet system is no excuse. Others—including others on the non-Communist Left—saw clearly what American Communists indignantly denied, that life under Soviet Communism in the Stalin era was defined by pervasive fear of an all-powerful repressive regime that routinely and on a massive scale employed spying, denunciation, imprisonment, torture, and murder against innocent victims.

By the 1930s and 1940s, Communists had proven themselves skilled organizers of powerful industrial unions that served hundreds of thousands of rank-and-file members well, while at the same time clinging to fundamental and tendentious misunderstandings and fantasies about the lives and political outlook of working people in the United States. No radical movement in the entire history of the United States built a larger institutional base rooted in the American working class than that the Communist Party enjoyed in the late 1930s and into the 1940s, chiefly through its role in the creation of the Congress of Industrial Organizations (CIO) labor federation. The unions under direct Communist leadership, like the United Electrical, Radio and Machine Workers of America (UE) and the International Longshore and Warehouse Union (ILWU), delivered to their members substantial gains in wages and benefits, better working conditions, and job security. These unions also supported progressive causes in the workplace, including the principle of equal pay for equal work and the hiring and promotion of minorities. In most of the unions in which they were influential, however, Communists rarely counted more than a handful of rank-and-file members. Workers in the Great Depression and the years that followed for the most part did not support, and often vehemently opposed, the radical restructuring of American society that Communists hoped to achieve. The Communists' belief that their being dedicated union organizers meant that their Party actually understood and represented the values of millions of working-class Americans was a delusion.

The Communist Party USA was an advocacy group entitled to normal constitutional guarantees of free speech, and at certain times and places it was also a criminal conspiracy. Communists were in theory revolutionaries, but in practice, for the most part, law-abiding reformists. They dreamed of a wholesale transformation of their society and economy, but devoted themselves to securing important but modest improvements in the lives of ordinary Americans. Although they rarely elected any of their own members to public office, it certainly wasn't through a lack of trying. Most of the Communists who were arrested and jailed, as thousands would be from the 1920s through the 1950s, were charged with activities that, committed by a Republican or Democrat, would have been seen as evidence of civic virtue rather than criminal behavior—that is to say, speaking out publicly for their point of view. However, by the late 1930s, a small group of Communists, perhaps a few hundred all told, with the approval and collaboration of top Party leaders, were engaged in espionage activities on behalf of the Soviet Union, activities which continued during the Second World War and involved the theft of the most important military secrets of the war. Revelations about this espionage network a decade later made it easier to persecute other Communists, those engaged in advocacy and nothing more, as members of a treasonous conspiracy.

Finally, in what is the central contradiction that both defined the character of American Communism and doomed its political prospects, it was a movement that claimed to be founded on a rigorously self-aware and self-critical rationalism, the "science" of Marxism-Leninism, but sustained itself over many decades through what proved to be the blindest of faiths. The Communists' resolute self-confidence in the path they were following allowed them to persevere through difficult years of repression and isolation; their inability to doubt their leaders and their dogmas led to intellectual atrophy and political irrelevance. The Communist Party, in Dr. King's words, proved to be a church that failed to remind its parishioners of their "moral responsibility to be intelligent."

What follows is not intended as a happy or inspiring story. It is a cautionary tale of what went wrong, and certainly not a blueprint for a contemporary American Left to follow, save to its own disadvantage. Studying the history of American Communism should be neither an exercise in filiopietism, the excessive veneration of ancestors, nor of demonology, the classification of malevolent spirits. Between 1919 and 1991, American Communists were caught in a political tragedy made of good intentions gone awry, as well as bad ideas and bad faith. What their story offers is not in any sense a "usable past," but rather an exercise in gaining historical perspective. As the late radical (and non-Communist) historian William Appleman Williams observed in his book *The Tragedy of American Diplomacy*, "Only by grasping what we were is it possible to see how we changed . . . and to gain some perspective on what we are." Williams wanted his students and readers to make a leap of historical imagination, to leave the present behind them as they explored the very different world of the past. The true value of the "historical experience," he believed, "is one of going back into the past and returning to the present with a wider and more intense consciousness of the restrictions of our former outlook."[5]

Finally, this book is an attempt to tell the story of American Communism, not as an encyclopedic, esoteric, or antiquarian dive into "Party history," but rather as an integral part of twentieth-century American history. Communists were an important part of that history, as social critics and agents of much-needed social change, and, for much of that time, as targets of official repression and mass hysteria. Understanding the causes for their triumphs and their failures might provide a measure of insight into the political challenges of our own era.

"I Speak My Own Piece": American Radicals

1900–1919

Promising, indeed, is the outlook for Socialism in the United States. The very contemplation of the prospect is a well-spring of inspiration.

—Eugene V. Debs, 1900

I'm in the labor movement and I speak my own piece.

—Elizabeth Gurley Flynn, 1906

While still a high school student in New York City, Elizabeth Gurley Flynn was already an accomplished speaker for radical causes; indeed, she had won a grammar school debate competition advocating the then-controversial proposition that women as well as men were entitled to the right to vote. When it came to street-corner public speaking, she wrote proudly in her autobiography, "I took to it like a duck to water."[1]

Born in 1890 in Concord, New Hampshire, and raised in a working-class Bronx household by parents who cherished both Irish nationalist and revolutionary socialist dreams, as a teenager Flynn was drawn to an eclectic mixture of Marxist, anarchist, and feminist ideas. Dark-haired, blue-eyed, slender, and animated, the young woman was arrested for the first of many times one evening in August 1906, while "soapboxing" on a street corner in Manhattan's theater district. Someone in her audience took offense at her revolutionary sentiments and summoned the police. The newspapers took note, not out of any particular sympathy for her cause, but because of the appealing figure she represented in her white shirtwaist blouse and long skirt, in the full flush of her youthful beauty, often compared to a "wild Irish Rose" such as the one celebrated in a popular song of the era.

Elizabeth Gurley Flynn, circa 1920
(Photo by Apic/Bridgeman via Getty Images)

Broadway producer David Belasco took notice and sent Flynn tickets to his current hit, a romantic melodrama set in the California Gold Rush era, *Girl of the Golden West*. She came to see the play with her mother, and afterward Belasco met with the two of them in his office. He thought she had the potential to be a great actress. Would she consider a career on the stage? "Indeed not," the sixteen-year-old firebrand replied, "I'm in the labor movement, and I speak my own piece."[2]

Flynn's insistence that she spoke her "own piece" reveals a defining characteristic of American radicalism in the years leading up to the outbreak of the Great War in 1914. Americans who committed themselves to the dream of replacing a rapacious capitalist system with a socialist cooperative commonwealth were following no one else's script for how to bring about that great change. They were certainly inspired by the success that fellow socialists in other countries were achieving, particularly in Germany, where the Social Democratic Party (SPD) won over a third of the vote in the 1912 elections and became the largest single party in the lower house of the German parliament.[3] But admiration was different than imitation, let alone subordination. American radicals understood that they had to find and follow their own political path. Their radicalism was experimental, often highly individualistic, sometimes extremely naive, but distinctly native-born and of their own devising. And, for a brief, optimistic decade and a half their movement, as represented by two overlapping left-wing groups, the Industrial Workers of the World (IWW) and the Socialist Party (SP), seemed on the ascendant. What they did not expect was that events taking place thousands of miles from American shores, in a society dramatically different than their own, would alter the prospects for and the character of the radical movement in the United States for much of the century to follow.

Flynn spoke her piece through the Industrial Workers of the World. Although a devoted student, within a year of that first arrest she dropped out of high school and departed for the not-so-golden West of mining ranges and lumber camps as an itinerant IWW organizer. The IWW, founded in 1905 in Chicago, was a revolutionary labor federation. Its vision of how socialism would come about, shared with many Western European unionists of the era, was known as "syndicalism" and emphasized building militant unions committed to using direct-action tactics, both in the immediate interests of their members and with the ultimate goal of overthrowing capitalism. The Wobblies, as they were called, were not necessarily opposed to voting for Socialist candidates (some of them were also members of the SP) but believed that the achievement of socialism would in the end be realized by means of a general strike by the nation's workers.[4]

The main labor organization in the United States in the early years of the twentieth century, the American Federation of Labor (AFL), founded in 1886, differed from the IWW in two important ways. First, it espoused a commitment to "pure and simple" unionism that shunned political commitment to any party, radical or conservative. And second, most of the unions belonging to the AFL sought to organize workers like carpenters and masons into *craft unions*, that is, unions limited to those who shared a particular craft or skill. The federation did include some *industrial unions*, which united all workers employed in a given industry like the United Mine Workers, but industrial unionism was never a priority for the AFL leadership, and for the most part it ignored the far-more-numerous ranks of workers considered unskilled. Socialists did vie for influence within the AFL. However, they lacked the strength to change the direction set by the AFL's founder and longtime president Samuel Gompers, who, once he had shed his own youthful enthusiasm for the teachings of Karl Marx, became a bitter foe of labor radicalism of all stripes.[5]

The IWW, in contrast to the AFL, embraced as its mission organizing the unskilled as well as the skilled, women as well as men, immigrants as well as native-born, and Black as well as white workers, into what it called "One Big Union." Although the Wobblies led many strikes in the years between

1905 and 1917, they failed to create a stable, ongoing labor organization on a national (or in most places, even local) level and thus never proved a serious challenge to Gompers's "pure and simple" craft unionism. Nevertheless, as movement and myth, the IWW captured the hearts of a generation of radical activists. Its spirit shines through in the poem written by Wobbly journalist Ralph Chaplin in 1915, later to be enshrined in the labor anthem "Solidarity Forever" sung to the tune of "Battle Hymn of the Republic":

When the union's inspiration through the workers' blood shall run,
There can be no power greater anywhere beneath the sun;
Yet what force on earth is weaker than the feeble strength of one,
But the union makes us strong.[6]

That vision of working-class solidarity leading to a better world inspired Elizabeth Gurley Flynn and many others in the opening decades of the century.

In 1912, twenty-one years old and by then a seasoned organizer, Flynn was back east taking part in the IWW's greatest strike, when 30,000 textile workers from scores of ethnic backgrounds, a majority of them women and children, walked off their jobs in the mills in Lawrence, Massachusetts, to protest pay cuts. This was the famous "Bread and Roses Strike," so named for the banner carried by some of the women strikers, "We want Bread and Roses, too." The Lawrence workforce was typical of the ethnically and religiously diverse American working class of 1912, a year when 60 percent of industrial workers in twenty-one leading industries were foreign-born, and another 17 percent were the children of immigrants.[7]

Mary Heaton Vorse, like Flynn a socialist and feminist, traveled to Lawrence from her home in New York City to cover the strike, the beginning of her long career as a labor journalist. She went to strike headquarters, where a meeting was in progress. IWW leader "Big Bill" Haywood spoke briefly. Then another organizer came to the podium:

When Elizabeth Gurley Flynn spoke, the excitement of the crowd became a visible thing. She stood there . . . the picture of a youthful revolutionary girl leader. She stirred them, lifted them up in her appeal for solidarity. Then at the end of the meeting, they sang. It was as though a spurt of flame had gone through the audience, something stirring and powerful, a feeling which has made the liberation of people possible.[8]

After two months of hardship, facing down a bayonet-wielding state militia, the strikers were victorious (one of the rare IWW strikes that secured substantial gains for its members, although the IWW itself, all too typically, was unable to secure a permanent place in the Lawrence mills).[9]

Flynn's fellow IWW organizer, Joe Hill, shortly before he was executed on a frame-up murder charge in Utah in 1915, wrote a song believed to be inspired by her, which he titled "The Rebel Girl." Hill's song ended with the chorus:

We've had girls before, but we need some more
In the Industrial Workers of the World.
For it's great to fight for freedom
With a Rebel Girl.[10]

The year of the Lawrence strike was also the year of the Socialist Party's greatest electoral triumph. As Theodore Draper noted, "A Socialist of 1912 who dared to foresee the ruin of the party in seven short years would have been accused of morbid hallucinations."[11]

The Socialist Party of America was founded in 1901, drawing together a coalition of revolutionary and reform-minded political activists from big cities, small towns, and even isolated rural communities across the country, cherishing high ideals about the kind of imagined socialist community they would build in the future but also proving remarkably effective at practical electoral politics in the here and now.

America's best-known socialist in those years was Eugene Victor Debs. Born in Terre Haute, Indiana, in 1855 to French immigrant parents, Debs grew up in modest circumstances, his father a local businessman. Debs dropped out of school before turning fifteen and went to work in the local railroad yards. He mastered the craft of locomotive fireman, then considered a skilled and relatively prestigious calling, but his talents led him down another path. By the time he was twenty-five, he was editor of the national magazine of the Brotherhood of Locomotive Firemen. By thirty he had won election as a Democrat to the Indiana legislature. Given his intelligence and eloquence, his future seemed unbounded.[12]

Debs's views in those early Indiana days were anchored in contemporary and essentially conservative values celebrating self-sufficient manhood, as well as a desire to see social harmony prevail between labor and capital. By the early 1890s, however, he had come to feel that craft unionism was a dead end for the labor movement. Instead, he turned to industrial unionism, and in 1893 he helped organize and became president of the American Railway Union. The ARU enjoyed phenomenal early success, climaxing in the great Pullman strike of 1894 when a quarter million railroad workers in two dozen states shut down the nation's railroads in solidarity with striking workers who built Pullman sleeping cars in a Chicago factory. It was the greatest demonstration of labor solidarity up until then in American history.

In the end, however, the strike was broken by federal troops, and Debs was thrown in prison, supposedly for interfering with the mails, in reality for challenging the power of the railroad corporations. The union's demise sent Debs on a political trajectory that in a few years' time saw him emerge as the presidential standard-bearer for a small but growing Socialist movement. Running for president in 1900, he attracted a mere 100,000 votes. But that first of five presidential campaigns was just the beginning. As the

Eugene V. Debs, circa 1910
(Photo by Fotosearch/Getty Images)

Socialist Party's standard-bearer twelve years later, he won nearly a million votes, some 6 percent of the total. In some states, such as Oklahoma, Washington, and California, the Socialist share of the vote climbed into double digits.[13]

In the years between 1900 and 1912, Debs took on the status of a kind of secular prophet in the eyes of many of his followers, as he thundered condemnation of capitalism's sins in tones reminiscent of the prophet Jeremiah in the Old Testament. Debs belonged to no church. Even though he once declared he was uninterested in playing the role of Moses leading the Israelites to the Promised Land ("because if I could lead you in, someone else could lead you out"), he was comfortable speaking in the idioms of midwestern American Protestantism.[14] Debs read his Marx and Engels; he believed in class struggle, and international working-class solidarity, and the cooperative commonwealth. At the same time, his aspirations for America's socialist future were based on moral principles about democratic citizenship and individual responsibility that he had imbibed as a young man in Terre Haute. Like Elizabeth Gurley Flynn, he too spoke his own piece. "Despite his Socialism," Debs's biographer Nick Salvatore argued, "a fierce individualism fueled his core vision."[15]

In the years from 1901 to 1912, the Socialist Party expanded from 10,000 to nearly 120,000 members, its ranks swelled by Oklahoma dirt farmers, Montana copper miners, and Greenwich Village writers and artists, among many others. Self-identified revolutionary socialists coexisted in the same party with so-called sewer socialists (which is to say, reformists and gradualists, who sought incremental improvements in urban life). While the Socialist Party was not immune to the racism endemic in turn-of-the-century America, Socialists were among the founders of the National Association for the Advancement of Colored People (NAACP). The ideas of the Socialist movement attracted a growing following on college campuses, in church groups, and in the settlement house and women's suffrage movements. Twelve hundred Socialists were elected to public office in 1912, including mayors from communities as diverse as Flint, Butte, and Berkeley. Socialists Victor Berger from Milwaukee and Meyer London from the Lower East Side of Manhattan served in Congress, although not overlapping in office. The socialist press reached hundreds of thousands of readers. By 1912 the New York–based Yiddish-language *Jewish Daily Forward* (or *Forverts*) had a circulation of 120,000, while the Kansas-based weekly *Appeal to Reason* had a circulation at the same time of over a half million.[16]

The SP's successes fed a determinist strain in the movement's outlook that assumed the embrace of socialism by a majority of Americans was inevitable. "We know," declared a front-page article in a 1908 issue of the *Rochester [NY] Socialist*, "that the private ownership of the means of production and distribution will give way to the collective ownership of these things. . . . We arrive at this through a careful study and application of the great law of economic determinism."[17]

The Socialist Party, reflecting the habitual fractiousness of the organized Left, was by no means a peaceable kingdom. There were heated debates over questions of strategy and tactics. In 1912, at the same national convention that nominated Debs as the party's presidential candidate, a majority of Socialist delegates voted to oust IWW leader Big Bill Haywood from the SP's ruling executive committee for advocating the use of "sabotage" in strikes (a tactic that the IWW almost never employed, in reality, but a provocative term for which the organization's leaders had an inexplicable rhetorical fondness). There were sporadic bombings and assassinations by anarchists in the first years of the twentieth century, acts of terror condemned by Socialists yet resulting in suspicion being cast on all radical groups, including the SP and the IWW. Nonetheless, the Socialist Party kept growing, and both revolutionaries and reformists within its ranks regarded Debs as a guiding influence (for his part, Debs was an unapologetic revolutionist, but also had confidence that socialism would come via the ballot box, rather than through violent upheaval).[18]

The Socialist Party's internal organization reflected the country's mainstream political culture in its localism and lack of central control. The party depended on volunteer labor, with few paid positions, either in its national office or in local organizations. Socialist-affiliated newspapers, publishing houses, schools, and fraternal and cultural groups were for the most part organizationally independent of the SP, under their own leaders and with their own financing. The party's structure was grounded upon the American political map, with town- or city-based chapters overseen by representative bodies at the county and state levels and an elected National Executive Committee. As a by-product of the tremendous wave of immigrants arriving in America from eastern and southern Europe in the first decade and a half of the twentieth century, a parallel structure developed in those years around various ethnic groups organized into foreign-language federations, starting with a Finnish grouping in 1904. By 1917 their number had expanded to fourteen, representing nearly half the total SP membership.[19]

When war broke out in Europe in 1914, it shattered comforting assumptions about international working-class solidarity, as well as about the inevitable triumph of the socialist cause. In peacetime, German, French, and British Socialist leaders had pledged that their supporters would never allow themselves to be used as cannon fodder in an imperialist war. And yet, in all the belligerent powers except for Russia, Socialists now vowed support for their own country's war aims. Living initially in a neutral nation, American Socialists held to their traditional opposition to militarism. But their consistency brought little comfort. For SP leader Morris Hillquit, the beginning of the Great War represented "the collapse of human reason and the ugly sight of the world denuded of its thin veneer of civilization."[20]

SP membership dropped by almost 25,000 in the months right after the onset of hostilities. In 1916 Debs took a sabbatical from running for president, and journalist Allan L. Benson headed the Socialist ticket. Campaigning against the growing call for "preparedness" in case of US entry into the war, he won just over 590,000 votes, 3.19 percent of the total, less than two-thirds the amount Debs had received four years earlier. Many of those who dropped out of the movement were native-born Americans, resulting in the proportion of immigrants in the party climbing to over half the total membership.[21]

The war in Europe was mired in bloody stalemate for three years, during which millions of soldiers died, and the conflict seemed like it would go on forever. In 1917, however, things began to change. In April US president Woodrow Wilson, who had campaigned the previous year under the slogan "He Kept Us Out of War," went before Congress asking for a declaration of war against Imperial Germany. Congress voted for the declaration on April 6, although there were six votes against it in the Senate and fifty in the House of Representatives, one of the latter cast by Meyer London, the Socialist congressman from the Lower East Side. The Socialist Party, meeting in an emergency convention in St. Louis the day after the United States entered the conflict, adopted a resolution proclaiming "its unalterable opposition to the war just declared by the government of the United States."[22]

That was a momentous decision, its impact magnified by another development, the outbreak of revolution in tsarist Russia in the early spring of 1917. Twelve years earlier, in 1905, restive workers and peasants, and mutinous soldiers and sailors, had come close to bringing to an end the autocratic rule of Tsar Nicholas II over Russia and its empire. The tsar had survived that challenge, first through concessions, later through renewed repression. But the Russian army's defeats on the eastern front between 1914 and 1917, and shortages of food on the home front, led to the tsar's overthrow in March 1917 and the establishment of a provisional government that included representatives of the Mensheviks, Russia's moderate socialists. In the months that followed, American radicals in the SP and the IWW began to hear reports about another, more radical socialist party, the Bolsheviks, led by a heretofore-obscure Russian revolutionary leader named Vladimir Ilyich Lenin.[23]

In a 1902 pamphlet entitled *What Is to Be Done?* Lenin called upon fellow Russian socialists to create a "party of a new type," an organization composed of trained and disciplined professional revolutionaries prepared to act decisively and, if need be, ruthlessly, as the "vanguard of the proletariat." True revolutionaries, Lenin argued, needed to abide by a principle of internal party organization called "democratic centralism." In theory, open and unfettered debate about policy was permitted until a decision was reached—at which point discussion ceased, and the resulting "party line" was to be carried out without dissent. Lenin did not argue that this model would fit all countries and political situations;

his was a party specifically designed to operate in a country like Russia, where organizing mass, legal opposition was impossible under the tsarist autocracy.

The Bolsheviks (or "one of the majority") and their more moderate rivals within the Russian Social Democratic Labor Party (RSDLP), the Mensheviks ("one of the minority"), split in 1903 over just how centralized and clandestine an organization was required to carry on the struggle; their factional names were fixed when delegates from Lenin's grouping outvoted their opponents on the question of instituting a more exclusive definition of party membership at the RSDLP's Second Congress, held that year in Brussels and London. Lenin wanted a tightly disciplined organization, while his opponents favored a looser, larger group. Of course, émigré revolutionaries were always squabbling over such matters, usually to no lasting effect. Both sides expected the split to be temporary (they would meet again as a united party in London in 1907 to hash out the meaning of Russia's near-revolution of 1905), and it was only in 1912 that what had been regarded up until then as two factions within a single party formally reorganized as separate parties with distinct and opposing identities. Even after their split, they were not necessarily enemies on all issues. In 1914, most of the Mensheviks, like the Bolsheviks, opposed the war, although unlike Lenin did not call for turning imperialist war into civil war.[24]

And yet, fundamental and irreconcilable principles grew out of the fracturing of the Russian socialist movement. The Mensheviks remained democratic socialists who regretted the necessity for conspiratorial measures under the tsar; the Bolsheviks found in those measures the essence of their political identity. Another Russian revolutionary leader, Leon Trotsky, did not fully commit himself in the years leading up to 1917 to either the Menshevik or Bolshevik camp. But in 1904, then aligned with the Mensheviks, he warned prophetically that "Lenin's methods" would kill the democratic aspirations of socialism: "The party organization at first substitutes itself for the party as a whole; then the Central Committee substitutes itself for the organization; and finally a single 'dictator' substitutes itself for the Central Committee."[25]

In the years before the revolution, and even at the start of the 1917 revolution, Lenin's Bolshevik party was by no means fully "Leninist" as that term later came to mean. Lenin was in exile in Western Europe for much of the time between 1900 and 1917, thus was often out of touch with his party's rank and file. The Bolsheviks who remained within the borders of the Russian empire, those that were able to escape jail or exile in Siberia, operated with considerable local autonomy rather than centralism, democratic or otherwise.[26]

The full extent of the differences separating the Mensheviks' views and Lenin's came to the fore only with the overthrow of the tsar. In Russia in the spring of 1917, the Mensheviks (along with another party of the Left, the Socialist Revolutionaries) enjoyed greater popular support than the Bolsheviks. In the judgment of historian Orlando Figes, "The Mensheviks were democrats by instinct and their actions as revolutionaries were always held back by the moral scruples which this entailed. This was not true of the Bolsheviks."[27]

Constrained by their scruples, along with the belief that Russia needed to go through a period of capitalist development, a "bourgeois revolution," before being ready to advance to socialism, the Mensheviks did not attempt to seize power in their own name. Instead, they lent their support to the provisional government representing a coalition of anti-tsarist parties. In those early spring days in 1917 before Lenin returned from exile, Bolshevik leaders, although not similarly wedded to democratic principles, shared the belief that the provisional government would remain in power for the foreseeable future, even if they opposed it. That would change only when Lenin returned from exile in Switzerland to Russia in April and set his comrades on the road to a second revolution.[28]

Leon Trotsky also was in exile and far away when the tsar was overthrown. Trotsky had arrived in New York City on January 13, 1917, settling with his family in an apartment in the Bronx, expecting a long stay. He was a celebrity among Russian-born socialists in the city, who remembered his leading role in the 1905 revolution, which saw the creation of "soviets," or workers' councils, in Saint Petersburg and other cities. He had a busy speaking schedule in New York, Philadelphia, and other cities. He was famously unimpressed by the American socialist leaders he met during his stay, with the exception of Eugene Debs, dismissing the moderate Morris Hillquit, for example, as "the ideal socialist spokesman for successful dentists."[29]

In the second week in March, Trotsky's expectations of a long sojourn in the United States came to an abrupt end when news arrived of the abdication of Tsar Nicholas II. He and other exiles set sail for home on March 27, arriving in Petrograd (Saint Petersburg's wartime name) in mid-May. Lenin and Trotsky were now in agreement, committed to an attempt to seize absolute power, supposedly for the "soviets," in reality for the Bolshevik Party. Before the year was out, to the astonishment of the world, in the space of a just few days in early November, they succeeded.[30]

American radicals knew little about the Bolsheviks, except that on taking power they pledged an immediate armistice to end the fighting on the eastern front, and favored a peace settlement based on the principle of self-determination. That was enough to secure the admiration and sympathies of their American comrades, at least at first. The Socialist Party's National Executive Committee declared in February 1918, "The revolution of the Russian socialists threatens the thrones of Europe and makes the whole capitalist structure tremble. . . . We glory in their achievement and inevitable triumph." Eugene Debs declared at the start of 1919, "Every drop of blood in my veins is Bolshevik."[31]

No one played a more influential role in shaping this early favorable impression of Lenin and Trotsky's revolution among American leftists than radical journalist John "Jack" Reed. Born in Portland, Oregon, in 1887, and raised in a wealthy household, he came east to attend prep school, and then enrolled at Harvard in 1906. There, in addition to his studies, he attended meetings of the Harvard Socialist Club, where he was influenced by Walter Lippmann, later to become a Pulitzer Prize–winning journalist.[32]

After graduating Harvard, Reed decided he too would try his hand at journalism, moving to New York City's Greenwich Village, where in 1913 he became an editor of *The Masses*, the monthly magazine that served as the iconoclastic voice of prewar radical bohemia, a forum for socialists, anarchists, Wobblies, feminists, and other freethinkers. It was a busy and formative year for the young journalist; he was arrested in Paterson, New Jersey, where he went to support an IWW-led strike of textile workers. Later the same year he traveled to Mexico and established a national reputation as a war correspondent sending back colorful and sympathetic accounts of the Mexican Revolution. When war broke out in Europe, he headed for the front and reported from both France and Germany. Back in the United States in 1915, he fell in love with Portland journalist Louise Bryant, who abandoned her husband to join him in Greenwich Village.[33]

Reed became a mythic figure for many of the American Left in the coming decade, especially among its bohemian wing (as well as, many years later, the lead character in the single American feature film ever explicitly devoted to the history of American Communism, Warren Beatty's 1981 epic *Reds*). In some ways, Reed was an unlikely champion of a hard-line group of disciplined ideologues like those who shaped the Bolshevik Party. As his biographer Robert Rosenstone noted, Reed influenced artistic, intellectual, and radical political circles in the United States that "optimistically proclaimed a revolution on the way," one that "would free society from the hand of the past and usher in a new age of self-fulfillment."[34] Self-fulfillment did not rank high on the Bolshevik virtues scale.

In September 1917, six months after the overthrow of the tsar and the same month that the Petrograd and Moscow soviets elected Bolshevik majorities for the first time, Louise Bryant and John Reed arrived in Petrograd (Reed as correspondent for *The Masses*, Bryant for an independent news syndicate). Reed's dispatches were published in the newly founded magazine *The Liberator*, successor to *The Masses* (suppressed by the US government in 1917 for its anti-war views). Collected and expanded, they would form the basis for *Ten Days That Shook the World*, published in 1919, which became the classic journalistic account of the Bolshevik Revolution.

On November 7, 1917, Reed was in the Smolny Institute, headquarters of the Saint Petersburg soviet. Around the Russian capital, armed groups of workers, soldiers, and sailors, calling themselves Red Guards, seized government offices, telegraph offices, railway stations, bridges, and other vital institutions in a coup d'état. In the Smolny building, Reed was present to witness the moment when Menshevik and other socialist opponents of the Bolshevik seizure of power walked out in protest. Left-Menshevik leader Julius Martov and a few others remained, still hoping against hope for a compromise, until Trotsky ("standing up with a pale, cruel face," in Reed's description), delivered his famous contemptuous dismissal: "Let them go! They are just so much refuse which will be swept into the garbage-heap [sometimes rendered as 'the dustbin'] of history!"[35]

From there Reed, Bryant, and three other American companions rode in the back of a truck filled with armed Bolshevik "Red Guards" to the Winter Palace, ex-residence of the tsar and last stronghold of supporters of the provisional government. The fighting, which was very brief and limited given the stakes involved, was over. The Americans strolled through the splendor of the palace halls before taking a cab back to Smolny. Finally, exhausted, they stumbled out onto the city streets at six in the morning on November 8, a moment that Reed somewhat ambivalently recalled as one of "the shadow of a terrible dawn grey-rising over Russia."[36]

In the months following the revolution, as Irving Howe noted, "hardly anyone in America really knew what was happening in Russia," since most of what appeared in the non-radical press was "drenched with malice" and could hardly be credited, at least by radicals who had seen how they themselves were being slandered in the same newspapers. "Once, however, John Reed started filling the pages of the *Liberator* with his brilliant narrative about 'ten days that shook the world'—an account of the Bolshevik revolution with the imperial simplicities of myth—then the American radicals could find a source of guidance and inspiration: *this is how it happened, this is how it's done.*"[37]

The seeming triumph of shared socialist ideals in the new revolutionary state in Russia was all the more stirring because American radicals were themselves under siege, accused of being (simultaneously) pro–Bolshevik Russia and pro–Imperial Germany. President Woodrow Wilson is supposed to have remarked in April 1917, "Once lead this people into war, and they'll forget there ever was such a thing as tolerance."[38] The rise in vigilante violence in the following months certainly suggested as much. More than seventy people were murdered by mobs in 1917–1918 in the United States for suspected disloyalty.[39]

Putting his liberal regrets behind him, if indeed he had any, Wilson proceeded to establish and preside over the official repressive machinery that enforced the suppression of civil liberties over the next few years. The administration-backed Espionage Act was introduced into Congress in the first days of the war. The core of the bill was the provision that anyone who "shall willfully cause or attempt to cause insubordination, disloyalty, mutiny or refusal of duty in the military or naval forces of the United States, or shall willfully obstruct the recruiting or enlisting service of the United States" could be arrested and sent to prison for up to twenty years. Another provision allowed the postmaster general to ban what he determined to be treasonable matter from the mails, a power used to suppress dozens of socialist newspapers and magazines. And, if that wasn't enough, the Sedition Act, passed by Congress the following year, authorized long prison sentences for anyone who dared to "utter, print, write, or publish any disloyal, scurrilous, or abusive language about the form of government of the United States," the Constitution, or even "the uniform of the Army or Navy." All told, nearly 2,000 Americans would be arrested for violation of the Espionage and Sedition Acts.[40]

Among their number was Eugene Debs. On June 16, 1918, speaking before a large crowd in Canton, Ohio, where he had come to support local Socialists jailed for opposing the war, he declared, as frowning federal agents on the scene scribbled down his words: "The man of Galilee, the carpenter, the working man who became the revolutionary agitator of his day, soon found himself to be an undesirable citizen in the eyes of the ruling knaves and they had him crucified."[41]

Debs devoted just one paragraph of his lengthy Canton address to expressing his opposition to the war. "The master class has always declared the wars," he noted, while "the subject class has always fought the battles." But that was enough under the Espionage Act to bring his indictment and conviction.[42]

Debs spoke as a class-conscious Marxist, but consciously or not, in his Canton speech he also drew on a strain of Protestant radicalism stretching back to the founding days of the Massachusetts Bay Colony, when Anne Hutchinson challenged the authority of the established ministry in that theocratic state in the famous "Antinomian controversy." Antinomianism, literally "being against or opposed to the law," was a term of abuse applied by orthodox Puritans to those who dared to assert a direct communication from God—or personal revelation—as the basis for their dissent. Two centuries later, another Massachusetts radical, the abolitionist William Lloyd Garrison, promised in the first issue of his newspaper *The Liberator* to be "as harsh as truth, and as uncompromising as justice." Frederick Douglass, John Brown, Elizabeth Cady Stanton, and Margaret Sanger followed in the same tradition. Theirs was a morally charged radicalism, in which they spoke their own piece. As did Debs.

In difficult debates within the Socialist movement, of which there were never any shortage, Debs spoke in private letters of the necessity of following "the inner light that God put there to guide through dark places."[43] In 1918, speaking to the court after being sentenced, he thundered in the voice of Hutchinsonian/Garrisonian revelation: "Your Honor, years ago I recognized my kinship with all living beings, and I made up my mind that I was not one bit better than the meanest on earth. I said then, and I say now, that while there is a lower class, I am in it, and while there is a criminal element, I am of it, and while there is a soul in prison, I am not free."[44]

Approaching age sixty-four, Debs began serving his sentence in April 1919 in a state prison in West Virginia, and after two months was transferred to Atlanta Federal Penitentiary. In his cell in Atlanta the only picture he hung on the wall was of Christ on the cross. In the end, pardoned by the newly elected president Warren G. Harding, Debs served less than three years of his ten-year sentence, but his health was broken.

It wasn't only left-wing revolutionaries who faced the fury of official repression. Victor Berger was a founding member of the Socialist Party, a congressman, and the most famous "sewer socialist" in the prewar socialist movement. Though a believer in reform, not revolution, he was nonetheless an outspoken opponent of the war when it came in 1917. Indicted under the Espionage Act in February 1918, he was convicted in January 1919 and sentenced to twenty years in federal penitentiary (ten years longer than Debs's sentence). In the meantime, he had won reelection to his old seat in Congress. The House of Representatives twice refused to seat him after he was elected by Milwaukee voters in 1918 and 1919. Finally, in 1922, after his Espionage Act conviction was overturned by the US Supreme Court, Berger was once again elected to Congress and allowed to take his seat.[45]

If that was how the courts treated moderate elected officials, the outspoken revolutionaries of the IWW could hardly expect anything less, even though the Wobblies did not officially campaign against the war. However, supporting strikes in wartime was treated as a species of treason. Some, like IWW organizer Frank Little, brutally lynched by a mob in Butte, Montana, on August 1, 1917, paid with their lives. The IWW leadership, 101 all told, including Big Bill Haywood, were convicted of violating the Espionage Act in a mass trial in Chicago in 1918; Haywood and fourteen others got twenty-year sentences, while the others were given sentences of between one and ten years.[46]

The Red Scare continued in full force through the spring of 1920, and took many forms, including the mass arrest of thousands of foreign-born radicals—Russian, Jewish, Italian—and the deportation of hundreds, including famed anarchist Emma Goldman. Many of those arrests were overseen by a young Washington bureaucrat with boundless ambitions named J. Edgar Hoover, who in 1919 became director of the federal Justice Department's "Radical Division," forerunner of the Federal Bureau of Investigation (FBI), which was established in 1924 with Hoover as its first and only director down to his death in 1972.[47]

In late January 1919, Soviet Commissar for Foreign Affairs Georgi Vasilievich Chicherin, a veteran Russian revolutionary who had spent many years in exile in Western Europe, invited left-wing groups around the world to convene later that spring for the founding of a new international federation of revolutionary parties to replace the Socialist International. Among those invited were representatives of the Industrial Workers of the World and "the Left Wing of the American Socialist Party." No Americans, as it turned out, were able to attend the resulting gathering in Moscow that March, and indeed, very few of the delegates who attended from thirty-odd countries represented organized revolutionary parties in their homelands, an inauspicious beginning. Still, the founding of the Communist International, better known as the Comintern, would have a major impact on the future of American radicalism. (The Comintern would also be referred to as the "Third" International. The "First" International was the International

Workingmen's Association, founded in London in 1864, which foundered in 1876 due to quarrels between the followers of Karl Marx and rival socialists and anarchists; the "Second" International was the Socialist International, founded in Paris in 1889.)[48]

A great strike wave unfolded in the United States in the first year after the end of the war, starting with a general strike of Seattle's workers in February 1919, and eventually including steelworkers, coal miners, and even the Boston police force, 4 million workers all told, or a fifth of the workforce.[49]

Even in this moment of intense class struggle, America's radicals were largely absent, either defending themselves from official repression or engaged in fierce internal factional battles within the Socialist Party. The party's left wing, centered in the foreign-language federations, wanted to emulate the Bolsheviks and sought to take control of or split from the existing Socialist Party. The party's reformist wing was determined to prevent either outcome by suspending or expelling the organizations controlled by the left-wingers. That list eventually added up to seven of the language federations, and a number of state organizations. As a result, between January and July 1919, the SP's membership fell from nearly 110,000 to under 40,000.[50]

The decisive split took place between August 30 and September 2, 1919, in Chicago, where the Socialist Party held its national convention. The official SP delegates, carefully selected to keep out the left-wingers, met in a hall on South Ashland Boulevard starting on August 30, while those future Communists who had already given up on the SP would meet two days later in the Russian federation headquarters on Blue Island Avenue. A third group, led by John Reed and Benjamin Gitlow, planned to attend the Socialist gathering before moving on to their own separate meeting, but they were unceremoniously removed by police when they sought to take seats in the SP's auditorium on the first day. The following day the ousted delegates reconvened—in the same building on a different floor—to found what became the Communist Labor Party (CLP). Meanwhile, the other Communist delegates, those who had already given up on the SP, began their convention on September 1, but not before the Chicago police raided their hall and tore down pictures of Marx, Trotsky, and Lenin. They then founded the Communist Party of America (CPA). Both parties, the CLP and the CPA, were outspokenly revolutionary in outlook, disdaining reform of any sort, favoring the establishment of "the dictatorship of the proletariat" in the United States, and opposing cooperation with any non-Communist groups. Both pledged allegiance to the newly founded Communist International. Despite their seeming similarities, desultory unity negotiations between the two rival parties came to nothing.[51]

The Debsian era of American radicalism was at an end. And so was a certain innocence that had characterized the movement from 1900 until the Great War. Debs, of course, was in prison in 1919 and played no role in the splintering of the Socialist Party that year. Helpless to intervene, in failing health and spirits, he wrote in an undated note from Atlanta Penitentiary to his lover Mabel Curry, relating a dream he had as he slept uneasily on the cot in his cell: "I was walking by the house where I was born—the house was gone and nothing left but ashes. All about me were ashes. My feet sank in them and my shoes filled with them. . . . I awoke. Outside it was thundering and lightning and rain was falling. I did not go to sleep again—The house was gone—and only ashes—Ashes!"[52] As Debs languished in prison, what, if anything, would arise from the ashes of the Socialist movement in years to come remained to be determined.

CHAPTER 1

The Flood or the Ebb?

1919–1927

The memory of the spring of 1919 has not faded. . . . Any spring is a time of overturn, but then Lenin was alive, the Seattle general strike had seemed the beginning of the flood instead of the beginning of the ebb.

—John Dos Passos, prelude to the reprint
of his 1921 novel *Three Soldiers,* 1932

Once the Communist movement matured, it became the prisoner of its own development. It gradually created precedents, traditions, rituals. But there was a time when everything was new, fresh, and sponta-neous. Every crisis was the first crisis. Every move was unrehearsed.

—Theodore Draper, *The Roots of American Communism,* 1957

For many on the Left in the United States, 1919 seemed the begin-ning of the flood tide. The Bolshevik Revolution was a year and a half old; a spirit of working-class unrest was abroad from Seattle to Berlin. For revolutionary-minded socialists, syndicalists, and anarchists in the

United States, recent events in Russia served as a combination of prophetic inspiration and practical how-to manual.

In October 1919, barely a month after the founding of the Communist Party of America (CPA), its newspaper *The Communist* proclaimed that the strikes convulsing the nation's steel towns could well prove "the turning point of the American working-class movement . . . the 1905 of the American proletarian revolution."[1] But 1919 did not turn out to be the American 1905, the prelude to the final victory. The great steel strike, supported by hundreds of thousands of workers in that brutally exploitative industry, failed to secure union recognition, let alone spark proletarian revolution (which was not its goal). And yet, a year later, undaunted, Communists in New York City responded to a far smaller strike involving a thousand workers at the Brooklyn Rapid Transit Company with the same enthusiasm for extravagantly misinformed historical analogy. "Broaden and deepen your strike," the CPA's leaflets in the fall of 1920 exhorted the transit workers (whose demands were concerned only with such trivial issues as better pay and working conditions). "Make it a political strike. Get ready for armed revolution to overthrow the Capitalist Government and create a Workers Government—as your brothers did in Russia."[2]

"Get ready for armed revolution"? With the benefit of hindsight, it's hard to avoid responding with a dismissive question. How could anyone be so delusional? Any number of plausible answers readily come to mind: naivete, fanaticism, ignorance.

But impatience with those who came before us doesn't serve our understanding of what seem, from a distant vantage point, their manifest shortcomings. As former British Communist E. P. Thompson wrote of the "obsolete," "utopian," and "deluded" English working-class radicals of the early nineteenth century, it was necessary to rescue them from "the enormous condescension of posterity."[3] In the case

Bolshevik soldiers marching through the streets of Moscow, circa 1919
(Photo by HUM Images/Universal Images Group via Getty Images)

of American Communists, a similar leap of historical imagination is required if we are to understand the expectations of millennial transformation they displayed in those early days of spontaneous and unrehearsed responses to unprecedented events in a faraway land. Consider the grainy black-and-white photographs from Petrograd (the wartime name of Saint Petersburg) and Moscow of crowds of workers and armed soldiers bearing banners with Bolshevik slogans in the days leading up to and immediately following the revolution of November 1917. Such images represented the fulfillment of a dream, long cherished, but only half-believed until then. Like Christianity, the appeal of the Russian Revolution lay in a compelling narrative, a story of righteousness triumphant. If a tiny minority of Bolsheviks, no more than 24,000 strong in the first months of 1917, could be ruling vast and distant Russia less than a year later, why couldn't the same near-miraculous outcome happen closer to home? Karl Marx had been a great admirer of William Shakespeare, and some of Marx's disciples in that revolutionary season of 1917–1919 must have been reminded of Brutus's proclamation in act 4 of *Julius Caesar*: "There is a tide in the affairs of men / Which, taken at the flood, leads on to fortune."[4]

What's more, the revolution in Soviet Russia, a country that had chosen a wonderfully exotic and evocative name for what was proclaimed to be its new democratic government, embodied the finest aspects of socialism's traditional egalitarian promise. Or so it seemed. Twenty-three-year-old American writer John Dos Passos, recently discharged from the US Army after wartime service as an ambulance driver in France, at work on what turned out to be his breakthrough novel, *Three Soldiers*, wrote hopefully in 1919 to a friend about events in Russia. "One has to remember," he cautioned, "that all that is published in the [capitalist] press is propaganda." The truth, Dos Passos believed, was that "the *Bolsheviki* are . . . moderate social revolutionaries," and the system of government they had created in Russia was "pure democracy," based as it was on the principle "that every man shall take part in the direct government of the country." Dos Passos had little political experience before 1919. But his hopes regarding the new Russia were shared by untold thousands of more politically sophisticated radicals, in the United States, Europe, and elsewhere.[5]

Barbara Rosenblum, a Hungarian Jewish immigrant living in Denver, was among their number. She responded to the reports from Russia by signing up as a charter member of the Communist Party in 1919. Before becoming a Communist, she had been a Socialist Party member, and an IWW sympathizer. Democracy and human equality taken to their full measure were the political values she cherished and were what drew her, pre-1917, to the movements led by Eugene Debs and Big Bill Haywood. She loved to recite the closing stanza of Percy Bysshe Shelley's "The Masque of Anarchy," composed a century earlier in 1819 to commemorate the working-class martyrs of that year's Peterloo Massacre in Britain:

Rise like lions after slumber
In unvanquishable NUMBER!
Shake your chains to earth like dew
Which in sleep had fall'n on you:
YE ARE MANY—THEY ARE FEW.[6]

The Romantic poets and historical imagination notwithstanding, revolutionary lions in unvanquishable number were not roused from slumber by the Bolshevik triumph, certainly not in Denver, nor even in New York City. Outside the realm of poetry, how could it have proven otherwise?

In reality, the Russian Revolution was singular and exceptional, in no sense prophetic of the impending demise of capitalism, particularly American capitalism. In its final decades, the tsarist regime was both brutal and decrepit, discredited by repeated military defeats, unable to count on the loyalty of its own army or navy, overseeing a faltering and largely agricultural economy. The United States, in contrast, was a nation whose star was in the ascendant. It was an emergent global power, the financial and manufacturing capital of the world, basking in victory gained in its first European war, home to a flawed democracy divided by stark class and racial inequalities that nonetheless commanded the widespread allegiance of its citizenry, including ordinary working people.

In any case, 1919 did not prove the beginning of the left-wing flood in the United States or elsewhere. As that tide ebbed, it was right-wing reaction, inspired by the real or imagined threat of homegrown Bolsheviks, that reached flood stage in the industrialized capitalist world. Socialism, by grim necessity, would need to be built in a single country, Russia. And prospects there looked none too promising, as the Bolshevik seizure of power was followed in the next half decade by civil war, foreign intervention, peasant revolts, epidemics, and famine, not to mention the new regime's own policies, all too often foolhardy, bungled, and inhumane.

Most Americans drawn to Communism by the heroic example of 1917 in Russia soon decided the movement either was not for them, or had no future in the United States. Of roughly 40,000 members of the two rival American Communist parties in the autumn of 1919, barely 12,000 remained two years later, and their numbers continued to decline thereafter.[7] The history of American Communism might have ended in the early 1920s, a brief fizzle of misplaced enthusiasm saved from obscurity only by the derision those gaudy rhetorical excesses provoked among subsequent generations of historians. "Get ready for armed revolution," indeed.

And yet, in that first crisis of faith in the American Communist movement, a hard core of believers proved immune to doubts and disillusionment. Denver's Barbara Rosenblum was among their number; her then-five-year-old daughter Dorothy, later known as Dorothy Healey, would grow up to become an important Communist leader. That the final conflict was postponed, the Bolsheviks' American admirers reluctantly came to accept, but their belief in its eventual triumph remained intact. Indeed, with the international revolutionary wave receding, they clung all the more fiercely to the hopes they had invested in the lone outpost of proletarian power.

The Communist movement in the United States in its first few years consisted largely of veteran radicals drawn from what had been notably freethinking organizations like the SP and IWW. And in the beginning, as Theodore Draper noted, "American Communism was not very different in its methods and make-up from other American radical movements." Despite taking inspiration from abroad, the first Communist conventions "were wide open, the discussions free, the leaders democratically chosen." In many ways, Draper concluded, the movement "still reflected more of the movements of the past—socialism and syndicalism—than of the future, communism."[8]

Benjamin Gitlow, a New Jersey–born son of Jewish immigrant parents, was among those coming from a socialist background into the leadership of the new Communist movement. He had joined the Socialist Party at age eighteen, and seven years later in November 1917, he had been elected to the New York State Assembly on the SP's ticket. Gitlow would not always prove in later years the most reliable chronicler of his days within the Communist Party. But there is a ring of sincerity to his judgment of his time in the Socialist Party: "American radicalism," he wrote, rested in the prewar years on "the bedrock of individual liberty and recognition of the rights of man."[9]

Had there been no Bolshevik Revolution, or had that founding generation of American Communists passed away before 1919, they would be remembered today as homegrown radicals like the SP's Eugene Debs and the IWW's Big Bill Haywood, rebels against oppression and exploitation, gutsy defenders of human rights, and honored accordingly at least in historical memory, if not always in their own lifetimes. That was not their destiny.

The first generation of rank-and-file American Communists was mostly working-class, European-born or descended, and male. The largest ethnic grouping within the movement in the mid-1920s was Finnish, located mostly in insular communities in Michigan, Minnesota, and the Pacific Northwest. Jewish members were also numerous, and more visible because they were concentrated in cities like New York, Philadelphia, Chicago, and Los Angeles. Communists from Lithuania, Ukraine, Russia, Poland, Yugoslavia, and Bulgaria could be found in big cities, especially Chicago and Detroit, but also in smaller coal-mining communities like Scranton and Wilkes-Barre in eastern Pennsylvania, and Uniontown and Bentleyville in the western side of the state. There were Germans in Milwaukee and Cleveland—Italians, Greeks, and others in New York City. There were almost no Communists in the southern states, or in the non-coastal states of the West. Although a distinct minority, there were some native-born, Protestant old-stock Communists, scattered across the country from New England to San Francisco. There were also a few (very few) Black members too, many of them, including four out of the first five members to join the Communist movement in Harlem, born in the West Indies. That included Otto Huiswoud, born in Suriname in the Dutch West Indies, who was the sole Black delegate attending the founding meeting of the Communist Party in September 1919. There were some prominent women in the Communist Party, including feminists like California women's suffrage activist Charlotte Anita Whitney (also worth noting as one of those rare old-stock Americans), but the Communists showed little interest in women's issues in the 1920s and made next to no effort to recruit female members, who remained a distinct minority for the first two decades of the movement.[10]

For the few thousand American Communists who did not depart the movement in its first years, Soviet Russia (after December 30, 1922, known as the Union of Soviet Socialist Republics, or the USSR, or the Soviet Union) became the unquestionable authority on left-wing strategy, tactics, and organization. Prose supplanted poetry as a hard-edged "Leninism" replaced romantic lyricism. A road to the promised land, embodied in a code of righteous and rigorous personal and organizational conduct, took form in the imagination of revolutionaries. In the flood times of revolutionary upheaval, the Communist Party would be the organizers of victory; in the ebb times of reaction (the latter far more frequent and protracted as things turned out in the twentieth century) the Party's primary mission lay in keeping faith with a new phenomenon on the revolutionary Left known as Leninism.

Authoritarian hierarchy, not democratic egalitarianism, was the essential organizing principle of Leninism. In the two years that followed the Bolshevik Revolution, the Soviet government banned the Mensheviks, shut down their newspapers, and exiled or jailed their leaders. Socialist Revolutionaries, Jewish Bundists, anarchists, and other non-Bolshevik leftists met the same fate.[11] Communists (the name the Bolsheviks took for themselves once in power) thought of themselves as soldiers at war, and there was no reason to regret the casualties inflicted on those outside their ranks, even if they were fellow revolutionaries. The "foundation of Leninism," as Joseph Stalin defined it in a series of lectures delivered following Lenin's death in 1924, was the understanding that "the working class without a revolutionary party is an army without a General Staff." The Party, he declared in words that became the basic catechism of Communism for millions of followers around the world in years to come, was "the military staff of the proletariat."[12]

Another military term destined to become common, first in the Soviet Communist Party and then throughout the international Communist movement, was "cadre." In an army, the cadre consists of the officers and noncommissioned officers who are in charge of training the subordinate ranks. Communist cadre assumed comparable responsibilities within the Party. The military analogies, with all that they implied about obedience and self-sacrifice, were not chosen casually. "We must train people who will devote the whole of their lives," Lenin wrote in the revolutionary newspaper *Iskra* in 1900, "not only their spare evenings, to the revolution."[13]

James Patrick Cannon was one of those Americans who early on heeded Lenin's call. Born in 1890 to English immigrants of Irish stock in a suburb of Kansas City, Kansas, by the time he was a teenager he was supporting himself by working ten-hour days in a packinghouse. At age eighteen, in 1908, he joined the Socialist Party, then a few years later became an itinerant agitator for the IWW—a "foot-loose Wobbly rebel," as he later nostalgically described his younger self.[14] The Bolshevik Revolution led him to rejoin the Socialist Party, so that he could be part of the left-wing forces tugging it into the revolutionary camp. He then became a founding member of the Communist Labor Party. A talented speaker with impeccable working-class credentials, he rose quickly in the movement's hierarchy. As he did so, his kinship with his footloose youth faded to sentimental memory.

Some years later, Cannon sought to explain the distinction between the Communists of his own generation and earlier Socialists: "The leader typical of the old Socialist Party," he wrote with obvious contempt, "was a lawyer practicing law, or a preacher practicing preaching . . . who condescended to come around and make a speech once in a while." Echoing Lenin, he declared that, for Communists, "the principle was laid down that these leaders must be professional workers for the party, must put their whole time and their whole lives at the disposal of the party."[15]

In coming decades, American Communists embraced many policies and slogans, often contradicting those that came before. What remained unchanged was the imperative to "Build the Party!" Every new member recruited represented progress toward the ultimate revolutionary goal, even if the numbers remained tiny compared to the overall population.

But first there had to be *a party*, a single party, instead of several squabbling claimants for the name of "Communist." A mind-befogging succession of splits and mergers befell early American Communism, leaving behind a multitude of defunct organizational acronyms. There is, of course, nothing new about factional battles in radical history. In the nineteenth century, American abolitionists, suffragists, and socialists each repeatedly split off from old organizations to form rival groupings. Splits could, on occasion, revive movements that had been in decline or stalemate. The vibrant Debsian-era Socialist Party itself came into existence thanks to a split at the beginning of the twentieth century within an earlier socialist group, the moribund Socialist Labor Party led by Daniel De Leon. Those who joined the Communist movement in its early years expected that their own willingness to part ways with former comrades would have a similar effect.

Instead, between 1919 and 1923, the splitters wandered through a desolate sectarian wilderness, where internal bickering replaced meaningful political engagement. Briefly, in the spring of 1920, there were two rival claimants for the title of being *the* official American Communist party.

One was the Communist Party of America (CPA), dominated by the Russian language federation. Although overwhelmingly foreign-born in composition, it included some native-born English-speaking leaders, including Charles E. Ruthenberg. The other contender was the Communist Labor Party (CLP), smaller in number than the Russian-dominated CPA, but with a somewhat larger contingent of native-born English speakers and leaders, including John Reed, Benjamin Gitlow, and James P. Cannon.

For the first months after coming into existence in 1919, both the CPA and the CLP functioned aboveground, starting publications, holding open gatherings, and maintaining public headquarters. In a message to the Communist rivals in January 1920, Comintern president Grigory Zinoviev called for their unification—but also for the creation of a parallel underground organization. What the Soviets had not envisioned was that their American comrades would abandon their aboveground activities for the underground—and then prefer to remain there. That meant keeping to a strict minimum public activities, gatherings, campaigns, and identifiable members. As Cannon confessed at a Comintern meeting in 1922, the American Communists' clandestine existence "is regarded by the masses as a good deal of a joke. They think [the Communist movement] is illegal because we want to be illegal."[16]

Over the years, Communists rewrote their history to eliminate its more embarrassing aspects. Joseph Freeman, who joined the movement in the early 1920s and became a prominent figure in the Party's literary establishment, argued in his 1936 memoir *An American Testament* that Communists faced only two choices in the 1920s: "political suicide," or "to exist as best they could in secret until their right to normal political activity was restored." With the end of the Justice Department raids rounding up foreign-born radicals in 1920, "the Communists began to take steps toward the formation of an open Communist Party."[17]

Freeman's account wasn't completely wrong: in the face of ferocious repression, the Communists' decision to curtail aboveground activities took place in circumstances not of their own making. But Freeman failed to note that the Socialist Party, of which he had previously been a member, still continued to the best of its abilities in the early 1920s to function openly and aboveground, despite the fact that its most prominent leader, Eugene Debs, was in federal prison; scores of other officials were facing federal charges; the US Congress refused to seat the duly elected Socialist congressman from Milwaukee, Victor Berger; and the New York State Assembly gave the same treatment to five elected Socialist assemblymen. At the Red Scare's height, in other words, Socialists chose to conduct themselves in a manner consistent with faith in the ultimate restoration of democratic norms.

The Communists' decision to go underground in 1920 reflected their rejection of those norms. The democratic rights that they were unjustly being denied were, it turned out, rights that they no longer honored themselves. In January 1921, Communist leader Robert Minor declared, in a debate in New York City with Socialist leader James Oneal, that a true revolutionary "will take a position of free speech when it is the bourgeois dictatorship that is on top, and he will take a position against free speech when it is the workers on top."[18] That was not an argument ideally suited to rally civil libertarians to defend persecuted Communists, although many principled liberals, including members of the newly established American Civil Liberties Union (ACLU), did so. Joseph Freeman, who worked as publicity director for the ACLU in the 1920s, nevertheless came to the conclusion that "under capitalism democracy was an illusion." Constitutional rights "were ours only so long as we did not exercise them against the propertied classes."[19]

While imprisoned, and in the few years remaining to him following his release from prison, Eugene Debs attempted to avoid polemics with the Communists. "Mistakes have been made on all sides," Debs wrote in April 1920. "I can fight capitalists but not comrades."[20] Nevertheless, in time he grew disenchanted with the Bolshevik Revolution itself. "There is certainly something that is radically wrong with the policy of Soviet Russia in dealing with those who are not in accord with its program," he wrote shortly before his death in 1926. "I have heartily favored Soviet Russia from the hour it was born and have supported it with my pen and from the platform to the full extent of my power, but I have been utterly opposed to the cruel Soviet policy which has proscribed the expression of opinion and made a crime of all honest opposition."[21]

In contrast to Debs, who fully understood that civil liberties in the United States were at best conditionally available to left-wing dissenters and yet remained a defender of traditional democratic rights, the belief in the illusory nature of "bourgeois democracy" helped Communists justify in their own minds their support for proletarian dictatorship in Russia (being "against free speech when it is the workers on top"). It also blinded them to the possibilities for securing a meaningful role for themselves within the existing political system in the United States. They turned abstention from active political engagement in those early years into a hard-and-fast revolutionary principle. Clinging to underground existence, the Communists were reduced to small groups of like-minded comrades, meeting occasionally and clandestinely in one another's homes, unwilling to recruit new members who they felt could not be trusted. American Communism in the underground era bore little resemblance to a movement setting forth to remake the world.[22]

Although 1920 was an election year, the two Communist parties did not support a single candidate for office, not even their former comrade Debs, who was running for president while a prisoner in Atlanta Penitentiary. Instead, Communists passed out leaflets with the slogan "Workers Don't Vote! Strike! Boycott This Election!"[23]

What seemed a more pressing question in 1920 than any election was which of the rival Communist parties would win Moscow's recognition as the official franchise of the Communist International. The contestants were themselves unstable coalitions, and in April the Communist Party of America split in two, with Ruthenberg and a young associate, Jay Love-stone, chafing under the dominance of the Russian federation, forming a rival group. That meant that now there were three Communist parties in the United States, two of them bearing the name Communist Party of America and one the Communist Labor Party (and all underground). Their number was again reduced to two when the Ruthenberg-Lovestone CPA merged with the Reed-Gitlow-Cannon CLP to form the United Communist Party (UCP).[24] And that's when the story begins to get complicated.

Moscow invoked its authority to force a merger between the CPA and the UCP. After many twists, turns, splits, ultimatums, and telegraphic cables zinging back and forth from Moscow to New York (famous riddle in left-wing circles from the era: "Why is the Communist Party like the Brooklyn Bridge?" Answer: "Because it is suspended by cables"), a single aboveground Workers Party of America was founded over the course of 1922–1923, opening its headquarters in Chicago in September 1923, and counting some 15,395 members.[25] In 1925, the party's name was modified to the conglomerate Workers (Communist) Party, and again changed in 1929 to the name it would bear thereafter (with the exception of a few months in 1944–1945), the Communist Party USA.[26]

Charles Emil Ruthenberg, known to intimate friends and comrades as "C. E.," was named to the highest post of the united party, executive secretary (the title would be changed to general secretary in 1925, reflecting Soviet usage). Forty years old when he took office, Ruthenberg was born in Cleveland to German immigrant parents. A bookkeeper by trade, he joined the Socialist Party in 1909 and became a frequent candidate for local public office on the Socialist ticket. In 1917, he won a quarter of the votes in the Cleveland mayoral campaign. He became a national leader in the SP's left wing in 1919, and a leader of the Communist Party of America later that year. He had none of the personal charisma of a Eugene Debs, but he possessed genuine organizational skills, which he applied to the advantage of the Party, and also to keeping his own faction in control.[27]

When the underground era began, Communists were instructed to destroy their Party membership cards. With the gradual return to public existence in the mid-1920s, they were again issued cards, on which were recorded their monthly dues payments. The cards issued in 1925 to members of the Workers Party proudly affirmed, "The undersigned declares his adherence to the program and statutes of the Communist International."[28]

And what of the Communist International, to whose program and statutes American Communists pledged adherence? On its founding in 1919, it was not yet clear to foreign admirers of Bolshevism how the new international federation would differ from the old Socialist International. Before the war, individual Socialists varied in their interest in the doings of the Socialist International; Eugene Debs, for one, never bothered to attend any of the regularly scheduled congresses of the International in those years.

No Americans were present for the founding meeting of the Communist International in Moscow in March 1919. Only two attended the Second World Congress in 1920, Louis Fraina from the CPA and John Reed from the CLP. Four American delegates attended the third Comintern congress the following year. Thereafter, the numbers of Americans increased dramatically. By 1928 their delegation to the Sixth World Congress was twenty-nine strong.

Along with greater numbers came an increasing time commitment for those journeying to Moscow. The congresses themselves lasted a month, and often American Communists would remain afterward for additional consultations. Cumulatively these regular sojourns in Moscow represented the formative experience of a generation of Communist leaders from around the world.

For those aspiring to Party leadership, attendance at the Moscow gatherings represented a necessary rite of passage, as well as what was probably a welcome break from routine. Communists who back home met in shabby offices and halls, subsisted on meager wages, and knew themselves to be a despised minority were now traveling on a regular basis, all expenses paid, as honored guests of the new Soviet state. In the summer of 1920 when Fraina and Reed arrived in Saint Petersburg for the opening sessions of the Second Congress, they proceeded to their seats in the Opera House auditorium with the other foreign delegates, while a two-hundred-member band played "The Internationale." Moving on to Moscow for subsequent meetings, the delegates were welcomed by a quarter million workers, let off from their jobs on paid holiday for the occasion, who gave the appearance of being very happy to see them. The delegates were housed in hotels on Tverskaya Street, in what had been the most fashionable district in Moscow in tsarist times. The status accorded them in Soviet Russia offered a glimpse of what might one day be their lot in a Soviet America. Enjoying privileges not available to ordinary Soviet citizens, they were inclined to overlook the queues for food, the children begging in the street, and the increasingly all-prevailing fear of the secret police.[29]

Starting in 1923, the Party stationed a full-time representative to the Communist International in Moscow. Others were soon given the opportunity for extended stays as apprentice revolutionaries in training. In 1926, at the initiative of the Comintern, the International Lenin School opened and welcomed seventy Communists from Western Europe and North America as students. For the next dozen years, until it was shut down in 1938, the Lenin School enrolled and trained around 3,500 students from around the world, including over 200 from the United States. The school offered a yearlong course of study in revolutionary theory, economics, history, and political strategy and tactics, which was sometimes extended to two or more years. Lenin School credentials often led to assignments in the Comintern's international operations, where practical lessons were learned about clandestine organization. Upon returning to the United States, the Lenin School/Comintern-underground graduates often enjoyed a swift rise in the CPUSA's hierarchy, their ranks including two future Party general secretaries, as well as at least twenty-nine future members of the Party's Central Committee.[30]

From the movement's earliest days, the Communist International supported American Communism with secret financial subsidies, the infamous "Moscow Gold" that Communists always strenuously denied receiving. John Reed was arrested in Finland in the spring of 1920 while he was en route to the United States with diamonds worth roughly $14,000 in his possession. Over the next several years jewels and other valuables, worth nearly 3 million rubles in total, were smuggled by one means or another into the United States.[31]

The Second World Congress of the Communist International, which ran from July 19 through August 20, 1920, has been described by historians of the Comintern as its real founding.[32] In 1919 the delegates were a ragtag assemblage of foreign radicals who happened to find themselves in Moscow. The 1920 gathering drew together delegates from already-established Communist parties, or from significant independent parties considering affiliation.

First on the congress's agenda was the adoption of the requirements for parties joining the Communist International, better known for their total as the "Twenty-One Conditions." The most important was number sixteen, which declared unequivocally, "All decisions of the Congresses of the Communist International and decisions of its Executive Committee are binding on all parties belonging to the Communist International." In 1914, the old Socialist International had been unable to take a unified stand against the onset of World War I because each party went its own way, most choosing to back their own countries. The Communist International was designed to prevent such disunity from ever happening again.[33]

The Second Congress made it clear that international Communism was a movement open only to disciplined revolutionaries. At the very same time, it tested the discipline of its adherents by taking a cautious step backward from the revolutionary pronouncements of the First Congress in 1919. In the year between those two gatherings, Lenin had begun a critical reexamination of his earlier assumptions about the prospects for world revolution. Revolutionary upheavals in Germany, Hungary, and elsewhere met defeat, while the Red Army's attempt to spread socialism from Russia to neighboring Poland on the tips of its bayonets had been hurled back. Ever the political realist, Lenin had no compunction about deploying a tactical retreat when circumstances demanded. His polemic *"Left-Wing" Communism: An Infantile Disorder*, published in April 1920, condemned foreign Communists who believed that they should reject any political engagement short of revolutionary agitation.[34]

Lenin drew on examples from Germany and Britain to illustrate those infantile disorders, and said nothing about the two American Communist parties, although he could easily have done so. In any case, the new line, which tiptoed back toward something resembling the detested reformism of the old Socialist Party, came as a shock to American Communists who thought they had left all that behind. They had no choice but to go along. Charles Shipman, a young American attending the second Comintern congress as a delegate from the Mexican Communist Party (he had been living in Mexico to avoid the draft during the war), recalled that he and other delegates "were openmouthed, almost scandalized, as they read the pamphlet. Any author but Lenin—the expounder, organizer, and engineer of revolution—they would have proclaimed an arrant opportunist."[35] A retreat from revolutionary adventurism thus represented at one and the same time a sensible embrace of a more pragmatic perspective and a fateful tightening of Soviet control over the Comintern's member parties.

Another decision announced at the Second Congress had a dramatic impact on the nascent American Communist movement. That was the surprise ruling that "dual unionism" was henceforth forbidden to Communists, and "boring from within" existing trade unions was the correct labor strategy. In the United States that meant that Communists should no longer simply abstain from involvement in trade union activities, the position of the CPA, or support the Industrial Workers of the World, the position of the CLP. Instead, they needed to devote themselves to working within the American Federation of Labor, an organization both rivals despised.

There was a reasonable argument to be made for this shift, insofar as it meant abandoning some Communists' lingering romantic attachment to the IWW. Although the heroic legends of its prewar days never disappeared on the Left, the IWW lived a shadow existence in coming decades. Wartime repression had effectively killed the organization, although contributing to its decline was the decision by its best-known leader, Big Bill Haywood, facing a twenty-year sentence under the Espionage Act, to seek refuge in the Soviet Union, where he remained until his death in 1928.[36]

John Reed was among the romantic revolutionaries who found it hard to part with the IWW. Reed reported to comrades in the United States following the Second Congress that he expected the Comintern's mistaken decision would be reversed at the following year's gathering in Moscow.[37]

It would not be long before such open dissent would be the occasion for immediate expulsion, but in 1920 it was still possible for someone like Reed, well-known to and indulged by Soviet leaders in Moscow, to get away with it. In any case, Reed died two months later in Moscow of typhus and was buried with high honors beneath the Kremlin Wall. He was just thirty-three years old. No one among the founding generation of American Communists had contributed more to the mythic appeal of the Bolshevik Revolution in the United States.[38]

The next three Comintern congresses, in 1921, 1922, and 1924, continued the relatively moderate policies ordained in 1920. The mid-1920s were seen from Moscow as an era of "capitalist stabilization" in which

Communists would have to bide their time. Even Leon Trotsky, uncomfortable with the new policy, admitted to the delegates at the Third Congress, "We told ourselves back in 1919 that [world revolution] was a matter of months, but now we say that it is perhaps a question of several years."[39]

These years also saw a moderation of Soviet domestic policies, with Lenin's announcement in March 1921 of the New Economic Policy, a strategic retreat from the rigid and economically devastating state control of the previous period. It worked, at least to the extent of bringing a modest increase in living standards over the next half dozen years.

The regime's new flexibility in domestic economic policy had no counterpart in political liberalization. In 1921 a rebellion by sailors in the port city of Kronstadt, where the Russian Baltic Fleet was based, sought to defend the democratic and egalitarian promise of the revolution that they had helped to make four years earlier. It was crushed by Red Army troops, whose assault on the rebels was personally authorized by Trotsky. This was also the year, not coincidentally, that the Tenth Party Congress of the Soviet Communist Party officially banned oppositional factionalism (supposedly "temporarily").[40]

The most important development in the early to mid-1920s, both for the future of the Soviet Union and international Communism, was the emergence of Joseph Stalin as Lenin's heir. An obscure figure in Bolshevik history before 1917, Stalin was appointed general secretary of the Soviet Communist Party in April 1922. At the time that was considered a relatively minor administrative post, with responsibility for overseeing party discipline and recruitment. However, it gave Stalin, who possessed the right personal combination of ruthlessness, cynicism, and cunning necessary to thrive in the Soviet leadership's predatory internal politics, the opportunity to build an unstoppable factional machine.

Few American Communists prior to 1924 would have picked Stalin as Lenin's successor. Leon Trotsky was far better known internationally, his name linked to Lenin's as the key figure in making the Bolshevik Revolution, an aloof but charismatic leader. Grigory Zinoviev, Lenin's closest coworker in the years leading up to the revolution, appointed head of the Comintern in 1920, was a skilled orator if an unsympathetic character. Trotsky or Zinoviev, rather than Stalin, seemed the logical candidate to succeed Lenin.[41]

But in the crucial months after Lenin died in January 1924, Zinoviev feared Trotsky as a rival more than he did Stalin. He and another of the veteran Old Bolshevik leaders, Soviet Politburo chairman Lev Kamenev, allied themselves with the Party's general secretary in the internal factionalism of 1924–1925. To the extent that the split in the Soviet leadership was about issues beyond personal power, Trotsky and his supporters (who constituted the "Left Opposition") remained committed to the idea that spreading the revolution abroad, or "permanent revolution," was necessary for the survival of socialism in Russia, while Stalin and his allies embraced the idea of "building socialism in one country," with no expectation in the near future of securing aid from revolutions in more advanced societies elsewhere.[42]

For all his brilliance as orator and writer, Trotsky proved an inept factionalist. He was a latecomer to Bolshevism, and although Lenin valued his contributions to the revolution's success, others regarded him as an interloper. Trotsky was fatally slow countering Stalin's consolidation of power. At the Thirteenth Party Congress in May 1924, under attack from the "troika" (Stalin, Zinoviev, and Kamenev), Trotsky disavowed any intention of going into opposition over policy differences, declaring that "in the last instance the party is always right. . . . One can only be right with the party and through the party."[43]

The Stalin-Zinoviev-Kamenev alliance unraveled in 1925, when Stalin no longer needed his erstwhile allies. Trotsky remained the archenemy, but Zinoviev and Kamenev were now cast into disgrace. Stalin made a new alliance with Nikolai Bukharin, who was identified with the moderate wing of the Soviet party. As a sign of his rising stature, Bukharin was promoted to Comintern president in Zinoviev's place in 1926. Throughout the years in which Stalin consolidated his power, American Communist leaders took careful note of who among the Soviet elite they should associate with and who should be shunned.[44]

And what of rank-and-file American Communists in the 1920s, those who did not enjoy the perquisites of all-expense-paid trips to Moscow, and never got to meet with any of the contenders for leadership of the Soviet Union? What sustained their loyalty through those bleak years?

Few rank and filers left memoirs reflecting on party life in the 1920s. One notable exception was written late in life by Peggy Dennis (wife of Eugene Dennis, the Communist Party's general secretary from 1945 to 1959). Dennis, born Regina Karasick in 1909 in New York City, was the daughter of Russian Jewish immigrant parents who came to the United States in the early years of the twentieth century. Cloakmakers, socialists, and ardent unionists, they clung to their revolutionary beliefs in their new home, first in New York and then in Los Angeles, where they moved when Peggy was three.

The Karasicks settled in a cottage in the working-class neighborhood of Boyle Heights, home to the city's burgeoning Jewish population, as well as Japanese, Mexican, Italian, and other immigrant groups. For many years to come, the neighborhood remained the center of Communist strength and left-wing trade unionism in Los Angeles. It was there, in 1922, that Peggy joined a Communist children's group, the Young Pioneers. The Karasick family was poor, and their offspring wore home-sewn clothes, but at least as Dennis chose to remember those days, she and her sister happily embraced her parents' values as part of "a vanguard far removed from mainstream America." The Karasicks, young and old, were "fiercely proud" of the things that separated them from their non-Communist neighbors: "For public occasions we wore the flaming red, embroidered shirts of the Soviet Russians, our songs pledged our lives to the International Soviet that would free the human race. We were confident that we alone were tapped by history to fulfill its mission for humanity's liberation from exploitation and oppression."[45]

Years later, arriving in the Soviet Union on her first visit to join her partner Eugene Dennis working for the Comintern, Dennis recalled, "I wanted to shout '*tovarich!*' to all Moscow. Six thousand miles from home, I was Home. Here everything was truly '*nahsh*'—ours, everyone was '*nahsh braht*'—our brothers."[46]

Comradeship, the promise of a redemptive future in which scientific and moral perfection went hand in hand, and above all an intense identification with the Soviet Union brought solace to rank-and-file Communists. The Party encouraged its members to think of the Soviet Union as their true homeland: it was the "Socialist Fatherland of All Workers."[47] The daughter of recent immigrants to the United States, uprooted and vulnerable in a society whose values she was taught to reject, Dennis found little in 1920s America to admire (at least nothing she mentions in her memoir); such feelings were saved for the achievements, real or imagined, of a distant "fatherland" she had never seen, that was still, somehow, populated by *nahsh braht*.

By mid-decade Communists began to create an aboveground political infrastructure, at first limited in scope and visibility, but surprisingly durable. In 1922, the Communists began publishing a daily Yiddish-language newspaper, based in Chicago, and edited by Moissaye J. Olgin. It was called the *Di Frayhayt* (in English, *Freedom*), renamed the *Morgn [Morning] Frayhayt* in 1927 when it moved to New York City. Committed in its early years to promoting both socialism and Yiddish culture, and featuring articles by prominent non-Communists as well as Party writers, it soon boasted a

circulation of 22,000, making it the largest-circulation Communist period-
ical of the decade, although with only a tenth of the readers of the socialist
Yiddish daily *Forverts* (*Forward*).[48]

In 1922, the Party also launched a weekly English-language newspaper, *The Worker*, at first based in Chicago. In 1924, the newspaper began
publishing six times a week and changed its name to become the *Daily
Worker*, the first English-language daily Communist newspaper in the
world. Like the *Morgn Frayhayt*, the *Daily Worker* moved to New York
City in 1927. With the demise of the socialist newspaper the *New York Call*
in 1923, the CP would be the only left-wing group in America with a daily
English-language newspaper. All told, the Communists published nine
daily papers and twenty-one weekly papers in the 1920s.[49]

In 1926, Communist and non-Communist writers in New York
collaborated in the founding of a new monthly literary and political
magazine, the *New Masses*. As the name suggested, it was meant to fill
the vacuum left by the demise of the original radical and free-spirited
Masses of the prewar era. It included orthodox Communists like Mike
Gold among its founders, but also some independent radicals like John
Dos Passos. Now settled in Greenwich Village after his return from
the war, Dos Passos exhibited an intense individualism and hatred of
authority, which both made him a rebel and prevented him from joining the Communist Party. As he declared in the second issue of the
New Masses, "I don't think there should be any more phrases, badges,
opinions, banners, imported from Russia or anywhere else."[50] He was,
however, still willing to work with Communists when their concerns
coincided, particularly in the defense of the many victims of political
repression in the first decade following World War I. "We have heard a
great deal in these last years," he wrote in *The Nation* in December 1920,
"of the duty of the individual to his government." But, he continued,
"it is time something were said of the individual to his own integrity."
American citizens, he thought, should form the habit "of loudly and

immediately repudiating every abuse internal and external of the government's authority and every instance of bullying and intolerance."[51] When Dos Passos spoke his own piece, it was very much in the voice of the prewar American Left.

Unfortunately for the future of the *New Masses*, and more broadly the American Left, it was the now-orthodox Gold, rather than the still-heterodox Dos Passos, who was destined to take over as editor of the magazine in 1928, by which time the original diversity of opinion on the editorial board was a thing of the past. Under Gold and subsequent editors the *New Masses* remained the CP's chief magazine of cultural and political commentary for several decades, switching to a weekly publication schedule in 1934.[52]

Other organizational initiatives in the mid-1920s included the creation of the Workers School in New York City in 1923, the first of a national network of adult-education schools in the 1930s and 1940s, in time offering classes in everything from dialectical materialism to platform-speaking to detective-story writing (the latter taught by best-selling mystery writer Dashiell Hammett). Working-class "self-education" had long been a staple of radical movements on both sides of the Atlantic, and the CP's emphasis on the importance of reading and discussion in a formal setting was one important way in which the Party remained true to earlier left-wing traditions. A noteworthy innovation of the curriculum in the Communist schools was the emphasis on Black history, in some cases taught by pioneering historians in the field, at a time when courses in the subject were rarely offered in the nation's leading colleges and universities. The Workers School was later renamed the Jefferson School of Social Science. By the 1930s the school enrolled thousands of students annually.[53]

The Party's main publishing outlet, International Publishers, was established in New York in 1924 by Alexander Trachtenberg. It offered works by American Communist writers, but its bread and butter lay in successive editions in English translation of Marx and Engels, Lenin, and

Stalin. Many of its books were sold through a network of party bookstores that opened in the United States by the 1930s.[54]

Also noteworthy was the creation in 1925 of the International Labor Defense (ILD), an organization that campaigned on behalf of those whom the Communists referred to as "class war prisoners," arrested in labor struggles or for political crimes. Under the leadership initially of James Cannon, the ILD maintained national headquarters in Chicago. It provided legal aid, publicity, and "prisoner's relief" in the form of spending money to those in jail, and funds to support their families. While under Communist control, it also aided defendants and prisoners who were not members of the Party (including a number of IWW prisoners during the 1920s), and maintained ties with others on the Left, including Socialists, Wobblies, and liberals. Eugene Debs, who otherwise kept organizational distance from the Communist movement, agreed to serve on its national board.[55]

The most important organizational initiative undertaken by Communists in the mid-1920s was represented by the Trade Union Educational League. The dominant figure in that effort was William Z. Foster.

Born in Taunton, Massachusetts, in 1881 to Irish immigrant parents, Foster grew up in the Philadelphia slums. He quit school at ten, and he was educated in the class struggle in some of the hardest, most dangerous, and worst-paid jobs in working-class America, from foundries to lumber camps to merchant ships. Foster was drawn to the Left, passing through the SP and the IWW before founding his own Syndicalist League of North America in 1912. Foster thought that the working class was potentially strongest in the workplace, or what radicals called "at the point of production," the site where workers—by a strategic withdrawal of their labor—could win the most gains for themselves in the short run, while in the long run threatening the very existence of the capitalist system. Foster also believed workers could exercise that power only if they built stable industrial unions. That, he decided, could best be achieved by working within the mainstream of the trade union movement in the United States, the American Federation of Labor.

Foster's vision found few supporters on the Left in the prewar years, and his syndicalist league soon disbanded. He continued to believe in the value of "boring from within" the AFL, and doing so himself he gained national prominence during the Great War by leading a successful organizing campaign under AFL auspices among Chicago packinghouse workers. In 1919, he headed up the AFL's steel-organizing drive, and although it ultimately failed, it was among the most ambitious attempts yet undertaken to organize a major American industry on a national basis.[56]

At the start of the 1920s, Foster seemed on track to become one of America's preeminent labor leaders. In November 1920, he founded a successor group to the prewar syndicalist league, this time with the more neutral-sounding name of the Trade Union Educational League (TUEL). The organization was based in Chicago, where Foster had strong ties with local union leaders. TUEL, like his earlier syndicalist league, sought to work within the AFL to spread the doctrines of industrial unionism.

The Communists initially regarded Foster as a lackey of the conservative wing of the trade union movement. When the Second World Congress of the Comintern in 1920 voted to repudiate dual unionism, however, the Communists reevaluated Foster, and he reevaluated them. At last, he thought, his own boring-from-within strategy had a chance of supplanting the IWW's hold on the imagination of labor's left-wingers.[57]

The new Communist trade union policy was directed by the Red International of Labor Unions (Profintern in its Russian abbreviation), in effect the trade union wing of the Comintern. Foster decided to attend its founding congress in July 1921. Returning from what turned into a three-month stay in Moscow, Foster secretly joined the Workers Party. Upon revealing his new allegiance in 1923, he was regarded as the leading Communist authority in trade union matters, and he would remain so for the next three decades. That made him a strong contender for Party leadership.[58]

Economically, the 1920s posed both challenges and opportunities for radical groups in the labor movement. The Comintern had decreed it an era of "capitalist stabilization"; in the United States it was more like capitalist utopia, with soaring corporate profits and low taxes benefiting the wealthy. A limited amount of this bounty trickled down to white working-class Americans, at least those employed in certain expanding industries (including auto and electrical manufacturing), in the form of increased real earnings. Single-family home ownership rose, and many homes, at least in non-rural areas, acquired electricity and indoor plumbing. Installment buying and other forms of credit made new appliances like radios, phonographs, and washing machines available to middle-class and at least some better-off working-class families. There was also a transportation revolution, with far-reaching economic and social consequences, as private automobile ownership expanded by 1929 to nearly half the country's families.[59]

In those same years, the pool of American workers available for employment was undergoing a demographic transformation. In the decade preceding World War I, over a million immigrants reached American shores annually, many of them finding employment in the nation's factories and mines. However, following restrictions imposed by Congress in 1921 and in 1924 with the still-more-stringent National Origins Act (both motivated by nativist and antiradical sentiment), the number of immigrants dropped dramatically. Only 700,000 entered the country in the entire decade between 1920 and 1930, with the restrictions particularly reducing the numbers coming from eastern and southern Europe. As a result, a more homogenous and assimilated white urban working class took form in the 1920s and 1930s.[60]

For employers, the good times of the 1920s were also measured by the declining fortunes of unions. In 1920, thanks to labor shortages during World War I, unions had reached an all-time high of over 5 million members, or 19.4 percent of nonagricultural workers. A short economic downturn in 1920–1921 slashed those numbers, as did an aggressive corporate drive called the "American Plan," which set out to destroy unions and restore the nonunion open shop. Industrial unions were particularly hard-hit, including the near collapse of the formerly powerful United Mine Workers (UMW). By 1929 overall union membership had fallen to under 3.5 million, representing just 10.2 percent of nonagricultural workers.[61]

There were weak spots in the American economy in the 1920s, and, potentially, openings for radical organizers. Even growth industries like automobile manufacturing were plagued by seasonal unemployment. Workers in older, ailing, technologically backward industries like textiles saw declining wages and worsening work conditions. Rural areas in general, especially in the South, and African-Americans, both southern and northern, did not share in the general prosperity.[62]

The AFL's longtime president Samuel Gompers died in 1924, but the federation's leaders continued to display indifference to organizing industrial unions. Most AFL affiliates in the 1920s were craft unions, almost exclusively enlisting skilled, native-born, white, and male workers. That, potentially, created a constituency for left-wing unionists among those workers the AFL scorned to organize.

Despite AFL hostility, for a few years TUEL gained recruits and influence among railwaymen, miners, and metalworkers, preaching the need for organizing in the mass-production industries, and amalgamating existing craft unions into industrial unions. TUEL showed particular strength in some already-existing industrial unions in the New York City garment industry, particularly the International Ladies' Garment Workers' Union (ILGWU). ILGWU president Morris Sigman (a onetime IWW organizer, so no stranger to the Left) banned TUEL and expelled Communist leaders soon after taking office in 1923. And yet, although there were fewer than 500 Communists in the ILGWU in the mid-1920s, for a moment they seemed on the verge of capturing the union, which would have given them a powerful enclave in the AFL, since it was then the federation's fourth-largest affiliate. By 1925, the Party controlled the three largest ILGWU locals in New York City and also had developed followings in union locals in Boston, Philadelphia, and Chicago.[63]

In 1926, in a bold move to expand their power in the union, the Communists pushed through a strike resolution for the New York cloakmakers. The strike commenced on July 1, with 40,000 workers walking out. Two months later they were on the brink of reaching an agreement with employers that would have brought substantial gains to workers. The Party's strike leaders, Charles "Sasha" Zimmerman, Joseph Boruchowitz, and Rose Wortis, were skilled organizers who had risen from the union rank and file. But before they could agree to the settlement, they needed to win official approval from the Party leadership. Therein lay the fatal weakness of Communist trade union activism in the 1920s. For reasons having little to do with the interests of the striking workers, two factions then vying for control of the CP decided to oppose the settlement, supposedly to hold out for a still better agreement down the road, but in reality seeking to impress Moscow with a display of their own faction's militancy. The settlement offer was withdrawn, and the strike continued for four more months, bankrupting the ILGWU in the process. That proved the end of Communist influence in the garment industry, outside of the furriers' union, where they had a gifted young leader in Ben Gold, who had led his union in a successful strike earlier in the year. Strike leader Zimmerman, who had been a charter member of the Communist Party of America (CPA) in 1919, would be expelled from the CP in 1929, but went on to a long career as an anti-Communist leader of the ILGWU's Local 22 in New York City, and close ally of the next ILGWU president, David Dubinsky.[64]

That same year, 1926, Communists were involved in another major strike, this one across the Hudson River in the northern New Jersey city of Passaic, which proved the largest and longest textile strike of the decade. A young Communist organizer, Albert Weisbord, led a walkout by more than 16,000 textile workers, almost all immigrants, half of them women—the kind of workers that the established AFL unions regarded as unorganizable.

Weisbord, son of Russian Jewish immigrants, was a graduate of both City College, not unusual for recruits to the Communist movement in those days, and Harvard Law School, which was definitely out of the ordinary. Short, balding, and bespectacled, but nonetheless possessing a charisma based on his obvious dedication and intelligence, the twenty-five-year-old Weisbord was the kind of organizer the AFL should have been assigning to bring the gospel of industrial unionism to places like the Passaic textile mills. Instead, it was left to the Communists to do so.[65]

The Passaic struggle began on January 25, 1926, when 6,000 workers at the Botany Worsted Mill struck, enraged by an across-the-board 10 percent wage cut the previous October. It soon spread to a number of nearby mills. Strikers demanded not only a restoration of cut wages but a 10 percent wage increase, a forty-four-hour week with time and a half for overtime, and union recognition. The AFL's United Textile Workers union, which only had a few members in the mill, refused to support the strike. As a result, the Communist-organized United Front Committee, an ad hoc organization headed by Weisbord, functioned in effect if not by choice independently of the AFL, issuing membership cards and collecting dues.[66]

Millowners refused to consider the strikers' demands. The strikers held out in the face of mass arrests, attacks by club-wielding police, and fire hoses turned on their picket lines in freezing cold weather by the local fire department. The harsh tactics employed against the strikers at first created public sympathy for their cause. Prominent supporters, including Rabbi Stephen S. Wise, founder of the American Jewish Congress; Norman Thomas, Eugene Debs's successor as head of the Socialist Party; and Elizabeth Gurley Flynn, the "Rebel Girl" of the prewar IWW (and not yet a Communist), all came to lend support. For a while, the Passaic struggle brought back memories of the IWW's iconic 1912 Lawrence and 1913 Paterson strikes. Weisbord wisely kept the focus on bread-and-butter issues; as the American Civil Liberties Union reported, "Communism is not being taught" to the strikers.[67]

Mary Heaton Vorse, who began her career as a labor journalist in Lawrence in 1912, had initially been repelled by the Communists she met in the early 1920s (a brief and unhappy love affair with Party leader Robert Minor at the start of the decade didn't help). Communists, she confided in her diary, all seemed to have "closed minds, so certain, so dull. . . . They *bore me, bore me, bore me.*"[68] And yet, sometime before she arrived in Passaic, she secretly joined the CP. Like Weisbord, she did her best as the strike's publicist to keep the focus in her press bulletins on immediate issues, and on the strikers themselves. The unusual thing about the strike meetings in Passaic, she wrote, "is the number of women. The seats are almost all taken up by them. . . . Young women, pretty rosy girls, older women, tired women. What a gap between the young women and the older women. Hope on the young faces, fatigue on the old ones. . . . How few years in the mills wipe out the color in a woman's face and dim her eyes, and make all the muscles of her body sag!"[69]

The Communists' International Workers Aid organization set up soup kitchens and relief stores, and provided a financial stipend for the strikers and their families. The Party's fundraising efforts brought donations from sympathetic unions and individuals across the country, turning it into one of the best-known labor struggles of the decade.[70]

But the millowners remained unbending, and the Communists' resources were running out. In September, nine months into the strike, with no progress in negotiations, Weisbord agreed (reluctantly, and on instructions from the Party) to give in to demands from both the employers and the AFL's United Textile Workers union that he personally withdraw from strike leadership. The UTW took over negotiations, and in the end it reached a settlement that rescinded the wage cuts but failed to gain union recognition. The most militant strikers were blacklisted. Unlike the cloakmakers' strike in Manhattan, the Communists made no major errors in the Passaic strike. They were simply overpowered by the power of the millowners and the local authorities. Even though they had repudiated dual unionism, Communists were replaying the IWW pattern of heroic strike leadership in doomed struggles that ultimately achieved nothing.[71]

Just as American Communists revised their union strategy in the early 1920s under Comintern prodding, so too they changed their electoral strategy. When locally organized labor parties emerged right after the war, the Communists regarded them as a distraction from the revolution. Following Lenin's condemnation of electoral abstention, however, they looked more favorably on the creation of a national farmer-labor party.[72]

The most promising such initiative in the early 1920s was undertaken by John Fitzpatrick, an Irish-born blacksmith who was the longtime president of the Chicago Federation of Labor. Fitzpatrick was a rare maverick radical in the AFL hierarchy, distinguished both by his support for industrial unionism and his interest in independent labor politics. He was an admirer of William Z. Foster, having worked closely with him on the 1917 packinghouse workers and 1919 steelworkers organizing drives, and he took a benign view of TUEL's efforts to build influence within the AFL.

Looking for allies in launching a national farmer-labor party in 1923, Fitzpatrick offered the Communists an invitation to join the effort. The Communists had done little in the years since their founding to suggest they were reliable partners in such an enterprise, and Fitzpatrick, with long experience in the hard school of Chicago labor politics, was hardly a naive idealist. Yet he knew Foster's abilities and that of his lieutenants in TUEL. He may have believed that the Communists would appreciate the opportunity to prove that they could function as responsible partners—albeit junior partners—in a broad third-party coalition. In any event, when Fitz-gerald sent out the call for a national convention to meet in Chicago the weekend of July 3–5 to found the new party, he saw to it that the Workers Party received an official invitation. The Communists sent ten delegates, including Foster.

The Workers Party also sent scores of other delegates to the convention, not as open Communists but as supposedly independent representatives of an assortment of obscure labor and farm groups. Altogether, they added up to between one-third and half the total delegates. Fitzpatrick, alarmed by this attempt to dominate the proceedings, turned against his Communist allies, but too late. With their artificial near-majority, the Communists proceeded to run roughshod over all others in attendance, ensuring their control of the convention and the "Federated Farmer-Labor Party" it created. Except, in reality, they created nothing but ill will. Pariahs to the conservative Right as a threat to capitalism, they now became pariahs to the labor Left as a threat to progressive politics. A furious and humiliated Fitzpatrick bitterly declared that the Communists had "killed the Farmer-Labor Party . . . and the possibility of uniting the forces of independent political action in America." The new party did not survive the year.[73]

The demonstration of a narrow kind of organizational prowess, packing the convention, proved that the Communists could be ruthlessly efficient in such efforts; the willingness to make an enemy out of a valuable ally like Fitzpatrick, to gain such a meaningless victory, proved that they could also be startlingly shortsighted.

Foster wrote a long self-justifying analysis of the Communist role at the convention for the next issue of the *Labor Herald*, TUEL's monthly magazine, calling it a "landmark in the history of the working class."[74] That it was not. But it does represent, in retrospect, a landmark in the history of American Communism, as one of the first public displays of a form of belligerent organizational aggrandizement that would become a trademark of the movement. This was not to be the last time that the Communists, through behind-the-scenes organizational maneuvering, had essentially captured themselves.

With the establishment of the Workers Party in 1923, the factional struggle between rival underground parties switched to rival groupings operating within the now-supposedly-united movement. The chief contenders for factional supremacy centered on three native-born leaders: Charles Ruthenberg, William Z. Foster, and James Cannon. Ruthenberg, allied with Jay Lovestone, could call on much of the party machinery to back them; Foster relied on supporters in TUEL; Cannon's supporters were found among ILD cadre. Foster and Cannon formed an on-again, off-again bloc against Ruthenberg and Lovestone. Other lesser figures allied themselves with one or another of the dominant factions based upon personal ties, political belief, and shifting signals from Moscow.[75]

Factionalism took up much of the time and energy of the rank and file as well as the leaders. Out in Los Angeles, a Fosterite stronghold, Peggy Dennis joined the Party in 1925 and immediately plunged into the internal battles. "Our factional loyalties," she remembered, "turned all Party meetings into screaming, conniving sessions that often ended in fist fights. Strategy caucuses to outwit our Party opponents became our main activity, the common class enemy was quite forgotten." At age sixteen she became a skilled factionalist, "enjoying the intrigues and caucusing that went on constantly."[76]

All the leading factions united on one issue, in support of a major change in the Party's internal structure known as "Bolshevization." They hardly could do otherwise, since this was a directive from the Comintern, issued in 1924, and implemented throughout the international movement the following year. The Bolshevization policy was meant to restructure Communist parties along the lines of the Soviet Communist Party. The organizational terminology varied among parties, but in the United States, the line of authority now flowed downward from the general secretary, who met with a Secretariat of two other top leaders, and with a Political Bureau of a half dozen other leaders; beneath these groupings there was a larger Central Executive Committee consisting of representatives from Party districts (consisting usually of two or more states, depending on membership) across the country; and so on down to county, city, section (part of a larger city), and branch levels.[77]

More significant than changes in nomenclature were two new requirements. The first was to have the Communist Party's ground-level unit, the branch—the place where dues were collected, assignments handed out, and so forth—be based on place of employment whenever possible, rather than on place of residence. The second was to strip the foreign-language federations of the quasi-autonomy they had enjoyed since 1919.

Something needed to be done to revitalize the CP at the local level. The *Daily Worker* carried a devastating portrait of branch life in 1924, authored by Martin Abern, a young Chicago Communist and Cannon protégé:

Our party branches generally meet every two weeks, some less often. It's safe to say about one-half of the branch, at best, shows up at the meeting. A discussion takes place—where to sell or give away literature, the difficulty of collecting money. . . . A few comrades are awake to getting to work in the unions or on the job. But on the whole, life is desultory, they declaim: it will take a long time before the masses are awakened, and more of the same. With religious resignation many comrades continue to await The Day.[78]

Party leaders were confronted with the problem that many of their recruits weren't cut out to be the selfless, tireless, saintly ascetics imagined in Joseph Stalin's 1924 *Foundations of Leninism*. Abern's proposed solution, which anticipated the Comintern's Bolshevization decision, was to replace the existing territorial branches, based on the neighborhoods or cities where Communists lived, with branches whose membership was based on where Communists were employed—since, he argued, members would see each other every day on the job, be accustomed to working together, and be motivated by the class solidarity to be found at the point of production. However, even if that were true (and there was no evidence to suggest it was), creating these "factory nuclei" (the Soviet term) would prove a challenge for American Communists, given that there were few workplaces in the United States where Communists found themselves grouped together with many other comrades.[79]

An even more difficult problem was posed by the eighteen foreign-language federations representing the majority of members in the Communist movement in the early days. Since the beginning, these had functioned with a degree of separation from the main Party organization that was distinctly un-Bolshevik. In their prewar Socialist incarnation, the federations had focused on preserving the cultures of their various homelands, with little direct involvement in broader American culture or politics. Not much changed when they became nominally Communist. The foreign-language federations sponsored a host of organizations and activities, including their own publications, theater, dance, and choral groups, bookstores, libraries, schools, benefits, picnics, forums, and the like. All of this offered advantages and disadvantages to the Communists. Steve Nelson, born in Croatia as Stjepan Mesaros, immigrated to the United States as a seventeen-year-old in 1920 and soon afterward joined the Communist movement. By the mid-1920s he had moved to Detroit, where he settled into the life of a party activist. "Between the Party and the surrounding fraternal organizations," he recalled in a memoir, "one didn't have to look far for recreation." There was a cooperative restaurant run out of a hall maintained by Yugoslav Communists, a summer camp on a local lake maintained by the Finns, plus singing societies, athletic teams, and other opportunities for socializing with comrades. "The drawback of this," however, "was that we rarely reached beyond the immigrant radical community and had little contact with native-born workers."[80]

While the language federations were a source of Party strength and stability, they were viewed by Communist authorities, as Nelson suggested, as a hindrance to growth in the longer term. Doing away with them, it was thought, would both encourage the assimilation of foreign-born members, because they would be interacting with members from other ethnic backgrounds and make the Party more attractive to English-speaking recruits. Another consideration was that the federations controlled sizable capital assets, including halls, print shops, and newspapers; as Foster told the Comintern in 1925 with an acquisitive emphasis not entirely seemly for a Communist leader, "The question is how shall the Party get control of this property."[81]

Not surprisingly, the foreign-language federations did not welcome the prospect of being bolshevized. Their members were quite happy sticking with their own kind. When told that the federations were going to be abolished, and that the decision came from the highest levels in Moscow, a member of the South Slavic federation in Milwaukee asked defiantly, "Is it impossible for the Communist International to make mistakes?"[82] Many responded by voting with their feet. When Bolshevization was pushed through in 1925, three-quarters of the former members of the Finnish federation failed to reregister as members of the Workers Party. Membership in District 9, which included Minnesota, Wisconsin, and Upper Michigan, the center of Finnish strength, dropped from 1,662 in 1925 to 599 a year later. Overall membership in the party dropped from about 16,235 in 1925 to 7,597 in 1926.[83]

In time, the Communists found a way to bring some of the disaffected foreign-born members back, with the creation in 1930 of the International Workers Order (IWO), a federation of ethnic mutual-benefit fraternal societies, the largest of which was the Jewish People's Fraternal Order. The IWO offered affordable health and life insurance policies and other benefits, as well as a wide range of cultural, educational, and recreational activities, including dozens of adult summer resorts and summer camps for children (the most enduring of the latter was Camp Kinderland in Upstate New York). At its height, in the mid-1940s, the IWO enrolled nearly 200,000 members. While most IWO members were not Communists, the federation was under firm Party control, with Communist leader Max Bedacht its director for most of its existence.[84]

The Red Scare is usually described as ending by the time Warren G. Harding became president, or shortly afterward. The large-scale raids, staged for maximum publicity by federal and state authorities, ceased after 1920. But Communists continued to be jailed, if under less dramatic circumstances.[85]

Communist leaders took the possibility of imprisonment as an occupational hazard. Before he was a Communist, Charles Ruthenberg had served ten months in prison in 1918 for violating the Espionage Act. As a Communist leader, he served an additional year and a half (of a five-to-ten-year sentence at hard labor) in 1921–1922 for violating New York State's "criminal anarchy" statute, which made it illegal to advocate the overthrow of the government by unlawful means. Benjamin Gitlow, brought up on the same charges in an earlier trial, was also sentenced to five to ten years in New York state prison, and he served nearly three in Sing Sing penitentiary before his release.[86]

It wasn't just hardened Party leaders who faced draconian sentences. Nineteen-year-old Yetta Stromberg, a student at the University of Southern California and counselor at a Communist summer camp in the San Bernardino Mountains of Southern California, was arrested in 1929 when the local district attorney raided the camp. She was charged with overseeing the ceremonial raising of a red flag in the morning, a camp ritual and violation of a 1919 state law that banned the display of such flags. She was convicted and sentenced to ten years in state prison for her crime. In her appeal, the Supreme Court ruled seven to two in May 1931 that California's red-flag law was a violation of the First and Fourteenth Amendments. But the courts could not be relied on for protection; six years earlier the Supreme Court had upheld Gitlow's conviction by a seven to two margin.[87] Whatever else one might say of American Communists in the 1920s, they had the courage of their convictions, with the convictions to prove it.

In the long run, the most important legal defense effort with which Communists were involved in the 1920s was one that did not involve their own members. Instead, it was the case of two immigrant anarchists, Nicola Sacco and Bartolomeo Vanzetti.

Nicola Sacco and Bartolomeo Vanzetti following their arrest in 1920
(Photo by Photo12/Universal Images Group via Getty Images)

On April 15, 1920, a factory guard and a paymaster were murdered during a payroll robbery of a shoe company in Braintree, Massachusetts. Suspicion fell on local anarchists, and two of them, shoemaker Sacco and fishmonger Vanzetti, were arrested on May 5, 1920. They were convicted on July 21, 1921, and sentenced to death. Six years of appeals followed to no avail, and their execution was scheduled for August 23, 1927. Arguments still are heard about Sacco and Vanzetti's guilt or innocence, but there is little question that their politics and immigrant background influenced the verdict.[88]

A diverse if fractious coalition of anarchists, Socialists, Wobblies, liberals, and Communists took up their cause. The Communists were but one element among many of Sacco and Vanzetti's supporters domestically, but internationally they were dominant. As the execution date neared, the Communist International coordinated protests around the globe demanding freedom for the condemned men, the first time that it had demonstrated its power to act on that scale, with demonstrations in cities across Europe, South America, Japan, Africa, and Australia.[89]

The Party portrayed the fight to save Sacco and Vanzetti as one of working-class solidarity, which wasn't absent, but many who joined the protests did so out of sympathy for fellow immigrants or fellow Italians, or on civil-libertarian grounds. In the United States, the case attracted considerable sympathy among middle-class intellectuals and writers, a constituency that the Communists had done little to attract in the past. John Dos Passos wrote about the case for the *New Masses*. Carrying credentials as a reporter for the *Daily Worker*, he also joined the last-minute picket lines in Boston protesting the impending execution, and he was arrested by Boston police, along with a number of other well-known writers.[90]

The appeals and the protests were in vain. On the night of August 23, a crowd of about 5,000 supporters gathered in Union Square in New York City to keep a silent vigil. Shortly after midnight, two signs were posted in the windows of the *Daily Worker* offices on nearby Twelfth Street—first,

"Sacco Murdered," and then a little while later, "Vanzetti Murdered." As the deaths were announced, one observer recorded, "A throaty wail of anguish arose."[91]

Shortly after the executions, Dos Passos was back in New York where he began writing his *USA* trilogy, three novels appearing between 1930 and 1936 offering a biting critique of American society in the early twentieth century. The climactic chapters in the final novel, *The Big Money*, centered on the campaign to save Sacco and Vanzetti. In the best-remembered section of the entire 1,000-plus pages of the trilogy, Dos Passos offered his thoughts on the meaning of the case in a stream-of-consciousness prose poem (a technique he called the "Camera Eye" and employed repeatedly in the trilogy, overturning the constraints of traditional narrative). It captured the sentiments of many of the anarchists' supporters on the night of their execution:

> all right you have won you will kill the brave men our friends
>   tonight . . .
> America our nation has been beaten by strangers who have turned
>   our language inside out who have taken the clean words our
>   fathers spoke and made them slimy and foul
> their hired men sit on the judge's bench . . .
> they have built the electricchair and hired the executioner to throw
>   the switch
> all right we are two nations
> America.

The phrase "you have won" was a cry of defeat and despair. And yet, the message of Dos Passos's Sacco-Vanzetti Camera Eye was more complex—one of alienation, to be sure ("all right we are two nations"), but at the same time of a kind of affirmation and renewal, giving a different meaning to "Americanization":

do they know that the old words of the immigrants are being
  renewed in blood and agony tonight do they know that the old
  American speech of the haters of oppression is new tonight in the
  mouth of an old woman from Pittsburgh of a husky boilermaker
  from Frisco who hopped freights clear from the Coast to come
  here in the mouth of a Back Bay socialworker in the mouth of
  an Italian printer of a hobo from Arkansas the language of the
  beaten nation is not forgotten in our ears tonight
the men in the deathhouse made the old words new before they
  died.[92]

Sacco and Vanzetti were not forgotten. The memory of the case lived on among working-class Americans of immigrant backgrounds, and it also helped move a generation of American intellectuals leftward in the coming decade. Dos Passos's "beaten nation" would be heard from again, as the ebb tide of the 1920s came to an end.[93]

Whether the Communist Party would play any significant role in the renewal of American radical prospects over the coming decade remained an open question. Ten years after the Bolshevik Revolution, the Communist movement in the United States remained small, isolated, and sectarian. Its leaders had learned to follow obediently political priorities established in Moscow, while displaying little understanding or even interest in adapting their movement to American political realities. In the next few years, they would wander even further from those realities in following Soviet dictates. The future of American Communism did not look bright.

CHAPTER 2

"Toward Soviet America": The Third Period

1928–1934

They used to tell me I was building a dream, with peace and glory
    ahead,
Why should I be standing in line, just waiting for bread?
Once I built a railroad, I made it run, made it race against time.
Once I built a railroad; now it's done. Brother, can you spare a dime?
                                    —"Brother, Can You Spare a Dime?" (1932),
                            lyrics by E. Y. "Yip" Harburg, music by Jay Gorney

LIKE a tornado the present economic crisis struck the capitalist world.
. . . Only the Soviet Union is immune. And as Stalin says, "The crisis
has struck deepest of all at the principal country of capitalism, its cit-
adel, the USA." The crisis is setting in motion forces that threaten the
very existence of the capitalist system.

                            —William Z. Foster, *Toward Soviet America* (1932)

When the American stock market crashed in October 1929, the Communist response was initially muted. The "gods of American finance are defeated in the effort to control the forces of the business 'universe' over which they rule," the *Daily Worker* gloated in a front-page editorial on October 29. Capitalism had demonstrated its underlying irrationality. The chief victims of the crash, those deluded enough to pursue wealth through speculation, were getting their just comeuppance. But what exactly that meant in the coming decade for American workers—and for the political prospects of American Communism—went unmentioned for the moment. By the new year, however, the dimensions of the economic disaster became clearer to the Communists, as it did to many others. "The leading capitalist statisticians say that the workers will be faced with severe unemployment for at least ten years," the *Daily Worker* reported on January 1, 1930. "That means that the 5,000,000 now unemployed will grow into many millions."[1]

All too accurate a prophecy. Unemployment, standing at 3.2 percent of the workforce in 1929, grew to 8.7 percent in 1930, 15.9 percent in 1931, and in the autumn of 1932 was nearing a quarter of the workforce. Pay cuts and reduced hours spread the misery even further. Meanwhile, the federal government under President Herbert Hoover provided no aid to the jobless, while state, local, and private relief proved entirely inadequate.[2]

Though scant comfort in dire times, the 12 million unemployed acquired their own popular song in 1932. The lyrics were by Edgar "Yip" Harburg, born Isidore Hochberg in New York City in 1896. The son of Russian Jewish garment workers, he grew up on the Lower East Side. After graduating from City College and embarking on a career as a small businessman, he went bankrupt at the start of the Great Depression. He proved more successful at songwriting. In 1932, he collaborated with composer Jay Gorney, a Russian immigrant and fellow socialist, on songs for a musical revue called *Americana* that opened on Broadway shortly before the November presidential election. One of the songs that Harburg and

Gorney contributed, "Brother, Can You Spare a Dime?," became wildly popular in versions recorded the next year by Bing Crosby and Al Jolson, among others. And this, despite the fact that Harburg and Gorney's contribution was far from the cheerful escapism of most Broadway show tunes.

"Brother," its tune based on a Russian Jewish lullaby that Gorney recalled from childhood, opens in a minor key suggesting hopelessness. Harburg's lyrics, however, were intended to offer a hint of rebellion. What the man asking for the dime was "really saying," he told an interviewer, was "I made an investment in this country. Where the hell are my dividends?" The song conveyed neither pity nor contempt for its subject, reduced through no fault of his own to poverty. In Harburg's view he was instead "a dignified human being, asking questions—and a bit outraged, too, as he should be."[3]

Harburg went on to win an Oscar in 1939 for Best Original Song, *The Wizard of Oz*'s "Over the Rainbow." As a lyricist, he had a gift for wistful

Jobless New Yorkers selling apples on the pavement, Great Depression, 1930
(Photo by Historica Graphica Collection/Heritage Images/Getty Images)

melancholy that linked his early and later 1930s hits. Although leftist in sympathies, Harburg wasn't organizationally inclined enough to join the Communist Party. But "Brother, Can You Spare a Dime?" posed the right question at the right time, quietly indicting a failed economic system, and has remained over the years the song that best evokes the feelings of despair and displacement of the early Depression.[4]

It was by no means apparent when "Brother, Can You Spare a Dime?" was first being heard on the radio, that the Communist Party would emerge as *the* major party of the American Left in the 1930s. The central contradiction of American Communism in the early 1930s was that, while being offered an unprecedented opportunity to make its case against capitalism, it remained committed to a political stance isolating it from all but a narrow slice of American workers. Communists entered the decade convinced that through sheer determination they could bend reality to their will, forcing a revolutionary crisis in the United States and creating a "Soviet America" based on a strategy derived from the experience of revolutionaries who lived in a society that bore little resemblance to their own. That proved an exercise in futility. The ebb tide of the 1920s was at an end; the flood tide of the 1930s was waiting for the Communists to avail themselves of it.

In March 1927, the Communist Party lost its first General Secretary, Charles E. Ruthenberg, who died from acute peritonitis. He was the second leader of an American left-wing party to die in six months. Socialist leader Eugene V. Debs never recovered his health after his imprisonment and in October 1926 died in a sanitarium in Illinois. His body was returned to his hometown of Terre Haute, Indiana, for burial, the funeral service delivered from the front porch of the family home, his cremated ashes buried under a simple stone marker in a local cemetery. The Socialist Party's five-time presidential candidate was an uncommon man, but his funeral was commonplace by design.[5]

Ruthenberg's mourning rites were more grandiose. They began with two days of lying in state in Chicago's Ashland Boulevard Auditorium. Following cremation, his ashes were transported to New York for a memorial meeting in Carnegie Hall. From there, in the most un-Debsian turn imaginable, Ruthenberg's remains were shipped to Moscow and interred in the Kremlin wall next to John Reed's remains and near Lenin's tomb. He was the only general secretary of the American Communist Party and the next-to-last American to be so honored (Big Bill Haywood's ashes would also be deposited there the following year). Despite the fuss made over him upon death, and again unlike Debs, Ruthenberg was almost immediately forgotten by his comrades.[6]

Ruthenberg performed a final service for the Party, or rather for Jay Lovestone, who reported his alleged last words, "Tell the comrades to close their ranks, to build the Party."[7] The ranks went unclosed, but in the inevitable inner-party struggle that followed, Lovestone prevailed. He would be both the youngest (at age twenty-nine) to win the designation of general secretary and the one destined for the shortest tenure in office.

Born Jacob Liebstein in 1897 to Jewish parents in Lithuania, Lovestone accompanied his family to New York City as a child in 1907, growing up in the Bronx. He entered City College in 1915, where he joined the Intercollegiate Socialist Society. In 1919, he started law school at New York University.

Inspired by the Bolshevik triumph in Russia, he abandoned law for a career as a professional revolutionary, becoming a leading figure in the combative left wing of the Socialist Party in New York. In the Communist movement, Lovestone allied with Ruthenberg, serving as his lieutenant in seven years of faction-fighting, the political activity at which he proved most gifted. Unlike Ruthenberg, who gained the grudging respect of Party rivals for his organizational skills, Lovestone was personally loathed by his opponents. One of them, Charles Shipman, remembered him as "a contemptuously glib whiz kid."[8]

Among Lovestone's first decisions in office was shifting Party head-quarters from Chicago back to his hometown. The Communists pur-chased a nine-story office building at 35 East Twelfth Street, two blocks south of Union Square. Party leaders had their offices on the top floor of the Twelfth Street building; accordingly, within the movement, it became customary to refer to them as the "ninth floor." The Union Square area was already home to Socialist Party headquarters and many of the SP's affili-ated organizations and publications, as well as the central offices of unions like the Amalgamated Clothing Workers. With this dense concentration of labor and radical influences, the square was the site of innumerable left-wing gatherings in years to come, including annual May Day parades that attracted tens of thousands of participants and spectators.[9]

Lovestone's control of the Party seemed unassailable. When an Amer-ican delegation visited Moscow to attend the Tenth Plenum of the Comin-tern following Ruthenberg's death (plenums were enlarged meetings of the Comintern's executive committee held between congresses), Stalin invited Lovestone and allies to a private three-hour meeting at his office in the Kremlin. Benjamin Gitlow was among their number, and according to his recollection, Stalin offered some cordial advice to the Lovestoneites: "Sta-lin insisted that the most important problem for the Communist Party in the United States was the fight for . . . the betterment of the workers' condi-tions. He told us that the proletarian revolution in the United States could wait, that it was a long way off."[10]

The meeting cemented Lovestone's status as the leading figure in the American Communist movement. He also enjoyed the patronage of another top Soviet leader, Nikolai Bukharin, president of the Comintern and Stalin's latest ally in the battle against Trotsky.[11]

During his time in exile living in New York in 1916–1917, Bukharin was impressed by the vitality of American capitalism. He shared in the ultrarevolutionary dreams of the early Soviet years, but he soon came to a more sober appraisal of political possibilities both in the Soviet Union and abroad. As he wrote in 1926, "American capitalism is the stronghold of the entire capitalist system." That meant that the Communists' role in the US was, by necessity, "still very modest."[12] Lovestone agreed, declaring in 1927 that "objective conditions" were simply not "favorable for the development of a mass Communist party" in the United States in the near future.[13]

The proposition that postwar American capitalism was, if only temporarily, an exception to the rule that capitalism was in decline worldwide became known in a phrase coined by Stalin as "American exceptionalism." With the two top Soviet leaders apparently in agreement, Lovestone and his allies became exceptionalists.

As became apparent in the 1920s, however, what was truth one moment in Moscow was apt to become heresy the next. Late in 1927, Joseph Stalin made several public statements suggesting that a new revolutionary upsurge was developing in Europe. By the time some 500 delegates gathered in Moscow for the Sixth World Congress of the Comintern from July 17 to September 1, 1928, Stalin had clearly turned on the Soviet Party's Right, just as he had previously turned on its Left. There would be no more alliances between Stalin and one or another Old Bolshevik in which there was any genuine shared power and influence. From now on, Stalin was sole and absolute ruler in the Soviet Union. In terms of domestic policy, Stalin's reversal signaled his intent to abandon the mild concessions to market forces represented by the New Economic Policy initiated by Lenin. In its place, he announced a new era, a Five Year Plan of rapid industrialization and the full collectivization of agriculture. This radical turn would also determine the Comintern's international line: there would be no more talk of a period of "capitalist stabilization." Instead, the new orthodoxy insisted that the world had entered a "Third Period," characterized by the impending global collapse of capitalism, including in the no-longer-exceptional United States. Stalin, heretofore the cautious advocate of building socialism in one country, became Stalin the uncompromising international revolutionary.[14]

All of this was welcome news to the anti-Lovestone factions in the American CP. Lovestone, hitherto so politically agile, was caught flat-footed by the latest developments in Moscow, repeating as late as December 1928 that as far as he was concerned, "comrade Bukharin represents the Communist line."[15] But Lovestone's downfall was temporarily delayed by another development in the American CP's ongoing internal battles, the split over Trotskyism.

As Trotsky's fortunes fell in the years after Lenin's death, with his removal from command of the Red Army in January 1925, his ouster from the Soviet Party's ruling Politburo in October 1926, his expulsion from the Soviet Communist Party in November 1927, and his forced exile in Alma-Ata, capital of Soviet Kazakhstan, in January 1928, all American Communist factions vied to be seen by Moscow as the most vehemently anti-Trotskyist. To say a kind word for the once glorious, now fallen hero meant instant expulsion. "Trotskyism" in the United States might have survived only as an obscure epithet attached to the memory of a failed contender for Soviet leadership, had not James Cannon arrived with the rest of the American delegation for the Comintern's Sixth World Congress in the summer of 1928.

In Moscow, Cannon was teamed up with Canadian Communist Party chairman Maurice Spector as members of a commission charged with developing a formal program to guide the Comintern in coming years. Along with other commission members, who were expected to rubber-stamp decisions already taken by Soviet leaders, the two North Americans received a packet of documents considered relevant to their task. Through some accident, it included an English translation of a critique by Trotsky of the program draft. In a densely worded argument, Trotsky contended that the cause of world revolution was being betrayed from within the Soviet Communist Party, as witnessed by his own downfall and exile: "The growth of the economic and political pressure of the bureaucratic and petty bourgeois strata within the [Soviet Union] on the basis of defeats of the proletarian revolution in Europe and Asia . . . was the historical chain which tightened around the neck of the Opposition during these four years. Whoever fails to understand this will understand nothing at all."[16]

Trotsky's jeremiad struck Cannon and Specter with the force of revelation. The failures of their own national parties to achieve significant political gains at home were, they now believed, linked by a "historical chain" to the failure of the Comintern to spread the revolution internationally, a failure that in turn was chained to Stalin's rise and Trotsky's fall from power in the Soviet Union. And all those problems, at home, abroad, and in the Soviet Union, could be remedied by restoring Trotsky to his proper place in the leadership of the world revolution, the purity of the original Bolshevik vision restored. (It did not occur to Cannon or Specter to ask a further question, which was if the historical chain that had choked the life out of the Trotskyist Opposition between 1924 and 1927 might somehow have been linked to the chain which Trotsky himself helped to forge, choking out the life of the Mensheviks, the Kronstadt sailors, and other dissident voices in the newly established workers' state in the years between 1918 and 1924.)

In any event, the two converts kept their thoughts to themselves for the moment. Safely home in New York in September 1928, Cannon shared a smuggled copy of Trotsky's critique with a select few trusted comrades, starting with his wife, Rose Karsner, and then with Max Shachtman, editor of the International Labor Defense's *Labor Defender*, and Martin Abern, the Party's Chicago-based district organizer. Other recruits joined Cannon's band by ones and twos, mostly in New York, but also in a few other outposts such as Minneapolis, which became a center of relative strength for the movement. Meanwhile in Canada, Spector was quietly assembling his own circle of sympathizers.[17]

If Communists had proven efficient at one thing over the past decade, it was at sniffing out heresies. A few weeks after returning from Moscow, Cannon was ordered to appear before the Party's top leaders to respond to disturbing rumors of disloyalty. He stalled, hoping to gain more recruits, until at the end of October he conceded the charges and proclaimed his new allegiance. Lovestone welcomed the opportunity to demonstrate his own loyalty to Stalin by cracking down on the Trotskyists, expelling Cannon, Shachtman, Abern, and others. (The same thing happened to Spector in Canada.) The *Daily Worker* warned Party members that sympathy for their former comrades would not be tolerated: "Any opposition to the expulsion of Cannon and his associates in the name of 'freedom of expression of opinion' amounts to an objective support of Trotskyism and helps to organize a Trotskyist group within our Party."[18]

Cannon and his followers promptly launched the Communist League of America (Opposition). The inclusion of "opposition" in parentheses was meant to suggest that they expected before long to be contesting for power *within* the American Communist Party. That proving impossible, the following year they dropped "Opposition" from the name, but as a saving remnant of true Leninists, at least in their own minds, expected in the not-distant future to replace the Communist Party as the major party on the Left. In 1938 Trotsky, from foreign exile in Mexico, hailed the decision by his followers in America and Europe to organize a new international federation to challenge the Stalinist Third International. "During the next ten years," he told them, the "program of the Fourth International will become the guide of millions and these revolutionary millions will know how to storm earth and heaven."[19]

Trotsky's prophetic powers were waning, for earth and heaven remained unstormed, at least by his followers. As of 1938, there were no more than a thousand or so members of the Trotskyist group in the United States, by then called the Socialist Workers Party. And that number dwindled following Trotsky's assassination in 1940, as his political heirs split (repeatedly) over the correct way to interpret his legacy.

Absorbing as the Communist Party's internal factional wars proved to its members, the class war still needed to be waged. Here too a complication arose in the closing years of the decade. At the outset of the 1920s, "dual unionism" had been forbidden by the Comintern, and "boring from within" the American Federation of Labor became the official strategy. But at a Moscow conference in March 1928, Solomon Lozofsky, founder of the Red International of Labor Unions, or Profintern, astonished American delegates by attacking their fidelity to "boring from within." Shortly afterward, the English-language edition of the *Communist International*, the Comintern's official journal, arrived in New York with an article by Lozofsky chastising American Communists for "dancing a quadrille . . . around the AFL."[20]

Accordingly, before year's end the Party established two new independent and overtly revolutionary unions, the National Miners' Union, led by Communist miner Pat Toohey, and the National Textile Workers Union, led by Albert Weisbord of Passaic strike fame, followed in January 1929 by the Needle Trades Workers International Union, whose central figure, if not official leader, was fur-worker organizer Ben Gold. The following August, the Trade Union Educational League (TUEL), founded at the start of the 1920s under Foster's leadership, was transformed at a convention in Cleveland into the Trade Union Unity League (TUUL), intended as a full-fledged rival to the American Federation of Labor. The new red federation claimed to represent 50,000 members in 1930, eventually growing to a dozen unions claiming over 100,000 members.[21]

The return to dual unionism offered Communists some potential advantages. Boring from within the AFL for the past seven years had yielded minimal gains in influence within the existing labor movement. And it wasn't as if the AFL was prepared to respond to the unprecedented challenges posed by the Great Depression. As *Fortune* magazine, not known for its leftist sympathies, commented in 1933, "the Federation has been suffering from pernicious anemia, sociological myopia, and hardening of the arteries."[22] AFL membership, which had reached 4 million in 1920, declined throughout the 1920s, and then plummeted in the early 1930s. By 1933 the federation had just over 2 million remaining members.

Given that record, what claim did the AFL have to exclusive rights to speak for American workers? Why not strike out in a new direction?[23]

To strengthen TUUL's claim to represent a viable alternative to the AFL, the Communists needed a dramatic labor-organizing victory. That drew their attention southward. Strikes were frequent in southern textile mills in the late 1920s, with dozens breaking out in 1929, almost all spontaneous, and often violent. Between the spring of 1929 and the fall of 1930, seven strikers died in such struggles in the Piedmont (the area between North Carolina's coastal plain and interior mountains, literally "foot hill"), and not a single one of their killers was brought to justice.[24] Despite the labor unrest in the industry and the region, the AFL United Textile Workers union had been all but driven out of southern mills, and it showed little interest in taking on the challenge of organizing in such an unpromising setting. That seemed to provide an opening for the Communists to step in and create an independent and openly revolutionary union.[25]

The place they decided would provide the breakthrough in their efforts was the Piedmont town of Gastonia in North Carolina, a classic company town. The Loray Mill company's five-floor red-brick mill, the South's largest textile factory, was situated on a slight rise, surrounded by an iron fence, looming fortress-like over the surrounding company-owned cottages in which many of its 2,200 workers were housed. The textile industry was suffering hard times in the late 1920s, and the Loray management responded with measures that increasingly restive workers called the "stretch-out"—cutting the workforce by a third, instituting longer hours, pay cuts, and piecework (that is, work paid for according to the amount produced, instead of a flat rate per hour of work).[26]

The southern states, especially the rural and mill-town South, were a long way from Union Square. It was only in 1928 that Communists ventured to stage public gatherings in some of the larger southern cities like New Orleans and Atlanta, supporting the Party's candidates for president and vice president, William Z. Foster and Benjamin Gitlow, in that year's national election.[27] All the more remarkable that six months later, the CP would, in its first open effort in the South, launch what turned out to be the most famous labor struggle of the decade. It was the first major strike Communists had ever led among native-born workers of old American stock, and the first strike in which Party organizers confronted the race issue. As historian Glenda Gilmore noted of Gastonia, North Carolina, "Had the Communists searched the South over for a tougher place to start, they could not have found one."[28]

Fred Erwin Beal was chosen by the Party and the National Textile Workers Union (NTWU) to tackle that daunting assignment. Like Albert Weisbord three years earlier in Passaic, he was a talented organizer. He also had impeccable proletarian credentials, his life resembling a character in one of John Dos Passos's novels. He had gone to work in the textile mills of Lawrence, Massachusetts, at age fourteen, taken part in the IWW strike of 1912, and become a devoted follower of Big Bill Haywood. In the 1920s he joined the Socialists, but in 1928 switched his allegiance to the Communist Party. Recognizing his abilities, the Party sent Beal to New Bedford, where he led a strike (large, if unsuccessful) that same year. Although he was a Massachusetts Yankee, his appealing personality, plus the fact that he was, as William Z. Foster noted, a "real American," that is, not an immigrant, nor Jewish, made him the best candidate the Communists had to spread their message south of the Mason-Dixon line. However, he carried little weight in determining strike strategy.[29]

Beal arrived in Gastonia in early March 1929 and pulled together a skeleton organization of four dozen members within the mill. They drew up a set of demands, focusing on bread-and-butter issues, including union recognition, a wage increase, a forty-hour workweek (the existing workweek was sixty hours or longer), better company housing, an end to piecework, and equal pay for women.

Beal would have liked longer to prepare, but when management began firing union activists at month's end, he decided the moment for action had arrived. By April 1, two thousand workers had heeded the NTWU's strike call, leaving behind only a few hundred supervisors and non-striking workers in the mill. The latter were mostly African-Americans confined to the most menial jobs, who did not trust the goodwill of their fellow white workers. That, of course, did not help Beal's arguments for interracial unionism. The absence of Black workers on the picket line did not prevent the anti-strike camp from posting handbills demanding to know, "Would you belong to a union which opposes White Supremacy?"[30]

The strike attracted support, not just among Loray workers, but from sympathizers at neighboring mills. Among those flocking to the union's cause was Ella May Wiggins, a twenty-nine-year-old mother of nine (four of whom had died of diphtheria and pellagra by the time of the strike) who labored for nine dollars a week, with a seventy-two-hour workweek, on the night shift as a textile worker at the American Mill in Bessemer City, which had its own walkout. Among her other contributions to the cause, she began writing and performing pro-union songs to bolster the spirits of her fellow strikers. Years later, Beal remembered Wiggins performing "Mill Mother's Lament," one of twenty songs she wrote during the strike:

> She would stand somewhere in a corner, chewing tobacco or snuff and fumbling over notes of a new poem scribbled on the back of a union leaflet. . . . Then in a deep, resonant voice she would give us a simple ballad like the following:

> *How it grieves the heart of a mother*
> *You every one must know,*
> *For we can't buy for our children*
> *Our wages are too low.*[31]

Long-established techniques of strikebreaking were quickly brought into play by state and local authorities. North Carolina's governor O. Max

Gardner (himself a millowner) sent the National Guard to Gastonia on April 3 to police the strike, preventing picketers from approaching nearer than a block away from the mill. But the guardsmen were a relatively benign presence compared to the strike's other foes.

The violence directed against the strikers, and the desperation of their situation, were of epic proportions. A fifty-year-old woman named Ada Howell was in the wrong place at the wrong time on April 22, when fifty rifle-bearing police assaulted a peaceful parade of 500 strikers, beating and arresting dozens. Howell was just passing by on her way to the relief store, but she was assaulted nonetheless by a blackjack-wielding cop. The ILD lawyers who interviewed her afterward asked her not to wash her bloody dress, so it could be displayed as evidence of police brutality. She was unable to do so, because as she explained, "I didn't have enough dresses to lay these clothes aways."[32]

Before the third week was over, the picket lines were broken. The families of those who remained on strike were evicted from company housing, and they took refuge in a union-erected tent colony built on a sympathizer's property. Although the strike was effectively lost, the CP prolonged it for several more months. Here's where the problem lay with the CP's labor strategy in the Third Period—not in dual unionism, *per se*, but in the narrowly sectarian political calculations that underlay and too often distorted Communist strike strategy. The Gastonia conflict had become an international cause célèbre, thanks to the Comintern's publicity efforts. That raised the stakes considerably. Fred Beal remained nominally in control, but control of the strike passed to senior NTWU leaders, who undid much of Beal's work in establishing rapport with the local workers by shifting the focus away from their immediate demands to purely political aims.

"The communist leaders here are for the most part youngsters," Paul Blanshard wrote in a report from Gastonia for *The Nation* at the end of April. Blanshard, a Socialist, was sympathetic to the strikers, but skeptical about the direction the campaign was taking: "When the National Guard came to town, the Communist leaders produced an appeal to the soldiers to revolt, an appeal which had all the ear-marks of the propaganda kindergarten of the Third International: 'Workers in the National Guard, we, the striking workers, are your brothers. Our fight is your fight. . . . Fight with your class, the striking workers.'"[33]

The CP publicized the strike as a "Citadel of the Class Struggle in the New South," notable not simply as a local battle for better wages and shorter hours, in the words of *Daily Worker* editor William F. Dunne, but as "a symptom of the world crisis of capitalism which leads straight and fast to a new imperialist war, to the direct danger of an imperialist attack on the Soviet Union, the fatherland of the world's working class."[34] Fred Beal's misgivings increased as the strike dragged on. He did not regard efforts "to bring out the political nature of the conflict" as helpful.[35]

This being the South, with its tradition of official and vigilante violence, sooner or later someone was going to get killed. Beal had forbidden strikers from carrying guns on the picket lines, but he could do nothing about the guns the workers kept at home. On June 7, 1929, when the chief of police Orville Aderholt and four officers showed up at the tent colony and attempted to take a strike supporter in custody, there was a shoot-out. Although who fired the first shot remained unclear, the police got the worst of it. When the shooting stopped, Chief Aderholt lay dead. Within days almost a hundred strikers and supporters had been arrested, including Beal. He and fifteen others were charged with first-degree murder.[36]

The first trial of the union defendants began in Charlotte in August. The *Charlotte News* editorialized that strike leaders "must be given a fair trial, although everyone knows they deserve to be shot at sunrise."[37] Surprisingly their trial did not end with anyone shot at sunrise, but in a mistrial. The millowners and their thugs responded with even more violence. On September 14, a truckload of strike supporters from Bessemer City set out for a strike rally in Gastonia. Among their number was Ella May Wiggins, who was scheduled to sing to the gathering. Gunmen were waiting for them outside Gastonia, and Wiggins died in a fusillade of gunfire, a bullet lodged in her spine. Mary Heaton Vorse, who was heading to the rally that day in a separate vehicle, believed that Wiggins was targeted for assassination because of her prominent role in the strike. Seven of the ambushers were arrested; the millowners paid their bail. The trial of Wiggins's murderers ended, predictably, in acquittal.[38]

Meanwhile the second trial of the union defendants arrested for the June shoot-out took place at the end of September. This time the jury found seven of the original defendants, including Beal, guilty of second-degree murder. All the defendants received heavy sentences, with Beal and several others facing up to twenty years in prison. Five of the seven jumped bail, fleeing to the Soviet Union.[39]

Three of the Gastonia defendants eventually returned to the United States, including Beal in 1933. He had been appalled by, among other horrors, the mass starvation he witnessed in Ukraine, in the midst of a famine deliberately induced by the Soviet government. On surrendering to police in the United States he declared, "I would rather be an American prisoner than a free man in Russia." He served five years in prison.[40]

The history of American Communism, like its Soviet inspiration, is characterized by the string of onetime heroes who wound up reduced to the status of pariahs or nonpersons in the Party's subsequent retelling of its own past. It's revealing that all three leaders of the most dramatic Communist-led strikes in the 1920s—Albert Weisbord of the Passaic textile strike, Charles Zimmerman of the New York cloakmakers strike, and Fred Beal of the Gastonia strike—wound up as outspoken opponents of American Communism. Readers of William Z. Foster's *History of the Communist Party of the United States*, published in 1952, would have no idea that they were once celebrated in the Party press as skilled and devoted organizers of militant unions. Foster dismissed Weisbord as "a weakling" who played no important role in the leadership of the Passaic strike, while Zimmerman was written off as someone who "did not boldly rally the strikers" in the cloakmakers strike. Fred Beal suffered the most complete erasure, airbrushed out of history completely, unmentioned in Foster's account of the Gastonia strike.[41]

Gastonia lived on in left-wing memory as a heroic legend, but nothing came out of it remotely justifying the sacrifices made by local strikers and Communist organizers. The following year, when Communists showed up in Bessemer City, North Carolina, where a new strike was in progress, workers ran them out of town.[42]

While the Gastonia tragedy played itself out, the Party was caught up in yet another factional drama. In March 1929, when the Workers Party met for a national convention, Lovestone thought he had secured his control of the Party by ensuring that the overwhelming number of delegates attending were in his camp. That turned out not to matter, because two foreign observers dispatched by the Comintern were also in attendance, bearing instructions that Lovestone step down from the post of general secretary and report to Moscow for a new and unspecified assignment. In effect, he was being kicked upstairs, with Foster lined up to succeed him as general secretary. Still failing to understand the gravity of his situation, Lovestone agreed to step down, but not for Foster. Instead, he proposed that his ally Benjamin Gitlow assume the post of general secretary.

Stalin was not in the habit of compromising with those challenging his authority. Lovestone and other Party leaders were summoned to Moscow to appear before the Comintern's American Commission in mid-April. Lovestone argued that his faction, with its majority, deserved to remain in power. Stalin decided it was time to put an end to such nonsense. Addressing Gitlow in a meeting on May 14, he made the logic of democratic centralism brutally clear: "You had a majority because the American Communist Party until now regarded you as determined supporters of the Communist International. . . . At present you still have a formal majority. But tomorrow you will have no majority."[43] Indeed, when Lovestone finally was allowed to return to New York City, he found he had no majority left and was expelled, along with the few score of Communists who still adhered to his cause, just as he had expelled the Trotskyists the year before.[44]

Like the Trotskyists, the Lovestoneites initially maintained themselves as a separate group. Originally known as the Communist Party (Majority Group), and going by several other names over the next decade, the Lovestoneite organization finally disbanded in the 1940s. Lovestone found more secure employment in time as an American Federation of Labor functionary, specializing in battling Communist influence in European labor movements, an endeavor in which he worked following the Second World War with the Central Intelligence Agency. Lovestone associates Gitlow and Ben Mandel became prominent figures in anti-Communist circles in years to come, Gitlow as the author of ever-less-reliable accounts of his years in the Party, Mandel as a staffer for the House Un-American Activities Committee and the Senate Internal Security Subcommittee.[45]

Lovestone's 1929 expulsion brought to an end a decade in which the history of American Communism was dominated by internal factionalism. Tensions between rival leaders remained a constant, but it was another quarter century before organized factionalism would reemerge as a major factor in the history of the CPUSA.

With Lovestone's downfall in 1929, William Z. Foster seemed poised to assume Party leadership. He was the best-known American Communist, having twice run as the Party's presidential candidate, in 1924 and 1928. He looked the part of the revolutionary tribune. Al Richmond, a veteran Communist, recalled the first time he heard Foster speak at a mass meeting in 1930 (writing in the present tense, but looking back many years later): "He is a tall, slender, handsome Irishman, then a few days past his forty-ninth birthday. He has physical vitality and great platform poise.... Foster is a hero of mine. He is the embodiment of the American working class, the living confirmation of the historic mission of the proletariat."[46]

In the end, it made no difference how popular Foster was with the rank and file. As American Communists had just been forcefully reminded, they were not in a position to choose their own leaders. That was up to Stalin, who had other plans, perhaps still doubting Foster's reliability because of his previous alliance with the Trotskyist renegade Cannon. Instead, Foster was relegated to a distinctly subordinate role as one of a four-man Party Secretariat, with Max Bedacht designated the interim general secretary. However, Bedacht also had liabilities, being German-born and a former Lovestoneite, and in June 1930 he was replaced by a newcomer to the Party's highest circle, Earl Russell Browder. Browder would serve in an interim capacity as Party leader for four years until, fully tested, he was promoted to general secretary in 1934. Over the next decade, he would oversee an unprecedented period of growth and change for the Party.

Born in Wichita, Kansas, in 1891, the son of a schoolteacher with socialist sympathies, and a freethinking mother who read aloud to her children from Thomas Paine's *Age of Reason*, Browder presented himself as a quintessential heartland American. He certainly sounded like one. As historian David Shannon noted, in his Kansas twang Browder pronounced the word "cadre" as though it rhymed with "ladder."[47]

Browder joined the Socialist Party at age sixteen, shifting his allegiance a few years later to Foster's Syndicalist League of North America. He won election to the Kansas City (Missouri) Central Labor Council, and the presidency of the local AFL Bookkeepers, Stenographers, and Accountants Union. Opposing American participation in the Great War in 1917, he was convicted for failing to register for the draft and, in a separate count, for urging noncompliance by others with the Selective Service Act. He served two prison sentences for these offenses, one for eleven months and the other for sixteen months. Of course, left-wing bookkeepers are not the stuff of legendary class struggle, and unlike Foster, he was not personally charismatic. One unfriendly observer in the 1930s said Browder reminded him of "a harassed small town lawyer."[48] Beneath the provincial demeanor, however, the bookkeeper from Wichita harbored both ambition and shrewdness.

In between wartime stints in jail, Browder rejoined the Socialist Party and sided with those who sought to align the party with the newly founded Communist International. Upon release from prison in 1920 he moved to New York. Helping recruit the much better-known Foster into the Party in 1921 was Browder's first major achievement, and for the next few years he served as Foster's lieutenant in the Trade Union Education League.[49]

Browder found the opportunity to step outside of Foster's shadow when he was sent overseas on clandestine duties. In 1926, he traveled to China, to direct the Profintern's apparatus overseeing Communist trade union organizing in China. He remained there for two years, working closely with the Chinese CP's leadership until anti-Communist repression drove the Profintern out. As Browder's biographer James Ryan notes, Browder acquired a reputation in Moscow in those years as a dependable cadre, who "established himself internationally before becoming widely known at home."[50] No longer Foster's protégé, he had developed his own ambitions for Party leadership.

In 1919, the American progressive reformer Lincoln Steffens made a three-week visit to Soviet Russia, and on his return famously remarked to a friend, "I have seen the future, and it works."[51] Other writers and intellectuals, like John Dos Passos, were similarly intrigued by the utopian prospects opened by the Bolshevik Revolution in its early days. Many lost interest in the next few years, some out of disillusionment, others from boredom. Nothing much seemed to be happening in Russia worthy of notice in the mid-1920s except for endless quarrels among Soviet leaders over obscure doctrinal issues.

In the later 1920s, however, Western intellectuals again began paying sympathetic attention to what was sometimes called the Soviet experiment—and this even before the stock market crash and the ensuing crisis of world capitalism. One marker of this renewed interest could be found in the vogue for Soviet films, like Sergei Eisenstein's 1925 *Battleship Potemkin*, and his 1928 *Ten Days That Shook the World*, two of some forty Soviet films commercially distributed in the United States in the second half of the decade.[52] Travel to Russia was also becoming significantly easier, no longer the arduous and forbidding adventure it had been in the early days of Bolshevik rule. World Tourists, a travel agency founded in New York City in 1927, with close links to the Communist Party (and in time to Soviet espionage), offered travel packages to the USSR, including an all-inclusive bargain tour costing $187.50.[53]

In the summer of 1928 Columbia University philosopher John Dewey led a delegation of educators, including several college presidents, on a tour of Leningrad and Moscow. On his return to the United States, Dewey wrote a six-part series for the *New Republic* about trends in Soviet education and arts. "Perhaps the most significant thing in Russia," he commented, "is not the effort at economic transformation, but the will to use economic change as the means of developing a popular cultivation" of a new culture and aesthetics, "such as the world has never known."[54] Dewey had no use for Leninist doctrine. In that, he was fairly representative of those beginning to take pilgrimages to the Soviet Union. Admiration for Soviet achievement among visiting intellectuals like Dewey tended to focus on cultural and social achievements only incidentally associated with socialism, let alone the dictatorship of the proletariat. They were more likely to visit a theater than a factory.[55]

Toward the end of the 1920s, the Communist Party's disdain for intellectuals, generally dismissed until then as unreliable, wavering, and petit bourgeois, began to change. The CP already had a number of affiliated writers' groups, thanks to its foreign-language federations and clubs, but literary efforts in Yiddish or Russian had little political impact in the United States outside of immigrant enclaves. What shifted in the Party's estimation was the importance of intellectuals, writers, artists, and others who brought political and cultural legitimacy to left-wing causes, such as the Sacco-Vanzetti case. Accordingly, Communists began to devote more attention and resources to what they referred to, in the militarized language of Party strategizing, as the "cultural front."

In 1929, Communists established their first organization for English-speaking writers, the John Reed Club. It proved an unexpected success, soon dwarfing the foreign-language groups in size and visibility. By 1932 that first club, based in New York City, had grown into a national organization with chapters in a dozen cities and about 800 members. While the *New Masses* remained the Party's flagship publication on the cultural front, many of the chapters founded their own literary magazines, including Chicago's *Left Front*, which published the earliest writings of an aspiring young Black novelist named Richard Wright.[56]

Unlike Wright, most of the writers drawn to the John Reed Clubs were little known and destined to remain so. Proletarian literature was a worthy goal in the eyes of the Party's cultural commissars, but non-proletarian writers who attained greater public recognition also had their uses, and were increasingly courted. In 1932, a group of fifty-three writers and other intellectuals formed the League of Professional Groups for Foster and Ford (referring to William Z. Foster and James W. Ford, the Communist candidates for president and vice president in that year's election), their number including such well-known figures as novelist Theodore Dreiser and literary critic Edmund Wilson. Though the group was short-lived, it proved the advance guard of a much larger collection of famous writers who would come to the aid of causes supported by the Communists later in the decade.[57]

The onset of the Great Depression drew new contributors to the *New Masses*. Among them was a young Columbia College–educated writer named Whittaker Chambers. He had joined the Party in 1925, dropped his Party membership when Lovestone was purged in 1929, but rejoined in 1931. He was chosen as editor of the *New Masses* in May 1932 largely on the strength of a short story he contributed a year earlier, "Can You Hear Their Voices?," dramatizing the impact of the Dust Bowl and the Depression on Arkansas farmers. It received widespread attention outside of Party circles and was rewritten as a play that was performed by radical theater groups across the United States, and around the world.[58]

Chambers was not destined to remain long with the *New Masses*. Sometime in the summer of 1932, he was summoned to the office of Max Bedacht, who after stepping down as acting general secretary of the CP played an unpublicized role as a recruiter for the Party's "special institutions," which meant underground activities. This underground bore no resemblance to the romantic playacting that Communists had engaged in during the early 1920s, but instead represented the beginning of one of the more successful spy networks in the history of espionage. Chambers, an unworldly and disheveled character, seems like an odd choice by Bedacht for a post as sensitive as espionage agent, but for whatever reasons the offer was made and accepted. At first, he worked for the OGPU (Russian acronym for Unified State Political Directorate), the Soviet central intelligence agency, and later for the GRU (acronym for Main Intelligence Directorate), the Red Army's military intelligence operation.[59]

On March 6, 1930, four and a half months after the stock market crash, the Communists led demonstrations in cities across the country to observe what the Comintern designated "International Unemployment Day." The most impressive took place in New York City's Union Square. The *Daily Worker* called it "the greatest demonstration ever seen in New York." The *New York Times*, in contrast, labeled the event "the worst riot New York has seen in recent years."[60]

It was certainly the largest assemblage ever held under American Communist auspices, probably more than the 35,000 credited by the *New*

York Times if less than the 110,000 claimed by the *Daily Worker.* The crowd filled Union Square and spilled over into side streets. The rally proceeded peacefully until shortly after 2:00 p.m., when Party leaders called on those gathered to march downtown to City Hall to present their demands for unemployment relief. According to the somewhat self-contradictory report in the *New York Times,* the "mob was led by a group of women and children holding aloft banners and singing The Internationale." They did not get far. The police moved in, some on horseback, wielding clubs and blackjacks, and as the *Times* reported, "in fifteen minutes of spectacular fighting scattered [the crowd] in all directions," inevitably prompting cries of "Cossacks!" That same day, tens of thousands more gathered in Boston, Chicago, Detroit, San Francisco, Los Angeles, and other cities, often violently dispersed by the police.[61]

One of those who helped organize the March 6 demonstration across the country in Oakland, California, was a fifteen-year-old member of the Young Communist League named Dorothy Rosenblum (later Dorothy Healey), the precocious daughter of Barbara Rosenblum, the early Denver Communist. By then Dorothy and her family were living in Berkeley, where she was a high-school student. But the lessons she was taking to heart were not those taught in public school. The lead-up to that demonstration in the late winter of 1930 proved, Healey recalled, "a formative moment for those of us in the YCL." Like the teenaged Elizabeth Gurley Flynn a generation earlier, her real education came on urban street corners, standing on a soapbox in front of a crowd of strangers in Oakland's skid-row district. Never having spoken publicly in her life, she was terrified at first, but learned "to speak naturally, as if it were all coming off the top of your head," and learned as well how to hold her own when her listeners heckled—"there was a lot of heckling." There were other practical tasks to learn, like how to run a mimeograph machine. But most importantly, for her, and for her youthful comrades, they were unconsciously "absorbing the organizational habits that came to characterize my generation of radicals":

We took the question of organization very seriously. . . . You started with small demonstrations in relief offices, or in various neighborhoods around the city, and then built up to a big central demonstration. That's the way to turn out a mass following, so you're not just bringing out your own militants each time. . . . We brought new people to demonstrations as a way of increasing their knowledge of the power of collective endeavor.[62]

Those lessons came slowly, for the YCLers and for the adult Party members, with many stumbles along the way. In the summer of 1930, the CP organized a conference in Chicago to create a new national organization known as the Unemployed Councils, which soon opened branches in every city where the Party had a presence. True to the spirit of Third Period ultra-leftism, they combined practical demands for increased relief payments, or blocking evictions, with calls to "Defend the Soviet Union" and the like, which limited their appeal. Still, keeping at it, day by day, month after month, Communist organizers drew in new recruits, by ones and twos, who then learned from their recruiters how to become organizers themselves. Steve Nelson was one of the Communists involved in early unemployed organizing in Chicago, a city where in the first five years of the Depression Communists organized over 2,000 demonstrations. "It was from involvement in the daily struggles," he recalled, "that we learned to shift away from a narrow, dogmatic approach to what might be called a grievance approach to the organizing."[63]

One thing there was no shortage of in the Depression years was grievances. Communists became well-known in poor urban communities for blocking the evictions of tenants who were about to be displaced for being unable to pay the rent. In Chicago, sociologist Horace Cayton Jr. noted in a study of the Black community in the 1930s, when "eviction notices arrived, it was not unusual for a mother to shout to her children, 'Run quick and find the Reds!'"[64] The CP's Unemployed Councils never achieved much organizational

William Z. Foster of New York (left), James W. Ford (right), Communist Party presidential and vice-presidential candidates, May 28, 1932 (Getty Images)

stability, and their political clout was limited. There were difficulties inherent in attempting to organize people with no fixed place of employment, and often no fixed abode. But the movement was important as the training ground where Communists learned valuable skills that they would draw upon later in the decade in more consequential organizing campaigns.

In 1932, the year of "Brother, Can You Spare a Dime?," the United States held its first presidential election since the start of the Great Depression. William Z. Foster ran for the third time as the Communist Party's presidential candidate. The last time he had run, in 1928, he received a mere 21,181 votes. In 1932, his vote increased fivefold, to 102,991. Less encouraging for the Communists was the increase in the vote for the Socialist presidential candidate that same year, with Norman Thomas receiving 918,000 votes, up from 289,000 four years before.[65]

Of course, both left-wing candidates trailed far behind the winner, Democratic candidate Franklin D. Roosevelt, with 22,821,277 votes. But the Communists, for the moment, were more concerned with closing the gap with the Socialists than with the seemingly inconsequential victory of this or that capitalist candidate, even one promising a "New Deal." "Roosevelt to Carry on Hoover Hunger Rule," shrugged the *Daily Worker*'s headline the day after the election.[66]

The Party's Third Period stance, in theory, emphasized class consciousness and class struggle, with "Class Against Class" a frequently employed slogan. It might have been more accurately rendered as "Communists Against Everyone." Since 1928, in accordance with the policies set down in Moscow, American Communists had denounced Socialist Party members as "social fascists," which is to say that, socialist label notwithstanding, their rivals were "objectively" doing the work of fascism. In fact, in some ways, the SP social fascists were even worse than the real fascists, since their appeals confused workers who would otherwise (so the argument went) find their way into Communist ranks.[67] The Communists' definition of coalition with other groups on the Left was through what they described as "united fronts from below," which meant enticing socialists and others to abandon their social fascist misleaders and join the Communist Party.[68]

The Communists' go-it-alone belligerence was on full display in William Z. Foster's 1932 book *Toward Soviet America*. Foster's frank discussion of what the Communists intended to do if and when they came to power in the United States became a lasting political liability for the Party. In the book's closing chapter, entitled "The United Soviet States of America," Foster argued that when the revolution came to America, it would duplicate in every important respect the pattern set in Russia in 1917. Thus a "revolutionary American working class" would create "Soviets" on the Russian model, whose decisions "are enforced by the armed Red Guards of the workers and peasants and by the direct seizure of the industry through factory committees." The resulting American Communist dictatorship "necessarily will have to hold firmly in check the counter-revolutionary elements who seek to overthrow or sabotage the new regime. . . . The mildness or severity of the repressive measures used by the workers to liquidate this class politically will depend directly upon the latter's resistance." Naturally, "all the capitalist parties—Republican, Democratic, Progressive, Socialist, etc.—will be liquidated," leaving "the Communist Party functioning alone as the Party of the toiling masses."[69]

The language Foster employed in *Toward Soviet America* was deliberately inflammatory: "armed Red Guards," "repressive measures," "liquidated," and so on. And also, as so often, it sounded like a literal translation from the original Russian—American "peasants"? Of course, in the early 1930s a term like "liquidated" carried an abstract meaning, at least for Americans, not yet fully equated with mass murder. The rhetoric of tough-minded despotism justifying one-party dictatorship had for some time coexisted in Communist publications with gentler images of a workers' government exercising fair-minded paternal authority. Like Saint Augustine's doctrine of "righteous persecution," which held that Christian love for the sinner might occasionally require physical chastisement or even execution to save them from eternal damnation, Bolshevik righteous persecution punished its opponents, especially its working-class opponents, strictly for their own good, or so Communists liked to believe. As another Party leader, Moissaye Olgin had written in the *Frayhayt* a few years earlier, "Dictatorship forces the individual worker to follow proletarian rule like a father forces his child to take medicine that tastes bad to him, but will make him healthy."[70] Who could take issue with a form of government that embodied a father's stern but loving authority backed by medical/scientific expertise?

Communist readers, in any case, didn't necessarily take Foster's bloody-minded threats seriously. Some may have regarded his words simply as a kind of provocative reworking of Shelley's *Ye are many—they are few*, a bit of bold rhetorical swaggering, not an actual blueprint for American Communist rule. However, for those less inclined to grant Foster poetic license, his language sounded more ominous. In posing the "choice" between "a prosperous happy Soviet Russia" and a "decaying doomed capitalist world," declared *New York Times* reviewer Joseph Shaplen (who had covered the Russian Revolution as a reporter in 1917), "Mr. Foster does not really intend to wait for the reader to make a choice. He boldly predicts the coming of the day when the choice shall be forced upon him in accordance with accepted Communist principles."[71] Promise or threat, as a matter of practical politics in a year in which Foster was asking Americans to vote for him for president of the United States, the message conveyed by *Toward Soviet America* was self-defeating, or, as Lenin might have said, "infantile."

The early 1930s were lean times for union organizers. Those workers lucky enough to retain jobs in those first years of the Depression, by and large, were understandably cautious, unwilling to risk being fired, either for striking or even joining a union.

TUUL, the Party-organized rival of the AFL, led a few large-scale strikes at the start of the new decade. The decline of the United Mine Workers offered Communists an opportunity, as spontaneous strikes by formerly unionized and increasingly impoverished miners broke out in the coal fields in the early 1930s. At the end of May 1931, responding to a call from TUUL's National Miners' Union, miners in western Pennsylvania, Ohio, and West Virginia went out on strike protesting recent wage cuts; at its height, organizers claimed 40,000 on strike, and thousands joined the National Miners' Union. It was the largest strike yet conducted under Communist leadership. It was, of course, met with violence by the authorities and a stubborn refusal to negotiate by mine owners, and eventually petered out without any permanent gains for either workers or TUUL.[72]

California agriculture was another place where Communists scrambled to get a foothold among desperately poor workers. After learning the ropes as an organizer in the unemployed struggles at the start of the 1930s, Dorothy Healey became a union organizer for the TUUL Cannery and Agricultural Workers' Industrial Union (CAWIU) while still a teenager. She was involved in a cannery-workers strike in San Jose in the summer of 1931, and a lettuce-workers strike in the Imperial Valley in January 1934, the latter leading to her arrest and a six-month jail sentence for disturbing the peace. Both strikes went down to defeat, and left behind no active union presence. In the early 1930s, Healey recalled, "the Party's attitude was that strikes . . . had an importance in themselves, regardless of outcome." Strikes were never considered "lost" because "each strike supposedly was a revolutionary training experience." Communists, like the Wobblies before them, "didn't understand the need for consolidating our gains, to make our unions serve the workers as a union, to provide leadership and continuity."[73]

In 1933, with some exceptionally talented organizers in the field, and a new Communist district organizer in California, Sam Darcy, who had a more realistic approach to labor struggles, the CAWIU led twenty-four strikes in the San Joaquin valley and elsewhere in the state, involving over 37,000 workers, the majority of whom won wage increases. In terms of workers who struck under the union's banner, it was, as historian Justin Akers Chácon notes, "the largest farmworker union in history." But the strikes failed to build a stable, ongoing organization in the fields.[74]

The future of industrial unionism would have to be secured elsewhere. In a few TUUL unions in the early 1930s, Communist organizers were learning to focus their efforts on the mundane tasks of building institutional strength over time, rather than staging pitched battles in costly and premature adventures. The latter generated headlines; the former built unions. Despite Comintern orders to cease "dancing quadrilles" around the American Federation of Labor, some Communist organizers, thinking for themselves, late in the Third Period began pushing at the edges of the politically permissible.

When Franklin Roosevelt introduced his New Deal policies intended to end the Depression in the months following his March 1933 inauguration, Communists condemned the program in its entirety, including the National Industrial Recovery Act (NIRA). Enacted in June 1933, the NIRA sought to enlist American industry in promoting economic recovery through a voluntary system of "fair competition," including production restriction, price-fixing, and similar measures. The measure was largely ineffective and its key provisions were invalidated by the US Supreme Court two years later.

But one provision, designated Section 7(a), included as an afterthought in the bill at the insistence of New York senator Robert F. Wagner, proved of immense consequence. It put the federal government for the first time on record as recognizing the right of American workers to organize for the purpose of collective bargaining "through representatives of their own choosing." Section 7(a) lacked an official enforcing mechanism and was ignored or resisted by industry. It nonetheless helped spark a wave of successful union organizing in 1933–1934.[75]

The *Daily Worker* denounced the NIRA, including Section 7(a), as the "industrial slavery act."[76] Communists remained convinced in 1933 that there was absolutely nothing the capitalist state even in its most liberal incarnation could offer that could possibly be of benefit to working people. When Senator Wagner proposed a bill in the spring of 1934 that would take Section 7(a)'s abstract endorsement of the right to collective bargaining and give it real enforcement teeth, Communist William Dunne was among the witnesses (most of the others representing business interests) opposing the measure. "We are against the bill just as we were against clause 7(a)," Dunne declared, "because it is intended to be used as another will-o'-the-wisp to dance before the eyes of the working class [to] trick them further into the swamp of starvation wages and permanent mass unemployment."[77]

Rank-and-file workers had other ideas, and through their actions demonstrated who was really in the vanguard of the labor struggle in those early

New Deal years. In the summer of 1933, a longshoreman in San Francisco named Henry Schmidt, who may have been a Communist Party member by then, signed up with the AFL's International Longshoremen's Association union (ILA), which until that time had been largely ineffective and inactive in organizing the docks. "We sort of streamed into the office," Schmidt said of himself and many others who were joining the union that summer. "It was the right time and the right place. It also had something to do with that thing that was called the National Recovery Act, NRA, Section 7a."[78]

Three years earlier, the Communists had founded the Marine Workers Industrial Union (MWIU), affiliated with the Trade Union Unity League, as a catchall organization for waterfront workers, including both sailors and longshoremen. Drawing on a long tradition of maritime syndicalism, MWIU militants were direct-action oriented, as shown by the frequent strikes they led on ships in the early 1930s. Their efforts contributed later in the decade to the founding of the powerful National Maritime Union (NMU) representing seamen sailing out of East Coast ports.[79]

The MWIU's efforts to organize West Coast longshoremen, however, languished. As Sam Darcy, the Party's district leader in California in the early 1930s admitted, TUUL had "not a single worker on the docks" in San Francisco when Henry Schmidt signed up with the ILA in 1933.[80]

Darcy, born Samuel Dardeck in Ukraine in 1905, was brought by his family to New York at age two. He joined the Young People's Socialist League at age eleven. He switched to the Communist camp and was a founder of the Young Workers League in 1924, later spending a year in Moscow as representative to the Young Communist International. Back in New York by the start of the decade, he was one of the principal organizers of the unemployed demonstration in Union Square in March 1930. But he ran afoul of Earl Browder, who didn't like Darcy's refusal to join in the constant chorus of praise from other Party leaders that the up-and-coming general secretary considered his due. As a result, Darcy was exiled to California in 1931, the West Coast then considered a backwater in its importance to the Party. As the new district organizer, Darcy proved himself a maverick, willing to support initiatives from below that were not quite in line with prevailing orthodoxy back on the East Coast.[81]

In December 1932, San Francisco Communists active in the Marine Workers Industrial Union launched a mimeographed newspaper called the *Waterfront Worker*. It focused on workplace issues, keeping its left-wing politics visible but understated. The newspaper spoke in a direct and earthy dockside vernacular, attacking the hated morning "shape-up," where workers gathered on the docks to be chosen for a day's employment, with this little ditty:

> *There once was a gang-boss named Dink*
> *Who from all his men ask'd a drink*
> *"If you give, you get hired*
> *If you don't you're fired."*
> *It's no wonder his name stink.*[82]

In the summer of 1933, the newspaper broadened its appeal as it came under control of a left-wing caucus in the ILA including both Communists and non-Communists, known as the Albion Hall group for its usual meeting place. With Darcy's approval, the paper urged longshoremen to join the International Longshoremen's Association, while criticizing the union's conservative leaders. The MWIU faded into oblivion in the pages of the *Waterfront Worker*. The paper's constant refrain in the spring of 1934 was that the "Rank and File must take a more active part in the affairs of the Union," by which it meant the ILA, "if they are not to be SOLD OUT."[83] The key figure in the Albion Hall group was a thirty-two-year-old Australian-born militant named Harry Bridges, who had arrived in the United States in 1920, spent several years as an able seaman and Wobbly agitator aboard merchant ships, and since 1922 worked on the San Francisco docks as a longshoreman.[84]

The Albion Hall group, with Bridges and a number of Communists in the lead, organized an ILA strike supported by 10,000 to 15,000 longshoremen that shut down the docks along the entire West Coast of the United States for eighty-three days in the spring and summer of 1934. That, in turn, sparked a general strike in solidarity honored by well over 100,000 San Francisco workers. California's Republican governor Frank Merriam sent in the National Guard to break the strike. Up and down the coast, violence by guardsmen, police, and vigilantes cost a half dozen lives among the strikers and their supporters. Nevertheless, in the end the strikers won a resounding victory, including wage gains, and a union-controlled hiring hall to replace the morning shape-up. Their victory led in a few years to the formation of the International Longshore and Warehouse Union (ILWU), with Harry Bridges as union president, and Henry Schmidt as president of ILWU Local No. 10 in San Francisco. The longshore strike, an epic American labor struggle, was a dramatic and long-lasting success. The ILWU for years stopped work annually on the anniversary of the day that two strikers lost their lives in San Francisco on what was remembered as "Bloody Thursday" in the Big Strike of 1934. Nothing before in the history of Communist-influenced strikes was remotely comparable in scope or importance. The lives in Gastonia in 1928 had been thrown away for nothing. The deaths on the waterfront six years later, while tragic, counted.[85]

The victory on the docks happened because rank-and-file workers, including some Communists, pushed in a direction that stretched the existing Party line to its limits. Both the Comintern and the CPUSA had been inching toward abandoning dual unionism since 1933, but on the eve of the longshore strike Browder would only go so far as to say that Communists should "build revolutionary opposition groups" in the AFL unions.[86] The longshore strike pushed Communists to work within the AFL to build strong industrial unions without the explicit and extraneous revolutionary goals. As the CPUSA reported with no little pride to the

Comintern in August 1934, "The reason for our strength in San Francisco, as distinguished from other strike situations where the Party stood on the outside of the struggle is because ALREADY in the middle of 1933, when the majority of the workers showed their desire to belong to the AFL, we actively participated in the organization of the AFL local among the long-shoremen."[87] TUUL, launched in 1929 at the start of the Third Period, was disbanded early in 1935, and there were few mourners in the CPUSA.

Unlike the dual-unionist adventure, sometimes the Comintern got something right. Decisions announced at the 1928 Sixth World Congress of the Comintern forced American Communists for the first time to pay serious attention to the "Negro Question," that is, to the plight of African-Americans in the United States, in a way that no previous socialist movement or other predominantly white-led political movement had done since the era of the abolitionists.

The old Socialist Party had a mixed record in the struggle for Black rights. Eugene Debs, who personally favored racial equality, nonetheless declared that socialists "have nothing special to offer the Negro, and we cannot make special appeals to all races. The Socialist party is the party of the whole working class, regardless of color."[88] This color blindness was thought at the time to be the essence of principled racial egalitarianism, certainly by Debs's white comrades, but it can be seen in retrospect as a blind spot for failing to recognize that the problems of African-Americans went beyond class. And not everyone in the SP was as color-blind as Debs. Black members recruited in the South were relegated to segregated locals.[89]

The Communist Party's original members, foreign-born workers in northern industrial centers, had little contact with African-American communities before the split within the Socialist Party. However, those northeastern and midwestern cities were undergoing significant demographic changes in the course of the 1920s, due to the Great Migration of the war years, as African-Americans abandoned the rural South for the urban North. As the "Red Summer" of 1919 ("red" in this case the color of blood, not the revolutionary flag) proved, racial violence was no longer confined to the Deep South, with deadly rioting breaking out between whites and Blacks in Chicago and other cities. Still, American Communists continued to rely on the ideas they had inherited from the socialist movement, declaring in 1921 that "the interests of the Negro worker are identical with those of the white."[90] But the Comintern pushed them to reconsider.

Before the revolution, the Bolsheviks had taken the position that the separate nationalities constituting the tsarist empire would, come the revolution, have the right of self-determination and independence. Stalin was the Bolshevik specialist on nationality issues, writing a pamphlet, "Marxism and the National Question," in 1913. The promise of self-determination was not fulfilled in the years after 1917 within the Soviet Union (an independent government in Georgia, established by the Mensheviks, was overthrown by force of arms in 1921), but the sentiment lived on in Comintern pronouncements that were meant to apply elsewhere. At the Comintern's Second World Congress in 1920, Lenin and Indian Communist M. N. Roy called on Communists to support national liberation struggles both in colonized countries and national minorities "among those without equal rights," specifically citing Black Americans. Two years later in 1922, at the Fourth World Congress, Jamaican-American poet Claude McKay, who had joined the Workers Party the previous year, gave a presentation about racism in the labor movement, in which he did not spare the Left. "This is the greatest difficulty that Communists of America have to overcome," he declared, "the fact that they first have got to emancipate themselves from the ideas they entertain towards the Negroes."[91] Among the American delegates to the Fifth World Congress in 1924 was Lovett Fort-Whiteman, born in Dallas in 1889, and among the first American-born Black activists to join the Communist movement.

He delivered a report to a Comintern audience including Joseph Stalin on recent developments among African-Americans. Black people, he argued, "are not discriminated against as a class but as a race." That was unorthodox; Black oppression, Communists believed, was first and foremost class oppression, although they were becoming more aware of the importance of the racial dimension. Fort-Whiteman urged the American Communist Party to begin organizing among Black southern sharecroppers.[92]

Finally, at the Sixth World Congress in 1928, the Comintern passed a resolution recognizing the right of African-Americans in those regions of the South where they constituted a majority to "self-determination," including the possible creation of a separate Black republic, independent of the United States. African-Americans were, the Comintern decided, in essence a nation within a nation, and as such entitled to secede from the United States in order to rule themselves. This became known as the "Black Belt" thesis. The proposal remained vague on practical details. (Black majority districts were not contiguous, but more of a patchwork, so how would the borders for the hypothetical new republic be drawn?) Considering that the Communist Party had no more than fifty Black members in 1928, it seemed beyond presumptuous for it to offer such a bold and improbable solution to America's racial issues. Still, for all its problems, the Black Belt thesis proved a turning point in the way that Communists understood the importance of the struggle for Black equality in the United States. And it made it imperative that the Communists begin organizing among Black southerners. As historian Mark Solomon noted: "By defining the Negro question as a national striving for self-determination, the theory elevated the Black movement to an elevated position in the Leninist pantheon: as an indispensable ally of proletarian revolution and, moreover, as a movement that was revolutionary in itself."[93]

Among the members of the special Comintern "Negro Commission" assigned to draw up the resolution was a Black Communist named Harry Haywood. Born Haywood Hall Jr. in Nebraska in 1898 and raised in Omaha and Minneapolis, he served in France with a segregated US Army regiment in World War I. Returning home, he joined the African Blood Brotherhood, a Harlem-based Black-nationalist group founded in 1919 that allied with the Communist Party soon after and then, in 1925, he joined the Party itself. He was dispatched as a student to Moscow that same year. On returning to the US in 1930 he played a major role in Communist efforts to recruit in the Black community over the next half decade.[94]

Following the dissolution of the African Blood Brotherhood in the early 1920s, the Communists organized a group called the American Negro Labor Congress (ANLC). As the name suggested, its focus was consistent with the traditional left-wing emphasis that viewed problems affecting Blacks exclusively through the prism of class. The Party identified racism as an enemy to be confronted, but chiefly because it divided white and Black workers and facilitated the exploitation of both. Like all Communist initiatives, the ANLC faced hostility from the official trade union movement, and that included Black union leaders like A. Philip Randolph, the socialist founder of the Brotherhood of Sleeping Car Porters. Never more than a paper organization, the ANLC did little to end the isolation of Communists from the African-American community, and it was disbanded in 1930. Its successor, the League of Struggle for Negro Rights, had a more politically inclusive name, but it too met little success in attracting Black supporters.[95]

Before it could agitate for a Black republic in the Deep South as mandated by the Comintern, the Party needed to build an organizational presence there. Accordingly, in late 1929, the Communists designated two new district organizations, with one headquartered in Charlotte, North Carolina, consisting of North Carolina, Virginia, and South Carolina, and the other headquartered in Birmingham, Alabama, encompassing Alabama, Georgia, Louisiana, Florida, Tennessee, and Mississippi.[96] Birmingham was the center of Alabama industry; its iron and steel industry, and the mines that supplied that industry with coal, were hard-hit by the

Depression. Before long, Communists were organizing unemployed groups in the Black community. Their most effective tactic involved sending delegations to the city's relief office on behalf of unemployed families. "We always taught our Party members and people who went on these committees to keep a calm head when they talk to these welfare officials," Black Communist organizer Hosea Hudson recalled, but they let it be known that "the neighbors in the community was waiting back there to see what the committee would have in getting the person some food or coal."[97]

Early on the Communists gained a valuable recruit in eighteen-year-old Angelo Herndon, born in Ohio and in 1930 employed in Birmingham as a miner. He joined the Party after reading a pamphlet about the Gastonia strike, and was drawn to its vision of interracial unionism. Herndon became an organizer and was arrested in Atlanta the following year, charged with promoting "insurrection," and sentenced to twenty years of hard labor. Herndon's case, handled by the ILD, drew considerable publicity, and appeals would go all the way to the Supreme Court, which invalidated the Georgia insurrection law in 1937. Another important Black recruit came to the CP via the Herndon trial. Benjamin Davis Jr., whose grandparents had been enslaved and whose father was a prominent Atlanta newspaper editor, grew up in the Atlanta Black elite, graduating from Amherst College and Harvard Law School. One year into his law career, he agreed to defend Herndon. He told the all-white jury in his summation that the prosecuting attorney "knows as much about communism as a pig does about a full dress suit." Not that anything Davis could say could possibly sway the white jurors, some of whom sat with their backs turned toward him as he spoke. Before the trial concluded, Davis too joined the Communist Party.[98]

Birmingham was no safe haven for the Communists, but they soon pushed on to even more dangerous territory in rural Alabama. Their goal was to organize sharecropper unions among landless Blacks, and their focus was rural Tallapoosa County. Here too they made valuable recruits, including Ralph Gray, the grandson of a Reconstruction-era state legislator. Of necessity, the Alabama Communist Party was a largely underground organization. As historian Robin D. G. Kelley wrote, "Two separate parties were formed—a large, broad-based organization of Southern Blacks and a tiny cadre of Northern whites . . . which met together occasionally in secret hideaways or in streets and parks during open demonstrations."[99] This underground was truly necessary, for as far as the democratic rights of African-Americans were concerned, 1930s Alabama might as well have been prerevolutionary tsarist Russia. Still, for all the dangers, the Party grew in Alabama in the early 1930s, comprising nearly 500 members, almost entirely Black, by the end of 1933.[100]

On March 25, 1931, white and Black "hoboes" riding on a Memphis-bound freight train in Alabama got into a fight, with the whites being forced off the train. The ejected whites went to the local police to complain. The police called ahead to have the train intercepted at its next stop, a small town called Paint Rock, Alabama. There, the local police (with an angry white mob gathering behind them) searched the train, and took into custody nine young African-Americans, whose ages ranged from thirteen to twenty. The police also found two young white women, Victoria Price and Ruby Bates, on the train and questioned them to see what they knew about the fight. Fearing that they might face charges of vagrancy or prostitution, the two women sought to divert attention away from themselves by accusing the nine Blacks of rape. There was no physical evidence that they had been assaulted, but in the Deep South in the 1930s in a case where white women were the accusers and Black men the accused, there was no question that the authorities would believe their story. The lives of the young Black men were now in jeopardy, and within three weeks eight of the nine were convicted in a series of rapid trials before all-white juries in the courthouse in Scottsboro, Alabama (the case of the ninth defendant, the thirteen-year-old, ended in a mistrial). The eight convicted men were sentenced to die in the electric chair on July 10. There was nothing out of the ordinary in this all-too-typical act of racial injustice in the Jim Crow South of the early twentieth century. The rush to "justice" in the case was unusual only in that the defendants had been spared meeting their fate at the hands of a lynch mob. They would surely have gone to their deaths in the electric chair, except for one new factor, the presence, nearby, of Communist organizers.[101]

Twenty-four-year-old Sol Auerbach, whose pseudonym was James S. Allen, in 1930 took on the assignment of publishing a weekly newspaper, the *Southern Worker*, based in Chattanooga, Tennessee. Philadelphia-born, Allen was the son of Russian Jewish immigrants, his father a veteran of the 1905 revolution. He had never before ventured south of the Mason-Dixon line. The first issue of the *Southern Worker* appeared on August 16, 1930. The paper had few subscribers (they were mailed their copies in plain envelopes to protect them from being identified as Communist sympathizers). Allen and his wife subsisted on a spotty subsidy from the national CP, sufficient neither to keep them in groceries nor to assure the printer was paid. He grew discouraged, and contemplated giving up the assignment and returning north.[102]

But it was Allen who, hearing the news about the arrest of the nine Black alleged rapists on March 25, 1931, alerted the International Labor Defense office in New York of the incident, suggesting that this might turn into the next Sacco-Vanzetti case.[103]

That is pretty much what happened. Thanks largely to the Communist Party, the nine men charged in the Scottsboro case became nationally and internationally famous as the "Scottsboro Boys," or sometimes the "Scottsboro Nine." While the Communists had been part of a broader Left coalition campaigning for Sacco and Vanzetti's defense, this time they were first on the scene. The NAACP was slow to awaken to the importance of the case, and by the time it sent its representatives to Alabama to contact the defendants, they found the ILD firmly in control. And not just in the courtroom. The Communists organized countless Scottsboro defense meetings and marches, from Camp Hill, Alabama, to Harlem, while their comrades abroad did the same. (At the Camp Hill protest meeting in July 1931, organized by the newly created sharecroppers' union, white vigilantes attacked the gathering and killed union leader Ralph Gray.) In a particularly dramatic development in the case, Ruby Bates recanted her accusations in 1932 and began appearing at ILD rallies in support of the defendants. By 1937 the trials and appeals, which went all the way to the Supreme Court, drew to a close, and although none of the cases ended in acquittals, several defendants were freed by then. The last convicted Scottsboro Boy, by then middle-aged, was released from jail in 1950.[104]

The Communists did the most of any group to save the lives of the Scottsboro Nine and reaped the political benefits. A generation of Black Communists, including some of its most important female leaders like Trinidad and Tobago–born Claudia Jones and Chicago-born Louise Thompson, were first drawn to the Party through involvement in the Scottsboro case. The Party also made enemies in the Black community, particularly as it battled with the NAACP for control of the defense campaign. This being the Third Period, the invective unleashed by Communists against their rivals in the Black freedom struggle was unrestrained. W. E. B. Du Bois, to take one prominent example, had been a founder of the NAACP in 1909, editor of its monthly journal *The Crisis* ever since, and since the publication of *The Souls of Black Folk* the leading African-American voice for civil rights. His example, and sometimes his mentorship, had helped shape a number of young Black activists who joined the Communist movement in the 1920s and 1930s, including Louise Thompson, who became a key Party organizer in Harlem in those years.[105] None of which saved Du Bois from coming under assault in the CP press as a "judas" and "lickspittle" of capitalism. He retaliated in the pages of *The Crisis*, declaring that the NAACP, which had been defending

Black rights long before the CP finally got around to sending its organizers south, could do a better job than the Communists in defending the Scottsboro Boys, and further that "American Negroes do not propose to be the shock troops of the Communist Revolution, driven out in front to death, cruelty and humiliation."[106]

As a result of the Scottsboro campaign, the efforts of the Unemployed Councils, and some union drives among Black workers, and notwithstanding the conflict with Du Bois and the NAACP, Communists began to attract support in the African-American community. Black churches, previously closed to Communist-sponsored gatherings due to the Party's atheism (which it was beginning to tone down), opened their doors. Harry Haywood, back in the United States after his prolonged sojourn in Moscow, recalled: "White comrades doing work among the unemployed [in Chicago] told us that the case was really an entrée into the community. Once people knew they were communists, they were accepted because communists were always associated with Scottsboro."[107]

The *Chicago Defender*, the premier Black newspaper in the country, ran an editorial entitled "Why We Can't Hate Reds," that noted its disagreement with much of the Communist program, but concluded, "there is one item with which we do agree wholeheartedly" with the CP, "and that is the zealousness with which it guards the rights of the Race."[108] Not hating the Reds wasn't the same thing as loving or supporting them. Still, this represented high praise for a group that remained a pariah in the eyes of most Americans as well as a measure of how on one central issue that had vexed the nation throughout its history, the Communists were indeed acting as a vanguard.[109]

Slowly the Party began to grow. From fewer than 7,000 in 1930, the number of registered Communists grew to 10,496 at the end of 1931, 13,949 by the spring of 1932, and 22,800 by the fall of 1934.[110] That year the

Communists claimed the distinction of becoming the largest party on the American Left, surpassing the membership of the Socialist Party, which began losing members due to its own internal factional wars in the 1930s. Still, five years into the Great Depression, the CP's membership, less than a fifth of those belonging to the Socialist Party two decades earlier, remained unimpressive. Sectarianism continued to hamper the CP's potential for growth.

In 1933, George Charney joined the Communist Party in New York City. He was twenty-eight, a graduate of New York University Law School, recently admitted to the New York bar. Rather than practice law he was drawn to full-time work as a Communist organizer. In 1934, six months into his time in the Party, he began to feel a vague sense of dissatisfaction with the extravagant leftism of its Third Period line. He had a weekly assignment of leafleting workers entering and leaving the Sunshine Biscuits factory on the Queens end of the Fifty-Ninth Street Bridge. The leaflets that he and a comrade distributed urged the workers to unionize and closed with the then-customary slogan, "For a Soviet America." One week, when they prepared to run the leaflets off on a mimeograph machine, they ventured to drop the business about Soviet America, because they "didn't like the sound of it grating on American ears," plus "it seemed so utterly farfetched to discuss wages and shop grievances, and end with this slogan."

Word got around, and at the next meeting of their Party unit, their leader, a veteran Communist from the early 1920s, "gave us our come-uppance," accusing them of opportunism. "It came right out of the 'book,' any book—*What Is to Be Done?*, *Foundations of Leninism*, *The Proletarian Revolution and the Renegade Kautsky*—in which the cardinal sin is the reluctance or failure to link immediate demands (wages) with the ultimate solution ('For a Soviet America')." The two youthful Communists were crushed by the criticism, particularly since their "petit-bourgeois origins," education, and class status were all cited as part of the comeuppance.

They had no choice but to submit. "The slogan 'For a Soviet America,'" Charney recalled in a memoir of his years as a Communist, "survived our challenge, and we stood in the corner like school children who had disobeyed the teacher."[111]

And then, a year later, in 1935, "For a Soviet America" disappeared from Communist leaflets, and suddenly everything changed.

CHAPTER 3

"Double-Check American": The Popular Front

1935–1939

Chorus: *Are you an American?*
Narrator: *Am I an American?*

I'm just an Irish, Negro, Jewish, Italian,
French and English, Spanish, Russian, Chinese, Polish,
Scotch, Hungarian, Litvak, Swedish, Finnish, Canadian,
Greek and Turk and Czech and double-check American.

—"Ballad for Americans" (1939),
music by Earl Robinson, lyrics by John La Touche

The strikers were coming out of Chevrolet, No. 4, flags preceding them.
There were flags on the steps and flags on the street. . . . The big flags
punctuated the crowd with color. They shouted to the rhythm of "Free-
dom, Freedom, Freedom!"

—Mary Heaton Vorse, *Labor's New Millions* (1938)

When Paul Robeson, the celebrated African-American singer and actor, returned to the United States in mid-October 1939 after a dozen years abroad, he was flooded with offers for bookings, including one from Norman Corwin, producer of the newly inaugurated CBS Radio series *Pursuit of Happiness*. A nationally broadcast half-hour show in the prime listening slot of Sunday late afternoons, it featured music and spoken word celebrating American democracy. Corwin asked Robeson to provide the lead voice for the performance of a cantata featuring music by Earl Robinson and lyrics by John La Touche. Originally titled "The Ballad of Uncle Sam," Corwin renamed it "Ballad for Americans."[1]

Earl Robinson, born in Seattle in 1910, arrived in New York in 1934 to study composing with Hanns Eisler and Aaron Copland. Musical and political interests led him to the Composers' Collective, a Communist-affiliated group in New York that promoted (without great success) a vision of "American proletarian music" heavily influenced by European modernism. In its early days, the collective disdained all forms of popular music, including the folk genre (a little ironically since one of the group's main figures, composer and musicologist Charles Seeger, was father to future folk singers of note, Pete, Peggy, and Mike Seeger). Robinson, who spent summers as a counselor at a Communist-run camp in Upstate New York, came to disagree with the Composers' Collective on the merits of folk music. In 1936, he wrote a song for a camp performance, with words by poet Alfred Hayes, memorializing the IWW songwriter/martyr Joe Hill. "I Dreamed I Saw Joe Hill Last Night" became a beloved staple of the folk song repertoire in succeeding generations.[2]

John La Touche, born in Baltimore in 1914, shared Robinson's political sympathies, and affinity for popular music. Robinson and La Touche collaborated on "The Ballad of Uncle Sam" for *Sing for Your Supper*, a production of the Federal Theatre Project satirizing anti–New Deal politicians. It became a target for the newly founded House Un-American Activities Committee (HUAC), and unintentionally sounded the death knell for the beleaguered Theatre Project, which lost its funding in 1939. This did not suggest much of a future for "The Ballad of Uncle Sam."[3] But the composition took on a second life, thanks to Robeson.

Since the early 1930s, Paul Robeson had made no secret of his own left-wing sympathies. He was also, politics aside, extraordinarily talented and, as biographer Martin Duberman noted, treated "his gifts and his worldly success not as ends in themselves, but as instruments for helping the [Black] race."[4]

Born in Princeton, New Jersey, in 1898, his father an escaped slave who became a Presbyterian minister, Robeson excelled academically and professionally. He earned an undergraduate degree from Rutgers, winning recognition as an All-American football player and a Phi Beta Kappa scholar. After graduating from Columbia Law School, he turned his talents to theater. By age thirty he had achieved international celebrity with starring roles in shows as varied as the musical *Show Boat* and Shakespeare's *Othello*. Radicalized in the 1930s, he visited the Soviet Union in 1934 and 1937. Robeson's prestige within the Black community proved invaluable to the American Communist Party following his return to the United States.[5]

Robeson's CBS broadcast took place on Sunday, November 5, 1939, before a studio audience of 600 listeners. "Ballad for Americans" offered a brisk tour of US history, starting with the American Revolution and continuing down to its own time. Included in the thirteen-minute historical procession were Jefferson's proclamation in the Declaration of Independence of the self-evident truth that "all men are created equal" and Lincoln's pledge at Gettysburg to preserve "government of the people, by the people, for the people." All through Robeson's recital of the national past, the initially skeptical chorus questioned his identity: "Who are you anyway, Mister?" "What's your racket?" Gradually his listeners (in the chorus and in the audience) were led to understand that he was nothing less than the universal American representing, most importantly, all national backgrounds.

To later generations that may sound like a sentimental and familiar celebration of the virtues of diversity. For many American listeners in 1939, not two decades removed from the anti-immigrant hysteria of World War I and the Red Scare, and the racist violence of the Red Summer of 1919, it was a more daring proposition. In Robeson's voice, there was congeniality—but also the proud self-assertion of his identity as a "double-check American." And in its final stanza, "Ballad for Americans" offered a testament to the nation's essential, underlying promise:

> *Our country's strong, our country's young,*
> *And her greatest songs are still unsung. . . .*
> *For I have always believed it, and I believe it now,*
> *And now you know who I am.*
> **Chorus:** *Who are you?*
> **Robeson:** *America! America!*

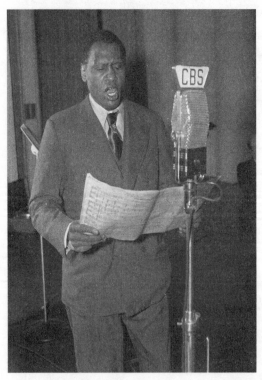

Paul Robeson at rehearsal for his second radio performance of "Ballad for Americans," December 31, 1939

(Photo by CBS via Getty Images)

On that note, the studio audience stood and cheered. Robeson was invited back to the program for a repeat performance on New Year's Eve, and "Ballad for Americans" became a standard in his concert repertoire. The song proved right for the moment, mixing themes of national self-celebration with social idealism, capturing the convictions and anxieties of a country still emerging from economic catastrophe while standing on the verge of global conflict. "Ballad for Americans" was so popular that, notwithstanding its left-wing origins, white baritone singer Ray Middleton was invited to perform it at the Republican National Convention in the summer of 1940. *Time* magazine, although unsympathetic to Robeson's politics, nonetheless found the choice of Middleton in his place surprising: "The Republicans were reported to have considered inviting Robeson to sing, decided against it because of his color."[6] Of course, for some listeners, what saved the song from being just another exercise in American self-absorption was the fact that its defining performance was given by a powerfully inspiring Black soloist, and not a white singer. Robeson and Bing Crosby both recorded versions of "Ballad for Americans" in 1940, and Robeson's version sold twice as many copies as Crosby's.[7]

Richard Hofstadter, a leading American historian in the post–World War II years, and briefly a member of the Communist Party while a graduate student at Columbia University in the 1930s, once observed that the United States was the only nation that had been "born in perfection and aspired to progress."[8] His wry insight helps explain the popularity of "Ballad for Americans" as well as the appeal of the more inclusively democratic political stance adopted by the Communist Party in the United States in the four years leading up to Robeson's broadcast. In both could be found a message that felt at once radical and redemptive, patriotic and progressive, harkening back to John Dos Passos's "Camera Eye" meditation on the death of Sacco and Vanzetti a dozen years earlier ("do they know that the old American speech of the haters of oppression is new tonight"), although considerably more upbeat. United States history in the reading offered by "Ballad for Americans" was a struggle to realize the promises made by admirable forefathers, promises that the United States would one day truly become the land of equality and of government by, and for, the people—and, for the first time, for all the "double-check American" people.

One way to think about the Popular Front, as the Communists called their new outlook, is as an attempt on their part for the first time to build bridges between themselves and other Americans, whereas always before their inclination had been to erect barricades. Instead of revolutionary upheaval, they now sought to assemble the broadest possible coalition, both domestically and internationally, against the spread of fascism. Just how American Communists came to embrace the politics of the Popular Front, the period that proved the high point of their political influence, is a question whose answer must be sought both abroad and at home. It starts in Germany.

In 1932, the Communist Party of Germany (KPD) was the world's largest outside the Soviet Union, with 200,000 members. Germany seemed the most likely place for the next Communist revolution to take place. Instead, on January 30, 1933, Adolf Hitler was appointed the country's chancellor, a position he swiftly invested with dictatorial powers. Over the next few months, the Nazi government outlawed both the Communist and Social Democratic parties, shut down their press, and threw their leaders into concentration camps. In 1932, the votes of the two left-wing parties together exceeded that of the Nazis by a million and a half. Yet the rivals were incapable of effective resistance: even as Nazi tyranny destroyed Germany's democracy, the KPD clung to its go-it-alone slogan, "Nach Hitler kommen Wir" (After Hitler—Our Turn!).[9]

On February 1, 1933, a front-page editorial in the *Daily Worker* responded to Hitler's accession to power—the most disastrous political development of the twentieth century—by attacking Germany's Socialists. "Fascism could not have come to power," the editors proclaimed, "without the aid of the Social Democratic Party leaders."[10]

Four months later, on June 1, 1933, the *Daily Worker* denounced French Socialists for voting to expand their nation's military. Why should anyone care which side prevailed in some future conflict between France and Germany, the Communist editors demanded to know:

> What is this "democracy" for which the socialist leaders are prepared to fight and which they urge the workers to defend? . . . It is the bourgeois parliamentary democracy which serves as the mask for the ruthless exploitation of the workers by the capitalist class. . . . The socialists want to defend the democracy of French imperialism against the fascism of the German ruling class. As if there were any difference between the capitalist class of Germany and the capitalist class of France.[11]

Communists in the early 1930s subsumed their opposition to fascism within their general opposition to capitalism, often to the point where the anti-fascist component was barely visible. In 1933 the Party launched a new group called the American League Against War and Fascism, an example of what later came to be referred to, pejoratively, as a "front organization." These groups, created at the Party's initiative, attempted to mobilize supporters around a set of broadly popular issues, usually with a prominent non-Communist as official leader while effective control remained discreetly lodged in Communist hands. In this instance Harry F. Ward, a Methodist minister associated with the Union Theological Seminary, served as chairman of the league, which also listed some other non-Communists as members on its letterhead. The league's name seemed straightforwardly anti-fascist. But, reflecting the Party's political priorities in those years, its founding manifesto was more concerned, as measured in column inches, with the Roosevelt administration's military expenditures than with the danger to democracy posed by any actual fascist powers. Nazi Germany was mentioned in a single sentence, Fascist Italy not at all.[12]

In line with Third Period political priorities, Communists conducted a rule-or-ruin strategy in the anti-fascist struggle. When Socialists planned a rally in Madison Square Garden on February 16, 1934, to show solidarity with the working-class neighborhoods of "Red Vienna," strongholds of the Austrian Socialists then under armed attack by the right-wing Austrian dictatorship, the *Daily Worker* called on its readers to join them in the name of anti-fascist unity. But unifying the Left was not the Communist objective. The *Daily Worker* accused the two main speakers invited to address the Socialist meeting, Matthew Woll of the AFL and New York City's newly elected mayor Fiorello La Guardia, of being "agents of fascism" and declared they "must not be permitted to speak." Accordingly, the thousands of uninvited Communists who showed up that evening disrupted the proceedings, booing and chanting, some getting into fistfights with the Socialist ushers. In the ensuing chaos, neither Woll nor La Guardia took the podium, which the Communists counted as a success. In the topsy-turvy logic of Third Period sectarianism, the next day's *Daily Worker* front-page account proclaimed triumphantly, "Despite Provocations of SP Leaders, Workers Unite for Garden Meet."[13]

At higher echelons of the Communist movement, however, the go-it-alone logic of the Third Period, exemplified by the Madison Square Garden fiasco, was beginning to seem misguided. Hitler's accession to power in Germany forced Stalin to reconsider the advantages of finding allies among the Western democracies. In July 1934, the French Communist Party, with Moscow's blessing, signed an agreement with French Socialists forming a coalition against fascism. For the first time, this was an alliance at the top, not simply an attempt by the Communists to poach a few members from their rivals under the misleading slogan of creating united fronts "from below." A few months later, the Communists extended the offer of anti-fascist cooperation to the French Radical Party, opening up the possibility of an anti-fascist coalition extending beyond the traditional confines of the Left to include non-Marxist "bourgeois" allies. Meanwhile the Soviet Union joined the League of Nations in September 1934, an organization it had previously denounced as the ringleader of European imperialism. And in May 1935 the Soviets signed a military pact with France.[14]

All of this prepared the way for a dramatic shift in the international Communist movement's priorities, announced at the Seventh World Congress of the Comintern in Moscow in August 1935. A ten-member delegation of CPUSA leaders, including Earl Browder and William Z. Foster, were among those in attendance at the first Comintern congress to be held in seven years. The meeting was presided over by a new leading figure, Bulgarian Communist Georgi Dimitrov. He had been arrested in Berlin in March 1933 and charged with plotting the Reichstag Fire (the Reichstag, Germany's parliamentary building, burned down the previous month under mysterious circumstances that proved convenient to the Nazis in justifying their crackdown on political opponents). Dimitrov ably defended himself in the subsequent trial in Leipzig which ended, rather remarkably, with his acquittal in December 1933. On his release he was given a hero's welcome in Moscow.[15]

At the Seventh Congress's opening session on August 2, 1935, Dimitrov drew a stark distinction between bourgeois democracy and fascism, calling for an alliance—dubbed a "Popular Front" or a "People's Front" of all anti-fascist forces, left and center, against the danger on the right. Coalition-building became the new Comintern watchword. During the Third Period, the most damning thing that could be said about fellow Communists was that they had engaged in "opportunist" behavior, downplaying revolutionary principle to curry favor with those espousing more moderate views. Now the gravest political errors Dimitrov denounced were those associated with clinging to outmoded orthodoxy.[16]

"In our ranks," Dimitrov proclaimed, "there were people who intolerably underrated the fascist danger."[17] Later in the Congress, he singled out the CPUSA for reproach for having denounced President Roosevelt as a "fascist." This was, he declared, a prime example of a "stereotyped approach." It was FDR's enemies, "the most reactionary circles of American finance capital," who represented the real fascist threat. To believe otherwise, was "tantamount to misleading the working class in the struggle against its worst enemy."[18] At the conclusion of the congress Dimitrov was appointed as the Comintern's general secretary.

It was not immediately clear how dramatically the Communists' political stance would change in the aftermath of the Seventh Congress. On his return to the United States, Browder insisted that the Popular Front represented no sudden about-face, declaring that the CP's goals remained "proletarian Revolution and socialism."[19]

What did change precipitously was the Communists' attitude to the no-longer "social fascist" American Socialist Party. "We shall do all in our power to make it easier, not only for the Social Democratic workers, but also for those leading members of the Social Democratic parties and

Norman Thomas (left) and Earl Browder (right) at Madison Square Garden debate, November 27, 1935 (Getty Images)

organizations who sincerely desire to adopt the revolutionary class position, to work and fight with us against the class enemy," Dimitrov had
emphasized in his closing remarks to the Comintern congress.[20] Accordingly, American Communists took the initiative in sponsoring a series of
cordial debates between Browder and Norman Thomas in the fall of 1935,
including one before an audience of 20,000 in Madison Square Garden
on November 27, scene of fistfights between Communists and Socialists
the previous year. This time adherents of the two parties joined together
at evening's start to sing "The Internationale." For all the show of fraternal good cheer the Communists now sent their way, Socialists responded
cautiously. Thomas, labeled a social fascist in a thousand *Daily Worker*
headlines in past years, joked to Browder that recently, "I do not recognize
myself when I read the 'Daily Worker.'"[21]

Two decades later, Irving Howe and Lewis Coser wrote in their history of
the CPUSA that the Party's success in the Popular Front years was the result
of a "kind of Machiavellian inspiration—the inventiveness that sometimes
comes from total cynicism."[22] That was not entirely wrong but, as Howe
would acknowledge subsequently, insufficient as a way of understanding the
Popular Front, particularly in its appeal to the younger recruits to the Communist cause. George Charney, who joined the CP in 1933 and remained a
member for the next quarter century, offered a different perspective in his
memoir. He had been slapped down by the guardians of Third Period orthodoxy when he ventured to drop the slogan about "Soviet America" from
a leaflet in 1934. He recalled of the advent of the Popular Front in 1935:

The very speed with which we adapted ourselves to the new line
. . . was an indication not so much of our mercurial temper as the
fact that it reflected what many of us really believed but could not
articulate. We were prepared to live, even sluggishly, with the old

policies, if that was the will of the party. But we were so much happier to live with a policy that was natural, that heeded reality, and that could unleash our creative talents and energies.[23]

Unlike some of their elders, younger Communists were predisposed to embrace the new policy. Prior to 1935 they had on occasion, without setting out self-consciously to overturn the prevailing orthodoxies, engaged in what might be called premature Popular Frontism. This was most evident in what had been for American Communists the previously unexplored political terrain of campus activism.

The Communist Party's youth affiliate, the Young Workers League, wasn't designed to attract student members, as its name suggested. Nor did it show much interest in that constituency when the name was changed to the Young Communist League (YCL) at the end of the 1920s. The YCL had about 3,000 members in 1930, but no formal campus presence. The Socialist Party, in contrast, had long maintained both a youth affiliate, the Young People's Socialist League (YPSL), and a campus affiliate, the Intercollegiate Socialist Society. The latter, founded in 1905, changed its name to the League for Industrial Democracy in 1921. It attracted only a handful of students in the decade that followed, since most seemed preoccupied in those years with football and fraternities; the only laws they sought to overturn were those associated with Prohibition.[24]

That changed in the early 1930s, to the benefit of both campus Communists and Socialists. Although the Depression saw a national decline in enrollments in higher education, New York City students continued to attend the city's tuition-free public colleges: City College of New York, Hunter College, and Brooklyn College. The city also had a private institution, Cooper Union, that students could attend tuition-free. Those four institutions, along with Ivy League Columbia University, proved the birthplace of the first large-scale student radical movement in the history of American higher education.[25]

Free-speech issues were an early and continuing rallying point, since many college and university administrators hated the noisy radicals who were beginning to appear on their campuses and did their best to crack down on them, with suspensions and expulsions. By the fall of 1931, YCLers and sympathizers from the city's campuses banded together to form the New York Student League, which the following spring joined with similarly minded students from other campuses, mostly in the Northeast, to form the National Student League (NSL). Around the same time, Socialist students began to revive their own campus presence under the auspices of the Student League for Industrial Democracy (SLID). [26]

The NSL espoused the standard Communist Party line on most issues of the day. And yet, as historian Robert Cohen noted, precisely because the Party and the YCL attributed little importance to student activism, from the beginning the NSL "was able to formulate policies that were based more on campus realities than Comintern dogma."[27]

The most important expression of the NSL's realism was its willingness to cooperate with non-Communist students, including Socialists, in common endeavors, starting in 1932. Their most impressive joint venture proved to be a series of annual one-hour student strikes against war, held every year between 1934 and 1937. The first, on April 13, 1934, drew 25,000 participants, the largest single student protest in American history to that point, with most of the turnout in New York City (this was, it's worth remembering, less than two months after adult Communists disrupted the Socialist Party's anti-fascist rally in the same city). The 1935 strike the next April claimed 175,000 participants on campuses across the nation.[28]

In December 1935, the NSL and SLID merged to form the American Student Union, with Socialist Joseph Lash as executive secretary and Communist James Wechsler as editor of its magazine. Over the next few years, it grew to 20,000 members, a number not topped by any similar organization until Students for a Democratic Society in the late 1960s.[29]

In another act of nascent Popular Frontism, the YCL and the YPSL cooperated in 1934 to gain control of a newly established umbrella organization of youth and student groups called the American Youth Congress (AYC). The AYC, founded under vaguely liberal auspices before it was taken over by the radicals, aspired to act as the voice of all the country's reform-minded youth organizations. Following its capture by the YCL and YPSL, the AYC went on to become one of the most influential front organizations of the 1930s in the United States, lobbying for federal spending for higher and vocational education and other youth-oriented causes. It secured the informal patronage of Eleanor Roosevelt, who attended the AYC's annual conventions in the summer of 1938 and 1939.[30]

The Young Communist League itself grew sevenfold in the 1930s, to some 22,000 members by decade's end. Among the reasons for the YCL's success was the leadership of Gil Green, who had joined the Young Workers League as an eighteen-year-old in 1924 and oversaw Communist youth organizing until the end of the 1930s. He displayed considerably more flexibility than other ham-fisted Communist apparatchiks left over from the 1920s, as displayed by his willingness to refrain from cracking down when YCLers active in student and youth politics pushed at the outer boundaries of the politically permissible.[31]

The YCL's growth represented a demographic watershed within the Communist movement, insofar as most of its new members were native-born, if often of immigrant parents. Attending public schools where they mixed with youngsters from different ethnic and religious backgrounds, and used to the rough-and-tumble of city streets, the YCL generation's influence served to "Americanize" the CP in the years to come. As they graduated to leadership positions in the adult organization, they tipped the percentage of native-born Party members from less than a third in 1933 to over half by the end of 1936.[32]

The YCLers were the radical edge of a much-larger rising wave of first-generation Americans, restlessly inhabiting the urban immigrant neighborhoods into which they were born, eager to find a place within the larger society. In a curious way, the life of a Communist activist would provide a select minority of that generation a crash course in American assimilation. Nat Ross provides an instructive example. Born to Russian Jewish immigrant parents in New York, he joined the CP in 1929. Over the next several years he served as a Party organizer in southern Illinois, then as a section organizer in Indianapolis, followed by a stint in Birmingham, Alabama, as district organizer for the Deep South, before moving to Minnesota, where he oversaw a dramatic increase in Communist membership as the Party allied itself with the Minnesota Farmer-Labor Party.[33]

Young Communists dispatched to Indianapolis, Birmingham, and Minneapolis soon learned that if they were to have political success they couldn't get by with the kind of dogmatic assertions that might go unquestioned on the Lower East Side of New York, or similar heavily foreign-born enclaves. In the 1920s, young Communists like Peggy Dennis felt estranged from their adopted homeland, vesting their feelings of patriotic identification with the distant, idealized Soviet homeland, which was "*nahsh*"—ours. That identification with the Soviet Union didn't weaken in the 1930s, but for many of the next Communist generation their own country was also becoming "ours" emotionally in a way that hadn't been the case a decade earlier. As National Student League founder George Watt recounted to an interviewer some decades later, "Those of us in the youth movement were working with university groups all over the country, with a lot of liberals, non-Marxist youth, and we began to feel that we were really part of the American scene." Browder's slogan, "Communism Is Twentieth Century Americanism," signaled to Watt when it was introduced in 1936 that his feelings were not only politically acceptable but a guide to how the movement should orient itself in the future.[34]

Much of the Communist effort to drape their movement in the trappings of previous generations of respectable American patriots, especially those of the Revolutionary War era, owed more of a debt to P. T. Barnum than to Tom Paine. In one famous example from 1937, the New York City chapter of the Daughters of the American Revolution (DAR) neglected to commemorate the anniversary of Paul Revere's ride. Young Communists pounced, hiring a horse and rider (the latter in Revolutionary War costume) to ride up and down Broadway, with a sign that declared, "The DAR Forgets But the YCL Remembers."[35]

Still, for some young Communists, the Party's pivot toward performative patriotism represented something more than just a stunt. In the space of little over a year, the shift from "Toward Soviet America" to Browder's new slogan brought tangible political gains, a lesson not lost on the YCLers. They regarded it as a permanent change in the Party's outlook and practice, rather than just an expedient maneuver.[36]

A potent symbol of assimilation into American society for the children of immigrants in the early twentieth century, by no means limited to young Communists, lay in the decision to abandon the foreign-sounding names they had been born with for other, more "American" names. George Watt was a case in point. Born Israel Kwatt, he felt little attachment to his given name, which had already gone through one change (from Kievkavsky) when his father emigrated to America. The son changed his own name when he became a student organizer.[37] As a rule, the children of immigrants joining the American CP in the 1930s tended to choose generic, Anglo-Saxon-sounding names: thus Abraham Richman became Al Richmond, and Joseph Cohen became Joe Clark. These were names designed for blending in to a country with which they had come to identify far more strongly than their elders, parental and political, could have imagined.[38]

With the onset of the Popular Front, the Communist Party cleaned house of organizations that had outlived their usefulness. Among those disbanded in 1935 were the League of Struggle for Negro Rights, which despite its involvement in the Scottsboro campaign had found only limited support in the Black community, and the John Reed Clubs, too closely identified with the Party's campaign promoting a stillborn vision of "proletarian literature" to be taken seriously by more influential writers and intellectuals.

Following the demise of the League of Struggle for Negro Rights, Communists and other figures from the Black civil rights and labor movements initiated the National Negro Congress (NNC) at a Chicago convention in February 1936. A. Philip Randolph, a Socialist whose role as the founder of the Brotherhood of Sleeping Car Porters made him the most important Black trade unionist in the United States, was elected president. That would seem to fit the usual Communist front pattern of organizations with a prestigious but pliable front man, while the real power was wielded behind the scenes by obscure Party functionaries. But not in this instance. Randolph was no ideological naïf and could hold his own in internal struggles, and the Communists were for the moment more willing than in the past to share a measure of organizational power. And the time was right for a group that was devoted to civil rights causes with a labor emphasis, as the number of Black members of American unions increased fivefold in the second half of the 1930s.[39]

When the NNC came under attack from some quarters of the Black community after its founding for including Communists, Randolph responded with a withering editorial in the *Chicago Defender*. Red-baiting, he declared, was a useful weapon for racists to "condemn those who aggressively fight for human and race rights."[40] In the next few years the congress organized chapters in more than seventy cities, and in some places its chapters proved more representative of local Black communities than the middle-class-oriented NAACP.[41] The congress spun off a youth affiliate, the Southern Negro Youth Congress (SNYC), in 1937, which functioned independently and attracted a group of talented young Black organizers to the Communist cause like James E. Jackson and Esther Cooper Jackson. While solidly under Party control, the SNYC displayed an unusual political creativity anticipating the spirit and mission of youthful Black activism in the 1960s, including launching a voter registration drive in 1940 and encouraging Black artistic expression.[42]

In another Popular Front initiative, the League of American Writers was established as successor to the John Reed Clubs. Unlike many front organizations, the league did not make use of the device of organizational affiliates to inflate its actual membership. It was going for quality not quantity in its recruitment strategy, restricting membership to writers with established professional credentials, as measured by reputation and publications. In the first two years following its founding in New York City in 1935, the league grew to a total of 250 members—not many compared to the 5 million "affiliated" members the American Youth Congress claimed that same summer. But the league's 250 were all bona fide members, who had taken the trouble of sending in a personal application, received the league's newsletter, and to one extent or another subscribed to its stated goal of supporting the Popular Front against fascism. Poet Archibald MacLeish, soon to be appointed as librarian of Congress, gave the keynote address at the league-sponsored Congress of American Writers in 1937, its second national gathering. Although not a Party member, MacLeish derided those who feared being "used" by Communists in collaborating against fascism. "The answer is," he declared, "that the man who refuses to defend his convictions for fear he may defend them in the wrong company has no convictions."[43]

Mike Gold boasted in 1939 that "Red-baiting this League is now like Red-baiting the reading taste of the American mind."[44] That certainly seemed the case when league member John Steinbeck's *The Grapes of Wrath* was published in 1939. The novel recounted the exodus of a displaced sharecropper family from Oklahoma to California where, instead of the promised land, they find only hardship and exploitation. *The Grapes of Wrath* sold 400,000 copies within a year of publication, and won Steinbeck the Pulitzer Prize. In 1940, it was the basis for an equally popular

Hollywood feature film starring Henry Fonda, which won two Academy Awards. More than any other artist, Steinbeck shaped the way subsequent generations of Americans remembered the Great Depression.[45]

Steinbeck dedicated *The Grapes of Wrath* to his first wife Carol, who was a member of the Communist Party. But Steinbeck was not a Communist himself and was not inclined to view them sentimentally. In 1934, he interviewed Cicil McKiddy, a migrant "Okie," Cannery and Agricultural Workers' Industrial Union organizer, and devout Communist, and made him the model for the protagonist of his first novel about a strike, *In Dubious Battle*, published in 1936. He admired the young man's selflessness, but found him poor company. "I don't like communists," he commented in a letter to a fellow writer in February 1936. "I rather imagine the apostles had the same waspish qualities. . . . Some of these communist field workers are strong, pure, inhumanly virtuous men. Maybe that's another reason I personally dislike them."[46]

Steinbeck's example suggests being a "fellow traveler" in the era of the Popular Front was not necessarily a synonym for being a naive puppet, or useful idiot, or the other pejoratives often attached to the term. A member of the League of American Writers, he supported the Communists when he felt they shared common interests. But he did so with his eyes open, without fully identifying with or even "liking" them, remaining independent in his own worldview and convictions. When their viewpoints diverged, as they eventually did, he went his own way.

Entirely by coincidence, just as the Communists began to move away from the ultra-sectarian policies of the Third Period in 1934–1935, the Roosevelt administration, strengthened by sweeping Democratic gains in the midterm elections of 1934, was turning leftward in its policy orientation. The New Deal's goal, notwithstanding accusations by conservative critics that it was leading the country toward Soviet dictatorship, was the revitalization and strengthening of an ailing capitalist system. What historians have labeled the Second New Deal, beginning in 1935, saw the creation of FDR's "alphabet soup" agencies, including the Works Progress Administration (WPA), the Resettlement Administration (RA), and the National Youth Administration (NYA), all of which sought to spur economic recovery by creating jobs or providing other benefits for unemployed workers and displaced farmers. The Social Security Act established a system of social insurance that for the first time offered Americans federally administered old-age pensions and unemployment insurance. And the National Labor Relations Act, better known as the Wagner Act for its principal architect Robert F. Wagner, created the National Labor Relations Board (NLRB), which committed the federal government to actually enforcing the right of employees to collective bargaining. Taken together, these measures had a transformative impact on American society, offering millions of working-class Americans an unprecedented measure of economic prosperity and social mobility.[47]

The New Deal's leftward course in the mid-1930s was both product of and spur to the phenomenal growth of labor militancy in those years, as embodied in the organization of the Congress of Industrial Organizations (CIO), which for the first time in the twentieth century created an effective rival to the American Federation of Labor. As labor historian Robert H. Zieger concluded, "The CIO stands at the center of the history of twentieth century America," representing "the largest sustained surge of worker organization in American history."[48] American Communists played a major role in creating and building on that surge.

John L. Lewis of the United Mine Workers, Sidney Hillman of the Amalgamated Clothing Workers, David Dubinsky of the International Ladies' Garment Workers' Union, and other leaders of industrial unions, all longtime critics of the AFL's lethargic conservatism, met in early November

1935 to found the Committee for Industrial Organizations (the designation "Committee" suggesting it intended to remain, for the moment, part of the AFL). However, the AFL leadership's hostile response, and the growing ambitions of CIO leaders, led to the CIO's emergence as a rival independent labor federation (renamed the Congress of Industrial Organizations in 1938), committed to spreading industrial unionism throughout America's mass-production industries, in steel, auto, rubber, electrical manufacturing, and beyond.[49]

At the Comintern's Seventh Congress in August 1935, Georgi Dimitrov cleared away any remaining doubts about the end of the Third Period's endorsement of dual unionism: "We are definitely for the re-establishment of trade union unity in each country. . . . We are for one union in each industry. We are for one federation of trade unions in each country."[50] In theory, then, American Communists should have opposed the decision to create the CIO as a rival to the AFL. But they quickly came to recognize its importance, and although this was technically at variance from Dimitrov's pronouncement, building the CIO became the Party's number-one domestic priority in the second half of the 1930s. Their support was welcomed by the CIO founders, who recognized the Party's potential as a source of dedicated organizers.

Daily Worker editor Clarence Hathaway reported to the Comintern in September 1936 that he personally "had met with [John L.] Lewis less than a week before I left" for Moscow. He proudly reported that "we now have 45 or 50 Communists on the full-time organizing staff" of the newly created CIO Steel Workers Organizing Committee (SWOC).[51] Higher up in the CIO's hierarchy, Lewis appointed Len DeCaux as editor of the *CIO News* newspaper and Lee Pressman as the new federation's general counsel, both of them, as he surely was aware, secret members of the Communist Party.[52] Publicly, Lewis pretended not to know how many Communists the CIO had on its payroll, declaring, "I do not turn my organizers . . . upside down and shake them to see what kind of literature falls out of their pockets."[53]

Within the CIO's inner circles he was more forthright. When questioned by the ILGWU's David Dubinsky about the Communists they both knew were well represented on CIO organizing staff, Lewis famously replied, "Who gets the bird—the hunter or the dog?"[54]

As Lewis suggested, just because they were being hired as organizers didn't mean Communists necessarily had any real power in the unions that they were helping to build. Philip Murray, president of the SWOC (a post he retained when it was renamed the United Steelworkers of America), made sure that Communists were kept out of office in the new union, and had laid off many of the Party's organizers by the spring of 1937. And yet, Communists also benefited organizationally from the arrangement, retrieving their own share of the "birds," for they were simultaneously building their influence within other CIO unions where they had greater sway than the Steelworkers, like the newly established United Electrical, Radio, and Machine Workers union (UE).[55]

Apart from the National Maritime Union and a few smaller unions, Communists counted relatively few members among the rank and file. Their strength within unions was lodged instead in elected and staff positions. Top Communists in the labor movement, or "influentials" as they were referred to, were given considerable leeway to run their unions as they chose, as long as they conformed to the general contours of Party policy. Most of the Communists who occupied high office in the new industrial unions kept their membership secret, although there were exceptions like William Sentner, who was elected president of the UE's District 8 in St. Louis in 1937, a position he held for over a decade.[56]

It later became a commonplace among congressional investigators and other anti-Communists to speak of Communist "infiltration" of the labor movement. The term is misleading, firstly because the most successful of the "infiltrators" had been instrumental in creating the unions they led, and secondly because their radical affiliations were, if unadvertised, not much of a secret to the rank and file. Few longshoremen in the ILWU, for example, were likely in ignorance of Harry Bridges's affinity for (if not formal membership in) the Communist Party.[57]

While the Communists influenced the new CIO unions, *at the same time* the new CIO unions influenced the Communists. The Party had always attracted idealists, who dreamed grand dreams about perfect uto-, pias to come; now, in addition, it began to attract pragmatists, who saw it as an organization that got things done in the here and now. What seemed most important to Communist union organizers in those years was that American workers were gaining a sense of their own rights and power, not that they were necessarily ready to embrace revolutionary socialism. For the first time since 1919, American Communists began to think about the actual dynamics of working class politics beyond the boundaries of the usual hand-me-down pieties and catchphrases about class conscious- ness. As Browder wrote in 1937, the "transition" from day-to-day struggles around demands for higher wages and better working conditions to the eventual achievement of socialism would "not come from empty slogans disconnected from everyday life" but rather through precisely the kind of bread-and-butter victories being won in workplaces across the country: "It is not a discouraged, defeated, and demoralized working class that will take up and realize the great program of socialism: it is the enthusiastic, victorious, and organized workers who will move forward from victories in the defensive struggle to the offensive and finally to socialism."[58]

The most decisive CIO victory in its first years came in the sit-down strike in Flint, Michigan, in 1936–1937, a historic achievement in which Com- munists along with other radicals played a vital role.[59]

The leadership of the United Auto Workers (UAW), formed in 1935, represented a coalition of Socialists, Communists, and others, nomi- nally presided over at the outset by an eccentric Baptist minister named Homer Martin who, when the time came for decisive action in Flint, was conveniently shunted to the side by more competent (and radical) UAW organizers.

CIO leaders hoped that winning bargaining rights for workers in one of the fiercely anti-union auto corporations would spur the success of the industrial union drive in other major mass-production industries. As their initial objective, CIO and UAW strategists boldly picked General Motors (GM), not only the largest auto manufacturer but also the largest corporation in the United States, with over 170,000 hourly workers employed in sixty-nine plants spread across fourteen states.[60]

In 1936, of the 150,000 residents in Flint, Michigan, 47,000 were employed by GM. The Fisher Body No. 1 plant in Flint was GM's Achilles' heel. It produced the dies used in other factories to stamp out body parts, which meant that a prolonged strike there could shut down nearly all the corporation's auto production nationally. UAW leaders chose Wyndham Mortimer to head up the GM drive, and in June 1936 he moved to Flint to begin preparations. Mortimer was a Communist who had worked in auto plants since 1917.[61]

Like other auto manufacturers, GM maintained an extensive network of spies in Flint and elsewhere to intimidate their workers. Those workers identified as union supporters could be fired with impunity. The city was as much a company town as the mill towns of the South, with the police chief a former GM detective.[62] Strict secrecy was thus necessary when the union began its organizing campaign. Here the old CP underground experience proved to be of some practical use. Communists working in the GM plants in Flint (estimates range from sixty to a hundred) provided Mortimer, and Communists Bob Travis and Henry Kraus, who arrived in the city later, with their initial contacts. Communists Bud Simons, Walter Moore, and Joe Devitt, by lucky chance, were employed in Fisher Body No. 1 plant and would prove invaluable to the organizing efforts that followed.[63] UAW president Martin, who distrusted Mortimer for his Party ties, forced him to leave Flint after he had laid the groundwork for the strike, but Bob Travis remained in local command, assisted by Socialist Roy Reuther.[64]

Union strength in Flint grew in the fall of 1936, with membership reaching 4,500 by year's end. Although that was barely one-tenth of the number of GM workers in the city, many of the new members worked in the critical Fisher Body No. 1 and Fisher Body No. 2 plants. The growth in union numbers reflected not only the UAW's efforts in 1936, but also the landslide reelection in November of President Roosevelt and (of considerable importance in events to come) the election of liberal Democrat Frank Murphy as Michigan's governor. Ballot-box victories reinforced the confidence of the UAW rank and file in the possibility of workplace victories to come. As UAW organizers urged the Flint's autoworkers, "Get a New Deal in the shops."[65]

A new tactic also strengthened labor's hand. Typically, when workers went on strike, they walked off their jobs and out of their workplaces, setting up picket lines outside to discourage management's importation of replacements, or "scabs" in labor parlance. That left the strikers, as at Gastonia in 1929, at the mercy of the local police, who broke up picket lines with violence and arrests. But in a sit-down strike, when workers quit work they stayed in the workplace indefinitely, which both prevented the employment of scabs and put valuable company property at risk in a violent confrontation.

The sit-down tactic grew out of a wave of international labor militancy. In France in May and June 1936 sit-down strikes involving several million workers shut down factories. There too worker militancy was reinforced by victories at the polls, with the accession to power of a Popular Front government in June. The success of the French strikes, securing union recognition, higher wages, and a forty-hour week, caught the eye of militant American unionists and inspired similar tactics in Indiana and Akron, Ohio.[66]

The sit-downs began in Flint on December 30, 1936, in Fisher Body No. 2, and later that day in Fisher Body No. 1, timed to begin after Christmas and

Frank Murphy's swearing-in as Michigan's governor. The UAW presented GM with a list of demands for better wages and working conditions, the creation of a grievance procedure, and union recognition. The union's goal was to win a national agreement with GM, in which the UAW would be the exclusive bargaining agent for all of the corporation's production workers. GM swiftly obtained an injunction from a local circuit-court judge ordering the evacuation of the factories, a legal maneuver discredited a few days later when CIO legal counsel Lee Pressman discovered that the judge granting the injunction owned GM stock valued at over $200,000, a substantial fortune at the time.[67]

The sit-downers elected a strike committee for each occupied plant, with Bud Simon the chairman in Fisher Body No. 1. Daily mass meetings in the plants voted on the proposals of the strike committee, meetings

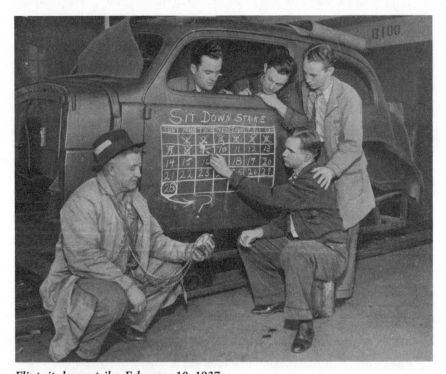

Flint sit-down strike, February 10, 1937
(Photo by Tom Watson/NY Daily News Archive via Getty Images)

that began and ended with a round of the old Wobbly anthem, now adopted by the CIO, "Solidarity Forever." Rules were established to maintain order, and strikers were told to be respectful of company property. There was a lot of time to read, and newspapers and magazines (including the *Daily Worker*, as well as mainstream publications) were shared by the strikers.[68]

The strikers' sense of solidarity would soon be tested. As the sit-down approached the two-week mark on January 11, 1937, Flint police and deputies from the county sheriff's office attempted to drive the workers out of Fisher Body No. 2, the less strongly held of the occupied plants. The police deployed tear gas and firearms; the strikers responded with fire hoses, and a barrage of auto parts, stones, and other missiles. Thirteen strikers and supporters were shot, none fatally. In the end, in what the strikers derisively named the "Battle of the Running Bulls" ("bull" being, at the time, derogatory slang for police), the strikers prevailed.

The next day Governor Murphy ordered 1,200 National Guard troops into Flint, but unlike the San Francisco longshore strike three years earlier, guardsmen were dispatched not to break the strike but to keep the peace. Seemingly neutral, Murphy showed he was in fact on the side of the workers by allowing the strike to proceed without state interference, as the workers sitting in at the GM plants understood. President Franklin Roosevelt also refused to intervene in the strike on the grounds that what happened in Michigan was of purely state concern. Freed by the Popular Front from the necessity of defending the orthodox belief that bourgeois democracy was simply a pro-ruling-class swindle, Communists now acknowledged the importance of electing liberal Democrats to office. As the *New Masses* commented editorially in mid-January, "If [Alf] Landon was in the White House and a Republican in Lansing, GM would be feeling a lot more confident."[69]

Rather than sitting passively inside the plants they had already seized, UAW strikers stayed on the offensive. On February 1, a month into the strike, Bob Travis directed a military-style operation that seized another auto plant, Chevy No. 4. This escalation of the struggle broke the stalemate and ultimately led to GM's surrender ten days later, on February 11, a month and a half after the strike began.[70]

The UAW didn't get all that it asked for, but what it got provided a secure base for gains to come. The agreement signed on February 11 covered just seventeen of GM's sixty-nine plants, and its recognition of the UAW as the exclusive bargaining representative in those plants was limited to the next six months. Nonetheless, having seen the UAW humble mighty GM in a true David-and-Goliath battle in Flint, auto workers who until now had taken a wait-and-see attitude poured into the union. UAW national membership jumped from fewer than 90,000 in February 1937 to 400,000 that October. Chrysler agreed to a contract recognizing the UAW in early April, leaving only Ford among the major automakers still holding out (Ford would sign its first contract with the UAW in 1941). The Flint victory helped inspire a wave of strikes that proved the greatest since 1919, with nearly 5 million workers going on strike in 1937, including hundreds of thousands who employed the sit-down tactic. Other major corporations learned from GM's misfortune, with US Steel recognizing the CIO's Steel Workers Organizing Committee as bargaining agent for its workers without a strike, less than three weeks later. The tide in the battle for industrial unionism was turning.[71]

Nowhere was that more evident than in Flint on February 11 when GM capitulated. At 5:00 p.m. the bearded, weary, but triumphant sit-down veterans marched out of Fisher Body No. 1, led by Communist Bud Simons, carrying American flags. They marched to Chevy No. 4 and Fisher Body No. 2, where they were joined by the other jubilant strikers. Choruses of "Solidarity Forever" bounced off the walls of the evacuated factory buildings. Mary Heaton Vorse was there, as she had been at the Lawrence textile strike in 1912, the steel strike of 1919, the Passaic strike of 1926, the Gastonia strike of 1929, and so many other conflicts where labor had known outright defeat or, at best, gained impermanent victories. She had been in Flint since mid-January chronicling the strike and bearing witness. She ended her account of the strike with a nod to labor's past and future: "The joy of victory tore through Flint. It was more than the joy of war ceasing, it was the joy of creation. The wind of Freedom had roared down Flint's streets. The strike had ended! The working people of Flint had begun to forge a new life out of their historic victory!"[72]

In the spring and summer of 1937, in the midst of the most successful worker insurgency in American history, it must have seemed to the Party's supporters as if they had found their way out of a long, dark maze of perennially lost causes, into newfound legitimacy and relevance. Vorse's invocation of the "wind of Freedom" making itself felt in the streets of Flint was not just poetic hyperbole. Outside of the ballot box, no force did as much to democratize American society and culture in the 1930s and 1940s as the labor movement, especially the new industrial unions of the CIO. They broke the near-autocratic control of employers in company towns. A proud, self-assured working class, many of recent immigrant stock, were no longer willing to accept a status relegating them to less-than-full citizenship. The "double-check Americans" were on the march.

However, as Robert Zieger noted in his history of the formative years of the CIO, the workers rallying to the new industrial unions in the 1930s were overwhelmingly "angry, not alienated." Their militancy "was directed above all else at the attainment of security, stability, and dignity at work."[73] Once those essential yet politically limited goals were reached, what role would remain for Communists to play in determining the future of American labor?

With the advent of the Popular Front, Communists and Socialists cooperated organizationally on a number of fronts, including the labor movement. But in electoral politics Communists and Socialists headed in opposite directions. Now it was the Socialists who proved the more sectarian of the two parties, continuing to run candidates on their own ticket against New Deal Democrats. Norman Thomas's nearly 900,000 votes in the 1932 presidential campaign declined to fewer than 200,000 in 1936, as his earlier supporters switched votes to Roosevelt. Socialists active in the labor movement, like the UAW's emerging power broker, Walter Reuther, found themselves politically embarrassed when the SP ran candidates against valued Democratic allies like Michigan governor Murphy (Reuther quietly resigned from the SP in 1938).[74]

In any event, the Communists regarded further efforts to achieve unity with the shrinking Socialist Party irrelevant. By 1936–1937 they had more ambitious goals, angling to play a role as the effective if unacknowledged left wing of the New Deal, what they would start to call the "Democratic Front."

In March 1936 Communist leaders, including Browder, Foster, and Sam Darcy, returned to Moscow to discuss the coming American presidential election. Foster, supported by Darcy, favored direct endorsement of Roosevelt in his reelection campaign. Browder wanted the Communists to run their own presidential campaign with himself as its presidential nominee. In the past, Foster had upheld orthodoxy against Browder's innovations. This time, however, he seemed to be tacking right by calling for the endorsement of a bourgeois candidate, with Browder taking the more militant stance by holding out for an independent Communist campaign. But Browder's position was more nuanced. He warned, with reason, that a direct Communist endorsement of FDR would cost the president votes. Instead, with Browder as their nominee, the Communists could run a campaign that focused its political fire on the Republican Party while implicitly supporting Roosevelt's reelection. Browder's plan was approved. The CP's stance in the coming election was much ridiculed by its left-wing rivals, and the 80,000 votes Browder received in November was 20,000 fewer than Foster had received four years earlier. In the end, nevertheless, the somewhat-clumsy stratagem spared FDR the onus of an outright Communist embrace, while still signaling a turn in Party strategy away from its past sectarianism.[75]

The Communists, over the next several years, proved remarkably effective at working for the first time within the realm of mainstream electoral politics. "In the twinkling of an eye," George Charney recalled of the later 1930s, when he served as the Party's organizational director in Harlem, "the orientation changed: everyone became an expert on election strategy, and predicting results became the favorite indoor pastime of all functionaries."[76]

By 1938, the Communists emerged behind the scenes as a well-entrenched minority within the California and Washington Democratic parties, the Minnesota Farmer-Labor Party (which would subsequently unite with the state's Democratic Party), and the New York State American Labor Party (ALP), in which they maintained a close working alliance with the ALP's sole congressman, East Harlem's popular independent radical Vito Marcantonio. (In the 1930s the ALP represented an uneasy collaboration between Communists and other groupings on the Left, including anti-Communist social democrats; by the mid-1940s it had effectively fallen under CP control.) They also occasionally backed Republicans, like New York City mayor Fiorello La Guardia in his successful 1937 reelection campaign. Though the Party lacked a single officeholder elected as an open Communist in the 1930s, it did have some secret members in public office, including Congressmen John Bernard (FLP, Minnesota) and Hugh De Lacy (Democrat, Washington). The Party continued to run candidates in its own name where their campaigns did not threaten the election of New Deal aspirants. Charlotte Anita Whitney, in a California 1936 race for state comptroller, and Israel Amter, in a 1938 New York election for congressman-at-large, each received more than 100,000 votes.[77]

The Party skillfully mobilized behind the scenes on behalf of its political allies, as was evident in the triumph of Culbert Olson as governor of

California in November 1938. Strongly pro-labor, Olson was attacked by Republicans as pro-Communist, and indeed he did have the backing of the CP, as well as the unions it influenced. "Keep California out of the 'Red,'" the incumbent governor Frank Merriam warned in his campaign ads. "Vote *Against* Olson and CIO Domination." But Olson won handily, becoming the first Democrat elected to the governorship in the state since 1894. In one of Olson's first acts in office, he pardoned labor organizer Tom Mooney, one of the longest-serving political prisoners in the country, convicted in 1916 on dubious charges of setting off a bomb at a Preparedness Day parade in San Francisco. "Free Tom Mooney!" had been a perennial Party slogan for nearly two decades; his release was seen by Communists as both a long-sought victory for civil liberties and a vindication of the Popular Front strategy. As Browder told a radio interviewer following the fall elections: "We Communists helped to build the united progressive and democratic front everywhere. . . . We are learning how to take our place within the traditional American two-party system . . . even though the real two parties now cut across all the old party labels, and can be more realistically identified as the New Deal party and the anti–New Deal party."[78]

In another measure of its redefined vanguard role, in the autumn of 1938 the Communist Party became one of the first voices calling for a third term for President Roosevelt.[79]

As part of its attempt to appear less foreign inspired, the CP renamed its constituent units. The ruling Political Bureau (often referred to, Russian-style, as the Politburo or Polburo), the top seven leaders based in New York City who guided Party affairs on a day-to-day basis, became the Political Committee. The Central Committee, previously the Central Executive Committee, summoned from across the country to meet three times a year in New York, now became the National Committee. Where possible, geographically sprawling multistate districts were broken down into state organizations to better fit the existing American political structure. The most elaborate restructuring was carried out in New York, which became the New York state organization, accounting for roughly 40 percent of the national Party membership by the late 1930s. Below the state organization were county organizations, and below the counties, cities or sections were reorganized along assembly-district lines. At the base were branches, which in New York City were sizable neighborhood-based groups of about fifty members.[80]

Communist newspapers underwent similar changes. Editors swept away the opaque inner-party dispatches about what was decided at this or that meeting, such as the famously turgid paragraph in the *Daily Worker* in 1933 reporting that "The 15th Plenum of our Party clearly establishes that the resolution of the 14th Plenum of the Party remains the basic guide for examining the work of the Party in carrying out the line of the 12th Plenum of the ECCI."[81] Starting in 1935–1936, the newspapers added features like comic strips, a women's section, cheesecake photos of bathing beauties, and sports pages. Circulation began to rise, reaching 30,000 for the *Daily Worker*, and twice that for the new *Sunday Worker*, which began publication in 1936. Out on the West Coast, the former semiweekly *Western Worker* was similarly transformed in 1938 into *People's Daily World*, which featured a column submitted by folk singer Woody Guthrie. Woody Sez, with its comic Okie dialect, deliberate misspellings, and Guthrie's cartoon illustrations, would have been unimaginable in a pre–Popular Front Communist publication.[82] Mike Gold, whose Change the World column had long been one of the more accessible features of the *Daily Worker*, despite his often hard-line orthodoxy, declared that the CP's revamped journalism proved that "one can be a human being as well as a Communist," and that the CP wasn't "a little sect of bookworms or soapboxers."[83]

Leninist discipline, for those new to the Party and perhaps not inclined or available to become full-time cadre, grew less intense in the Popular Front era. Communists celebrated service and self-sacrifice to the cause, but not everyone was expected to become a saint or an ascetic. As a result of such changes, and a generally favorable political climate, the Party grew, year by year, notwithstanding its continuing problems with membership turnover. In the three years following the 1936 adoption of the Popular Front policy, membership rose by more than 10,000 a year, reaching 38,000 at the start of 1937, 54,000 at the start of 1938, and 66,000 at the start of 1939.[84]

The number of Party employees also expanded dramatically, reaching nearly 4,000 strong by the late 1930s, more than any left-wing organization before (or since) had ever employed. And they were better paid for their efforts. George Charney arrived in Boston as the organizational secretary in 1935, and in a good week he might receive $8 to $10 for his efforts, scraped together from quarters and dimes of dues collected and pamphlets sold. Within a year or so of the onset of the Popular Front, he was regularly receiving $20 to $25 a week, which, while still a modest sum, was enough to seem to him "affluence by comparison."[85]

People joined the Communist Party for all kinds of reasons over the years, but between 1936 and 1939, its greatest draw was almost certainly its commitment to the anti-fascist cause. That commitment went well beyond words, because American Communists were fighting and dying in a real war against fascism in those years, in defense of the Spanish Republic.

The Spanish Civil War began on July 17, 1936, when Spain's army, led by General Francisco Franco, launched an insurgency to overthrow the country's democratically elected Popular Front government, in power since the previous February. The "Nationalist" rebellion enjoyed the support of the country's fascists, its large landowners, factory owners, and the Catholic Church. The Nationalists were provided substantial aid from Mussolini's Italy and Hitler's Germany, in the form of tanks, planes, and tens of thousands of soldiers—making Spain fascism's training ground for the broader war of conquest to come. The Spanish Republic, or "Loyalists," supported by Socialists, Communists, anarchists, liberals, and the trade unions, fought back against Franco's professional soldiers, thwarting the rebels in their attempt to take over Madrid, Barcelona, and other big cities in northern and central Spain. Britain and France proved unwilling to intervene in the growing civil war, imposing an arms embargo on Spain's government, as did the United States. Only the Soviet Union and Mexico provided direct military aid to the republic.[86]

Denied aid from sister democracies, the republic attracted another source of support. At first spontaneously, political refugees from Germany and Italy and others (including a few Americans) came to Spain to join the various militias that had sprung up in defense of the Republican cause. In the fall of the first year of the Spanish Civil War, the Comintern issued instructions to its member parties to recruit volunteers to join what came to be called the International Brigades, eventually attracting 35,000 volunteers from fifty-two countries, who made up seven brigades in the Spanish Republic's army. By early November nearly 2,000 German, British, French, and other foreign volunteers organized and designated as the Eleventh International Brigade played a key role in the successful defense of Madrid from a fascist offensive.[87]

The first contingent of American volunteers, eighty-six strong, shipped out from New York Harbor on the passenger ship *Normandie* the day after Christmas 1936, bound for France. They were the first of nearly 3,000 from the United States. Mostly in their mid-twenties, few of the Americans had any previous military experience. They were, overwhelmingly, immigrants or the children of immigrants, mostly from urban backgrounds, one in five from New York City. A third of the volunteers were Jewish; about eighty were African-American. Half to two-thirds were already Communists or joined the Party during the war. None came to Spain because they were ordered to do so. There were so many American Communists who wanted to join the fight that their departure would have crippled organizing efforts at home, and many would-be volunteers were turned down.[88]

John Gates became among the best known of those who fought in Spain, arriving in February 1937, age twenty-three. Born in Manhattan in 1913 to Jewish immigrant parents, raised there and in the Bronx, he joined the Young Communist League at age seventeen while a freshman at City College. He moved to Ohio in 1932 as a TUUL organizer. Along the way, he changed his name from Solomon Regenstreif to John (more often known as "Johnny") Gates. Three weeks after arriving in Spain, having fired a total of three rounds of ammunition in training, he was sent to the front. Over the next year, he rose in the ranks, becoming battalion political commissar, the equivalent of colonel, in the spring of 1938.[89]

Once in Spain, the Americans reported to International Brigades headquarters in Albacete, where they were issued outdated rifles and outfitted in mismatched uniforms from Spanish and other European armies. Like Gates, their spirits were high, but their preparation for what was to come minimal.[90]

The famous Abraham Lincoln *Brigade* never existed as such. Instead, Americans who fought in Spain fought as one of four battalions in the Fifteenth International Brigade (the other three at the start consisting of a British, a Franco-Belgian, and a Balkan battalion). The Americans belonged to the Abraham Lincoln Battalion, the George Washington Battalion, or the mostly Canadian Mackenzie-Papineau Battalion. The Lincoln and Washington Battalions were merged in July 1937, as American casualties decimated both, but continued to be known popularly as the "Lincoln Brigade."[91]

In early February 1937, Nationalist forces, backed by artillery provided by the German Wehrmacht's Condor Legion, attempted a breakthrough across the Jarama River, intending to encircle Madrid a few miles to the north. They were driven back by Republican forces, but the threat on that front remained acute. On February 16, some 450 untested soldiers from the Abraham Lincoln Battalion were thrown into the counterattack. The Lincoln commander was twenty-eight-year-old Robert Hale Merriman.

He had been a graduate student teaching at Berkeley before spending a year in Moscow studying Soviet economics in 1936. When he got to Spain, he was appointed commander of the Lincoln Battalion on the basis of having been an ROTC student as an undergraduate.[92]

Advancing on the fascist lines on February 23, the battalion's raw recruits were pinned down by machine gun fire in an open field in their combat baptism. Making it back to their own lines after dark, they left twenty dead behind. Four days later, they were ordered to seize a hilltop held by the fascists. In what became an all-too-common feature of Republican attacks, the promised artillery, air, tank, and other support never materialized. Merriman's ROTC training was not much of a military background, but enough for him to know that an unsupported frontal assault on an entrenched position was suicidal. He argued against the attack with brigade commanders, but he was overruled. When the Lincolns went over the top on the night of February, Merriman was among the first of hundreds of casualties, falling wounded. (A brave and dedicated soldier, much admired by his men, he was promoted to chief of staff for the Fifteenth Brigade in August 1937. He was among the last Americans to die in battle in Spain in the summer of 1938, possibly executed after capture by the fascists.) All told in their first days in combat, out of the original 450, the Lincoln Battalion suffered 127 dead and over 200 wounded.[93]

Despite their losses, the Lincolns helped hold the line against the fascist advance at Jarama. American volunteers for the most part still believed in ultimate victory. The following month Loyalist forces, including other units from the International Brigades, turned another Nationalist offensive in the Battle of Guadalajara, once again saving Madrid. "We're all confident out here that the government forces will, in a very short time, be able to finally and completely crush the gangsters and mercenaries that compose the fascist forces," nineteen-year-old Lincoln volunteer Robert Klonsky, of Brooklyn, wrote to his family in late March from Spain. Klonsky had arrived in Spain on February 5 and was thrown into combat at

Jarama three weeks later. He hoped that "in a few months I will be back home with all of you celebrating victory together."[94]

More than 2,000 American volunteers arrived in Spain in the months following Jarama. From the start of March 1937, US passports were stamped not valid for travel to Spain. Pretending to be tourists or students, the volunteers were smuggled from France into Spain via coastal waters or by hiking across the Pyrenees in the dead of night. The reinforced Lincoln Battalion took part in five subsequent Republican offensives in 1937–1938: at Brunete in July 1937, Aragon in August, Belchite in September, Teruel in January and February 1938, and along the Ebro River beginning in March 1938 and continuing through the end of summer. Reflecting the overwhelming fascist advantage in men and material, most of the battalion's battles ended in stalemate or retreat. Roughly 600 more Lincolns would die in Spain, all told nearly one in every four of the volunteers in the battalion. Many others were wounded. At times, before new recruits arrived to take the place of the already fallen, the number of Americans left in the battalion dipped below a hundred. George Charney, who remained in the United States but had many friends among the young Communists who volunteered to fight in Spain, recalled that by the spring of 1938, "there was hardly a Communist family that did not have a relative or a friend on the casualty list."[95]

Republican Spain proved a magnet for left-leaning writers in 1937–1938, including Ernest Hemingway. He made four trips to Spain as a war correspondent and befriended many of the men fighting in the Lincoln Battalion, including Robert Merriman, who served as the model for Robert Jordan, the American protagonist in Hemingway's 1940 novel *For Whom the Bell Tolls*.[96] In the novel, Jordan reflected on the role the Communists were playing in Spain: "He was under Communist discipline for the duration of the war. Here in Spain the Communists offered the best discipline and the soundest and sanest for the prosecution of the war. He accepted their discipline for the duration of the war because, in the conduct of the war, they were the only party whose program and whose discipline he could respect."[97]

In the original passage, Hemingway had not written that Jordan was "under Communist discipline" for the duration, but that, like the actual Robert Merriman, "He was a Communist." By 1940, when the book came out, Hemingway would have had good reason not to have his protagonist self-identify as a Communist.[98] But even in the midst of the war, Hemingway's feelings about Communist discipline were more complicated than the lines he gave to his character to speak. At the Hotel Florida in Madrid, where many journalists covering the war stayed, Hemingway told *Daily Worker* correspondent Joe North in 1938 that "I like Communists when they're soldiers, but when they're priests, I hate them." North, offended, stiffly replied that Communists were good soldiers precisely because of their priestly self-discipline. Hemingway, unpersuaded, laughed and good-naturedly offered his Communist colleague a drink.[99]

George Watt, who arrived in Spain in August 1937, had a memorable encounter with Hemingway in early April 1938, in the midst of the fascist offensive driving down the Ebro River to the Mediterranean. In a desperate and ultimately failed attempt to blunt the fascist effort to split Republican Spain in two, the Loyalists launched their own counteroffensive across the river. In the face of the fascists' overwhelming superiority in tanks, artillery, and planes, the Lincolns were forced to retreat, losing many more men, killed or captured. A handful, including Watt and Johnny Gates, reached the west bank of the Ebro River on April 3, with safety lying on the far side. Using a wooden door as a raft, they launched it into the swollen river, but their little craft quickly foundered. Watt and Gates, through some miracle, reached the far shore. Shortly afterward, a car pulled up, and out stepped Hemingway and Herbert Matthews, the latter the *New York Times* correspondent in Spain. They knew the Lincolns were in trouble and drove to the Ebro hoping to learn of their fate. As Watt later recreated the encounter:

Matthews is busy taking notes. Hemingway is busy cursing the fascists. He is angry. He is optimistic. The Republic is in a fighting mood, stronger than ever, he tells us. The rear is mobilized, and the Ebro is being fortified. The Fascists will not cross the Ebro. We will get our revenge, he assures. He talks like one of us. We rejoin our brigade and wait for our men to return. We soon come to realize that most are not coming back. [100]

On September 21, the Spanish Republic's prime minister, Juan Negrín, announced that the International Brigades would be sent home, and three days later, the eighty or so remaining American volunteers were pulled off the line. The survivors paraded through the streets of Barcelona on October 29 along with 2,500 other International Brigade soldiers, as throngs of the city's residents, many weeping, turned out to salute their departure. The Americans, true to style, shambled out of step. "We've never been what you call good at parade marching," the battalion's last commander, Milton Wolff, admitted.[101]

In February 1939, Hemingway contributed a short piece entitled "On the American Dead in Spain" to the *New Masses*, commemorating the second anniversary of the Battle of Jarama. It proved an elegy not only for the volunteers who died in Spain, but for the Spanish Republic, which fell to Franco's forces a month later. It might also be read, at least in retrospect, as a requiem for the Popular Front, which would not long outlive the end of the Spanish Civil War. Hemingway predicted that Spain would someday find its way back to democracy—a prophecy that took nearly four decades to be fulfilled:

Our dead live in the hearts and minds of the Spanish peasants, of the Spanish workers, of all the good simple honest people who believed in and fought for the Spanish Republic. And as long as all our dead live in the Spanish earth, and they will live as long as the earth lives, no system of tyranny ever will prevail in Spain.[102]

"We believe," the *New Masses* editors noted, "it is one of the finest tributes yet paid to the boys who won't be coming back."[103]

"On the American Dead in Spain" might have provided a gently uplifting conclusion to an account of the Abraham Lincoln Battalion's history except the history of American Communism rarely provided such endings. When *For Whom the Bell Tolls* was published in 1940 it was denounced in the pages of the *New Masses* by Lincoln veteran Alvah Bessie as "a slander on the Spanish people."[104] The Spanish people actually come off rather well in the novel. Its real sin was its harsh treatment of French Communist leader André Marty, chief political commissar of the International Brigades. Hemingway portrayed Marty as tyrannical, paranoid, and incompetent ("está loco," as one of the Spanish characters in the book says of him with contempt).[105]

To attack the reputation of a noted international Communist leader was sufficient in the eyes of the American Communist Party to transform a celebrated ally like Hemingway into a hated turncoat. *Daily Worker* columnist Mike Gold, whose personal friendship with Hemingway extended back to the late 1920s, denounced the novelist for "petty-bourgeois renegadism." On a subsequent visit to New York, Hemingway dropped by Communist Party headquarters on East Twelfth Street and inquired if Gold was available. Informed that he was not, the novelist told the receptionist, "Tell Mike Gold that Ernest Hemingway says he should go fuck himself."[106]

In the last years of the 1930s American Communism would reach the historical high point of its strength and legitimacy. Those same years also proved seedtime for Soviet espionage in the United States, planting a harvest reaped during the Second World War.[107]

Of all the contradictions posed by the history of American Communism, this is the one where F. Scott Fitzgerald's praise for the ability "to hold two opposed ideas in the mind at the same time, and still retain the ability to function" provides the greatest challenge. Communists, especially the younger generation, thought of themselves as patriotic "double-check" Americans. At the same time, they belonged to an organization that recruited several hundred of their comrades as spies. While it is tempting to acknowledge one or the other of these clashing realities and ignore the other, both are part of the maddeningly complex history of American Communism, bound together as parts of a story that defies satisfying generalizations.

American Communist involvement in Soviet-directed clandestine operations began abroad in the 1920s and early 1930s. Two future general secretaries of the CPUSA, Earl Browder and Lenin School–trained Eugene Dennis, were involved in establishing and maintaining such operations in the Pacific region, via the Profintern's Pan-Pacific Trade Union Secretariat in Browder's case and the Comintern in Dennis's case. Many others participated in such activities, including Lenin School graduate Steve Nelson, who was dispatched to Berlin in 1933 carrying instructions from Moscow to the German Communist underground.[108]

None of these early examples involved espionage. In a number of cases, however, such clandestine foreign activities did break US law, especially in the widespread use of false passports, a practice that eventually landed Browder in legal trouble.[109]

Before the establishment of diplomatic relations between the two countries in 1933, the Soviet Union had limited opportunities and resources for spying on the United States government. With the opening of an embassy in Washington, and consulates in other cities, however, the professionals from the NKVD (the renamed OGPU, Soviet central intelligence) and the GRU (Red Army military intelligence) moved in. As the Party was accustomed to assigning its cadre as agents in clandestine operations abroad, when the call came to provide assistance to domestic espionage, it may have seemed to Party leaders a natural progression, one more way to fulfill the CP's perennial slogan, "Defend the Soviet Union."[110]

With the rank-and-file Communists who were recruited to do the spying, the story gets more complicated. By and large, they had no prior experience in clandestine operations. They needed training. They also needed persuasion that they were doing the right thing. Soviet spymasters were skilled at the incremental recruiting of amateurs. In handing out assignments to novice spies, rarely did they send even the most eager recruits after big secrets until they had gotten them used to the idea of handing over materials of little consequence. Harry Gold, later to gain notoriety for his role in the theft of atomic secrets, got his start in industrial espionage in the 1930s by stealing from his employer, a sugar company, information regarding the use of dry ice to keep ice cream from melting, and that was only after much soul-searching.[111]

Nathan Gregory Silvermaster, an economist employed in the Treasury Department during the Second World War, was praised by his NKVD handler as "a man sincerely devoted to the party and the Soviet Union . . . [who] understands perfectly well that he works for us."[112] Silvermaster embraced his role as spy for Soviet intelligence fully aware of what he was doing, for whom, and why. The agent's formulation suggests, however, that there were others providing documents who did not "understand perfectly well" that their information was going to Soviet intelligence. Some thought that it would wind up on Earl Browder's desk in New York, providing useful political scuttlebutt that would go no further. Or perhaps they understood that the information they handed over would be shared with Comintern headquarters in Moscow but again only to guide political decision-making. As one NKVD agent reported to Moscow in 1937 about Michael Straight, a source within the State Department: "He has very little experience and sometimes behaves like a child in his romanticism. He thinks he is working for the Comintern and he must be left in this delusion for awhile." "Delusion" is a good word to describe the state of mind of those Americans who worked on behalf of Soviet espionage in the 1930s, at least those who thought of themselves as good American patriots who just happened to be in a position to share some helpful knowledge with that other country they felt had a claim on their allegiance, the Soviet Union.[113]

The height of the Popular Front's era of democratic good feelings in the United States, 1936–1938, was also the height of Stalin's murderous purges in the Soviet Union. Estimates vary, but perhaps three-quarters of a million Soviet citizens were summarily executed in the Great Purge of the late 1930s, and a million more imprisoned under the harshest imaginable conditions in forced labor camps. The full scale of suffering would not be known for another generation.[114]

Communists in the United States acknowledged, without embarrassment, that people were imprisoned and sometimes shot for political crimes in the Soviet Union. Party publications sought to lend an aura of normalcy to what otherwise might have struck American readers as extreme and abhorrent. The topic came up casually, for example, in a *Daily Worker* story reporting on Paul Robeson's first visit to Moscow in December 1934. Filmmaker Sergei Eisenstein hosted a reception for Robeson, attended, as the *Daily Worker* reported, "by nearly all the celebrities in Moscow's theatre and art world." This occurred shortly after the assassination of the Leningrad party chief Sergei Kirov, a mysterious event used by Stalin as an excuse for the widespread purges of the later decade. Asked by Vern Smith, the city's resident *Daily Worker* correspondent, about reports of recent executions of "counter-revolutionary terrorists," Robeson replied offhandedly, "From what I have already seen of the workings of the Soviet government, I can only say that anybody who lifts his hand against it ought to be shot!"[115] While that seems an odd question to pose to an artistic celebrity in a brief interview at a crowded Moscow reception, it suggests the *Daily Worker*'s goal of legitimizing politically motivated executions, so long as the executioners had a red star on their uniforms.

In contrast to the mostly anonymous political murders of earlier years in the Soviet Union, the Moscow trials, a series of carefully choreographed show trials between 1936 and 1938, were intended as public spectacles. Old Bolshevik leaders like Grigory Zinoviev, Lev Kamenev, Karl Radek, and Nikolai Bukharin, men whose names were enshrined in early histories of the 1917 revolution like *Ten Days That Shook the World*, now stood accused by the Soviet state of the crimes of treason, espionage, and sabotage in the service of hostile foreign powers. They openly admitted their guilt, a peculiar feature of the trials taken at face value by American Communists. "Dimitroff out of the strength of his innocence," a writer in the *New Masses* commented in January 1937, "stood up at the Reichstag fire trial, denied the charges against him, denounced his prosecutors. If Zinoviev and his associates were innocent, they had ample opportunity to follow Dimitroff's example and to discredit the trial."[116] That the NKVD had persuasive means at their disposal to guarantee that such protestations of innocence would not be heard from defendants in the Moscow courtroom went unconsidered.

Most Americans in the late 1930s had long regarded the Soviet Union as a malevolent force in the world; the trials thus neither added to nor subtracted from its sinister reputation. If they paid attention at all, many doubtless regarded the proceedings as an obscure vendetta, where current leaders were killing off political foes who, had the situation been reversed, would doubtless have done the same to their own opponents. Who cared whether Stalin killed Trotskyists, or Trotsky killed Stalinists? One less Communist, either way.

Within the Communist movement itself, the defense of the trials was not simply a matter of defending the Soviet Union against its critics, but of defending the American CP against the possible emergence of yet another internal crisis. If the history of American Communism is a narrative of conversion and faith, it is also one of disenchantment and apostasy. American Communists were not born Leninists or raised in a society where obedience to Party authority automatically went unchallenged. Communism was an adopted and embattled faith and, as such, often precariously held. A few years before the trials, Mary Heaton Vorse confided to her diary, "I find myself in a bourgeois frame of mind about the kulaks." The "kulaks" was a reference to the fate of the so-called "rich peasants" she was reading about who in 1931 were being displaced from their land in the forced collectivization of Soviet agriculture in the first Stalinist Five Year Plan. "*Who cares which class rules so long as the sum of injustice remains the same?*" she asked herself in her diary, underlining the question to emphasize its importance. Later the same year she wrote in another confidential note, "I am a communist because I don't see anything else to be. But I am a communist who hates Communists and Communism."[117] As Vorse's example suggests, the values that drew Americans to the Communist movement, like those that drew an earlier generation to Eugene Debs's vision of socialism, or Big Bill Haywood's syndicalism, or Emma Goldman's anarchism, were, at least initially, democratic and egalitarian. Individual Communists had to find ways to rationalize the chasm between those values and the brutal realities visible to those who would see them behind the ramshackle facade of a supposedly benevolent workers' homeland.

To counter the doubts some Communists were developing about the trials, Party leaders insisted that they were a matter of simple, if stern, justice. Browder, characteristically, compared them to the history of the American Revolution: just as American patriots had been forced to contend with its Benedict Arnolds, so Soviet justice had dealt with its own traitors. Browder warned a meeting of New York City Communist cadre in March 1938 to remain vigilant lest fascist sympathizers in the United States use alleged injustices in Moscow to "split open the progressive and democratic forces, and set them to fighting one another so that the reactionaries may slip back into power."[118]

Americans stationed in Moscow had a firsthand view of the terror's impact on Soviet society. In 1937 Eugene Dennis moved to the city as the

CPUSA's representative to the Comintern, accompanied by his wife, Peggy. As she later wrote: "We knew that the Comintern had been decimated," but rationalized the killings "as part of the brutal realities of making revolution." In the end, she confessed, "We accepted the infallibility of our leaders, the wisdom of our Party," and suppressed their doubts.[119]

As long as the Soviet Union appeared to be the sole major power opposing the spread of fascism in Europe, the Moscow trials were not going to affect the willingness of Popular Front supporters in the United States to align themselves with Communist allies. Malcolm Cowley, an influential literary figure since the 1920s, as well as a founder and vice president of the League of American Writers, declared at the height of the trials that for people like himself, "The personal character of Stalin may seem relatively unimportant. Many of the policies for which he is praised or execrated may be regarded as the inevitable result of an effort to unify and strengthen the Soviet Union in the face of an international fascist alliance."[120] Cowley didn't need to be convinced by Earl Browder that Soviet justice was truly just, or that Nikolai Bukharin was really Benedict Arnold in modern Russian dress. He deliberately chose to ignore the issue because he feared Hitler more than he feared Stalin.

Others dissented. On May 27, 1939, the liberal weekly *The Nation* published a manifesto by the Committee for Cultural Freedom, a newly organized group of anti-Stalinist intellectuals, cofounded by John Dewey and Sidney Hook, both of whom, like many American intellectuals, had begun the decade with some sympathy for the Soviet Union. Now they set out to create a united front against the Popular Front, by challenging its most cherished assumption, that Communists and non-Communists could stand together to defend liberal values. Their manifesto declared that Germany, Italy, and the Soviet Union represented different examples of the same evils. "Unless totalitarianism is combated wherever and in whatever form it manifests itself," the CCF manifesto declared, "it will spread in America." John Dos Passos, in a final and decisive break with the

Communists, was among those adding his name to the list of ninety-six signatories.[121]

With the future of the Popular Front at stake, the Party called on its supporters in the intellectual community to respond in a letter to *The Nation*. Endorsed by 400 signatories, this counterblast to the Committee for Cultural Freedom's manifesto denounced the "fantastic falsehood" that the Soviet Union was in any sense comparable to the fascist powers. "The Soviet Union," the letter declared, "continues as always, to be a bulwark against war and aggression, and works unceasingly for a peaceful international order."[122]

By the time it appeared, in the issue of *The Nation* dated August 26, 1939, everything had changed yet again.

CHAPTER 4

"Welcome Back to the Fight"

1939–1945

Looking back today, we believe that our policy of the past two years has been vindicated. . . . In our struggle against fascism . . . there is an unbroken continuity even though the forms and tactics of this activity now require change.

—New Masses, July 8, 1941

Welcome back to the fight. This time I know our side will win.

—Victor Laszlo to Rick Blaine, *Casablanca*, 1942

First released in November 1942, the classic Warner Brothers film *Casablanca* continues to entertain new generations as a love story and thriller, and deservedly so. But viewed in historical context, the film offers a more complicated and historically richer message. Its political subtext, largely forgotten in subsequent years, was obvious to many viewers who saw it in theaters in 1942–1943, and certainly to Communists. *Casablanca* reflected a "serious understanding of the people's war," the *New Masses* reviewer declared enthusiastically.[1]

Set in the title city in the first week of December 1941, when the United States was not yet at war, and French North Africa was controlled by France's collaborationist Vichy government, the movie offered a parable for America's abandonment of isolationism and embrace of international solidarity. Humphrey Bogart's character Rick Blaine presents himself at first as just a cynical saloonkeeper, but as he is reminded by his friend, police prefect captain Louis Renault, as well as by several other characters, before he came to Casablanca he smuggled arms to Ethiopia when it was under attack by Italian fascism and fought for the Loyalists in Spain against the Spanish fascists backed by Hitler and Mussolini. Whether Rick had been a Communist in the 1930s isn't a question the film directly addresses (although it's intriguing that for some unexplained reason he can't return to the United

Anti-fascists: Humphrey Bogart (right) as Rick Blaine, and Paul Henreid as Victor Laszlo, in Casablanca, 1942 (Photo by Silver Screen Collection/Getty Images)

States), but in pre-saloon-keeping days he certainly seems to have been some kind of anti-fascist idealist, and thus, at the very least, a Communist ally during the Popular Front. Disillusioned or not, he still has the right enemies. He remains on the Nazis' blacklist. To underline the point, his nemesis, the sinister Wehrmacht major Heinrich Strasser, shows him his dossier the first time they meet, and if there was one thing Communists were likely to have, it was politically damning dossiers.

The customers who came to Rick's Café Américain represented a cross section of anti-Nazi refugees from all over Europe. At a crucial plot point the miniature United Nations assembled in Rick's gin joint rise together, teary-eyed and exhilarated, to sing the revolutionary anthem "La Marseillaise," musically overpowering a tableful of belligerent Nazis midway through their own rendition of the German nationalist anthem "Die Wacht am Rhein."

In the end, Rick puts aside his personal grievances to return to "the cause," sacrificing the chance to reunite with Ingrid Bergman's ethereally beautiful Ilsa Lund (Czech resistance leader Victor Laszlo's wife, and Rick's former lover) in the realization that "it doesn't take much to see that the problems of three little people don't amount to a hill of beans" when there's a people's war to be won.

Howard Koch, one of the three principal screenwriters, shared the film's Academy Award for Best Adapted Screenplay with cowriters Julius and Philip Epstein. Koch was responsible for what he called the "political elements" that were a minor theme in the original treatment. Koch himself never joined the Party, but he was involved in a number of wartime Communist-influenced groups in Hollywood. He would be blacklisted in the film industry in the 1950s, not for his contribution to *Casablanca* but for the misfortune of having been assigned script-writing duties for another wartime Warner Brothers film, *Mission to Moscow*, which offered a benign portrait of Joseph Stalin that played a lot better in 1943 than it would a decade later.[2] Had it not been so popular, *Casablanca* might also have been regarded in the McCarthy era as subversively inspired. While it may not have been the intent of Warner Brothers, the movie perfectly embodied the essence of wartime left-leaning anti-fascist idealism, a cinematic tale of individual commitment, collective struggle, and fervent internationalism.

Four years before *Casablanca*'s release, in the closing days of 1938, Earl Browder announced a startling new slogan for the American Communist Party, proclaiming its support "For National and Social Security." Of course, the demand for a system of social security, including old-age pensions and unemployment insurance, had been a staple of Party platforms for years. But never before had American Communists advocated military preparedness. Quite the opposite: in the past they had viewed spending on social welfare and spending on national defense as antithetical—every dollar wasted on preparing for war, they argued, was a dollar unavailable for necessary domestic expenditures.[3] In Browder's slogan, for the first time, the two forms of security, social and national, were depicted as complementary and equally crucial.

The Popular Front's call for international collective security to counter the threat of fascist aggression undermined the logic of the CP's long-standing anti-militarist stance. In 1936, the *Daily Worker* gave front-page coverage to an appeal by Spain's prime minister Francisco Largo Caballero for American arms to defend the republic against fascist insurrection. If the US government had subsequently shipped planes and tanks to the Loyalists (as the USSR was doing) instead of imposing an arms embargo, Communists certainly would have applauded the initiative. And if American arms were a good thing when deployed in defense of Republican Spain against domestic and international fascism, why wouldn't they be a good thing similarly deployed in defense of the United States?[4] The Party's principal front organization devoted to foreign-policy issues, the American League Against War and Fascism, changed its name in 1937 to the American League for Peace and Democracy, in part to project a more positive-sounding message, but also to avoid sounding like a pacifist group opposed to all wars.[5]

Browder, who had just returned from a trip to Moscow in the fall of 1938, would not have originated a slogan so at variance with past policy without assurance that it passed muster with Soviet leaders. Stalin may have hoped that American rearmament would stiffen British and French resolve to stand up to Hitler, with the promise of a powerful New World ally. "We cannot deny the possibility, even the probability," Browder told a meeting of the CP's National Committee in December 1938, "that only American arms can preserve the Americans from conquest by the Rome-Berlin-Tokyo Axis." Two decades earlier, Browder had been imprisoned for opposing the World War I. Now on the eve of a second global conflict, he embraced a very different perspective. Communists, he declared, needed to "clear away all remnants of the pacifist rubbish of opposing war by surrendering to the warmakers."[6]

Within months, however, disquieting hints of an impending shift in Soviet foreign policy emerged. On March 10, 1939, in an address to the Eighteenth Congress of the Soviet Communist Party, Stalin speculated on the motives prompting Britain and France to hand over Czechoslovakia's Sudetenland region to Germany the previous September. Was this simply a misguided bid by those governments to secure "peace in our time," as Neville Chamberlain proclaimed on returning from Munich? Or something more sinister, a plot by capitalist powers to whet the German appetite for conquests further eastward? The Soviet Union, Stalin declared, was not going "to be drawn into conflict by warmongers who are accustomed to have others pull the chestnuts out of the fire for them." Reports in the *New York Times* and elsewhere speculated about a possible German-Soviet diplomatic reconciliation.[7]

George Charney recalled uncertainty among fellow Communists sparked by Stalin's comments. Still, as spring turned to summer in 1939, he couldn't imagine a shift in Soviet policy so drastic that it would affect the Party's commitment to the Popular Front. As for those "chestnuts," Charney asked, "What was so clearly indicated in this cryptic phrase . . . as against the years of bloody conflict in Spain?"[8] The CPUSA's general secretary remained certain that anti-fascism and collective security were still linchpins of Soviet diplomacy. "There is as much chance of Russo-German agreement," he declared in July 1939, "as of Earl Browder being elected President of the Chamber of Commerce."[9]

Browder had lived through many reversals in Soviet policy. To commit himself with no path for retreat suggests he was certain in his own mind that the current line was there to stay. Had he been correct, and had the Party's position remained one of favoring both "National and Social Security" in the three years leading up to the Japanese attack on Pearl Harbor on December 7, 1941, the subsequent history of American Communism might, conceivably, have played out differently. That was not to be.

In Europe that spring and summer of 1939, it was increasingly evident that war was imminent. Five days after Stalin's "chestnuts" speech, German troops entered Prague. In April Italy invaded Albania. Hitler meanwhile demanded territorial concessions from Poland. The British and French governments finally abandoned appeasement, issuing a joint guarantee of Polish security. But Chamberlain made no serious attempt to devise a common strategy for collective security with Stalin, concerned that any such arrangements would result in an expansion of Soviet power in Europe.[10]

On August 22, 1939, the Soviet news agency TASS abruptly announced that Nazi foreign minister Joachim von Ribbentrop would fly to Moscow the following day to sign a nonaggression pact. *Frayhayt* editor Melech Epstein heard the astonishing news in the CP's national headquarters in New York: "The party building on 12th and 13th streets was hushed," he recalled. "Party functionaries avoided talking to each other. The worst sufferers were the switchboard operators. They were swamped with telephone calls all day long by worried Communists unable to credit their own eyes."[11]

Browder called a press conference the following evening on the ninth floor of Party headquarters. Uncertain as yet about the true meaning of the Pact, he described it as "a wonderful contribution to peace" that threatened neither Poland's security nor the continuance of the Popular Front. In fact, he suggested, the United States, Britain, and France should sign similar nonaggression pacts with the Soviets. As for the impact of the "latest international developments" upon the rank and file of American Communists, Browder declared their reaction was "one of rather complete understanding and agreement."[12]

Not at first, however, and especially not among the largely Jewish membership of the Party in New York City. Communists attempting to sell the *Daily Worker* or soapbox in Jewish neighborhoods in Brooklyn and on the Lower East Side were met with hostility and derisive cries of "Heil Hitler." Some prominent Communists, like *Frayhayt* editor Epstein and *New Masses* literary editor Granville Hicks, publicly renounced their party memberships, in Hicks's case with a widely noted resignation letter in the *New Republic* accusing CP leaders of advancing "apologetics completely devoid of clarity and logic" in defense of the Pact.[13]

Communists wavered in confusion in those last weeks of summer. Most current Party members had joined since 1936, when anti-fascism was often the primary cause attracting them to its ranks. In the end, however, few departed. On September 11, some 20,000 New York City Communists answered the call for yet another rally in Madison Square Garden. James Wechsler, whose own disenchantment with Communism had come two years earlier during the Moscow trials, covered the event for *The Nation*. There could no longer be any question, he told the magazine's liberal readers, that the majority of the Communist rank and file would remain loyal to their leaders, even if momentarily bewildered by the sudden reversal in Soviet foreign policy: "The thing that stood out in the meeting," he reported, "was the almost desperate huddling together of people confronted by a monumental world crisis, taking refuge in a reaffirmation of their own solidarity."[14]

For liberals who had supported the Popular Front in the second half of the 1930s, no similar satisfactions were available. In early September, the *New Republic* reported sardonically from "the Union Square Front" that the Party's fellow travelers were "dropping like ripe plums in a hurricane."[15]

Following the Pact, resignations poured into organizations like the American League for Peace and Democracy, which shut its office early in 1940. The League of American Writers lingered on, but it saw most of its famous members depart before year's end. Among the first to leave was poet W. H. Auden, who explained in his letter of resignation that the league was typical of political groups on the Left in which "the Liberals were lazy, while the Communists did all the work and, in consequence, won the executive power they deserved. This did not matter so long as the Popular Front was a reality; now it does."[16]

Despite Browder's praise for the Pact as a contribution to peace in Europe, the Wehrmacht invaded Poland from the west on September 1, followed by an invasion of eastern Poland by the Red Army on September 17 (in accordance with secret codicils to the "nonaggression" agreement between Moscow and Berlin). Britain and France declared war on Germany on September 3 but could provide no meaningful aid to the beleaguered Polish government, which in the face of overwhelming odds surrendered to the Nazis on September 27. The conflict, the CP declared, was in their view "the second imperialist war," no different in character than the first such war of 1914–1918.

The CP also endorsed the Soviet invasion of Poland, distributing leaflets in New York City in September headlined "USSR Defends

Poland." The *Frayhayt* reassured its Yiddish-speaking readers that in the Soviet-occupied zone of eastern Poland, "*at least two million Jews who were in mortal fear of Nazi oppression and degradation are to fear no more.*"[17] There was more to come along similar lines, as the Communists endorsed the Red Army's invasion of Finland in December 1939, and the Soviet Union's annexation of Latvia, Lithuania, and Estonia the following spring.

In the eyes of many American liberals, Nazi Germany and the Soviet Union were now allies in the conquest of weaker neighbors. Critics of the CPUSA coined the phrase "Communazis," suggesting that supporters of totalitarian regimes of the Left and Right were essentially members of the same political camp, blood brothers in their support for tyrannies built on terror and aggression. Brothers too in the threat they posed to the United States, each representing potential "fifth columnists," hidden agents prepared to strike at American national security through sabotage and other means when the right moment came.[18]

That the CP's position on the war in Europe followed in lockstep with Soviet foreign policy was a given. What that meant in terms of the Party's perspective on domestic politics was, at first, uncertain. Some orthodox Communists, after years of quiet dissatisfaction with the reformist outlook imposed on the Party by anti-fascist coalition-building, were not sorry to see the departure of erstwhile liberal allies, with their petty-bourgeois concerns. Among top CP leaders, William Z. Foster and Alexander Bittelman were eager to return to the familiar class-against-class rhetoric of the early 1930s. The Party's ruling Political Committee met in emergency session from September 14 to September 16 to discuss the international situation and its domestic implications. Bittelman argued that Communists should again emphasize their ultimate goal of the revolutionary transformation of American society, as they had during the Third Period.

Browder disagreed. On the defensive, he remained intent on salvaging some of the Popular Front policies with which he was so closely identified, insisting it was "very important that we keep [the] continuity of our line before the masses through every change." Browder criticized Britain and France for failing to respond to previous Soviet appeals for collective security, but he still reserved his harshest criticisms for the Nazis, "the immediate instigators and perpetrators of war."[19] He refrained from any direct criticism of Roosevelt, who was, after all, officially committed to maintaining American neutrality. In comments to a meeting of the National Committee, he even went so far as to call again for a third term for the president.[20]

However, coded shortwave messages from Comintern leader Dimitrov in late September chided Browder for failing to draw the proper conclusions from the Nazi-Soviet Pact, and thus "remaining a captive of tenets that were correct before the European war but are now incorrect." The onset of the war "changes our relationship to FDR," Dimitrov declared, because the main enemy now "is camp of imperialist bourgeoisie."[21]

Browder and his allies in Party leadership temporized for as long as they could. In the September meeting of the Political Committee, Eugene Dennis argued that the Party should not draw the "foolish conclusion that . . . a fascist regime is no different than a bourgeois democratic regime."[22] As the autumn wore on, however, the Communists ceased to single out the Nazis for blame for starting the war, and increasingly sought to erase the political distinction between "bourgeois democracy" and fascism, just as they had during the Third Period. Nazi rule in occupied Czechoslovakia was harsh and oppressive, the *Daily Worker* declared editorially in late November. On the other hand, the editors added, German atrocities against conquered peoples were in no way worse than the "equally monstrous crimes" that Britain had committed in India.[23]

The CP's insistence on the moral equivalence of the belligerents at times shaded over into the implication that the main enemy of peace since August 1939 consisted of Britain and France, rather than Germany. Hitler, after all, had made his peace with Stalin, while the Allies' intentions toward the Soviet Union remained unclear. American Communist leaders in October 1939 condemned British ruling circles for an alleged plot to "bring to power in Germany that section of the bourgeoisie which will immediately engage in military intervention against the USSR"—which was to say that they believed (or at least pretended to believe) in the bizarre notion that somebody was waiting offstage in Berlin who might take over the German government at the behest of the British and, once in office, prove *even worse* than Hitler.[24]

Having voluntarily surrendered the moral high ground of militant anti-fascism, and having endorsed every successive reprehensible action taken by the Soviet government from the Pact to the invasion of Poland and beyond, Communists once again, as in 1919–1922 and 1928–1934, found themselves political pariahs. They were encouraged by Party leaders to regard the hatred they engendered among former allies (whom they now excoriated as turncoats) as the true measure of revolutionary purity. In doing so they helped make themselves easy targets for opponents from across the political spectrum.[25]

In Washington, conservative Virginia Democratic congressman Howard Smith proposed the anti-Communist Alien Registration Act of 1940, better known as the Smith Act, which upon passage criminalized conspiracy to teach or advocate the desirability of overthrowing the US government. Although the Justice Department held off using the new law against Party members for the moment, it was unclear how lengthy a respite that would prove. In 1940 Congress also passed the Voorhis Act, named for its principal author, liberal Democrat and (former Socialist) California congressman Jerry Voorhis. Among other provisions, the act required organizations controlled by foreign powers to register with the Justice Department. The Voorhis Act prompted the Party to disaffiliate from the Communist International. In practice, American Communists continued to travel to Moscow to report to Comintern leaders as long as wartime conditions permitted.[26]

Congressional legislation proved less of a threat to the Communists, at least in the short run, than seemingly nonpolitical criminal cases brought by federal prosecutors. In late October, FBI agents arrested Browder for violating US passport laws when he had traveled abroad under assumed names as a Profintern agent a decade earlier. In a White House Cabinet meeting late in 1939, Attorney General Frank Murphy, a staunch liberal, as he had proven as governor of Michigan during the Flint sit-down strike, commented with satisfaction that "every possible effort is being made to indict any Communist who has violated the criminal laws in any respect."[27]

Following his conviction in January 1941, Browder surrendered to federal authorities on March 25 for transport to Atlanta to begin serving a four-year sentence. In his absence, his chief aide Robert Minor oversaw Party affairs on his behalf. Browder was imprisoned in the same federal penitentiary where Eugene Debs had been held two decades earlier. The Party launched a "Free Earl Browder" campaign on the model of many earlier campaigns to free political prisoners. But, unlike the Debs case, few Americans regarded Browder as a political martyr.[28]

Communists were targeted by state and local as well as federal authorities. Imitating the House Un-American Activities Committee chaired by Martin Dies, which had emerged since its founding in 1938 as a determined enemy of the Communist Party nationally, so-called "Little Dies Committees" were now established by state legislatures in California, Oklahoma, and Texas, which carried out investigations to harass local Communist officials. In New York, the state legislature established the Rapp-Coudert Committee (named for its two principal members) to investigate Communist influence in public higher education, in the most sustained attack on radicalism by state authorities since the Red Scare. More than 500 faculty, staff, and students from City College, Brooklyn College, Hunter College, and Queens College were subpoenaed to testify before the committee, and over fifty faculty and staff lost their jobs, not for any demonstrable classroom or professional misconduct, but solely for political affiliation.[29]

During the Popular Front years, liberal opinion would have been outraged by similar assaults on free speech. Some liberals did stand up for the besieged Communists. The *New Republic*'s chief political columnist Kenneth Crawford declared, in the fall of 1939, that "the price of maintaining civil liberties" for non-Communists "is stout defense of the civil liberties of genuine Communists themselves."[30] But he was in the minority. By the spring of 1941, a Gallup poll showed that over 70 percent of Americans favored laws outlawing the Party. Even the American Civil Liberties Union joined the attack, expelling Elizabeth Gurley Flynn from its board of directors for her Party membership in 1940, although she had been a charter member of the ACLU twenty years earlier.[31]

By late 1939, Communists were returning to a quasi-underground existence. Selected Communist leaders disappeared from public view and, in Party parlance, became "unavailable." CP leader Eugene Dennis, already seen as a future general secretary, was among them, disappearing from view in October 1939 and spending the next year and a half hiding out in backwoods cottages in Upstate New York. He was then dispatched to the Soviet Union, both for safekeeping and to report to the Comintern on the CP's activities since the start of the war.[32]

Following August 1939, the Communist Party suffered crushing reverses in almost every arena in which it lately had enjoyed success. As Dennis informed Comintern officials when he arrived in Moscow, the Party itself, which counted 65,000 "registered" members (that is, members who had officially renewed their membership with a Party club) in January 1939, was reduced to 50,000 members who had taken that step two years later, a reduction, if accurately reported, of nearly a quarter of its strength.[33]

The Communists' newly founded front group, the American Peace Mobilization, whose slogan was "The Yanks Aren't Coming," was designed like earlier efforts to build coalitions with non-Communist allies. The group, however, attracted few recruits outside Party ranks, even at a time when a majority of Americans declared themselves opposed to supporting the Allied cause in Europe. Isolationist sentiment in 1939–1941 mostly benefited right-wing organizations from which Communists were excluded, principally the 800,000 member America First Committee, whose most prominent spokesman was the pro-German, antisemitic Charles Lindbergh (a smattering of pacifists and Socialists, including Norman Thomas, also supported the organization). In liberal interventionist circles, Communists were mocked as the "Russia First" committee.[34]

There was one important exception to the collapse of Party influence. In the labor movement, Communists managed not only to hold their own but even gained power. Organized labor as a whole, apart from the heavily Jewish garment unions, displayed little enthusiasm for supporting the Allied cause in 1939–1940, which meant that the Communists' new anti-war line in and of itself did not make them outliers. Equally important, Communists sustained an informal alliance with CIO president John L. Lewis. He had no personal sympathy for the Party, but his views were both strongly isolationist and anti-Roosevelt, which reflected his rivalry within the CIO with Amalgamated Clothing Workers president Sidney Hillman, who in 1939–1940 was emerging as FDR's most dependable, and pro-interventionist, labor ally. The Communists, anti-FDR and anti-Hillman, were useful allies.

In February 1940, Lewis spoke at a Washington gathering of the American Youth Congress. Earlier that day on the White House lawn, President Roosevelt had scolded AYC delegates for passing a resolution opposing American aid to Finland, then at war with the Soviet Union. During his own speech that evening, Lewis excoriated FDR's criticisms. Who, he asked, had a greater right to question American foreign policy than the young men who "in the event of war will become cannon fodder?" He dropped hints about supporting a third party in the upcoming election, which delighted the Communists, although later in the year he instead endorsed the Republican presidential candidate, Wendell Willkie.[35]

When the Congress of Industrial Organizations met in Atlantic City for its annual convention in November 1940, Sidney Hillman championed a "Communazi" resolution, in an effort to ban Communists, along with Nazis and fascists, from holding office in the CIO. Lewis, who had given notice of his intention to step down as CIO president if Roosevelt was reelected, turned over the presidency to his ally, Steelworkers leader Phillip Murray, at the convention. He spent some of his remaining political capital blocking Hillman's anti-Communist resolution. It was referred back to committee where it was watered down to a more generic statement rejecting "policies emanating . . . from foreign ideologies such as Nazism, Communism, and fascism," which passed by unanimous standing vote. The resolution's passage, of course, included the votes of scores of Communist delegates from unions they controlled or influenced—symbolically humiliating, but in practical terms a toothless repudiation. Communist officeholders in the CIO, such as general counsel Lee Pressman and *CIO News* editor Len DeCaux, remained in their jobs.[36]

Though under assault by Hillman in the national CIO, and facing similar attacks from anti-Communist rivals in some of the CIO's constituent unions, especially from the Reuther forces in the United Auto Workers, the Communists saw new opportunities within a rapidly expanding labor movement. Ironically, it was expanding because of the very war they so vehemently opposed.

The Depression was finally coming to an end, and unemployment gave way to labor shortages as the American defense industry began receiving government contracts for tanks, planes, and battleships. The CIO was on the verge of sweeping away employer resistance to unionization in the major mass-production industries like steel, auto, and electrical manufacturing, and Communists were well positioned to take advantage of this wave of militancy. At the same time that the CIO was passing a resolution lumping together Communists and Nazis at its 1940 national convention, Wyndham Mortimer, the most prominent Communist organizer in the UAW, was leading a successful strike of workers at the Los Angeles Vultee Aircraft plant. The strikers were vilified in the press for sabotaging military preparedness (the plant produced training planes for the armed forces) at the behest of Communist conspirators. In response, Mortimer declared that "some people think that anyone who wants more than $20 a week is a Communist." The strikers held strong, and after twelve days the company capitulated, raising starting wages by 25 percent and instituting paid vacations and sick leave.[37]

These developments offered Communists a path forward at a time when few other avenues for political gain were available. William Z. Foster, who retained an element of his former syndicalist beliefs, took the lead in emphasizing the importance of workplace struggles for union recognition and economic gain. "The first thing we must clearly realize," he declared in December 1940 following the victory at Vultee, "is that economic questions relating to the living standards of the people are of decisive importance" at the moment, not only for their own sake, but because they could be used to "develop into the general struggle to keep America out of the war."[38]

Communist leadership of several bitter and prolonged strikes in the winter and spring of 1941, including one at the Allis-Chalmers plant in Milwaukee and another at North American Aviation in Los Angeles, was viewed by government officials as an attempt to sabotage military preparedness. President Roosevelt was sufficiently alarmed by June 1941 to recommend to his attorney general that the FBI expand efforts to investigate the "subversive control of labor." Thus encouraged, over the next few years the bureau greatly stepped up efforts to infiltrate the CP, which would have a dramatic impact on the Communist movement's fortunes in the postwar era.[39]

Of course, the UAW's decision in 1940 to organize aircraft workers in southern California had been supported by both the Communist and anti-Communist leaders of the union. Other unions securely controlled by Communists (which the UAW was not), and that were well-placed to sabotage defense efforts had that been the Party's actual intent, such as the West Coast longshoremen and the East Coast sailors, avoided strikes throughout 1940 and 1941. Not a single workday was lost due to a strike by the United Electrical Workers in 1941. And conservative unions, like the AFL's Seafarers' International Union, took advantage of demand for labor in the months leading up to American involvement in the war to go on strike to win better wages and conditions. That the Communists hoped to turn the strike wave to political advantage was hardly a conspiratorial secret since they proclaimed that intention again and again in Party publications. Through the struggles for union recognition, bigger paychecks, and better working conditions, Gil Green (soon to be appointed to the important post of New York district leader) wrote in the January 1941 *Communist*, "labor will emancipate itself from the Roosevelt myth, will learn who are its true friends . . . and will move in the direction of independent political action."[40]

Communists were prone to this kind of wishful thinking—workers, fighting for x, would naturally *move on* to agree with the Party's positions on y and z. Workplace militancy, in fact, rarely translated into anti-Roosevelt or anti-war sentiment. But it did lead to significant gains in union membership: the unions affiliated with the CIO and the AFL increased from just under 9 million members in 1940 to nearly 15 million five years later.

This rising tide lifted all boats in the labor movement, including those with Communist skippers. The Communist-led United Electrical Workers, for example, founded with just 30,000 dues-paying members in 1936, counted some 300,000 in 1941 on the eve of American involvement in World War II. Five years later, at war's end in 1945, the UE had more than doubled in size, achieving a membership of 750,000, securing its position as the third-largest affiliate in the CIO, surpassed only by the United Auto Workers and United Steel Workers. It became the largest left-led union in

American history, dwarfing the fabled Industrial Workers of the World at its height. Overall, Communists led eighteen CIO unions, with well over a million members among them, representing over one-fifth of total CIO membership, as well as a number of state and city CIO councils, from New York to Los Angeles. The CP also remained influential in other CIO unions they did not control, including the United Auto Workers. Whether or not the Yanks were coming, the war increased Communist influence within the labor movement.[41]

In Europe, the fighting took a dramatic turn in the spring and summer of 1940. Communists, like many other observers, initially expected the "second imperialist war" to follow the pattern set by the first one back in 1914–1918, that is, a prolonged stalemate that could last years before there was any decisive outcome. Instead, after seven relatively calm months of "phoney war" to the west of Germany, Hitler launched his Western Front blitzkrieg offensive in April, invading and conquering Denmark, Norway, Holland, Luxemburg, and Belgium in short order, and forcing France to surrender in late June. Britain came under sustained air assault in August, and the Germans prepared for a cross-channel invasion later in the year. The Nazi-Soviet Pact, initially justified by Communists as a necessary act of realpolitik buying time for the Soviet Union to strengthen its defenses, no longer seemed quite as good a deal. "Will not Hitler, in the event of a crushing victory over Great Britain and France, turn his armies against the USSR?" a reader asked the *Daily Worker* in June 1940. William Z. Foster replied, with an assured rhetorical shrug, that such an invasion would "provoke a general European revolutionary war" and "put the life of the capitalist system in jeopardy."[42]

In Europe in 1940–1941, however, the thunder was distinctly on the fascist right. Italy launched an ill-fated invasion of Greece in the fall of 1940, initially repelled by determined Greek resistance, aided by the

British. Then the Germans intervened in April 1941, forcing the British out and the Greeks to surrender. Bulgaria joined the Axis at the beginning of March, and the Germans pressured Yugoslavia to do the same. When the pro-Axis Yugoslav government prepared to do so, the army stepped in and installed a new government, which signed a treaty of friendship with the USSR on April 5. Enraged by this defiance, Hitler ordered the invasion of Yugoslavia.

In response to the military catastrophe unfolding in Europe, talk began to be heard in some quarters of the Party hinting at a partial return to an anti-Nazi outlook. Joseph Starobin, a veteran of the City College chapter of the National Student League in the early 1930s, and then an increasingly authoritative voice in Party circles on foreign affairs, argued in the *New Masses* in mid-April 1941 that the USSR should not be expected "to remain passive" in the face of German advances. The May issue of *The Communist* declared that "the attacked peoples" of Greece and Yugoslavia were "waging a valiant and just war of liberation."[43]

If Greeks and Yugoslavs were lauded by the Party for anti-fascist resistance, that didn't translate into a reconsideration of the overall nature of the war, which, logically, should have justified Communist support for the British, fighting their own battle for national survival. Without a definitive signal from Moscow, the CPUSA remained committed to the "Yanks Aren't Coming" line. Stalin, though warned by British intelligence and his own agents in Berlin of an impending German invasion, believed those were Allied provocations. The June 20 issue of the *Daily Worker* complained: "Reports of a 'break' between the Soviet Union and Germany . . . continue to flare up in capitalist newspapers. What is immediately noticeable . . . is the lying character of the stories being published as gospel truth."[44]

Two days later, on Sunday, June 22, German tanks smashed through the Soviet border defenses. "The first hour was awful," Mike Gold wrote in the

Daily Worker. "I shall never forget it. Now it had come—the thing we had feared for five, ten, twenty years."[45]

Comintern leader Georgi Dimitrov cabled American Communist leaders on June 26 declaring, "The primary task now is to risk everything to achieve victory for the Soviet people and the complete destruction of the fascist barbarians. Everything must be subordinated to this task."[46] When the CP National Committee met in emergency session two days later, there was none of the confusion seen in the first weeks of the Nazi-Soviet Pact. Every blow against the Nazi enemy, Gil Green declared, "is a blow in the interests of the Soviet people. . . . We must support these blows completely, for no matter who delivers them or for what reasons, they help to defeat and annihilate the main enemy of mankind."[47]

The invasion news shocked American Communists. "Defend the Soviet Union" had been the one slogan that never changed through all the other twists and turns of policy and rhetoric since 1919. And yet, there was another reaction, especially common among younger Communists who had come of age politically during the Popular Front, and it didn't originate with a cabled policy directive from Moscow. George Watt, former political commissar in the Abraham Lincoln Battalion, was summoned early on June 22 to a meeting of the New York City YCL called by another Spanish Civil War vet, John Gates, with whom he had swum to safety across the Ebro River in Spain three years earlier. What Watt remembered feeling was an overwhelming sense of relief at being released from the political burdens imposed by the Pact. "We felt like we had come home again," was how he put it.[48] "Home" had several meanings in this case, home to anti-fascism, as well as home to America. These young Communists were relieved, in other words, to return to a political stance that both made sense to them instinctively and might free them of the status of pariahs in their own country. "Many of us," Gates later recalled, "were ashamed now of the policy we had followed since August 1939 and were determined to make up for it."[49]

Shame was not the same thing, exactly, as clarity. "Wasn't the bourgeois democracy of the British during the imperialist war better than Hitler's fascism?" one reader of the YCL's *Weekly Review* asked in a letter to the editor after June 22. "Why didn't we support the British then?" Claudia Jones, recently appointed as YCL educational director, offered the new orthodoxy in reply: the war *had* been imperialist until June 22, but "Hitler's attack upon the Soviet Union as a bid for world conquest endangered the continued independence and existence of all nations and peoples."[50] Jones and other young Communist leaders did not repudiate the political choices they had made over the preceding two years. The YCL's internal culture did not exactly encourage critical self-reflection. Any criticism of the line that American Communists had adopted between August 1939 and June 1941 necessarily would have to be broadened into criticism of the Soviet leadership, unthinkable at any time, but particularly at the present moment when the very survival of the Soviet Union was in jeopardy. Few American Communists, young or old, were inclined to obsess over the shortcomings of the Party line during the Nazi-Soviet Pact. Rather, they did their best to dismiss the whole episode as just so much ancient history, no more worth dwelling on than, say, the dimly remembered revolutionary adventurism of the Third Period. Or, if they still felt qualms, they may have told themselves there would be time enough for a critical postmortem later on, when the immediate crisis passed. But the crisis never seemed to pass, as one desperately fraught moment was succeeded by the next.

The flip-flops of 1939–1941 were less easily forgotten or forgiven outside Party ranks. In the first issue of the *New Republic* to appear following the Nazi invasion, the liberal editors commented acidly, "The Communists will no doubt make another attempt now to set up a United Front; we doubt whether they will succeed with anybody whose memory is good enough to go back a couple of years."[51] The political damage inflicted by the Nazi-Soviet Pact would not prove such ancient history after all, with long-term consequences for the Communist cause in America.

Almanac Singers, 1941, Pete Seeger (center) with banjo, Woody Guthrie (left) with guitar (Photo by Michael Ochs Archives/Getty Images)

Communists once again changed direction, slogans, and allies. The change was also reflected in the musical accompaniment to Party gatherings in New York and elsewhere provided by a small coterie of Greenwich Village–based musicians. They called themselves the Almanac Singers and were the first significant urban folk group in the United States. Coming together in the winter of 1940–1941, the original Almanacs included Pete Seeger, Lee Hays, Millard Lampell, John Peter Hawes, and soon Woody Guthrie, as well as a number of others in a revolving cast of singers and guitar players who lived in or were regular visitors at the various communal apartments they rented in the Village (most famously the so-called Almanac House at 130 West Tenth Street). They were, from all accounts, an appealing group of young people: Seeger, a mere twenty years old, among the youngest; the oldest, Guthrie, not yet thirty. All men at first, but soon joined by Sis Cunningham and Bess Lomax Hawes, all white at first, but soon including African-American performers like Huddie "Lead Belly" Ledbetter, Josh White, Sonny Terry, and Brownie McGhee. They early on developed a gift for drawing their listeners to join them in singing, which became a staple of American folk-song performance in coming decades. They were idealistic, informal, earnest, unpolished, and creative, some of them quite talented, a few destined for greatness.

And not always well served by their political choices, certainly not in those early days. In the spring of 1941 none of them, except possibly Guthrie (and there the evidence is disputed), were card-carrying Communists, although Seeger had been in the YCL in his short time as a Harvard student in the late 1930s, and would join the CP in the summer of 1941.[52] Still, as they cobbled together a repertoire of topical songs in their first months together, they closely followed the then-prevailing Party line. In doing so, they performed some enduring labor anthems like Guthrie's "Union Maid," introduced on May 1, 1941, at a Madison Square Garden rally of 20,000 striking transport workers.

At the same time, the Almanacs became identified with some less enduring antiwar songs. In May 1941, they released their first album, entitled *Songs for John Doe*, which included "Ballad of October 16" (taking its title from the day the previous autumn when President Roosevelt signed into law the first peacetime military draft in US history). They had first performed the ballad at the annual gathering in Washington, DC, of the American Youth Congress the previous February, where it was received enthusiastically by the young delegates. The lyrics were written by twenty-two-year-old Millard Lampell, the son of Jewish garment workers from Paterson, New Jersey, later a prizewinning screenwriter. His ballad began with a cheeky challenge to Roosevelt:

Oh, Franklin Roosevelt told the people how he felt
We damn near believed what he said
He said, "I hate war and so does Eleanor
But we won't be safe 'til everybody's dead."[53]

A month or so later, following the events of June 22, the ballad permanently disappeared from the Almanac Singers' repertoire. As Woody

Guthrie remarked to Pete Seeger about that time, perhaps with a trace of self-mockery, "I guess we won't be singing any more of them peace songs."[54]

Four months or so later, in response to the October 31 torpedoing by a German U-boat of the US Navy destroyer *Reuben James* off the coast of Iceland with the loss of 115 crewmen, Guthrie wrote a new song for the Almanac Singers featuring stirring martial lyrics:

> *Now tonight there are lights in our country so bright*
> *In the farms and in the cities they're telling of the fight*
> *And now our mighty battleships will steam the bounding main*
> *And remember the name of that good Reuben James.*[55]

Guthrie added a motto to his guitar: "THIS MACHINE KILLS FAS-CISTS." The leading Almanacs would soon be making amends for their earlier views through service in the war effort: Seeger and Lampell in the army, Guthrie in the merchant marine (one of Guthrie's wartime voyages took him to the coast of Normandy in the summer of 1944; his ship struck a mine off Omaha Beach but managed to stay afloat).[56] In any event, the Almanacs could have avoided a lot of subsequent grief if they had postponed forming the group for a half year or so, until, say, July 1941; the legacy of their anti-war performances during the last months of the Nazi-Soviet Pact haunted and killed the group within a few years, just as it was on the cusp of mainstream commercial success.[57]

The CP's National Committee was meeting in New York City the first weekend in December, when news arrived on Sunday afternoon of the Japanese attack on Pearl Harbor. Robert Minor, quoting Marx, announced that the moment had come when "the weapon of criticism is replaced by the criticism of weapons."[58] The previous July, John Gates had told a gathering of young Communists, "Every YCLer must be ready to give his life to the great cause of defeating Hitler." On December 16, he went to his local recruiting office, and the following day the former lieutenant colonel in the Abraham Lincoln Battalion was sworn in as a private in the US Army. At a gathering that same night of several thousand Communists meeting in a New York hotel, he led the assemblage in reciting the Pledge of Allegiance, not previously a feature of Party gatherings. Three decades later George Charney wrote of the occasion, "I will never forget the meeting at which Johnny Gates announced that he had volunteered for the Army and saluted the flag. It released a tremendous emotional feeling, as though . . . we were atoning for the sins of the past."[59]

The war years were for American Communists, as for other Americans, a time of strong emotions, a swirl of hopes and fears, a sense of sharing a "rendezvous with destiny," as President Roosevelt had said some years earlier. For Communists, some of those feelings, as Charney suggests, had to do with casting off troubling memories of their official indifference to the outcome of the war against Nazi Germany. They reclaimed the mantle of anti-fascism, combining patriotism with the Party's trademark internationalism.

In the space of a few days in early December 1941 *Casablanca*'s cynical saloonkeeper Rick Blaine switched from isolationism to renewed anti-fascism with grace and dash. If only real life were as simple as the movies. With victory over Nazism now the absolute priority, the cause for which, as Comintern leader Dimitrov had declared, "everything must be subordinated," the Communists reevaluated their efforts in every field of political endeavor, not always so gracefully as the proprietor of the Café Américain. The latest turnaround in the Party line often involved awkward choices. In the labor movement, the Communists dropped their opposition to former arch-opponent Sidney Hillman (now a valued pro-war ally) and started attacking John L. Lewis (who remained isolationist in outlook, continued to lead strikes in the coal fields, and withdrew the United Mine Workers from the CIO). Communist union organizers became ardent supporters of the no-strike pledge adopted by both the CIO and the AFL in December 1941, encouraging workers in vital war industries to increase productivity in exchange for incentive pay. There they met with rank-and-file resistance, sometimes from other Communists. CP organizer Max Gordon recalled that Party members active in the Party unit at Schenectady's GE plant flat out refused to accept the new line on speedups: "The guys in the shop said to me, 'For Christ's sake, Max, if we go all out and quadruple our production, what happens after the war?'" Despite such tensions, the CP continued to recruit working-class members into its ranks, with a majority of its membership belonging to unions by 1943.[60]

President Roosevelt was no longer viewed as the servant of the economic royalists or a hypocritical warmonger, but as a valued leader in the fight against the fascist aggressor internationally, and against reactionary forces at home. When he commuted Browder's four-year sentence to time served, a diplomatic goodwill gesture on the eve of Soviet foreign minister Vyacheslav Molotov's arrival in Washington for consultations in May 1942, the grateful Communist leader released a statement to reporters waiting for him on his release from Atlanta penitentiary promising "to weld unbreakable national unity under the Commander-in-Chief." Within months of his release, having resumed his leadership duties, Browder published a book entitled *Victory and After* in which he argued that "support for President Roosevelt" was the "essential guiding slogan for our country in finding its way through this war."[61]

In the fall of 1941, the Communists won a small but heartening electoral victory that suggested the political opportunities opening up to them post–June 22. Peter V. Cacchione, Kings County chairman of the Communist Party since 1936, won election to the New York City Council from Brooklyn in November 1941. It was his third attempt (in 1939 he had been thrown off the ballot due to procedural technicalities), and he racked up 35,000 first-choice votes and 14,000 second-choice votes under the city's proportional representation system. It was the most significant election victory by an open Communist running on the Party ticket in the history of the movement. Another Brooklyn CP leader, one of the younger, native-born recruits from the 1930s, recalled the "wild exuberance" of the borough's Communists on election night when they learned of Cacchione's victory: "The feeling was that we had achieved citizenship. . . . We had used the system to get our guy in—not under a disguise, but as a Communist."[62]

Prioritizing victory over Nazism above other considerations posed a particularly difficult political dilemma for Communists in the movement for Black equality. Their alliance during the Popular Front with A. Philip Randolph fell apart during the Nazi-Soviet Pact. Randolph went on to organize the March on Washington Movement (MOWM), an all-Black organization that promised to bring tens of thousands of Black Americans to Washington to demand an end to racial discrimination in defense industries and in the US military, a campaign from which he excluded Communists. To head off Randolph's march, scheduled for July 1, 1941, President Roosevelt established the Fair Employment Practices Committee to supervise efforts to end discrimination in defense industry hiring (it did nothing to desegregate the military). Building on its partial victory, MOWM went on to hold large public protest meetings against racism in New York, Chicago, and elsewhere in 1942. Meanwhile, Black newspapers promoted a "Double V" campaign that raised the slogan "Victory over discrimination at home" to equal status with "Victory over the Axis abroad."[63]

For Communists, in contrast, the latter *V* ranked ahead of the former. In the October 1941 *Communist*, the Party's most prominent Black leader, James Ford, explained that from the Party's perspective, while demands for equal voting rights and the end of discrimination in the armed forces remained valid, it would be "wrong to press these demands without regard to the main task of the destruction of Hitler, without which no serious fight for Negro rights is possible."[64]

Some Black leaders at the time, and some historians since, have charged the Communists with abandoning the struggle for equal rights. In their influential history of the Party, Irving Howe and Lewis Coser stated flatly that "the CP believed the struggle for Negro rights should be suspended entirely during the war."[65]

"Suspended entirely" is an exaggeration. The Communists did not so much abandon the struggle for Black rights during the war, as seek to direct it into channels that would, at the same time, strengthen the war effort. They remained the most outspoken group within the labor movement pushing the fight for equal employment rights for African-Americans in major industries, as a wartime great migration brought tens of thousands of former sharecroppers out of the rural south and into the urban north. In the unions they controlled, Communists also consistently promoted Black members to leadership positions, and they fought hard in unions they did not control, like the United Auto Workers, to open up those offices to Black workers (in the face of opposition from their factional opponents).

The National Maritime Union, by 1941–1945 the largest seamen's union in the world, was particularly effective in expanding opportunities for its Black members in an industry that had a long tradition of restricting non-whites to the most menial positions aboard ships. In January 1942, when a New York shipping firm refused to accept twenty-five Black NMU sailors among a crew of 140 sent from the union dispatching hall, NMU president Joseph Curran warned the company that the ship would not sail without them. NMU vice president Frederick Myers, a Jamaica-born Black Communist Party member, told *Sunday Worker*, "This is not only a white man's war. . . . Every man regardless of the color of his skin will have a right to do his share to win this war."[66] The ship owners backed down, and Black and white crew members shipped out together. The NMU along with the National Negro Congress also fought to commission Black ship captains in the American merchant marine. Hugh Mulzac, a Black Communist who had earned his master's license in 1918 but who had had to serve as a steward for over two decades, was given command of the Liberty ship *Booker T. Washington*, sailing with an integrated crew under him recruited by the NMU. He made twenty-two transatlantic voyages as ship's captain during the war, transporting troops and supplies to the European front. His personal achievement opened the way for other African-Americans to become ships' officers.[67]

In the NMU, the CP enjoyed considerable rank-and-file support, even on potentially explosive issues like racial integration. In other Communist-led unions like the United Electrical Workers that was often not the case, and the push for equal employment opportunities for African-Americans led to violent opposition from the white rank and file in some locals. At the Westinghouse plant in East Pittsburgh and the Western Electric Company plant on Baltimore's Point Breeze waterfront, white workers disrupted production when newly hired Black workers joined them on the assembly line. UE officials would not back down, and at Point Breeze actually called on the government to take over the plant and end the walkout.[68]

In their Harlem stronghold, Communists reached their high-water mark among Black voters during the war years. The CP had long enjoyed a close political alliance with the Reverend Adam Clayton Powell Jr., the charismatic pastor of the powerful Abyssinian Baptist Church. They had supported his successful campaign for election to the city council in 1941. When he declined to run for reelection two years later (preparing a successful 1944 bid for election to Congress), the CP decided to run Benjamin Davis Jr. for the seat. With Powell's endorsement and the backing of the New York City CIO, Davis won handily (and in Brooklyn, in the same election, Pete Cacchione was reelected). Davis was the first Black Communist ever elected to public office in the United States. Harlem in those years regarded him as one of their own. The *Amsterdam News* praised him and predicted he would "be a real asset to the entire citizenry of New York."[69]

The Party's ongoing commitment to racial equality, even with its emphasis on preserving national unity in wartime, paid off in its recruiting drive in the second year of the war. In 1942 ten percent of the Party membership consisted of African-Americans; in 1943, one-third of the 15,000 members who joined that year were African-American.[70] In the end, as historian Mark Naison concluded in a balanced judgment, Black Communists during the Second World War retained respect in communities like Harlem "for their trade union and political connections and willingness to practice racial equality," but they "no longer stood on the cutting edge of black protest or possessed a monopoly on direct action techniques."[71]

The Party's efforts on behalf of racial equality were extended during the war to include another minority. Communists in Los Angeles played a significant role in defending the city's Mexican-American population, who were being victimized by police and white vigilantes. That young Mexican-American males favored a style of baggy oversized clothing called zoot suits was a strike against them, making them both easily identifiable on the streets and vulnerable to wartime intolerance. In the late summer of 1942, twenty-two young men, all but one Mexican-American, were arrested on dubious charges of murder when another young Mexican-American was found dead in East Los Angeles near a reservoir known as Sleepy Lagoon. Some of those arrested were beaten and intimidated by police detectives into making self-incriminating statements, but there were no witnesses, no murder weapon, and not even definite medical proof that the deceased had been murdered. The Hearst press in Los Angeles ran a series of inflammatory stories about a previously unnoticed crime wave by gangs of Mexican-American juvenile delinquents. Seventeen of the defendants were subsequently found guilty of murder. The Sleepy Lagoon Defense Committee, organized in October 1942 with significant Communist involvement, launched a national campaign modeled on the Scottsboro Boys defense to raise funds and publicize the case. Screenwriter Guy Endore (later blacklisted as a Communist) wrote a widely circulated pamphlet, *The Sleepy Lagoon Mystery*, highlighting the role of racial discrimination in the case. "We are seeking," he noted in the introduction, "to correct a social as well as a case of individual injustice."[72] Party lawyer Ben Margolis played a key role in the appeal process. Their efforts paid off when in October 1944 the convictions of all seventeen defendants were reversed by the District Court of Appeal. Historian Edward J. Escobar noted that through the efforts of the Sleepy Lagoon Defense Committee, for the first time "white society," or some sections of it, "came to see Mexican-Americans as an oppressed racial minority group."[73]

If the Party remained committed in substantial ways to the struggle for African-American and Mexican-American equality in those years, there was one racial minority in the United States whose rights Communists (like virtually all their countrymen) did indeed regard as expendable. That was Japanese-Americans. A month after Pearl Harbor, Mike Gold warned in his *Daily Worker* column against any "stupid, cruel and un-American persecutions and mob actions against aliens" living in the United States, including those of German, Italian, and Japanese-American descent.[74]

When the "stupid, cruel and un-American" persecution came at the hands of the American government and in the name of military necessity, however, Gold and the CP remained silent. In the months after Pearl Harbor, 120,000 people of Japanese ancestry living on the West Coast, two-thirds of them American citizens by virtue of being born in the United States, were removed from their homes by executive order of the president and interred in "relocation" camps run by the military in the interior of the United States. No evidence was ever produced that any of them, whether Nisei (native-born) or Issei (immigrants), posed a genuine threat to national security (or any more than that posed, say, by the thousands of Americans of German ancestry who had supported the Nazi regime in the 1930s, and who were left unmolested). Most of the "relocated" Japanese-Americans would not regain their freedom until near the end of the war.

A few of those sent to relocation camps were Party members. The CP had just over a hundred Japanese and Japanese-American members, most of whom lived on the West Coast (where their detention was required). Among their number was Karl Yoneda, a longshoreman and union organizer, and his white American wife, Elaine Black, who voluntarily accompanied him into incarceration. Notwithstanding the injustice of his family's "relocation," Yoneda remained loyal to the CP's national-unity line while imprisoned, writing in a letter to the *CIO News* in May 1942 that "those of us who are American citizens of Japanese ancestry are grateful to our government for the way this grave question of evacuation is being handled. What a difference from fascist-controlled countries." Yoneda was eventually released when he enlisted in the US Army, and went on to serve in Burma.[75]

Pete Seeger of the Almanac Singers, whose wife, Toshi Ohta, was half-Japanese, was not as sanguine. Because Ohta lived on the East Coast, she wasn't interned, and Seeger married her in 1943. But wartime hatred of all Japanese-Americans, interned or free, cast a dark shadow over the couple's future. When the California state organization of the American Legion passed a resolution calling for the postwar deportation of all people of Japanese ancestry living in the US, regardless of citizenship, Seeger sent a letter to both the Legion and the *Los Angeles Times* expressing his outrage:

> We, who may have to give our lives in this great struggle—we're fighting precisely to free the world of such Hitlerism, such narrow jingoism.
>
> If you deport Japanese, why not Germans, Italians, Rumanians, Hungarians, and Bulgarians?[76]

Military intelligence, aware of Seeger's musical and political background, routinely intercepted his correspondence with his young bride. As one War Department official familiar with Seeger's case wrote to J. Edgar Hoover in September 1943, he believed "that Subject will be further influenced along questionable lines by new wife." Seeger's "devotion to his wife was so strong before their marriage" that it led him to protest "what he considers to be the improper treatment of American-born Japanese."

For a Communist in the Army, even marital devotion could be considered evidence of potential disloyalty. As the letter from the military intelligence officer to Hoover concluded, "Their marriage will quite possibly fuse and strengthen their individual radical tendencies."[77]

Seeger was among 15,000 Communists who joined the US military in World War II, often not waiting to be drafted but volunteering for military service (usually in the army), and once in uniform, pressing for combat assignments. In the early years of the war, before the US was fully engaged, Communists were probably more likely to know someone who died in battle against fascism than the average American, given the hundreds of Abraham Lincoln Brigade volunteers who died in Spain, and the hundred Communist seamen, members of the National Maritime Union, who died in 1941–1942 when their ships were torpedoed by German U-boats. Many had volunteered for the dangerous run through the North Atlantic to carry American Lend-Lease supplies to the Soviet port at Murmansk.[78]

Communists who joined the US military during the Second World War officially took leave from the Party, which meant that there was no expectation they would carry out any political assignments beyond doing their duty as good soldiers. For the most part, they avoided drawing attention to their political allegiance, because to do otherwise could have negative consequences. Official army policy called for assigning "potentially subversive personnel," meaning Communists as well as fascists and enemy aliens, to units "in which there is minimum opportunity for damage." For Private Dashiell Hammett, who was forty-eight years old when he enlisted in the army in the fall of 1942, that meant being shunted from basic training to Camp Shenango in Pennsylvania, where the military dumped many suspect recruits who were deemed unsuitable for overseas service. In September 1943, he was transferred to Adak Island in the Aleutians, also considered a safe and even more remote place to deposit radicals for the duration. Hammett, one of the best-known literary celebrities associated with the CP before the war, the author of, among other classic mysteries, *The Maltese Falcon*, didn't pretend to be anything but what he was, a Communist. The local commander, a mystery fan, chose to overlook that liability, promoting him to sergeant and putting him in charge of editing the base newspaper. He also toured other bases in Alaska to give inspirational talks, not quite what the military intelligence officers who exiled him to the icy North had in mind.[79]

Growing needs for infantry replacements in the last year of fighting led the military to loosen the restrictions on deploying Communists overseas and in combat. John Gates, after his own stint in the Aleutians, arrived in Germany in late March 1945 to join the army's Seventeenth Airborne Division, in time to see the final collapse of Nazi resistance but too late to take part in the fighting. An estimated 500 Lincoln vets served in the military, and many did see combat, including Robert Thompson, who earned a Distinguished Service Cross fighting in New Guinea; Archie Brown, who served with the Seventy-Sixth Infantry Division in the Battle of the Bulge; Saul Wellman, who was severely wounded in the fighting at Bastogne with the 101st Airborne during the same battle; and George Watt, who bailed out over Belgium in 1943 when his B-17 was about to crash, and returned to Spain with the help of the European resistance. Black Lincoln vets, like their white counterparts, also served, though they found themselves discriminated against on the basis of race as well as politics. Tom Page, a Black volunteer who had rejoiced at being treated as an equal in the integrated Lincoln Battalion, served with a segregated US Army engineering unit in North Africa, Italy, and France. A number of Lincoln vets were recruited for the Office of Strategic Services (OSS), the newly created wartime intelligence agency, and took part in covert operations in Europe. When the FBI alerted the OSS director, General William Donovan, that he had Communists working for him, he is supposed to have replied, "I know they're Communists; that's why I hired them."[80]

The departure of so many young male Communists for military service had a dramatic effect on Party demographics. By October 1942, CP organizational secretary John Williamson warned, "We must be prepared to replace a majority of our functionaries in all state organizations." Women plugged the gaps. Thus Joe Clark, who was editor of the YCL's *Weekly Review* before leaving for the army in the spring of 1942, was replaced by Claudia Jones. (Clark served with distinction in the European theater, winning a Silver Star in combat in France.) By 1944 nearly half of all Party members were women, compared to just over 25 percent in 1936.[81]

Red Army soldiers were regarded as worthy comrades in arms by Americans across the political spectrum. Every country that the German Wehrmacht invaded between the autumn of 1939 and the spring of 1941 had surrendered within weeks. But that was not true of the Soviet Union after June 22, 1941. When it became clear in the closing months of that year and the beginning of 1942 that the Nazis were not going to reach Moscow after all, and in fact had suffered their first serious military reversal of the war, Soviet military prestige soared. In the spring and summer of 1942, Americans ranging in political views from CIO president Philip Murray to National Association of Manufacturers president William P. Witherow to General Douglas MacArthur celebrated the heroism of the Soviet peoples (usually referred to as "the Russians") and the Red Army. Admiration turned to adulation in the months during and just after the Battle of Stalingrad, which raged from August 1942 to February 1943. *Time* magazine chose Stalin as its "man of the year" for 1942, explaining to its readers that "Stalin's methods were tough, but they paid off." Shortly afterward, in a special issue devoted to the Soviet Union, and featuring a benevolent-looking Stalin on the cover, *Life* magazine paid the Russians the supreme compliment of being "one hell of a people," who "look like Americans, dress like Americans, and think like Americans."[82]

Wartime goodwill toward the Soviets did not necessarily entail any corresponding sentiments toward American Communists. Vice President Henry Wallace, who attended a "Salute to our Russian Ally" gathering of more than 20,000 in Madison Square Garden on November 8, 1942, organized by yet another successful front group, the Council of American-Soviet Friendship, confided to his diary around the same time that "a typical American Communist is the contentious sort of individual that would probably be shot in Russia without a ceremony," sounding a little wistful that American authorities were unable to resort to such straightforward measures.[83]

For many Communists who served in the US military in World War II, it was their first break in years from the all-encompassing world of Party culture and discipline. It taught some surprising lessons. George Charney, who joined the army in 1942 (serving in the Pacific, where he earned a Bronze Star) later said his military service helped him discover

> to my chagrin and amusement that I had no special authority or spoke from no dais in a pyramidal tent to summarize the discussion in the customary party style. What I had to say I had to get in edgewise, like the others, and sometimes shout to be heard. . . . After years of Communist separateness, in part self-imposed, the war reunited me with my fellow Americans.[84]

In Charney's case, it would take still more years before he fully absorbed the lessons of that experience. His fellow Communist Frank Straus Meyer drew more immediate and radical conclusions from his time in the Army in World War II.

Meyer's route to Communism was atypical. He was born in 1909 in Newark, New Jersey, to well-off parents of German Jewish ancestry. In 1930, he crossed the Atlantic to enroll at Balliol College, at the University of Oxford. The onset of the Great Depression broke the Meyer family fortunes, which may have been part of the reason why he started reading Marx and joined first the British Labour Party, and then the British Communist Party. He excelled at school, completing his bachelor of arts in 1932, while rising through the ranks of student radical politics. Highly regarded by his British comrades, he was recruited to the Central Committee of the British CP. He went on to study at the London School of Economics before being expelled for involvement in Communist activities.[85]

Two years later he returned to the United States to became first a YCL and then CP organizer in Illinois, rising to the position of educational director for the Illinois-Indiana district. The drab and demanding life of a full-time functionary wore him down. In 1942 he requested and was given leave from the CP to enlist in the army, which his biographer suggests represented a welcome relief from the toll that Party duties were taking on his spirits.[86]

Unfortunately, he was not up to the physical demands of military service, and in the fall of 1943 received a medical discharge. While awaiting his discharge papers to be completed, he spent his free time in the base library, reading widely in American history, including *The Federalist Papers*. He was impressed with its celebration of limited government and the separation of powers.

All that was on his mind when, a civilian again, Meyer wrote to Browder in November 1943. He still considered himself a Communist, he told the Party chief, but his "rather rude immersion among the American people in its most undifferentiated sense, which my Army career represented," had led him during his absence "to think very hard about the problems of our Party." He raised a number of somewhat abstract questions about the Leninist theories of imperialism and of revolutionary struggle, but the heart of his lengthy letter had to do with the relevance of the Bolshevik theory of organization to American society and politics. "Isn't the Leninist party," he asked, "designed for an immediate, sharp, and final struggle? Is it possible to build a mass Marxist party to meet the challenge that lies in front of us today on such a basis?"

The Bolshevik model of a disciplined cadre organization excluded most ordinary Americans who simply could not sacrifice the time and energy it took to be a Communist. As for those who chose to become professional revolutionaries, like himself in the 1930s, all too much of their time went to an endless round of "inner party" activities, which shut them off from meaningful contact with the people they were trying to influence. Meyer proposed a new kind of radical organization, whose members attended a limited number of meetings, perhaps quarterly, "received general guidance and education there," as well as from Party publications, but whose "one main task" would be to "think and act where he lives, works, plays, participates in the life of his community, as a Communist." This would no longer be a democratic-centralist party, but one basing its organizational structure on "traditional American concepts of democracy." The ideal organization he described sounded a lot like the British Labour Party, which he had joined all those years earlier in Oxford before becoming a Communist.[87]

A reader of official Party pronouncements in 1942–1943 would have some reason to think that Meyer's hopes for a radically restructured CP were not entirely unrealistic. Party organizational secretary John Williamson was an orthodox Communist through and through, who, unlike Meyer, showed few signs of independent thinking in his years as an inner-party functionary. However, even he, for purely pragmatic reasons, was beginning to rethink the Bolshevik model. For the first time since the late 1930s, the Party was growing again, nearing the level of its pre-Pact membership by 1944. Nevertheless, Williamson questioned whether the Communist Party as a whole was proving receptive to the new opportunities opening up to it. In a *Daily Worker* article in December 1942, he

Joseph Stalin (left), Franklin Delano Roosevelt (center), Winston Churchill (right), Teheran conference, December 1943 (Getty Images)

declared that it was important that Communists "appear publicly in their neighborhoods as political clubs setting an example of patriotic activity," and in doing so operate more "in accordance with the established organizational forms of all parties." In a reversal of the strict Leninist discipline governing Party members in the past, Williamson announced that individual attendance at branch meetings was no longer a requirement of membership. "Too often," he declared, "we want to set as standards for all members the yardstick of the professional revolutionist."[88] This distinction seemed to open the door to a two-tiered Party structure, with a majority of members who lent a hand when they could or chose to, and only a select cadre of "professional revolutionists" adhering to the traditional standards of giving "the whole of their lives" to the movement.

Still greater changes were in the offing for American Communists. In the last week of November 1943, Roosevelt, Churchill, and Stalin met together for the first time. At their conference in the Iranian capital of

Teheran, the "Big Three" agreed on a spring 1944 date for a cross-channel invasion of France by British and American forces. They signed a joint communiqué known as the Teheran Declaration, pledging that their nations would "work together in the war and the peace that will follow." Details were vague, and questions as to the political future of eastern European nations currently under Nazi occupation were barely touched on. After reading the text of the declaration, political columnist Dorothy Thompson joked that "never before in history had so few kept so much information from so many." But one American read a good deal more into the Teheran Declaration.[89]

In a speech to a Party gathering in Bridgeport, Connecticut, on December 12, 1943, Browder called the meeting of the Big Three "the greatest, most important turning point in history." In his exuberantly optimistic reading of the Teheran Declaration, he argued that the Western Allies had accepted the Soviet Union as a member of the family of nations, that the alliance would continue into the postwar era, that there would be no socialist revolution in the foreseeable future in liberated Western Europe, and that the United States would see a prolonged period of class peace. He concluded that "as a Communist" he would be "prepared to clasp the hand" of J. P. Morgan, should the famous banker support the Grand Alliance in war and the peace that followed.[90]

Three weeks later, on January 7, 1944, at a meeting of the CP's National Committee in New York City, Browder announced that in the postwar world, it would no longer make sense for Communists to run candidates under their own banner. The CP would be "in a long-term alliance with forces much larger than itself," and accordingly "should adjust its name to correspond more exactly to the American political tradition," dropping the designation that made it a separate party, and instead renaming itself as an "association."[91]

Browder seems to have enjoyed shocking the sensibilities of his followers. He could have chosen a way to announce his new views without offering to shake the hands of a predatory symbol of American high finance like J. P. Morgan (who also happened to be long dead). As general secretary, Browder had never made much of an effort to consult with his comrades about Party policies. Now he had come up with what must have seemed to him the best, and certainly most far-reaching, innovation of his career, and had done so entirely on his own. It had been over five years since his last trip to Moscow, and he had gotten used to the autonomy afforded him by wartime conditions. Abandoning his customary caution, he took the risk of reading into the Teheran Declaration his own fondest wishes.

Browder was emboldened by the decision of the Communist International to dissolve itself six months earlier. This wartime public-relations gesture was intended, as Stalin told a Western correspondent shortly afterward, to dispel the "calumny" that foreign Communists acted as agents of Moscow. Browder, however, took the gesture more seriously than it deserved, and in particular the declaration by the presidium of the Comintern's executive committee, dated May 15, 1943, that "Communists have never been supporters of the conservation of organizational forms that have outlived themselves."[92] If that was true of the Communist International, Browder reasoned, why shouldn't the same principle apply to the Communist Party USA?

Browder was raising some serious questions about the traditional Marxist understanding of American politics. In *Teheran and America*, a pamphlet published in the spring of 1944, he veered away from the orthodox view depicting Democrats and Republicans as simply rival representatives of "the executive committee of the ruling class," as Marx and Engels had characterized the state in *The Communist Manifesto* a century earlier. Browder argued that America's two-party system had to be understood in more complex terms. The Republicans and Democrats "are parties only in a formal and legal sense; they are not parties in the sense of representing well-defined alternative policies. They are coalitions of local and regional interests, diverse tendencies of political thought, and institutionalized politics." In a parliamentary system, such as prevailed in Europe, Browder noted, the constituent groupings that made up the Democratic and Republican parties "would be separate parties." In the United States, those who hoped to secure real political gains could only do so through the medium of the existing major parties. For Communists to continue to take their stand outside these messy, diverse coalitions, he suggested, was a formula for irrelevance. By choosing to become "one of the so-called 'minor parties,'" leftists permanently consigned themselves to the status of "a sect which has withdrawn from the practical political life of the nation." Accordingly, Communists would not seek power in their own name but only in broader coalitions formed around limited common goals. They would commit themselves for the foreseeable future to reform rather than to overthrow the capitalist state. Browder didn't put it quite like this, but in effect he was saying that the Communists' near-term goals had become evolutionary and social-democratic, rather than revolutionary and utopian.[93]

Browder moved some distance toward an understanding of what he called "American political tradition." But not all the way. For Browder, the Soviet Union still remained the idealized workers' state, the ultimate goal to which all societies should strive, even if the arrival of a Soviet America was postponed indefinitely. And that meant that Communists owed allegiance to the Soviet Union as much as they did to their homeland. Accordingly, Browder continued in 1944, as in years past, to oversee the theft of US state secrets to pass along to Moscow. In particular, he worked closely with an old Bolshevik and longtime CPUSA member named Jacob Golos, who with his lover Elizabeth Bentley ran the most important NKVD network in Washington during the Second World War. To the horror of NKVD professionals, Golos and Bentley passed stolen documents directly to Browder, who then forwarded them to Moscow, a serious breach of espionage tradecraft as well as common sense.[94]

For all his appreciation of the two-party system, and the need for Communists to take their place within it, Browder remained a Leninist.

Party or association, the old principles of democratic centralism were to remain in place to guide decision-making in Browder's new organization, certainly at the uppermost levels of leadership. This became apparent in the furious debate in the CP's Political Committee in the first weeks of 1944. Party chairman William Z. Foster and his longtime ally Sam Darcy (who in 1943–1944 served as organizer for the CP's eastern Pennsylvania district) jointly drafted a letter for consideration by the Political Committee. They disagreed with the premises of the proposed changes to the CP's traditional structure and outlook. While not challenging the policy of upholding national unity for the duration of the war, they argued that following victory a renewed depression in the United States would inevitably bring renewed class conflict. They predicted that the current harmony between the Western capitalist powers and the Soviet Union would also prove short-lived. American Communists needed to prepare for both eventualities and not be misled by "Comrade Browder's rather rosy outlook for capitalism."

The Political Committee met on February 8 to discuss the letter, although "discuss" is not quite the right word. Apart from Foster and Darcy, all who spoke condemned their defense of Party traditions as heresy. Browder patronized Foster for "being terribly confused. The world has become too complex for him." Browder warned, "We are not a friendly debating society. We are a political army engaged in the struggle for the world. . . . And if we are faced with the necessity of dealing with this question after tonight, that will be merely one more unfortunate casualty of a war that has had many casualties." A few months later Darcy was expelled on charges of factionalism. Foster, to prove his loyalty, was required to chair the commission that decided on his ally's expulsion.[95] The only concession to Foster that Browder offered was agreeing to forward a copy of his letter to former Comintern leader Georgi Dimitrov in Moscow. (Dimitrov sent Browder a mildly critical response, asking if he was "going too far" in dissolving the Party, a warning which Browder incautiously shrugged off.)[96]

None of the internal debate over Foster and Darcy's dissent was shared beyond the confines of the Political Committee. Browder's Teheran line promised, at least implicitly, a Communist organization that ran along more open and genuinely democratic principles, truly responsive for the first time to the ideas and concerns of rank-and-file members. However, as *People's Daily World* editor Al Richmond later observed, it represented "one of the supreme paradoxes of CP history that the metamorphosis into the CPA was effected with organizational practices that . . . were a negation of the political rationale for the CPA."[97] There was some unofficial grumbling at the grass-roots level, but no organized opposition. Some veteran Communists greeted the changes with genuine enthusiasm. Steve Nelson, serving as chairman of the party organization for Oakland, California, in 1944, had seen the Party run its own candidates in four presidential elections, and in scores of local and state elections, and had even been a candidate himself for Congress in 1936. He no longer saw any purpose in such exercises: "I thought we weren't really doing anything effective in those elections. It was a formality, a hell of a lot of work gathering signatures, and no results. The guys we called the *actives*, the second layer leaders . . . had all faced this business and to them Teheran was an attempt to remedy the situation."[98]

Outside Party ranks, Browder's initiative did not impress the few observers who noticed it at all. The *New York Times* editorial reaction to announced changes showed that the Communists continued to labor under the not-so-ancient history of the Nazi-Soviet Pact era: "We would feel more certain that a genuinely American, law-abiding left-wing move-ment were being born if the Party would retire the outstanding leaders who have wriggled and wabbled all over the political map. The men who sneered at Britain's agonies in 1940 . . . can hardly inspire confidence now."[99]

During the 1930s the Party had grown adept at the mechanics of staging public rallies. In New York City, in particular, the Communists could draw on a pool of talent, including left-wing scenery designers, composers, and choreographers. Browder took a personal interest in the stage management of these spectacles. The convention of May 20 to May 22, 1944, which ushered out the Communist Party USA and ushered in its successor, the Communist Political Association, was his theatrical masterpiece.

On Saturday morning, May 20, William Z. Foster, standing in front of a giant poster reproducing a photograph of Stalin, Roosevelt, and Churchill seated together at Teheran the previous December, called the meeting to order. The front of the podium from which he addressed the audience was covered by a red-bordered service flag with a gold star (displayed by families with a member killed in battle), a blue star (signifying a family member currently serving in the military), and the number 9,250 (the number of Communists then on leave for military service). Foster offered a brief address reviewing Party history, always "in the front ranks of every fight for freedom," and then recommended the assembled delegates endorse the proposal to transform the CPUSA into the CPA.

Browder followed him to the podium, offering the resolution for formal vote, which passed unanimously. A half hour after convening, and following a standing chorus of the labor anthem "We Shall Not Be Moved," the delegates took their seats and constituted themselves as the founding convention of the new association. At the final session on May 22, Browder was elected as the first president (not "general secretary") of the CPA. There was no longer a chairman, so Foster was demoted to one of eleven vice presidents of the group. In other concessions to American usage, the ruling Political Committee was now the National Board. The CPA's theoretical journal, formerly *The Communist*, was renamed *Political Affairs*. And when Browder addressed the delegates, he called them "Ladies and Gentlemen," instead of "Comrades."[100]

The CPA's first task was to go all in for Franklin Roosevelt's reelection to a fourth term in office. In March, Browder wrote, "President Roosevelt is the only political figure in our country whose election next November would constitute a guarantee that the policy of Teheran would guide our country in the ensuing four years."[101] No hint of any dissatisfaction with the president was heard from Communists. When Roosevelt dumped his sitting vice president in favor of the more moderate Senator Harry Truman of Missouri at the Democratic National Convention in July, Browder expressed satisfaction, saying it was "fortunate for the country" that the staunchly liberal Henry Wallace was passed over.[102]

Though the Communists did not have a single candidate of their own on the ballot, the 1944 election saw the greatest electoral effort of their history to date. They worked primarily through the CIO Political Action Committee (PAC), founded the previous year with Sidney Hillman as its chairman (and the first such organization created in US political history). With its satellite organization, the National Citizens Political Action Committee, the PAC conducted a massive voter-registration and get-out-the-vote campaign, as well as raising about a fifth of all the money Roosevelt spent in his campaign. In New York State, in alliance with Hillman, Communists took control of the American Labor Party, which made them powerful players in New York City and state politics. Republicans pounced on the Communist role within the president's reelection campaign, with vice-presidential candidate John Bricker declaring that "the great Democratic Party has become the Hillman-Browder communistic party with Franklin Roosevelt as its front." Roosevelt went on to win, but by the smallest margin of his four presidential campaigns. New York was the only state in which FDR's victory margin was greater in 1944 than in 1940.[103] Browder celebrated the election results and predicted in the *Daily Worker* that Communists would remain a "small, if important sector of the great patriotic coalition" in years to come.[104]

The next half year, from FDR's reelection in November through the last days of the Third Reich in April 1945, must have seemed to Browder the ultimate vindication of his Teheran gamble. Then in a single day in early May it all fell apart for him, and for the Communist Political Association. A copy of the April 1945 issue of the theoretical journal of the

French Communist Party (PCF), *Cahiers du Communisme*, was delivered to Browder in CPA headquarters in New York by two French Communists returning from the founding convention of the United Nations in San Francisco. The journal included an article whose title, when translated to English, read, "On the Dissolution of the American Communist Party." It was written by, or rather it appeared under the name of, Jacques Duclos, the PCF's second in command, and became known in American Party circles as the "Duclos Letter." The article's author outlined the "erroneous conclusions in no wise flowing from a Marxist analysis" that Browder had drawn from the 1943 meeting of the Big Three in Teheran. In doing so, "Duclos" quoted from published sources like the *Daily Worker*, and also unpublished sources like Foster's January 1944 letter to the CPUSA's Political Committee. After presenting Browder's position, the author listed the lessons he drew from the developments in the American Party. First, he argued, Browder's Teheran line had "ended in practice in the liquidation of the independent political party of the working class in the US." Second, this was a "notorious revision of Marxism on the part of Browder and his supporters . . . expressed in the concept of a long-term class peace in the United States." Third, American Communists were "deforming in a radical way the meaning of the Teheran declaration" by turning it into a "political platform of class peace."[105]

The message to American Communists could not have been clearer. Duclos was obviously not the real author of the article attributed to him, for he would not have had access to Foster's letter dissenting from the Teheran line that Browder had secretly forwarded to Moscow, expecting it would be consigned to a dusty file cabinet and forgotten. Instead, Foster's letter had found its way to readers whose reaction to it was quite different than Browder imagined. The Duclos Letter was a message from the only foreign authorities whose opinion really counted in the international Communist movement: Soviet Party leaders. Evidence in Soviet archives that only became available following the collapse of the USSR suggests that *Cahiers du Communisme* article was first written in Russian and circulated among Soviet and Comintern leaders, before being translated into French to appear under Duclos's name.

Stalin and his associates could have ordered American Communists to change course by means of shortwave broadcast, or by a private messenger. Since they chose to indicate their dissatisfaction in a public forum, it obviously would not suffice for Browder simply to write a new book explaining that Teheran did not, after all, mean long-term class peace in the United States. The CPUSA would have to be restored, Browder's influence checked, Foster's influence augmented. Stalin may also have intended to send a subtle signal to US policymakers in Washington, a reminder that newly powerful Communist parties in Western Europe, like the French and Italian Communists, could cause trouble for the Western Allies, if Soviet and American diplomatic ties were to continue to fray (as they had begun to do in the spring of 1945).[106]

When the CPA's leaders met in emergency session on May 22 to discuss the implications of the Duclos Letter, Browder still retained supporters. "It seems to me," Elizabeth Gurley Flynn declared, "that we should be able on the Board to arrive at the conclusion we were wrong by our own thinking and our own effort rather than have it suddenly catapulted at us by a Communist Party from another country." The meeting ended inconclusively and resumed the following day. Browder was in a defiant mood, declaring he was not going to become a "political zombie." Asked by Dennis to define "zombie," he replied, "A zombie is a modern myth about a dead person who has been raised up by some magical process and walks around under the control of another's will."[107]

That declaration of political independence did Browder no good. Over the next several weeks, his support collapsed, both among the CPA's leaders and the rank and file. He retained the title of CPA president, but a temporary three-man secretariat, consisting of Foster, Dennis, and John Williamson, took over daily supervision of association activities, including preparations for a special convention at the end of July to yet again revamp the future of the American Communist movement.

In the interim, the *Daily Worker* briefly opened its letters column to a discussion of the Duclos Letter and its implications. The overwhelming majority of the Communist rank and file had joined the Party during Browder's fifteen-year reign as Communist leader. Through all those years Browder had been praised in the Party press as a great and inspired figure. Now that he had been repudiated, it must have worried other Party leaders how ordinary Communists would react to this shocking reversal. However, only a minority of letters to the *Daily Worker* in the summer of 1945 were from those who continued to support Browder and the Teheran line; most who took a position condemned both. (Of course, the paper's editors might have been weighting the selection of published letters against Browder.)

The most interesting letters, in retrospect, were those that were neither pro- nor anti-Browder, but rather spoke to what the controversy revealed about the Communist movement's fundamental weaknesses. In the future, rank-and-file members "must be able to know and feel that they can disagree with older Communists or leading personnel," one writer argued, "without being classed as Trotskyites, Social Democrats, Nationalist Negroes, Ivory Tower Intellectuals, Male Chauvinists or disrupters. In other words, all must be made to know the difference between Marxist self-criticism and name calling." Another writer addressed the flip-flops of recent years: "Each period's 'line' is out of the blue; the slogans of the day are treated as though they were basic, and independent concepts. . . . We ride our slogans to death and they become 'at all costs' propositions."[108]

These were useful insights, but the discussion was closed long before the CPA met in an emergency convention in late July. The outcome of the convention was not in doubt. The delegates reversed the decisions of the last national gathering of Communists in May 1944, thus shutting down the CPA and restoring the CPUSA. Browder's leadership was repudiated, his legacy swept aside. Soon afterward, Foster was restored as Party chairman, and Dennis became the new general secretary.

Browder remained a nominal member of the Party for the next six months, until officially expelled in February 1946. Robert Thompson, who became leader of the Party's most important district, New York, expressed satisfaction with the vote to expel the man who had led the Party during its period of greatest growth and influence: "It will close the door with finality on the period in which our Party has been an arena of struggle between Browderism and Marxism."[109]

The direction the Party took in the aftermath of Browder's fall from power closed another door as well. This was the last moment in the history of the CPUSA when it represented a significant movement in American political life. American Communists were, thereafter, chiefly important as political victims, not as political actors.

CHAPTER 5

Speaking Their Own Sins

1946–1958

I speak my own sins; I cannot judge another. I have no tongue for it.
— Words attributed to Salem witch trial defendant John Proctor,
in Arthur Miller's *The Crucible*, 1953

The core of those who left was that whole generation of younger people who had come into the party from the YCL, the Spanish vets, and the people who had been active in the mass movements. Afterwards there just weren't any real know-how people left in the Party, and we weren't able to pick up the pieces.

— Peggy Dennis, 1978 interview with the author

John Proctor Jr., an English-born Puritan settler of Salem Village, Massachusetts Bay Colony, was convicted of witchcraft in a Salem court on August 5, 1692, and hung two weeks later. He was one of twenty men and women executed in the Salem witchcraft trials.

Roughly two and a half centuries later a character named for and loosely based on Proctor appeared as the protagonist of Arthur Miller's play *The Crucible*, which opened on Broadway on January 22, 1953. *New York Times* drama critic Brooks Atkinson, who had called Miller's 1949 Broadway offering *Death of a Salesman* "one of the best dramas" ever written by an American playwright, noted in a dry understatement in his review of *The Crucible*, "Neither Mr. Miller nor his audiences are unaware of certain similarities between the perversions of justice then and today."[1]

The Crucible would become Miller's most frequently performed work. But its reception in 1953 was mixed, and although it won a Tony Award for Best New Play of 1953, its Broadway run was limited to 197 performances (less than a third the number achieved by *Death of a Salesman* two years earlier).[2] A week after his initial review, Atkinson devoted a column in the *Times* to some second thoughts on the parallels implied in *The Crucible* between the "perversions of justice" in seventeenth-century Salem and mid-twentieth-century America. While there "never were any witches," Atkinson now felt compelled to point out, "There have been spies and traitors in recent days. All the Salem witches were victims of public fear. Beginning with [Alger] Hiss, some of the people accused of treason and disloyalty today have been guilty."[3]

Atkinson had been an outspoken critic of the House Un-American Activities Committee (HUAC) and Senator Joseph McCarthy. That he felt obliged, in effect, to review Miller's play a second time, and more critically than the first, is revealing of the political pressures and complexities that need to be considered regarding American anti-Communism in the McCarthy era. As Atkinson suggested in his initial review—and then seemed to take back in the follow-up—American Communists *were* being victimized in those years in ways that, like the Salem trials, and more recently the Red Scare of 1919–1920, represented a cruel miscarriage of justice. And yet, at the same time, Communists were not without their own sins. In the Red Scare of 1919–1920, none convicted under the misnamed Espionage Act had actually committed espionage, or anything like it. The "witches" of 1919–1920, like Eugene Debs, had been punished solely for dissenting opinions. However, charges of "espionage" in the 1940s and 1950s were not always instances of malicious hyperbole.[4]

The "McCarthy era" of American politics, known for the hurling of reckless partisan accusations of Communist subversion, is also somewhat misnamed, since the junior US senator from Wisconsin, Joseph McCarthy, only became associated with the issue when he charged in a highly publicized speech to a Republican gathering in February 1950 that scores of US State Department members (he was never very specific with either numbers or evidence) were currently card-carrying members of the Communist Party. By then, the post–World War II Red Scare was nearing the half-decade mark. It was an era of mass hysteria and official repression that wrecked lives and careers and tarnished the ideals of American democratic values in the name of defending them. It also went on and on, and would outlive its namesake, who died in 1957.

On June 19, 1953, the night that convicted atomic spies Julius and Ethel Rosenberg died in the electric chair in Sing Sing prison thirty miles north of New York City, *The Crucible* was nearing the end of its Broadway run. When John Proctor was executed offstage in the culminating moment of the final act, the audience rose and stood in silence, in a heartfelt demonstration of solidarity with the Rosenbergs, whom they believed were simply victims of injustice. But the audience's gesture did not reflect the opinion of the vast majority of Americans. When asked in a Gallup poll the previous February whether the death sentence was justified in the Rosenberg case, 76 percent approved, while only 15 percent expressed opposition.[5]

Christian tradition distinguishes between *sins of commission*, that is, overt violations of scriptural commandments, and *sins of omission*, a failure to do that which is required of the righteous, even when no commandment has been broken. While revelations of Americans spying on behalf of the Soviet Union dominated headlines in the McCarthy era, only a handful of Communists were guilty of such sins of *commission*. Most of the laws that Communists were accused in court of violating involved expressions of opinion, which should have been protected under the Bill of Rights. In retrospect, the Party's abiding sins (not just in the 1950s but throughout its history) involved the second category, sins of *omission*.

The principal form taken by those sins of omission was the collective failure by Communists to speak truthfully to others and, fatefully, to themselves. Communists, taken as individuals, could be altogether admirable people: intelligent, compassionate, self-sacrificing to a fault. And yet, whatever their personal qualities, the movement to which they devoted their lives was based on lies, not about everything, but certainly in regard to one central issue, the nature of the Soviet Union. *Daily Worker* editor John Gates noted in a memoir published in 1958 that he and his fellow Communists had "never mastered the art of persuading very large numbers of Americans, deceptively or otherwise." Instead, Gates suggested, the one deception they excelled at was self-deception, "the basic cause of [our] demise as an effective political trend."[6]

The moral complexities of speaking truthfully are at the heart of *The Crucible*. Arthur Miller, born in New York City to Jewish parents in 1915, grew up in privileged circumstances, living in an apartment with a view of Central Park, until his family's fortune was wiped out by the Great Depression. The Millers then moved to live in a more modest neighborhood in Brooklyn, and after finishing high school Arthur had to delay plans to attend college for two years due to tight finances. Finally, in 1934 Miller enrolled as an undergraduate at the University of Michigan. As a student journalist, he was drawn to the Left, covering the Flint sit-down strike of 1936–1937 for the campus newspaper, the *Michigan Daily*.[7]

Like many others, the Spanish Civil War gripped his imagination; nothing else, he would recall, was "as powerful in the formation of my generation's awareness of the world."[8] In the spring of 1937 Miller drove a friend, Ralph Neaphus, to New York City, where Neaphus, like John Gates a few weeks earlier, departed for Spain as a volunteer in the International Brigades. Gates survived; Neaphus did not. Captured by the fascists in the spring of 1938 during the chaotic retreat of the remnants of the Abraham Lincoln Battalion on the Ebro front, he was among a number of American volunteers summarily executed.[9]

Graduating from Michigan that same spring, Miller returned home to Brooklyn and perfected his craft as a playwright. During the early 1940s, he attended Communist-sponsored meetings in New York, wrote theater reviews for the *New Masses* under a pseudonym, and in the later 1940s lent his name to various Communist-supported campaigns. Despite all this, it seems that he never formally joined the Party.[10]

Miller secured his reputation as the foremost American playwright with the Broadway successes of *All My Sons* in 1947 and *Death of a Salesman* in 1949. The latter, directed by Elia Kazan, won him the Pulitzer Prize for Drama. Given his political past, Miller would have almost certainly drawn the hostile attention of anti-Communist witch-hunters sooner or later. His authorship of *The Crucible* guaranteed it.

Miller had wanted to write a play about the Salem trials since his college days, loyalty and betrayal being a recurring theme in many of his works. The HUAC hearings of the late 1940s and the Smith Act trial of top Communist leaders in 1949 inspired him to turn to the project again. He was preparing for a research trip to Salem in 1952 when he learned some disturbing news about his friend and colleague Elia Kazan. Like Miller, Kazan had been drawn to the Communist cause in the 1930s, and in his case had actually been a Party member for a year or so. Called to testify before HUAC in January 1952, he initially refused to name names of fellow Communists in the New York theatrical world in the 1930s. But faced with the assured end of a promising Hollywood career, he changed his mind. In a second hearing in April Kazan named eight former associates as Communists, including playwright Clifford Odets.[11]

Arthur Miller (right) testifying before HUAC, 1955 (Getty Images)

Before delivering his April testimony, Kazan asked Miller to visit him in his Connecticut home to hear the reasons for this morally fraught decision. Although Miller by this time, like Kazan, had abandoned his Communist sympathies, he could not abide the idea of betraying old friends and comrades. He never forgave Kazan for naming names.[12]

Kazan's subsequent career in Hollywood flourished. *On the Waterfront*, released in 1954, won him an Oscar for Best Director (the film, about corruption in the East Coast longshore industry, can be read as a counter-parable to *The Crucible*, a justification of informing in a good cause).[13]

Miller followed a different path. Broadway theater proved relatively immune to the anti-Communist pressures that ended the employment of scores of left-leaning Hollywood directors, screenwriters, and actors in those years, so he continued to see his plays performed on the stage. However, he spent the next few years embroiled in the legal consequences of writing *The Crucible*, starting with the revoking of his passport by the US State Department. In 1956 he was dragged before HUAC and asked why the Communists applauded his Salem play (a new production of *The Crucible* had opened on Broadway after the original production closed and was still playing when he was called to testify). And, of course, he was asked to name names. Unlike Kazan, he refused to do so, citing both the First Amendment protections of free speech, and his own personal sense of right and wrong. "I want you to understand I am not protecting Communists or the Communist Party," he told his inquisitors. "I am trying to and I will protect my sense of myself. I could not use the name of another person and bring trouble to him."[14]

Miller's pessimistic view of humankind may have been one of the reasons he never joined the Communist Party. In a biography of Miller, John Lahr wrote that in *The Crucible* John Proctor "is the messenger of disenchantment, embracing complexity, ambiguity and guilt."[15] From the play's opening act, the audience knows Proctor had an illicit relationship with the character Abigail Williams, a young woman formerly a servant in his house, who helped ignite the hysteria about witchcraft. Proctor finally confesses his adultery. He *is* guilty, just not of the crime of which he is accused. In Miller's stage directions for *The Crucible*, Proctor is described as "a sinner not only against the moral fashion of his time, but against his own vision."[16] His is a sin of both commission (adultery) and omission (dishonesty). The sin he will refuse to commit is to falsely accuse others of consorting with the Devil, even though to do so will save his life. Why not make the accusation? his puzzled interrogator asks. After all, the individuals he is being asked to denounce have already been named as witches by "a score of people." "Then it is proved," Miller has Proctor reply. "Why must I say it?"[17]

Truth-telling and informing are two very different things. For the purpose of Miller's play, Proctor's confession to his real sin, adultery, not witchcraft, redeemed him morally, even if it did not spare him the hangman's noose. Like Proctor, American Communists had their own sins to confess, just not, for the most part, those they were being accused of before official tribunals. "Complexity, ambiguity, and guilt" are not absent from the history of American Communism. As the worst of McCarthyism was coming to an end in the later 1950s, American Communists like John Gates became willing, at long last, to speak their own sins.

At the end of the Second World War, the Party felt optimistic about its prospects. In his history of the CP in the postwar era, former Communist Joseph Starobin wrote, "For the span of 1945–1949 as a whole, it is striking how many conditions could have been considered favorable to American Communism." In those years, he noted, Communists "were not swimming against the tide. They were swimming in turbulent waters—quite another matter."[18]

By 1945, the Communist Party no longer had to compete with any significant rivals on the American Left. The Socialist Party was in terminal decline, while the even-more-negligible Trotskyist movement had split into rival squabbling wings. In contrast, CP membership stood at 50,000 in 1945, a number which three years later had climbed to 60,000. George Charney, who on his return from the army in 1945, was appointed chairman of the Communists' thriving New York County organization, recalled:

> The national recruiting campaign in 1946 was very successful, especially in the larger cities. Our county membership in this period exceeded eleven thousand members. . . . Our sections were staffed by young, able people who labored without stint and with a remarkable élan. We had every reason to be pleased and even optimistic about the future.[19]

While New York City remained by far the largest center of Party strength, the CP also was a growing presence elsewhere. Between 1945 and 1949 the

Los Angeles Communist Party, for example, grew from just over 3,000 to 5,000 members, making Southern California the second-largest district in the Party.[20]

Over half the members of the Communist Party in those years were industrial workers, and two-fifths were union members. Communist-led or influenced unions were making breakthroughs in interracial organizing and attracting minority recruits to the Party in doing so, combining a commitment to labor and civil rights issues in campaigns among plantation workers and longshoremen in Hawaii, packinghouse workers in Chicago, copper miners in New Mexico, and tobacco workers in North Carolina (by 1946, for example, there were about 150 Communists in Winston-Salem, North Carolina, most of them Black members of the newly founded Local 22 of the Party-led Food, Tobacco, Agricultural and Allied Workers union).[21] The Party's ranks were now composed largely of native-born English-speaking US citizens. A substantial portion of its male membership were military veterans of the Second World War, a useful credential in countering those who would question their patriotism. Whatever else could be said of Communists in the years immediately following the Second World War, they represented a movement of native-born radicals, with deep roots in the labor movement, who felt at home in America.[22]

This homegrown generation of radicals made the Communist Party more capable in terms of practical politics than ever before in its history. The Party's "cadre," that key Leninist resource, was largely drawn from the YCL generation, those who had joined in the 1930s and had a decade or more of political experience under their belts. They numbered perhaps 10,000 or 12,000 all told, a small number in a country whose population topped 150 million. But they were the reliable hard core of the Party, the ones who stuck around while newer recruits came and went, and whose discipline and reliability magnified the impact of their contribution. With the exception of the Debsian Socialist Party at the height of its strength before the First World War, no left-wing group in American history had ever before assembled such a collection of seasoned, dedicated activists. These were the members who represented, as Peggy Dennis remembered, the "real know-how people."[23]

They also had the advantage of not having to start over from scratch. During earlier Party upheavals, like those precipitated by the proclamation of the Third Period in 1928 or the signing of the Nazi-Soviet Pact in 1939, Communists had junked existing organizations and alliances to keep pace with the changing Soviet line. Following Browder's downfall, his name may have become anathema, but his policies remained intact. In 1945–1947 Communists continued to play influential roles in mainstream politics in at least a half dozen states, from New York to California. In New York City, the Party's two representatives on the city council, Peter Cacchione and Benjamin Davis, were both reelected by comfortable margins in the November 1945 election. Several CP allies, including Transport Workers Union president Michael J. Quill, also served on the city council, elected on the American Labor Party (ALP) ticket. The ALP, controlled behind the scenes by the CP, averaged 13 percent of New York City's vote in elections between 1938 and 1949.[24]

The strength of organized labor, with nearly 15 million members, about a third of the nonagricultural workforce, also seemed to favor the Communist political agenda. A massive strike wave at home followed victory abroad, with over 3 million workers walking out in 1945–1946, including industry-wide strikes by the largest CIO unions, the United Auto Workers and the Steelworkers unions. It seemed like 1919 all over again except, this time, workers won many of the strikes. Party members remained in the leadership of a number of unions in the Congress of Industrial Organizations, including the third largest, the United Electrical Workers. The Communists controlled the CIO Greater New York Industrial Union Council, which represented a half million workers in 250 CIO locals in and around the city, and were influential in other CIO citywide councils across the nation. Communists maintained an informal working alliance with CIO president Philip Murray, and the politically influential president of the Amalgamated Clothing Workers, Sidney Hillman (until the latter's death in 1946).[25]

Finally, Communists were heartened by victories won by comrades abroad. The Soviet Union was no longer a lonely outpost surrounded by hostile powers, having taken its place as one of the world's two great superpowers following the defeat of Nazi Germany. In Eastern Europe, Communists allied with the Soviet Union ruled Poland, Hungary, Czechoslovakia, Yugoslavia, Romania, Bulgaria, Albania, and East Germany, nations which, with the exception of Yugoslavia, would later form the military alliance known as the Warsaw Pact. In Western Europe, the Communist parties of France and Italy were serious contenders for power, attracting the support of millions of voters. And, at a moment when the old colonial empires were crumbling, Communists were, or seemed to be, on the ascendant in many of the British, French, Dutch, and former Japanese colonies. After the Red Army occupied the northern half of the Korean peninsula at the end of the Second World War, Communist Kim Il Sung was installed as ruler of what became the Democratic People's Republic of Korea. In Vietnam, Communists led by Ho Chi Minh were fighting a guerrilla war to overthrow the French colonial regime, on their own and without the support of an invading army. Meanwhile, the Chinese Communist Party was waging a revolutionary struggle against China's decrepit Nationalist government, bringing Mao Zedong to power before decade's end.

William Z. Foster tallied the numbers in his 1949 book *The Twilight of World Capitalism*: "In the USSR, the first great socialist land, there are now well on to 200 million people; in the new democracies of Central and Eastern Europe, the second group of countries to begin the march toward socialism, there are 100 million more. . . . And now the overwhelming masses of China, 475 million strong, are also beginning to get under way."[26]

A tiny minority in their own country, American Communists were heartened to think of themselves a vital part of an international movement on the brink of governing the majority of the world's peoples. "Instead of socialism in one country," George Charney recalled of the view within the Party in those years, "there was socialism that reached half around the world; instead of capitalist encirclement, the prospect was one of socialist encirclement."[27]

All of that was seemingly in their favor, but in the end, none of it mattered. American Communism was heading for political disaster, in a revived Red Scare that exceeded the version of 1919–1920 in severity, comprehensiveness, and duration, and from which it never recovered.

Far from dwelling in William Z. Foster's imagined "twilight of world capitalism," American Communists lived in a nation embarking on an unprecedented era of economic expansion and social mobility. The Soviet Union was not a workers' paradise; nor, of course, was the United States a land of liberty and justice for all. Deep, ongoing injustices characterized American society, especially those based on race, and apart from the Communist Party few largely white organizations were as yet committed to their elimination. Nevertheless, for the majority of white Americans (who represented close to 90 percent of the US population in 1945), life had never been better.

America's industrial base, unlike that of other advanced capitalist powers in Europe and Asia, survived the war not only unscathed but vastly strengthened. In 1946 Party theoretician Alexander Bittelman predicted an economic crisis before the end of the decade "likely to dwarf the economic catastrophe of 1929–1933."[28] That did not happen. The economic pains of 1945–1946, with wartime price controls giving way to a round of inflation, and millions of military veterans rejoining the civilian workforce, were short-lived, and bore no resemblance to a return to Depression conditions. The Servicemen's Readjustment Act of 1944, or the "GI Bill," helped jump-start the collective postwar prosperity, subsidizing a vast expansion of home ownership, higher education, and small-business ownership. Pent-up consumer demand for civilian goods, and the increase in early marriage and birth rates that came to be known as the "Baby Boom," also contributed to economic expansion, as did a resumption of high levels of defense spending in the early 1950s. American gross national product, median family income, home and automobile ownership, and life expectancy all increased dramatically between 1950 and 1960.[29]

Prominent economists declared that America in the postwar years had become a classless society, which was a vast exaggeration. And yet, it was becoming a society in which radical consciousness of class differences and conflict was difficult to sustain. Most of the new homes being built were located in the suburbs, linked to urban centers and workplaces by a federally subsidized interstate-highway system. The old white ethnic working-class neighborhoods, from the Lower East Side to Boyle Heights, centers of radical sentiments and organizing, saw a wholesale flight of their long-established residents in the postwar years, and the neighborhoods they abandoned were soon populated by impoverished minorities. Manufacturers departed from the urban industrial heartland, moving to the suburbs, to the rural South, or overseas. After the 1945–1946 strike wave, big unions like the UAW and Steelworkers increasingly sought long-term contracts, with periodic cost-of-living increases built in, lessening the number of officially called strikes. Already in 1946, the Party's apparent strength within the labor movement began to erode, when anti-Communist Walter Reuther won election as president of the United Auto Workers union, and Joseph Curran, president of the National Maritime Union, broke with his longtime Communist allies and purged them from the union. Even if there had been no Cold War with the Soviet Union, and no return of the Red Scare, these were not the social and economic circumstances that favored the continued growth and influence of Marxist radicalism of any persuasion, Communist or otherwise.[30]

The Cold War further isolated the Communists. Perhaps Franklin Roosevelt would have found a way to lessen if not eliminate postwar tensions with the Soviet Union had he not died shortly before victory was achieved over Nazi Germany. His successor was not so inclined. President Harry Truman initiated an unprecedented set of economic, political, and military policies designed to contain the expansion of Soviet international power. In the Cold War, the Soviet threat was magnified in American popular imagination by fears that Communist sympathizers in the United States, open and hidden, undermined national security through subversion, sabotage, and espionage.[31]

It was not irrational for Americans to be concerned about Stalin's intentions in the later 1940s, but reason was adulterated with hysteria. Although home to much-larger Communist parties, and within plausible striking distance of an invasion by the Red Army in the event of a Third World War, Italy did not feel the need to establish an Un-Italian Activities Committee, nor did France establish an Un-French Activities Committee. As historian James Patterson noted, "American anger at the Soviet dictatorship went well beyond fears of appeasement." Americans had a sense of themselves as a kind of providential nation and "approached foreign policy in a highly moralistic way." This lent, Patterson contended, "a messianic feeling . . . indeed an apocalyptic tone" to the way Americans understood the Cold War against Communism, abroad and at home.[32]

For the most ardent anti-Communists, merely containing the spread of Communism was not enough. Instead, Republicans proclaimed, the goal should be to "roll-back" Communism, a popular position with Americans whose ancestral homelands in Eastern Europe had recently fallen to Soviet domination. But rolling back Communism in 1950 in the Korean War—that is, attempting not just to defend South Korea but to drive the Communists out of North Korea—led to intervention by Communist China, and a bloody stalemate that lasted until 1953. Rolling back Communism in Eastern Europe was never seriously contemplated because of the danger of provoking nuclear war with the Soviet Union. The *only* Communists who could safely be rolled back in those early years of the Cold War, literally driven from their strong points and punished for misdeeds real and imagined, were found within the borders of the United States. The Communist Party USA would, in the end, play a more significant role in US politics as scapegoat for reverses overseas than as a genuine threat to the existing capitalist order.[33]

As Brooks Atkinson said of *The Crucible*, this time there *were* witches, a few anyway. Fear of Communist subversion was overblown, of Communist sabotage spurious. The same cannot be said of Communist espionage. There *were* spies. In November 1945, Elizabeth Bentley, who ran a wartime espionage ring within the federal government that gathered information from more than three dozen well-placed sources, went to the FBI to confess. Her subsequent testimony before a federal grand jury in 1948 resulted in lurid headlines about the "Red Spy Queen." Bentley was erratic, but much of what she had to say was corroborated by other FBI sources, including Whittaker Chambers, who had himself defected from the Soviet underground network in 1938. In sensational testimony given before HUAC in 1948, Chambers identified Alger Hiss, a Harvard Law School graduate who was an important enough figure in wartime diplomacy to accompany Roosevelt to the Yalta summit with Stalin and Churchill in 1945, as a Communist and a spy. Hiss denied the accusation in countertestimony, but not persuasively. He was tried for perjury and found guilty in 1950, and sent to prison.[34]

And then, of course, there were the Rosenbergs, the couple at the center of the most famous spy case in American history, involving the theft of atomic secrets from the wartime Manhattan Project. Julius Rosenberg, an engineer in a war plant in Fort Monmouth, New Jersey, was recruited as a Soviet spy in 1942, and went on to recruit other Communists into his network, including his wife Ethel's brother David Greenglass, a soldier machinist, who was assigned to work in the Manhattan Project's Los Alamos laboratory in 1944. (Ethel's involvement in all this was peripheral, chiefly consisting of her knowledge of her husband's and brother's involvement in espionage.) Greenglass was not the only spy at Los Alamos, and others provided more valuable information to the Soviets. Still, while wearing the uniform of his country, he had passed military secrets in wartime to a foreign power, which could have resulted in his own death in the electric chair. His testimony in the Rosenbergs' trial in 1951 won him a reduced sentence, at the price of guaranteeing the conviction of his sister and brother-in-law and their execution in 1953, orphaning their two sons. The children of Party members from that era remember being terrified that next time their own parents would be taken away to be executed.[35]

Soviet intelligence achieved spectacular success during the Second World War, but the defection of Bentley, Chambers, and others led to its networks of spies in the United States being exposed or abandoned. While a few hundred Communists, to one extent or another, had been involved in espionage activities, the overwhelming majority, tens of thousands, had not. Ignorant of the existence of the Party's clandestine apparatus, most Communists sincerely regarded the charges against the Rosenbergs and others as just more witch-hunting. But they were wrong. Party leaders had betrayed them and their cause, implicating all Communists by association in crimes in which they had no knowledge or involvement. As a result, American Communism as a whole would never shed the stigma in popular memory of the fatal involvement of a few with Soviet intelligence in the 1930s and 1940s.

In 1944 Earl Browder proudly announced that Communists had taken their place within the country's two-party system. William Z. Foster was determined to change that strategy. In February 1946, in an article for the

CP's theoretical journal *Political Affairs*, Foster argued that workers, farmers, Blacks, and other progressive forces should unite in coalition around shared opposition to monopoly capitalism and imperialism "to culminate eventually in a broad third-party movement."[36] But when would "eventually" arrive? In reality, Communists were still committed to working in alliance, through unions and other groups, with the liberal New Deal wing of the Democratic Party. The Party's new general secretary, Eugene Dennis, more cautious by instinct than Foster, warned repeatedly in 1946 of the dangers of sectarian "self-isolation," which he defined as "the alienation of us Communists from our progressive non-Communist allies, especially in the labor movement."[37]

What would turn Foster's *eventually* into *right-now-this-very-moment* for a Communist-organized third-party movement was the mounting obsession within Party leadership with the "war danger," meaning an attack by the United States on the Soviet Union. In August 1946, Foster declared that "the world reactionaries, led by American monopoly capital, are already beating the drum for a new war," driven both by the imperialist imperatives described by Lenin back in 1917, and a new factor, "the need of haste . . . to make use of the atomic bomb before the Soviet Union can acquire for itself this lethal weapon."[38]

This became known within the Party as the "Five Minutes to Midnight" line. In Foster's apocalyptic view, time was running out not only for peace but for American democracy. The leadership of both the Democratic and Republican parties, in league with Wall Street, were preparing to outlaw the Communist Party as the first step in imposing a fascist regime in the United States. It followed (to Foster and, increasingly, to other Communist leaders) that the Party's primary responsibility lay in maintaining its ideological integrity, whatever short-term political costs that entailed. After the impending catastrophe of war and fascism had run its course, the CP would emerge from the ruins, fighting spirit intact and political honor unsullied, just as the underground Communist parties in Nazi-occupied

Europe had emerged triumphant from the resistance movements of the Second World War.[39]

Running under the slogan "Had Enough?" in the 1946 midterm congressional elections, Republicans regained control of the House and Senate for the first time since the start of the Great Depression, bent on undoing the policies and programs set in place over the dozen years of Franklin Roosevelt's presidency.

Two new organizations were brought into existence at the end of 1946 and the beginning of 1947, determined by their own lights to defend the achievements of the New Deal. The first was the Progressive Citizens of America (PCA), and the second Americans for Democratic Action (ADA). The former represented a revival of Popular Front–style politics, through the merger of two groups originally formed to back FDR in 1944, the National Citizens Political Action Committee and the Independent Citizens Committee of the Arts, Sciences, and Professions. It brought together left-leaning Democrats, union leaders, and, behind the scenes, some of the Communists' most politically savvy operatives. The PCA was designed to function as an advocacy group within the Democratic Party, not as the basis for a third party. Henry Wallace, Roosevelt's vice president during his third term, and in 1945–1946 Truman's secretary of commerce until forced out of the Cabinet over disagreements with the government's emerging hard line against the Soviet Union, was the group's champion if not its formal leader. Support for Wallace in 1946 and 1947 was widespread among liberal Democrats and was not necessarily indicative of any sympathy for Communism. Many liberals were genuinely worried that Truman was proving a weak leader, with little commitment to preserving the gains of the New Deal era. Believing that had FDR lived there would be no Cold War, the circles around the PCA found Wallace's criticisms of Truman's confrontational foreign-policy stance attractive.[40]

The anti-Communist liberals of Americans for Democratic Action, while not necessarily enamored of Truman, regarded the PCA as a Stalinist Trojan horse. With Protestant theologian Reinhold Niebuhr as its leader, and Eleanor Roosevelt its most prominent supporter, ADA's outlook was one of chastened liberalism, still in favor of using the power of the federal government on behalf of the common welfare, but suspicious of both the crusading fervor of the 1930s and of those inclined to apologize for Soviet aggressiveness. Communism and fascism were, in the words of ADA's founding manifesto, to be opposed equally as "hostile to the principles of freedom and democracy." Historian and ADA supporter Arthur Schlesinger Jr. argued in an influential 1949 book that what he called a "Vital Center," composed of the non-Communist Left and the non-fascist Right, was the only hope of those who "believe deeply in civil liberties, in constitutional processes and in the democratic determination of political and economic policies."[41]

The "Vital Center" in its own way embraced a hope as woolly-headed and utopian as any held by the most naive of Henry Wallace's fellow-traveling supporters. No consensus around supposed shared beliefs in civil liberties and so forth was possible between the Republican Right and the anti-Communist Democratic Left, when the fear of Soviet expansionism provided such a strong temptation for Republicans to tag their Democratic opponents with the label of being soft on Communism, and at the same time spurred Democrats to prove that they were every bit as concerned with countering the threat of foreign and domestic Communism as their hyper-partisan Republican opponents.

The new Republican majority in Congress pushed through the Taft-Hartley Act in the spring of 1947, a collection of anti-union measures long sought by business lobbyists, including a requirement that union officers file affidavits with the Labor Department swearing that they were not Communists in order to make use of National Labor Relations Board election procedures.[42] Although Truman shored up support with the labor movement by opposing Taft-Hartley (which passed over his veto), he sought to counter Republican red-baiting with new anti-Communist measures of his own, including an executive order on March 23 establishing official loyalty review boards to determine if government employees were members of or sympathetic to the Communist Party. Under the provisions of the executive order, over the next decade some 25,000 federal employees were subjected to investigations, close to 3,000 were fired, and 12,000 more resigned to avoid dismissal.[43]

That same spring, Truman's Justice Department released the Attorney General's List of Subversive Organizations, which branded tens of thousands of Americans, who in the 1930s and 1940s had joined groups like the League of American Writers, the National Negro Congress, the International Workers Order, the American Youth Congress, and scores of other groups, as untrustworthy, and made them subject to extralegal punishment through an unofficial but nonetheless devastating blacklist. "Without charging any illegal acts," political philosopher Garry Wills noted some years later, "without supplying the grounds for its proscription, without offering a machinery for individual reply, the government branded as putatively disloyal any citizen who belonged to a large number of organizations," a classification that was "used to deny people employment in *any* responsible position, private or public."[44]

Increasingly beleaguered, American Communists vacillated between clinging to their tried-and-true electoral strategy or striking out in bold new directions. John Gates, who in the immediate postwar years oversaw legislative issues for the CP, reported to a meeting of the Party's National Committee in June 1947 on political options in the coming year. While he did not rule out a third-party effort in the 1948 presidential election, he added that it should be launched only if supported by "such unions as the United Auto Workers and the Amalgamated Clothing Workers." In other words, it wouldn't be sufficient for Communist-influenced unions like the UE or the ILWU to favor a third party, if the rest of the labor movement was opposed. Eugene Dennis, searching for compromise between Party hard-liners and moderates, declared at the same meeting that while third parties should be encouraged at the local level, the ideal situation in 1948 would be for a progressive candidate to challenge Truman for the presidential nomination from within the Democratic Party in the primaries.[45]

Despite Foster's best efforts, at the start of 1947 most Communists remained wedded to the Browderite vision of working within the two-party system. Henry Wallace, who from his temporary perch as editor of the *New Republic* magazine was making an independent assessment of his political future, declared that the "problem now is to create, not a third, but a second party," that is, his own path in 1948 was to try to win the Democratic Party to truly progressive policies, at home and abroad.[46] As of the summer of 1947, a third-party challenge from the Left seemed unlikely in the coming presidential election. However, before the year was over, the Communists changed their mind, thinking incorrectly that in doing so they were carrying out a directive from Moscow.[47]

For Joseph Starobin, who witnessed the switch to the third-party strategy as a Party insider in 1947–1948, the "key catalyst" was a meeting in Poland in October 1947 of the leaders of nine European Communist parties, including the ruling parties of the Soviet Union, Bulgaria, Czechoslovakia, Hungary, Poland, Romania, and Yugoslavia, plus the powerful Communist parties of France and Italy, to form a federation called the "Information Bureau of the Communist and Workers' Parties," better known as the Cominform. Headquarters for the new federation were initially established in Belgrade, although that arrangement came to an abrupt end within six months when Yugoslav Communist leader Josip Broz Tito parted company with the Cominform and the Soviet Bloc.[48]

American Communist hard-liners interpreted the formation of the Cominform as a signal from Moscow to expect a general revolutionary upsurge in coming years. And if revolution wasn't on the horizon in the United States (they weren't that deluded), CPUSA leaders, with Foster the most determined proponent of this position, decided that the Soviets wanted them to intensify their own efforts with some bold initiative. A "cautious course" regarding the question of challenging Truman with a third-party campaign, according to Starobin, was now taken to mean "underestimating the readiness of the working class to struggle, and overestimating the power of imperialism."[49]

The decisions constituted the most calamitous policy reversal in the long entire history of policy reversals by the Communist Party. "Having set off on the crusade for a new third party . . . ," Dorothy Healey, who became leader of the Party in Los Angeles in 1945, reflected years later,

> we were abandoning one of the preconditions that we had set for its organization, which was a solid base within the labor movement. Our isolation from the working class in later years was not the product of our "right-wing opportunism" during the Browder period. . . . In this country, unfortunately, you don't lose contact with the working class by moving right. It's when you move to the left that you risk everything. That's what we decided to do in 1948.[50]

The new party, dubbed the Progressive Party, had no connection with the parties of that name that ran Teddy Roosevelt for president in 1912 and Robert La Follette in 1924. It was created from scratch, with Communists playing key roles behind-the-scenes, reversing a decade of commitment by the Communist Party (save for the Nazi-Soviet Pact era) to working in alliance with Democrats. While breaking with the Democratic Party in opposing Truman's foreign policy, the Progressive Party platform otherwise offered a fairly standard liberal wish list of planks, calling for an end to racial discrimination, the creation of a system of national health insurance, and a host of pro-labor initiatives, starting with repeal of the Taft-Hartley Act.[51]

Though the Progressive Party's stance was wholeheartedly pro-labor, that feeling was not reciprocated by the actual existing labor movement. The 1924 La Follette candidacy had attracted the support of the American Federation of Labor. But twenty-four years later, neither the AFL nor the more liberally inclined Congress of Industrial Organizations wanted anything to do with Henry Wallace's campaign. In its nearly three-decade existence, the Communist Party's greatest single achievement had been its contribution to the creation of the CIO, winning a share of power and legitimacy in the labor movement as a result. With the decision to launch a third-party campaign in 1948, the Communists threw those hard-won gains away.

Top CIO leaders were committed to securing Truman's reelection and regarded any support by the CIO's constituent unions for a third party as organizational treason. Up through 1947, CIO president Philip Murray had, to an extent, protected the Communists from other CIO leaders, like Walter Reuther, who wanted them ousted. That would no longer be the case. And it wasn't only the anti-Communists in the CIO who decided this was the breaking point. "Red Mike" Quill, president of the Transport Workers Union, and a close Party ally since the early 1930s, had once famously declared that he "would rather be called a Red by the rats than a rat by the Reds."[52] But when he was summoned to a meeting of left-wing unionists and learned about plans for an independent Wallace candidacy, he shouted, "To hell with you and your central committee." He publicly broke with the CP in 1948 and purged his union of its Communist staffers.[53]

Elsewhere in the left wing of the CIO, the third-party strategy was backed dutifully but unenthusiastically. The ILWU executive board gave

Wallace their endorsement, but left their locals free to do so or not. Harry Bridges did not actively campaign for Wallace. UE president Albert Fitzgerald served as co-chairman of the Wallace for President Committee, but the UE did not formally endorse him. That did not save either union from facing the wrath of the CIO national leadership soon after the 1948 presidential election.[54]

The CP's great gamble would not have been possible without a candidate as prominent and (as of late 1947) popular as Henry Wallace. President Truman would denounce "Henry Wallace and his Communists," but Wallace, for his part, thought of himself as an independent actor and FDR's true heir, having been part of the New Deal from the start, first as a Cabinet member and then as vice president. Through 1947 and into the early months of 1948, Wallace attracted substantial crowds to his events. He assumed his support among liberal Democrats would outweigh in importance the support he was being offered by the Communists, limiting their influence. When asked by reporters about his Communist allies, he replied, "I'm not following their line. If they want to follow my line, I say God bless 'em."[55] He also hoped that the Communists would refrain from the kind of heavy-handed behind-the-scenes manipulation they had brought to earlier electoral alliances. "I urge elimination of groups and factions in this new party movement," he declared in April 1948. He wanted a party "as broad as humanity itself," which would only be possible if Americans "realize that we do not represent one group. If we are going to be a party of 20 million, there are going to be many kinds of people in that party. Keep the door open."[56]

It was the Communists who determined how wide to open that door, since without the organizational resources they brought to the Wallace campaign, there simply would have been no Progressive Party in 1948. Neither Wallace nor the Communists thought he had any real chance of victory in 1948, but they hoped for a respectable third-place showing, perhaps in the range of 3 million votes. That would be more than enough to guarantee Truman's defeat, which seemed inevitable in any case. And if the election had been held in November 1947, it is possible Wallace would have attracted a substantial vote.[57] President Truman's personal approval ratings continued to spiral downward in the spring of 1948, bottoming out at an abysmal 36 percent. Upon Truman's defeat, Wallace's supporters would be in a strong position to either continue as an independent party, or, should they return to the Democratic Party, to influence the selection of its presidential candidate four years later.[58]

But ironically, the third-party campaign strengthened Truman's prospects in 1948, defusing Republican charges that he was in alliance with Communists or indifferent to the danger posed by Communist subversion. As Truman argued in a campaign speech, attacking Wallace's spoiler role, "The Communists want a Republican administration because they think that its reactionary policies will lead to the confusion and strife on which Communism thrives."[59] Stalin did not do Henry Wallace any favors as he ratcheted up international tensions, which suggests that the Soviets were not very invested in his campaign. In February 1948, Communists in Czechoslovakia overthrew the postwar coalition government in place since 1945. And in June, Soviet forces launched a blockade of West Berlin, an outpost of Western influence surrounded by Communist East Germany. Wallace blamed both developments on Truman's "get tough" policies, reinforcing the perception that he was indeed a Communist puppet who automatically excused Soviet misdeeds. Communists in the Progressive Party made matters still worse when they blocked a resolution from some non-Communist Vermont delegates to the July Progressive Party convention in Philadelphia that would have placed the new party on record as disavowing "a blanket endorsement of the foreign policy of any nation," a rhetorical gesture that might have gone some ways toward countering charges of a pro-Soviet bias on its part. The defeat of the "Vermont resolution" was widely taken to suggest that the open door that Wallace had called for was closing to all but his most ardent left-wing supporters.

Once again, the Communists proved unable to exercise self-restraint when presented the opportunity to dominate coalition efforts, and once again, the chief effect would be that they wound up capturing themselves.[60]

In the end, Truman pulled off a surprise victory, in which the Democrats retained the White House and regained control of both houses of Congress. The Progressive Party came in fourth in the balloting, behind not just the Democrats and Republicans, but also the "Dixiecrat" States' Rights Democratic Party ticket headed by segregationist Strom Thurmond. Wallace attracted only 1,156,103 votes nationwide, a dismal 2.37 percent of the total, half of which came from New York State (in contrast, out of a much smaller electorate, Robert La Follette had won nearly 5 million votes in 1924, or 16.6 percent). The results revealed conclusively the CP's weakness not only in politics but in the labor movement. Seven out of ten union members voted for Harry Truman in 1948. Truman, asked how he had prevailed against all odds in the election, replied simply, "Labor did it."[61]

The following year the national CIO leadership expelled ten Communist-led unions from the federation. Only three of them, the ILWU, the UE, and the smaller International Union of Mine, Mill and Smelter Workers, known as Mine-Mill, survived past 1955. The ILWU remained a power on West Coast docks, but the UE's membership was decimated by raiding from the newly chartered CIO International Union of Electrical Workers, harassment by the Catholic Church, HUAC, and manufacturers like GE, and finally a decision by the CP itself to shut down its efforts to keep the union alive and independent. By 1957 a mere 70,000 members remained in the UE, less than a tenth of its size a dozen years earlier, although it would ultimately survive. Mine-Mill, under similar attack, merged with the United Steelworkers in the 1960s.[62]

For nearly three decades, at least once past their early underground existence, Communists had devoted the bulk of their efforts to building the

Smith Act defendants, January 17, 1949; back row, left to right: Jack Stachel, Irving Potash, Carl Winter, Benjamin J. Davis, John Gates, Gil Green; front row: Robert G. Thompson, Henry Winston, Eugene Dennis, Gus Hall, John Williamson
(Photo by Irving Haberman/IH Images/Getty Images)

labor movement, which even in their most sectarian days was an outward-looking perspective. Starting in the late 1940s, as they lost their institutional base in the CIO and came under extensive and sustained official assault, they stopped looking outward. Their focus turned inward to the defense of the Party. Everything else had to be subordinated to the fight for self-preservation.

The turning point came on July 20, 1948, when FBI agents arrested five top Communist leaders at Party headquarters in New York City: Chairman William Z. Foster, General Secretary Eugene Dennis, Organizational Secretary Henry Winston, Director of Education, Agitation, and Publications Jack Stachel, and Trade Union Secretary John Williamson.

They were charged with violation of the 1940 Alien Registration Act, better known as the Smith Act, which made it a crime to conspire to teach or advocate the "duty, necessity, desirability or propriety" of the overthrow of local, state, or the federal government by force or violence. In the following week, seven more Communist leaders were taken into custody on the same charges, including New York City councilman and member of the CP's National Board Benjamin Davis, New York district leader Robert Thompson, *Daily Worker* editor John Gates, Illinois district leader Gil Green, National Board member and vice president of the Fur and Leather Workers Union Irving Potash, Michigan district leader Carl Winter, and Ohio district leader Gus Hall. Their number included two African-Americans (Davis and Winston), four Jews (Gates, Green, Winter, and Stachel), and three immigrants (Potash, Stachel, and Williamson). Two were Spanish Civil War veterans (Gates and Thompson). Hall, Potash, Thompson, and Williamson were Lenin School graduates.[63]

They would be brought to trial in the federal courthouse in Lower Manhattan's Foley Square in January 1949. While they were being tried, the Soviet Union detonated an atomic bomb, and Mao Zedong came to power in what thereafter became known to Americans as "Red China." These were not the best of times for Communists to come before an American court.

The Smith Act was first employed by federal prosecutors in a 1941 trial of the Trotskyist leaders of the Socialist Workers Party, including James P. Cannon, who was found guilty and sent to prison. The Communists had some qualms about the prosecution of their hated rivals, rightly worrying that the Smith Act might someday be used against them as well, but they didn't do anything to oppose their trial and imprisonment.[64]

Journalist I. F. Stone, although close to the Communist Party, opposed the prosecution of the Trotskyists, writing in an article for *The Nation* magazine, "For the first time in peace since the Alien and Sedition Acts of John Adams a mere expression of opinion is made a federal crime." The government's rationale for bringing a case against Cannon and his associates was "no different from the reasoning on which Trotskyists are jailed in the Third Reich or the Soviet Union."[65]

Stone was a loyal-enough ally or "fellow traveler" of the Communists to have signed the infamous August 1939 open letter to *The Nation* that denied the "fantastic falsehood" that Soviet Union was a totalitarian state, and for the next decade remained allied with the Party on many issues, including support for Henry Wallace in 1948. But, at the same time, he spoke, wrote, and thought in a morally driven American idiom, and was a consistent civil libertarian.

In 1949, Stone was a columnist for a left-wing newspaper in New York, the *Daily Compass*, and covered the Smith Act trial of the Communist Party leadership. On October 14, the day after the jury delivered its verdict, his column questioned the rationale for the trial, as he had eight years earlier in the Trotskyist case: "From first to last the government has not alleged or sought to prove that the defendants committed any act which was unlawful. They were not accused of trying to put a bomb under the Capitol or of inciting others to do so or of drilling a private armed force with which to march on Washington. They were accused of disseminating revolutionary ideas."[66]

Unlike Stone, most newspapers and most of the rest of the country thought the case against the Communists entirely justified. As John Gates later acknowledged, "Many people who believed that the Smith Act was unconstitutional, nevertheless did not support us; they were convinced that if we ever came to power we would deprive everyone, except the Communists, of their democratic rights."[67]

Much of the prosecution's case in the Smith Act trial consisted of reading aloud excerpts from books available for sale from International Publishers, the Party's main publishing outlet. Works of Marx, Lenin, and Stalin, as well as American Communist authors, including William Z. Foster's *Toward Soviet America*, were included as evidence for the Party's plans for the violent seizure of power. John Gates was called by the defense to testify to the Party's essentially peaceful commitment to social change, which he later characterized as a "futile attempt to prove that the classics of the Marxist writers meant what we said they meant, instead of what they plainly did mean, if taken literally." Instead, he thought in retrospect, the defense "should have concentrated on the civil liberties aspects of the case: the right to read, write, say and think any political thoughts we pleased."[68]

Lasting nine months, the Foley Square trial was the longest in American legal history. At its conclusion, presiding judge Harold Medina instructed the jury that a guilty verdict was the appropriate remedy should they agree that Communists were prepared to launch an armed uprising, if not in the immediate future, "as speedily as circumstances permit."[69] The jurors arrived at their verdict about as speedily as imaginable given the length and complexity of the trial, deliberating a mere seven and a half hours before returning guilty verdicts against all eleven defendants (the twelfth, William Z. Foster, was not brought to trial because of ill health). Judge Medina sentenced ten of the defendants to five years imprisonment, half the maximum of ten years he might have given them (although the Trotskyist defendants convicted in 1941 of violating the Smith Act had received relatively lenient sentences of a year to sixteen months). Robert Thompson received a reduced sentence of three years, in recognition of his wartime military record. The judge also sent all five lawyers for the defense to prison on contempt charges, which led in several cases to disbarment. It would not be an easy task to find lawyers willing to defend Communist defendants in future Smith Act trials.[70]

And there would be more trials, once the appeals process was concluded, which took another year and a half. In the meantime, in June 1950 the North Korean army invaded South Korea, and the United States was back at war, less than five years since the ending of the Second World War. Many Americans, including President Truman, believed it was the start of a Third World War. For its part, the *Daily Worker* hailed the North Korean invasion and its early victories, reporting on June 29, 1950: "Liberation forces of the Korean People's Republic yesterday freed Seoul."[71]

On June 4, 1951, the US Supreme Court announced its decision in *Dennis v. United States*, upholding the constitutionality of the Smith Act, in a six to two vote. Less than three weeks later, FBI agents began arresting the "second string" Party leadership, starting with Elizabeth Gurley Flynn and sixteen others in New York City, soon followed by more arrests. All told, between 1951 and 1954, one hundred twenty-six CP leaders were charged under the Smith Act. Of 105 actually brought to trial, 93 were convicted and sentenced to three to five years in prison.[72]

The result, as intended, was a crippled Communist Party. "Party meetings were increasingly concerned not with what was happening in the world . . . but only with the CPUSA," veteran Communist and blacklisted screenwriter Walter Bernstein recalled. "Its leaders were going to jail. It had no vision except staying alive. This only added to its irrelevance."[73]

The attacks on the Party weren't limited to the Smith Act trials. The Justice Department rounded up hundreds of foreign-born Communists for deportation, including some like ILWU leader Harry Bridges and UE leader James Matles who were naturalized US citizens (in their cases, the Supreme Court eventually reversed the deportation decision on technicalities). Many others, like Trinidad and Tobago–born Claudia Jones, an elected member of the Party's National Committee, were not as fortunate; the highest-ranking Black woman Communist in the United States, she was deported to England in 1955.[74] Steve Nelson, district secretary of the Western Pennsylvania CP and an important national leader, was held for denaturalization and deportation, sentenced to five years in prison under the Smith Act, and on top of that, convicted of sedition under a separate Pennsylvania sedition act and sentenced to twenty years in state prison (ultimately he was not deported, and the Supreme Court threw out the sedition conviction as double jeopardy).[75]

Victims were legion, some prominent, many obscure. The celebrated cases of political persecution, like that of the Hollywood Ten—movie industry producers, directors, and screenwriters, each sentenced to a year in prison for refusing to testify in HUAC hearings in 1947—are well-known to historians of the McCarthy era. More difficult to recover are the legal and human costs to thousands of ordinary people who made up the Party's rank and file who were also victimized, most often by being fired from their jobs as electrical workers, marine cooks, postal workers, and the like. One such case that did escape obscurity was that of a New York City–employed washroom attendant, who was fired in 1955 because he had been a Communist from 1936 to 1939; he was one of the fortunate ones, reinstated on appeal to the New York Supreme Court. Meanwhile some 300 public-school teachers in New York City were fired for Communist affiliations.[76]

The Supreme Court's decision in *Dennis* was taken by Communist leaders as the signal to implement plans to go underground, the third time in three decades the Party took that step. The eleven convicted defendants were ordered to report for imprisonment on July 2, 1951, but Henry Winston, Gil Green, Robert Thompson, and Gus Hall did not show up, confirming the Party's image in American public opinion as a criminal conspiracy. Eugene Dennis was supposed to disappear as well, but he was foiled in doing so by a mix-up over arrangements to go into hiding. Hall was captured in Mexico in October 1951 (originally intended to be a way station en route to refuge in Moscow), and Thompson in California in September 1953. Winston and Green were never found, but voluntarily surrendered to authorities in 1956, to be sentenced to an additional three years in prison, in addition to their original five-year sentences; they would not return to their families until 1961, ten years after they went underground. The additional years they served in jail proved pointless, a sacrifice to Party discipline that accomplished nothing.[77]

Several thousand additional Communists, who were not, at least as yet, facing charges, joined the fugitive Smith Act defendants in the underground, some forging new identities within the United States, others leaving the country. As Party leader in Los Angeles, Dorothy Healey was in charge of recruiting local members for the underground apparatus. For those who agreed, Healey recalled: "It meant they had to disappear, change their names, move to a new city, and have no contact with their family or friends for no one could say how long a time." From the start in 1951 and continuing through 1955 when it ended, Healey concluded, "The underground was a disaster. It was like a bad spy movie. . . . We were turning ourselves into a caricature of the conspiracy" that the Party's opponents "accused us of being."[78]

The members of the underground, for the most part, were drawn from the ranks of the YCL generation of the 1930s, the most trusted and experienced activists, precisely those who should have been representing the Party's public face and outward reach. At the same time, when recruiting new members was all but out of the question, thousands of loyal Communists were stripped of membership for a suspected lack of commitment, for alleged "white chauvinist" tendencies, or for other perceived vulnerabilities, like seeing a psychiatrist or psychoanalyst or being homosexual (the latter judged a problem on grounds of security, since it was feared gay members might be blackmailed by the authorities into acting as informers).[79]

By 1955 Party membership was reduced to no more than 20,000, a third of its size a half dozen years earlier. The Party's once formidable presence in the labor movement was all but destroyed. The prospects for Communist electoral relevance were equally dismal. The Progressive Party, which had scraped together a disappointing million or so votes for Henry Wallace in 1948, attracted just over a tenth that number in 1952 when it ran left-wing lawyer Vincent Hallinan as its presidential candidate.

Most of the Party fronts listed on the attorney general's subversive organization list were gone by the mid-1950s. At the moment when a new and dynamic civil rights movement was beginning to form in cities like Montgomery, Alabama, the Communist Party had no organizational presence in the movement. And the Party's most successful auxiliary organization, the International Workers Order, with its tens of thousands of members, excellent insurance policies, and network of clinics, newspapers, schools, and summer camps, was shut down by order of the New York State Insurance Department in 1953, despite being found fiscally sound.[80]

International Communism had not been contained, let alone rolled back in the late 1940s and early 1950s, but that could not be said of American Communism. The movement was effectively destroyed by the time Dwight Eisenhower took the oath of office as president in January 1953.

And then, just when things seemed most hopeless, there were signs of change, if nothing yet like renewal. The Stalin era, if not Stalinism, came to an end on March 5, 1953, when the Soviet dictator died. The CPUSA's National Committee cabled condolences to the Central Committee of the Soviet Communist Party, describing Stalin as "the best loved man on earth, enshrined in the hearts of people everywhere, to whose well being his life was selflessly devoted."[81]

Following a brief power struggle, Nikita Khrushchev became the new leader of the Soviet Communist Party. Khrushchev had joined the Bolsheviks in 1918 and emerged as a close associate of Stalin in the 1930s, and was responsible for the death of a good many fellow Communists during the purge era. Still, he took a number of steps that tempered the murderous paranoia characterizing his predecessor's rule. In his first years in power, he ordered the release of millions of prisoners held in the Siberian gulag. On the diplomatic front, he sought a reconciliation (as it turned out, temporary) between the Soviet Union and Yugoslavia. Khrushchev traveled to Belgrade to meet with Tito in 1955, and the two leaders adopted a joint declaration pledging that socialist countries would henceforth enjoy the freedom to follow their own paths to socialism. There also began to be vague references in the official press in Moscow to a problem in the past leadership of the Soviet Union having to do with a disembodied abstraction labeled "the cult of personality."

For American Communists, this was confusing. When Tito defied Stalin in 1948, they obediently repeated the Soviet charges that the Yugoslav leader was an American hireling, just as ten years earlier they had taken it as a matter of faith that Trotsky was an agent of the Gestapo. Now that Stalin's case against Tito had collapsed, or no longer seemed to matter, what were Communists to make of charges against such "Titoists" as László Rajk in Hungary, Rudolf Slánský in Czechoslovakia, and other Eastern European Communist leaders who had been tried and executed in the postwar purge trials? If those trials were frame-ups, what might that suggest about the legal proceedings on which they were modeled, the prewar Moscow trials? In 1951, *Daily Worker* editor John Gates had published a pamphlet with the resolute title *On Guard Against Browderism, Titoism, Trotskyism*. Now, just four years later, at least one of those terrible threats seemed to have been a mere misunderstanding between fraternal socialist powers. Had the condemnation ten years earlier of another of those threats, that of Earl Browder, been based on a similar misunderstanding?[82]

Domestic developments also began to undermine American Communists' faith in the wisdom of their leaders. Were American fascism and a Third World War with the Soviet Union all but inevitable? As the California Smith Act defendants prepared for their trial in 1952, they established a trial committee to decide on legal strategy. Dorothy Healey, one of the committee's six members, had her own doubts about the Party's "Five Minutes to Midnight" analysis, and she was surprised to discover at their first meeting that she was not alone:

> Remarkably, at our very first session, the trial committee came to the unanimous conclusion that the Party's estimate was mistaken.

... To speak about the onset of "fascism"—when our Party offices were still open, when our Party press was still publishing, when the labor movement was able to function legally, and there were the first stirrings of what would become the civil rights movement—seemed a perverse and inaccurate characterization. ... It was not the apocalypse.[83]

Healey and California state party leader William Schneiderman traveled to New York to argue for a broader trial strategy emphasizing civil-libertarian arguments, which would give a stronger basis for subsequent appeals to the Supreme Court. William Z. Foster was unimpressed, and told them to give up their "bourgeois legalistic illusions." They were not able to change the Party line, but they did change their courtroom strategy, abandoning the "political defense" employed in the 1949 trial. George Charney, awaiting his own second-string trial in New York, appreciated the difference: "The California case had preceded ours, and I remember how impressed I was with the testimony of [San Francisco CP leader] Oleta O'Connor Yates, the only defense witness. . . . It was clear that the California people had independently resolved to point their case in a new direction and give emphasis to the issue of civil liberties. . . . I secretly admired their gumption."[84]

Yates, Healey, Schneiderman, and the eleven other California defendants were all convicted, despite the new trial strategy. Nevertheless, the precedent they set in challenging Party orthodoxy had dramatic political and legal consequences. On June 17, 1957, the US Supreme Court ruled in *Yates v. United States*, in a six to one decision, to overturn their convictions. What the court decided, in Healey's words, was that it wasn't enough for the government to prove that she was a Communist leader and believer in Marxism-Leninism. Rather, it needed to prove "that I personally had participated in advocating that people go out and, say, buy guns and ammunition in preparation for the revolution. And that, of course, I had never done."[85] As Justice John Marshall Harlan, who wrote the majority decision, observed, "Those to whom the advocacy is addressed must be urged to *do* something, now or in the future, rather than merely to *believe* in something."[86] Harlan had previously voted to uphold the constitutionality of the Smith Act in the *Dennis* appeal. The court's new willingness to reconsider anti-Communist laws and procedures stemmed from many developments, including the appointment of liberal Earl Warren as chief justice in 1954. The decision also likely reflected recent political developments such as the reduction of Cold War tensions following Stalin's death, the end of the Korean War in 1953, and the US Senate's censure of Joseph McCarthy in 1954.[87]

California Communists were not the only dissenters from the official Party line. In some parts of the country, like New York, the state's underground leadership were the ones having second thoughts. Being a Party leader in normal times involved an endless round of organizational busywork. Without such responsibilities, underground leaders often found themselves with lots of time on their hands, time to read and, for some, to do some hard thinking. Like the California defendants, the New York underground leaders, including Spanish veteran George Watt, began to question the "Five Minutes to Midnight" line, and when the Party finally shut down the underground in 1954, they brought their questions back with them to their comrades in the aboveground.[88]

Joseph Starobin wasn't underground, but he too was removed from the hothouse inner-party atmosphere in the early 1950s by dint of being assigned to Paris as foreign correspondent for the *Daily Worker*, traveling widely in Europe and Asia, even reporting from Vietnam on the Communist-led struggle against French colonialism. During that time, he developed his own doubts, quietly refusing to reregister his membership in the CP on his return to the US in 1954. The following year he published a book with a Party-friendly but independent press describing his recent travels abroad, and the conversations he had with Communist leaders in Europe and Asia. In the guise of a travelogue, *Paris to Peking* raised questions about past Soviet and American Communist policies. In coming years, he suggested, it should be a "basic principle" that Communists in different countries "are going to take the Socialist path in their own context of historical development."[89] That was a modest enough proposal, but one that in the past would have been regarded as heresy. Not this time: he found sympathetic readers in the Party, including on the staff of the *Daily Worker.* Starobin later described the mood in American Communist circles in the mid-1950s as constituting "a vast intellectual black market in which many of us traded, half in a daze, unable to voice everything on our minds."[90]

In Atlanta Penitentiary, John Gates, serving his sentence from the Foley Square trial, was also trading in that intellectual black market, in his case by choosing to read George Orwell's *1984.* As a work of literature, Gates found the dystopian novel off-putting, and "despairing of humanity." But he found some of the parallels between the novel's "Big Brother" and Stalin disturbing. He tried to discuss his concerns with fellow prisoner Eugene Dennis, but found that Dennis's "absolute faith in the Soviet leaders" remained unshaken.[91]

Gates and Dennis, and five other of the original Smith Act defendants, were released from prison on March 1, 1955, having served three years and eight months of their five-year sentences. The conditions of their parole forbade them from engaging in political activities until January 29, 1956, when Gates once again assumed the editorship of the *Daily Worker,* and Dennis the post of general secretary of the Communist Party. "Just ahead," Gates recalled, "lay the biggest political storm of our lives."[92]

When the Soviet Communist Party met in Moscow in February 1956 for its Twentieth Party Congress, American Communists paid close attention.

In its public sessions, Khrushchev and other speakers repeatedly attacked "the cult of personality." Stalin's name was not mentioned, but it was not hard to conclude he was the implied target. The *Daily Worker*'s coverage and editorial response initially offered an upbeat account; mistakes had been made but now they were being corrected. Beneath the surface confidence, however, the paper's editorial staff was troubled.

For over three decades, the *Daily Worker* had been the authoritative voice of American Communism, tacking right or left, sometimes by minute degree, sometimes in dramatic reversals, depending on signals from Moscow. In the spring of 1956, however, the *Daily Worker*'s staff realized that they shared some political concerns that went beyond tinkering with the tone and emphasis of the standard "Party line." In a startling development, startling even to themselves, editor Gates, foreign editor Joseph Clark, managing editor Alan Max, and sports editor Lester Rodney, as well as other columnists and reporters, all veterans of the 1930s YCL generation, had begun to think independently.

Joseph "Joe" Clark's background in the Communist movement stretched back to 1930 when as a senior at Brooklyn's New Utrecht High School, he had organized a successful student boycott of milk cartons to protest a rise in their price.[93] He rose steadily in the YCL hierarchy in the following decade and then, following military service in World War II, joined the staff of the *Daily Worker*. From 1951 through 1953, he was the newspaper's correspondent in Moscow, and, of course, a consistent apologist for the Soviet regime. In a series of dispatches from Moscow, reprinted in a 1954 pamphlet entitled *The Real Russia*, Clark insisted that there was no antisemitism in the Soviet Union, no political terror, no harsh treatment of the few Soviet citizens sentenced to prison. "The Soviet penal system," he asserted flatly, "is based on labor rehabilitation."[94]

Nevertheless, it was Clark who in March 1956 broke the *Daily Worker*'s silence on the true significance of the just-concluded Moscow congress. In a March 12 column, he noted that East German Communist Party leader Walter Ulbricht had gone beyond the scope of Khrushchev's public comments about the "cult of the individual" by putting the blame for the practice on Stalin by name. That wasn't enough, Clark insisted: "Ulbricht would have been a lot more candid if he had only admitted that he himself had contributed to sponsoring the 'cult of the individual.'"[95] A mild criticism, perhaps, yet one that suggested that the problems revealed at the Moscow meeting went far beyond the failures of this or that past leader, and were instead systemic in the international Communist movement.

If Ulbricht had his own sins to account for, what did the *Daily Worker* have to say about those committed by American Communists? The answer came the next day in a column by managing editor Alan Max, entitled "US Marxists and Soviet Self-Criticism." Max's own involvement with the CP began in the early 1930s, during or soon after his time as an undergraduate at Columbia University. He joined the staff of the *Daily Worker* as a reporter in the late 1930s, and ran the paper while John Gates was in prison. In his March 13 column Max declared, "Any Marxist who says he has not been jolted" by the Twentieth Congress "is either not being honest with himself . . . or minimizes the extent of the developments now in progress in the Soviet Union." He admitted that American Communists had "glossed over" problems in the USSR, particularly the suppression of civil liberties, but pledged that would never happen again. Max concluded by asking readers to send in their own reactions to the Twentieth Congress as letters to the editor.[96]

This unprecedented request by the *Daily Worker* for an honest discussion of their own Party's mistakes and misdeeds emboldened rank-and-file Communists. Despite a warning by Party chairman William Z. Foster to avoid lending aid and comfort to "capitalist apologists" by criticizing comrades in the Soviet Union and elsewhere, hundreds of readers sent letters to the *Daily Worker* and other CP publications in the months to come, many directly challenging Foster's attempt to choke off free discussion. "At the time [the] Duclos letter on Browderism was published in France," one reader noted, "Foster did not feel that critical evaluation of another party concerning American affairs was ruled out." Another wrote: "We demand of the bourgeoisie that they permit free discussion of socialist ideas, quoting at them the dictum that truth has nothing to fear from free discussion. Too often we have failed to apply it within our own ranks. . . . A certain contempt for the rank and file is implied in the constant fear that 'destructive' criticism has to be stifled."[97]

CP general secretary Eugene Dennis also came under attack. Dennis tried to find a middle way between Foster's icy defense of orthodoxy and the new calls for reform, but in doing so he only reinforced his own reputation for indecisive vacillation, earning the enmity of both sides in the unfolding debate. "Alex Leslie" (most of the letters to the *Daily Worker* appeared under pseudonyms) wrote in to defend the paper's editors against another reader's accusation that its editors were guilty of "incorrect formulations" in criticizing the Soviet Union: "I would rather read one of those 'incorrect' editorials with their vivid communication of personal outrage," Leslie declared, "than a dozen wordy and passionless 'correct formulations' by Dennis," and other Party leaders. He demanded to know how Dennis really felt "about the lies you swallowed, about the years wasted in propagating those lies, about the innocent men and women destroyed." Communists, Leslie concluded, needed to go back to the origins of their movement, before the Bolshevik Revolution, when it had leaders of the caliber of Eugene Debs, who understood that "socialism is a moral movement, a movement against the cut-throat, belly crawling world of capitalism, a movement to exalt not this or that 'great leader' but all humanity."[98]

It wasn't just the inadequacies of the current leadership of the Party that were at fault. The very structure of the Leninist party bred destructive illusions, according to a letter from "A. W." printed at the start of May. Why, the writer asked, did Communists habitually refer to their own leaders as "'leaders of the American Working Class,' 'leaders of the Negro

People,' 'Great Women Leaders' etc."? The truth was that most "CP leaders and functionaries have been for most of their lives inner party functionaries, isolated from the people, and have no organizational ties with the mass organizations of the people."[99]

The forces of orthodoxy within the American Communist movement were on the defensive that spring and summer. And Party leaders learned on April 28, 1956, that Khrushchev's condemnation of Stalin at the Twentieth Party Congress had gone much further than was yet public knowledge. A copy of Khrushchev's "secret speech" to the delegates in a closed session of the congress was passed to the American CP via the Soviet embassy and read aloud at a 120-person gathering of the National Committee and other invited insiders in the auditorium of the Jefferson School in New York. Steve Nelson, thirty-year veteran of the Party, Abraham Lincoln Battalion commissar, and Smith Act defendant, chaired the meeting, which was devoted to a reading of a lengthy summary of the Khrushchev speech. Stalin, who the CPUSA had mourned as "the best loved man on earth" just three years earlier, was now revealed to the gathering as the bloodthirsty paranoid tyrant he had been in reality. In the Stalin era, Khrushchev declared, "Honest Communists were slandered, accusations against them were fabricated, and revolutionary legality was gravely undermined." Three-quarters of the 139 members of the Soviet Communist Party's Central Committee in 1934 had been arrested by the end of the decade, he revealed, as were over half the 1,966 delegates to the Soviet Party Congress that year. And there was much more.

Dorothy Healey was among those who wept as she listened to Khrushchev's denunciation of Stalin:

We had marched for so many years with the purity of the Soviet Union as our banner. It was not just a public thing, you felt it, believed it. You had no difficulty dismissing the stories that you were told about the Soviet Union as lies, nonsense. And here you were being told that not only were those stories true but that they went beyond anything you ever heard from enemies of the Soviet Union.[100]

She also thought of the old comrades she had voted to expel from the Party when they were accused of violating Party discipline or straying from the official line. "Would I have voted the same way," she wondered, "if we had been in power and it had been a question of life or death?"[101]

As the reading of the report ended, Nelson recalled, "I could see people, old Party leaders, crying in the audience. . . . I made the first comment. I said something like, 'This is not the reason why I joined the Party. From now on we have to reject this; we have to make our own decisions; there are no gods.'"[102]

The National Committee's other business at the April meeting was to vote on a report about the state of the Party by Eugene Dennis. The CP's "left-sectarian" direction in the past decade, he argued, grew out of shortcomings that were "basic, deep-seated, and longstanding." Since 1945, the Party had overestimated the danger of war and fascism and overlooked possibilities for "peaceful coexistence" between the United States and the Soviet Union. The Party had been mistaken in its belief that a major economic crisis would inevitably befall the United States. It had made a major blunder in insisting on making "foreign policy issues the acid test of all united front relationships," particularly in the labor movement. And, of course, the Progressive Party had proven a disaster. Beneath all of these mistakes lay the fact that Communists had failed "to understand the difference between that which is universally valid in Marxism and that which is peculiarly applicable to one country or another." That amounted to a comprehensive repudiation of everything the CP had done since Browder's fall. Of forty or so voting delegates at the meeting, only William Z. Foster, the man chiefly responsible for fostering the CP's left-sectarianism, voted in opposition.[103]

As for Khrushchev's speech, formally titled "On the Cult of Personality and Its Consequences," it would not remain a secret much longer, as it was publicly released on June 4, 1956, by the US State Department, which had obtained a copy through its own channels. It was immediately reprinted in a condensed 4,000-word version in the *Daily Worker*, under a headline unimaginable at any prior moment in the newspaper's publishing history, "Stalin's Repressions Spelled Out in Khrushchev Speech Made Public Here." It would then be reprinted in its full 26,000-word version in the following issue of *Sunday Worker*.[104]

American Communist dissidents seemed to have a mandate to reform the Party. They controlled the most important state organizations (including New York and California) and newspapers (including the *Daily Worker*, the West Coast daily *People's World*, and the daily *Frayhayt*). They were in the vanguard, not just in the American movement, but in the international movement. Joe Clark, as foreign editor of the *Daily Worker*, kept readers abreast of the latest developments in other Communist parties. In Poland the formerly disgraced and imprisoned CP leader Władysław Gomułka was returning in triumph to power, and apparently successfully facing down a Russian challenge to the liberalization of the regime; in Italy, Italian Communist leader Palmiro Togliatti (long admired by American Communists for his political innovations) was calling for a "polycentric" Communist movement, while challenging Khrushchev to explain how and why other Soviet leaders had allowed Stalin to acquire his despotic powers. Meanwhile, there was a steady stream of revelations about the crimes of the Stalin era, including the acknowledgment that the Eastern European purge trials had been frame-ups, and that Yiddish culture in the Soviet Union had been suppressed and many Jewish writers and artists murdered.[105]

Foster was not without resources of his own, including support among many Party old-timers. But his greatest strength lay in his opponents' weaknesses. Outside observers of the Party's inner battle, like the *New York Times*, wrote about something they called the "Gates faction," named for the *Daily Worker*'s editor, as if it were a tight-knit group with commonly agreed-upon goals, while the Old Guard found it useful to attack the "Gates-Starobin-Clark line" as the latest in a long string of heresies. In fact, Gates did little to organize his own supporters into a cohesive faction. "We were attempting to reverse the Party's deep-seated sectarian isolation," reformer Max Gordon recalled, "and what could be more sectarian . . . than a factional struggle within the Party?"[106] Nor did the dissenters share a common program. Some wished to retain elements of the Leninist tradition, as well as the name of the Communist Party; others, like Gates and Clark, wanted to dissolve the Party and start over with a new group, representing a clear break with vanguardist illusions. Foster had inertia on his side; the dissenters had to come up with alternatives, which only divided their ranks. "We had no difficulty," Dorothy Healey recalled of a meeting with John Gates in 1957 that did not go well, "in finding unity on what we didn't want."[107]

As a result, Foster's base remained in the Party, while the reformers' base increasingly was heading toward the exits. The CP's dissenting wing, Starobin later wrote, "had the votes and won the argument, but their Party disappeared."[108] And then came the Hungarian Revolution.

In Hungary, a reform-minded Communist, Imre Nagy, had emerged as an outspoken critic within the Hungarian CP of the purge trials in the early 1950s that had led to the execution of László Rajk in 1951. Mátyás Rákosi, installed as general secretary of the Hungarian Communist Party by Stalin, and the man who oversaw the purge trials, remained in power until forced from office and into exile in July 1956 in the face of widespread unrest. As Rákosi's power ebbed, Nagy's rose, and in October he was appointed prime minister. As Nagy's biographer Peter Unwin noted, "Nagy wrote in 1955 as a committed Communist [who] still believed that Marxism-Leninism held the key to the future [and] did not anticipate that the logic of his own argument might lead to a destination outside the Party"—words that can be applied as well to many of his American counterparts.[109]

Although uneasy about the more radical demands for regime change coming from university students and others, on taking office Nagy took steps to dismantle the repressive apparatus of the Hungarian regime, including dissolving the secret police. In a fatal step, he also withdrew Hungary from the Warsaw Pact. That was too much for Khrushchev, who sent Soviet tanks rolling into Budapest and other Hungarian cities on November 1. After a few days of brave but doomed fighting in the streets, the Hungarian resistance was crushed. Nagy was arrested, imprisoned, tortured, and finally executed in 1958.

Before the invasion, the American CP's National Committee had adopted a resolution declaring that Soviet military intervention would violate "the essence of the Leninist concept of self-determination." Foster did not attend the meeting, and Dennis, in an ominous portent for the reformers, abstained on the vote. A week later, while Hungarian freedom fighters were dying on the barricades, Dennis declared in a letter to the editor printed in the Daily Worker that the Red Army was entirely justified in eliminating "an imperialist salient threatening the vital security of all the peoples' democracies and the USSR." That Dennis had to resort to a letter to the editor to get his views expressed in the newspaper was itself unprecedented. In any case, his personal commitment to reshaping the Party along the lines favored by the reformers, always shaky, now collapsed.[110]

The CP's Old Guard, as so many, many times in the past, rallied around the battle cry "Defend the Soviet Union." When the National Committee met again on November 18, it found itself hopelessly deadlocked on the question of Hungary. According to rough notes that survive the meeting, Gates warned that "membership is questioning very basis of socialism" because of the Soviet invasion of Hungary. "Split here," he predicted, and "one view must prevail." But not all the reformers were ready to join Gates in unequivocal condemnation of the Soviet action, fearing a fascist resurgence in Hungary or Western intervention. In the end, the National Committee neither condemned nor endorsed the invasion.[111]

For George Charney, chairman of the New York State Communist Party, events in Hungary in the fall of 1956, even more than the Khrushchev secret speech, were the "final blow to the illusory structure we had created and lived with for a generation."[112] The suppression of the Hungarian Revolution hastened the departure of the reform-minded among the rank and file. As one New York Communist, identified by the initials "T. M." in their letter to the *Daily Worker*, wrote:

> I have been a member of the Communist Party for 19 years and of the YCL for five years before that. When the "Stalin revelations" broke last spring . . . I felt there was still hope, that if we really analyzed and corrected our mistakes we could still become the party to lead the American people to socialism. But now I do not want to belong to an organization whose members feel socialism should be imposed on the ends of bayonets.[113]

The CP held a national convention in New York City in February 1957, with the reform wing still nominally in control. But the most pressing issues facing the Party, including whether to reject the Leninist model for a new type of organization, were avoided, in a bid for unity among the competing factions. The convention adopted a resolution stating that American Communism was "based on Marxist-Leninist principles as interpreted by the Communist Party of our country," which Gates's followers voted for but disliked because they no longer considered themselves Leninists, and Foster's followers voted for but disliked because they disapproved of Communists in any country, outside the Soviet Union, feeling free to "interpret" Marxist-Leninism as they saw fit.[114] At the end, Gates,

Dennis, Foster, and Foster's ally Benjamin Davis stood together before the delegates, in a symbolic show of comradeship that fooled no one. Such gestures only hastened the departure of those who hoped to reform the movement. "This was our dilemma," Charney recalled. "We could not continue without compromises; we could not compromise without adding to the confusion and demoralization in our ranks."[115]

Foster won by outlasting his opponents. "The orthodox wing led by Foster," Starobin noted, "did not have the votes and did not win the argument. They had no Party left, either, but they held the franchise. To them that was all that mattered."[116] Lenin's maxim, "Better Fewer, But Better," as a guiding principle of recruitment to Bolshevik ranks was Foster's, taken to the extreme. As he remarked to Dorothy Healey, at the convention's end, "It's better to have fifty true members than fifty thousand people who are not genuine Communists."[117]

Numerically he was on his way to achieving that goal. The CP was reduced to only 5,000 members at the end of 1958, and only 3,000 by 1959. (It was by then one-seventh the size it had been three years earlier, one-twentieth of the size it had been a decade earlier.)[118]

In Los Angeles, the CP had survived the worst of McCarthyism better than the rest of the Party, retaining 3,800 members in 1955 of the 5,000 it had in 1948. But that number would be down to 1,500 by the end of 1957, and fewer than 500 a year or so later. In March 1958, twenty-six leading California Communists, including Oleta O'Connor Yates and four other California Smith Act defendants, publicly resigned from the Party. Dorothy Healey, who remained in the Party, recalled with regret:

> My generation was leaving, the generation that had grown up in
> the Young Communist League, that had a great deal of experience
> in both mass work and in Party leadership. . . . It was a far more
> significant thing than we'd recognized at the time, just in terms

of competency, just to be able to do . . . the ordinary things that preoccupied you 90% of the time as a revolutionary.[119]

California remained in the hands of the reformers, but by May 1957, enough reformers had resigned from the New York party organization for the Foster forces to regain control of the CP's largest district. John Gates soldiered on, declaring, "I have not lost hope . . . that the opponents of our new policies will be decisively defeated."[120] But Foster's allies starved the *Daily Worker* for funds, and the newspaper published its final issue on January 13, 1958, after thirty-two years of publication, to be replaced by a weekly *The Worker* under orthodox control (on the West Coast the *People's World* was also cut back to a weekly edition, although it remained somewhat more freewheeling than the East Coast paper). Gates finally announced his own resignation on January 10, 1958, declaring that the CP "had ceased to be an effective force for democracy, peace, and socialism in the United States."[121]

The CP National Committee with its new (old) Stalinist majority responded, "There is no place in the Party for a Gates or his ideology. The departure of such individuals will not injure but will strengthen the party."[122] In a curious echo of this claim, Congressman Francis Walter of Pennsylvania, chairman of the House Un-American Activities Committee, declared in 1958 that the Communist Party in the United States represented "a greater menace than before. It has long since divested itself of unreliable elements. Those who remain are the hard-core disciplined agents of the Kremlin on American soil."[123]

The reformers who left the Party in 1956–1958 were not drawn to the political extremes of some of their predecessors. Repudiating Stalinism and Leninism, many remained socialists, at least at first. They did not become FBI informers, or name names before investigating committees, or publish lurid confessions of real or imagined past misdeeds. Nor did they band together as a left opposition, having no desire to replicate the futile clannishness of the Trotskyists, and other ex-Communist sectarians. Many of the former cadre were distracted by more pressing questions of how to support themselves and their families, since credentials as CP functionaries or *Daily Worker* reporters did not exactly open doors of prospective employers in the late 1950s.

Some former Communists eventually found ways to become politically active again. As Irving Howe noted in the 1960s, in a number of centers of radical activism like New York City, ex-Communists functioned in informal networks, "based on common opinions, feelings, memories." As new political opportunities began opening up, through the civil rights and anti-war movements, "these people were present, ready and eager; they needed no direction from the CP. . . . They were quite capable of working on their own *as if they were working together.*" Mostly they provided support rather than leadership to the new movements of the 1960s. They shared skills and perspective with less experienced activists. Although few were wealthy, some, as Howe noted, could "put up in a pleasant New York apartment visitors from a distant state," a not-insignificant resource.[124]

Ironically, the most influential Old Left group in the 1960s may well have been this informal party of ex-Communists. It was a "party" that could accomplish many of the same things as a more formally organized left-wing organization—everything, that is, except recruit new members. In the aftermath of the de-Stalinization crisis of 1956–1958, for the first time in the twentieth century, the United States was left without any significant national organization espousing socialism. Speaking their own sins was redemptive for the YCL generation—but it marked the end of the road for American Communism as a meaningful movement.

CHAPTER 6

Ashes to Ashes

1959–1991

How long had we been operating out of our depth? We never had, never had lived, an alternative in America. The liberals did because they wanted, and want, the same mixture as before, only better. But we, we never touched that source of life which provides alternatives, meaningful, stark and immense.

—Clancy Sigal, *Going Away: A Report, a Memoir* (1961)

Hegel remarks somewhere that all great world-historic facts and personages appear, so to speak, twice. He forgot to add: the first time as tragedy, the second time as farce.

—Karl Marx, *The Eighteenth Brumaire of Louis Bonaparte* (1852)

The unnamed protagonist of Clancy Sigal's autobiographical novel *Going Away* drives from Los Angeles to New York in November 1956 in a borrowed convertible, checking in on friends along the way, his trip punctuated by reports on the car radio about fighting in Budapest between Hungarians and the invading Red Army. Twenty-nine years old, the son of radical union organizers, on the verge of nervous breakdown, he has spent the past decade on the margins of the Communist Party. The old comrades he encounters on his eastward journey are disillusioned and despairing. Halfway across the country, Sigal's protagonist telephones a woman he knew from a union-organizing drive in North Carolina years before: "Almost the first thing she said was, 'Have you been listening to the radio? We worked, turned mimeo machines, we argued and passed resolutions and made enemies out of friends, and look what we got for our pains; tell me what good it did.'"[1]

Clancy Sigal had joined the Communist Party as a teenager in 1942, the year of the Battle of Stalingrad, and left in 1948, disgusted by the

I. F. Stone and Todd Gitlin, Washington, DC, anti-nuclear-weapons demonstration, 1962 (Photo by permission of the Gitlin family)

Communist coup in Czechoslovakia. He wound up blacklisted when he moved to Hollywood as a screenwriter in the early 1950s, hanging on for a few more years working as a talent agent (Humphrey Bogart was one of his clients). By the mid-1950s he considered himself a Trotskyist, although not a very orthodox one. He left the United States in 1957 for a six-month literary fellowship in Paris. Instead of returning home at its conclusion, he stopped off in London and decided to stay, starting a tempestuous romance with novelist Doris Lessing. Lessing could have been a character in *Going Away*: she had joined the Communist movement in Rhodesia as a young woman in the 1940s before moving to London in 1949, and resigned from the British Communist Party following the Soviet invasion of Hungary in 1956. Recognizing a fellow-spirit in Sigal (in her autobiography she called him a "heroic figure" as he wrestled with both his mental health and his hatred for all things Stalinist), she would make him the model for the character Saul Green in her celebrated 1962 novel *The Golden Notebook*.

Sigal was better known in Britain, where he lived for the next three decades, than in his native land. But *Going Away*, published in 1961, took on cult status among some young radicals in the United States, serving as introduction to the complicated, contradictory history of American Communism. Todd Gitlin, a recent Harvard graduate, was among the readers encountering it in the early 1960s. Unlike Sigal, Gitlin had no family ties to the Left, although like many other young people in those years he found himself drawn to folk music when he was in college, sparking an interest in radical traditions. He read *The Golden Notebook* during his final semester at Harvard, before discovering *Going Away* six months later. This was shortly after he was elected president of the fledgling campus radical group Students for a Democratic Society, which in 1963 had all of 500 members scattered among a few elite liberal arts colleges in the Northeast and flagship public universities in the Midwest. "In my bookish way," he recalled years later,

I was seeking a "usable past" while struggling with an uneasy relationship between witnessing history and participating in it. In some way, I intuited that the dilemmas we were facing as young radicals were already built into the situation of being left wing in a country that was not. And I sensed that these were dilemmas about which Clancy Sigal would have something important to say.

Gitlin admired Sigal's yearning for a radical movement based on something more humane and reliable than dogma and discipline. He was drawn to *Going Away*'s vision of a political movement resembling a "circle of friends" very different from what the Communist Party had offered Sigal in younger days: "I loved the long sections he devoted to political sagas. . . . Above all, I was touched by his urgent need to know if it was 'possible to have a small circle of friends, friends of grace and purpose, not incestuously, but on a basis of mutual respect, work, and a kind of humorous, informal dignity in the United States.'"

Gitlin found *Going Away*, in equal parts, inspiring and tragic—and also reassuring: "I turned the final page and lay in bed thinking, *This will never happen to me.* My movement was different. Stalin and McCarthy were dead. The New Left was independent, unillusioned, rambunctious, joyful. Lucky me, I had the sixties to look forward to."[2]

The Communist Party also looked forward to the coming decade as a time of renewal. In 1959 it acquired a new general secretary who came into office promising to "foster in our Party a freshness, a boldness, a situation in which we are not afraid of probing new paths, new ideas, new angles, and of freely discussing them."[3]

Gus Hall would have a long time to fulfill that promise—forty-one years in total, from 1959 until his death at age ninety in 2000 (for the last fourteen years of that span, his title was changed to chairman, in place of the traditional general secretary). That was thirteen years longer than Joseph Stalin held the post of general secretary of the Soviet Communist Party, and roughly the same number of years that Mao Zedong, under various titles, led the Chinese Communist Party. Hall determined the shape of American Communism in those years as much as Stalin and Mao shaped their own parties, although the consequences in his case inclined, especially near the end, more toward farce than to tragedy.

Hall was born Arvo Kustaa Halberg in Cherry Township, Minnesota, in 1910 to Finnish immigrant parents who were active in the IWW and became early members of the Communist Party. He left school at fifteen to work as a logger in Minnesota's forests in support of his family (his father had been blacklisted from working in the Mesabi Iron Range mines for his leftist sympathies). Halberg joined the Communist movement as a teenager in 1927. In 1931 he was sent to Moscow for studies at the Lenin School, returning to Minneapolis in 1933 to lead the Young Communist League in

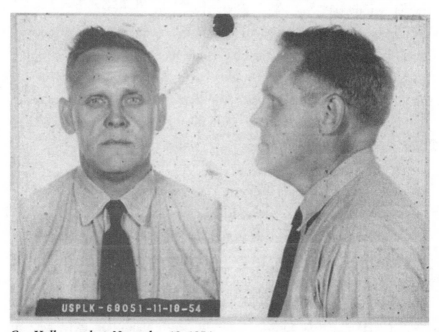

USPLK-68051-11-18-54

Gus Hall mug shot, November 18, 1954
(Photo courtesy of Bureau of Prisons/Getty Images)

the city. Having changed his name to Gus Hall in 1934, he was active in strikes in Minnesota and Ohio, and was one of several score Communists hired as organizers for the Steel Workers Organizing Committee drive in 1936. He was appointed leader of the Communist Party in Youngstown, and then in Cleveland, Ohio. In the final year of World War II, he served in the Pacific as a navy machinist's mate.

Discharged from military service in the spring of 1946, he became leader of the CP's Ohio district and in 1947 was appointed to the Party's ruling twelve-member National Board. One of eleven Communists convicted in the Smith Act trial of 1949, Hall went underground in 1951, only to be arrested later that year in Mexico. Released from federal penitentiary in 1957, having served a total of five and a half years of what had grown to an eight-year sentence due to his flight, he set out to replace Eugene Dennis as general secretary.[4]

Hall looked the part of a tough guy used to hard manual labor; he was just under six feet tall and barrel-chested. He wasn't an eloquent speaker or writer or, for all his hearty endorsement of the science of Marxism-Leninism as an infallible guide to understanding the world, much of a theorist. But that only added to his air of plainspoken proletarian authenticity. The intellectuals who flocked to the Party's banners in the 1930s were mostly long gone; Hall, the high school dropout, who had spent his time in prison lifting weights rather than reading Orwell, had proven his reliability.

Hall was absent during the Party's fiercest internal battles in the 1940s and 1950s (serving in the Pacific when Earl Browder was overthrown in 1945, and sitting in prison during the de-Stalinization crisis in 1956). This proved an asset in his bid for leadership because his political views were not well-known, and he could portray himself as a reformer to the reform-minded, and as a hard-liner to the unreconstructed.[5]

Once Hall's parole ended in 1959, he began his campaign for general secretary. He traveled around the country, including a two-week stay in

Los Angeles. Southern California was the most reform-minded district left in the CP after the mass exodus of 1956–1958, and Hall played to its preferences. At a meeting with district leaders, Dorothy Healey recalled: "We told him bluntly that to us the decisive question facing the Party was establishing its independence from Soviet direction. . . . 'Not only do I agree with you,' he said, 'but as a matter of fact I'm convinced that for the Soviet Union's own good we have to maintain our independent outlook.'"[6]

Hall accused Dennis of a cowardly violation of discipline (for supposedly flouting orders to join the underground in 1951), as well as skimming Party funds for his own use. For their part, the Soviets seemed content with Dennis's continued leadership. But he was not in good health, suffering a stroke before the Party's December 1959 national convention, which he could not attend. At the conclusion of the gathering, the CP's National Committee voted to replace Dennis with Hall, designating Dennis as national chairman, and William Z. Foster, also in ill-health, as chairman emeritus.[7]

The older generation of leaders was passing from the scene. Both Dennis and Foster died soon after, Dennis in his apartment in New York City in January 1961, Foster in a hospital in Moscow in September of the same year. Another venerable Party leader, Elizabeth Gurley Flynn, the "Rebel Girl" who succeeded Dennis as national chairman, also died in Moscow in 1964.[8]

In his keynote address to the Party convention in 1959, Hall quoted Mao Zedong on the need to adopt Marxism to Chinese conditions, suggesting that Communists in the United States should adapt their own thinking and practice to fit American realities. The *New York Times* reporter characterized Hall's speech as signaling "a sharp turn to the right" for the Party under his leadership, perhaps returning to the politics it had embraced under Browder fifteen years earlier.[9]

But that was far from the case, certainly not if what was meant by *turning right* was reforming the Party's undemocratic internal structure or acting with any real measure of independence from Soviet control. Gus Hall proved neither a rightist or a leftist in terms of the CP's internal politics, neither Browderite nor Fosterite. Within two years of taking office, he had expelled Alexander Bittelman, a seventy-year-old founding member of the Party, for espousing rightist views, and Milt Rosen, a younger Upstate New York labor organizer, for espousing leftist views. (Rosen, with a small band of former Communists would go on to found the Maoist-oriented Progressive Labor Party, which would play an outsize role in campus radical politics later in the decade.) Hall was, first and foremost, a "Gus Hallite," although that term was not used. What he valued in fellow American Communists was loyalty—personally to him, and, in terms of international politics, to the Soviet Union.[10]

McCarthyism was on the wane following the death of its namesake in 1957, and the Supreme Court decision that same year gutting the Smith Act. But it did not disappear. Well into the new decade the CP remained under official attack, and its top leaders, most of whom like Hall had served time in federal penitentiaries, were understandably concerned about the possibility of a renewed repressive crackdown. House Un-American Activities Committee hearings continued through 1969, although toward the end HUAC focused more on the New Left than the Communists. In 1956 the FBI launched a sustained political assault on the Communist Party under the rubric of COINTELPRO (short for Counter Intelligence Program), consisting of secret efforts to disrupt, sabotage, and discredit the Party's operations, often involving forged documents, the planting of false stories with reporters, and illegal surveillance. This covert campaign continued through the 1960s, only ending when a group of antiwar activists broke into an FBI office in Pennsylvania and released the COINTELPRO files they found there to the *Washington Post* and other newspapers. Here too the program's animus was increasingly focused in the 1960s on non-Communists (including Dr. Martin Luther King Jr., the Black Panthers, and campus activists).[11]

Communists were also targeted by the Subversive Activities Control Board (SACB) established by the 1950 Internal Security Act (better known as the McCarran Act after its principal Senate sponsor, Patrick McCarran of Nevada). In 1962 fifteen national and district Party leaders received letters from the US attorney general ordering them to register themselves with the SACB as members of an organization that was "a participant in a worldwide criminal conspiracy under the control of the Soviet Union." Failure to do so—in other words, failure to incriminate themselves as criminal conspirators and foreign agents—would subject them to imprisonment and fines. Communists fought back in the courts in what turned into a three-year struggle. In the meantime, to lower exposure of its members to McCarran Act provisions, the CP curtailed local meetings and national gatherings. The cases against Communist leaders were only dropped after a 1965 ruling by the US Supreme Court that the provision of the McCarran Act requiring registration was unconstitutional. By then, the postwar Red Scare had been in effect for twenty years.[12]

Although McCarthyism lingered, signs of new possibilities for American radicalism multiplied in the early 1960s, particularly on the nation's university and college campuses. This was a different kind of movement: innovative, locally based, committed to nonviolence and civil disobedience. Four Black freshmen at the Agricultural and Technical College of North Carolina, acting completely on their own, sat in at the lunch counter of a segregated Woolworth's store in downtown Greensboro, North Carolina, on February 1, 1960, refusing to leave when denied service. Hundreds more joined them in Greensboro the following week. As news of the sit-ins spread, tens of thousands more sat in at Woolworth's lunch counters across the South. Such direct-action tactics, "putting your body on the line" as it came to be called in movement circles, achieved results: that summer, the Greensboro Woolworth's quietly began to serve Black customers. Coming off the spring's upheaval, a new independent civil rights youth group, the Student Nonviolent Coordinating Committee (SNCC), was founded at a conference in Raleigh, North Carolina. SNCC's members came from a variety of backgrounds, but their inspiration was thoroughly indigenous to the United States, the greatest influence on the group in its early days being the Black church.[13]

The other major campus activist group emerging in the early 1960s, Students for a Democratic Society (SDS), had its roots in the socialist movement, growing out of the old Student League for Industrial Democracy. Its members were primarily white, but it too drew inspiration from the civil rights movement. Its only connection to the Communist Party came through the involvement of a number of "red diaper babies" in its formative days, including Steve Max, son of Alan Max (one of the reform-minded *Daily Worker* editors during the de-Stalinization crisis). But the offspring of Communists and ex-Communists who joined in the early days were drawn to SDS precisely because it seemed nothing like the old CP youth groups.[14]

The sit-ins of 1960 were followed by the Freedom Rides of 1961, followed by the Southern Christian Leadership Conference's Birmingham campaign in the spring of 1963 and the March on Washington in August of that year, followed by the Freedom Summer voter registration campaign in Mississippi in 1964, followed by the first major campus protest led by the Free Speech Movement at the University of California at Berkeley in the fall of 1964, followed by the Selma voting rights campaign in the spring of 1965. The spring of 1965 also saw a major escalation of the American war in Vietnam, as well as the first major demonstration against the war, a march on Washington in April organized by SDS. And all through that tumultuous time, there was a "folk revival," in which Pete Seeger emerged as a revered figure. "If I Had a Hammer," originally cowritten in

1949 by Seeger and Lee Hayes to honor the Smith Act defendants, became a hit for the newly founded trio Peter, Paul, and Mary, who included it on their debut album in 1962 and performed it in 1963 at the Newport Folk Festival and at the March on Washington before hundreds of thousands of enthusiastic listeners. This was only fourteen years since fans of Seeger and Paul Robeson had been assaulted as they departed from the concert grounds at Peekskill, New York. The times they were definitely a-changin', and Seeger (and some songs written while he was a Communist in the 1940s) lived on to serve other causes in the 1960s. Mary Travers liked to refer to her trio as "Seeger's Raiders."[15]

Young activists in the early 1960s embraced some older veterans of the Communist Left like Seeger (who had quietly resigned from the Party by the start of the 1950s), without endorsing, or knowing much about, the movement from which he came. New Leftists sometimes described themselves as being "anti-anti-Communist," which among other things meant that while they were not themselves Communists, they saw no point in continuing on principle to exclude Party members, current or past, from common political endeavors. Bob Moses, who pioneered SNCC's voter registration efforts in Mississippi, was the principal organizer for the Freedom Summer campaign in 1964. When it came under attack for accepting help from the National Lawyers Guild, a group that traced its roots to Popular Front days, Moses was unmoved. As he impatiently told a reporter in Jackson, Mississippi, that summer, Freedom Summer had no intention of imposing a political litmus test on groups and individuals contributing to the fight for voting rights: "We can't call up people in the field one day and say now the Communist issue will be imposed. . . . We really look upon all these things—the political arguments of the thirties and forties, the impressions of the whites—as impositions from the outside."[16]

That was a promising sign for the Party's prospects for a comeback. So were opportunities for Party leaders to bring their message directly to college and university audiences as the old bans on Communist speakers were repealed. In the early 1960s, Gus Hall spoke on dozens of campuses across the country and sometimes attracted audiences of several thousand students at a time. But the students who showed up were generally present out of curiosity, or as a demonstration of political tolerance—not pro-Communist, but anti-anti-Communist, which was different. If they were drawn to a left-wing group, it was not going to be the Communist Party, or its newly organized youth group, the W. E. B. Du Bois Clubs.

W. E. B. Du Bois, antagonistic to the Communists in the 1930s, drew close to them in the 1940s and 1950s. In 1961, age ninety-three, he joined the Party, shortly before moving to Ghana, where he died in 1963. Founded in his memory in 1964, supposedly but not really independent of the Party, the Du Bois Clubs never grew beyond a thousand or so members nationwide and collapsed in 1969.[17]

Some individual Communists found ways to contribute to the new insurgencies. Prominent among them was Bettina Aptheker, daughter of Herbert Aptheker, the latter a pioneering historian of American slavery and an important (and, at the time, highly orthodox) figure in Party leadership. Bettina, who got involved in civil rights protests while a teenager in Brooklyn and joined the Party in 1962, went on to become a leading figure in the Free Speech Movement (FSM) in Berkeley where she was an undergraduate. Her Communist affiliation was noted sourly by US Senate investigators (Headline: "Bettina Aptheker Identified as Figure in Berkeley Riot"), and with the whimsical sexism also typical of the era in a lengthy profile in the *New York Times* (Headline: "California Coed, 21, Is the American Communist Party's Foremost Ingenue"). When Berkeley students voted in 1965 for representatives to a newly established Campus Rules Committee to advise the university chancellor on the regulation of student political activities, the Rioting Ingenue turned out to be their top choice. However well-publicized her role in the movement, Aptheker was acting as an individual, not as the spearhead of some carefully thought-out Communist strategy to win young people to the cause. The Party, cool to the FSM campaign despite Aptheker's leading role, failed to reap any significant following among young activists. When she and her then husband Jack Kurzweil became active in a Party club in San Jose a few years later, they were the only members under the age of fifty.[18]

More often, it was ex-Communists, not current members, who contributed to the revival of protest in the early 1960s. They were not necessarily anti-Communist but no longer paid dues to an organization that they felt was too discredited to be worth their support. Among their number was Oliver Leeds, a Harlem-born child of Grenadian immigrants, who joined the Young Communist League in 1938, and after military service in World War II, the Communist Party. He and his wife Marjorie Leeds both left the Party in the mid-1950s. Marjorie got involved with the Brooklyn chapter of the Congress of Racial Equality (CORE) a few years later, and in 1960 invited her husband to join her on picket lines supporting the Woolworth's boycott. Still wedded to some of his old political assumptions, Oliver Leeds was initially suspicious of CORE as being too "social-democratic" (CORE traced its origins to a group organized in 1942 by Socialists and pacifists). Interviewed in 1988, a year before his death, he defined his politics as being "a communist with a small 'c.'" The political skills he had developed in his years as a Communist proved invaluable, and Leeds went on to become a key leader in the 1960s of what became one of the most militant and effective CORE chapters in the country. But, like Bettina Aptheker in Berkeley, his individual example brought the Party no political gains.[19]

It wasn't so much that the Communists' political stance on any given issue was wrong or unappealing to younger activists, but the very language in which they couched their understanding of the world seemed, in a word much favored among the young at the time, "irrelevant." At the start of the decade, the radical sociologist C. Wright Mills, older than but influential in New Left circles, urged the activists of the new generation to abandon the "metaphysic" left over from "Victorian Marxism," that is, the belief that the industrial working class was "*the* historic agency" of revolutionary social change.[20] In April 1965, SDS president Paul Potter gave the main speech at the anti–Vietnam War march in Washington, DC, calling upon his listeners to "name the system" that produced the war, and then somewhat surprisingly failing to do so himself. Explaining his omission later, Potter said, "I refused to call it capitalism because capitalism was for me and my generation an inadequate description of the evils of America—a hollow, dead word, tied to the thirties."[21]

The New Left, centered on groups like SDS and SNCC, grew from small beginnings to include hundreds of thousands of adherents in the later 1960s. Some older Communists, like Dorothy Healey and Gil Green, welcomed the movement's growth as a healthy development. Hall, in contrast, regarded the new generation of student activists with suspicion, dismissing them for representing "petit bourgeois ideology."[22]

Some older Communists seemed to go out of their way to antagonize their younger counterparts elsewhere on the Left. The CP prided itself on its interracial tradition, symbolized by the veteran Black Communist Henry Winston's appointment as Party chairman in 1966, a post he would hold until his death twenty years later. But younger Black activists were increasingly unwilling to work in or with racially mixed groups like the Communist Party, a problem exacerbated by the Party's hostility to the politics and symbols associated with "Black Power." *The Worker*, the weekly newspaper edited by Black Communist James Jackson, was highly critical of Malcolm X's racial separatism, even after he broke with the Nation of Islam. When SNCC, inspired by Malcolm's vision, founded an independent political party to mobilize Black voters in Lowndes County, Alabama, in 1966, and chose as its symbol a snarling black panther (their effort predated and was separate from the California-based Black Panthers), the fifty-two-year-old Jackson condemned SNCC's choice of animal avatar. As the *New York Times* reported, "James E. Jackson, a leading Negro Communist . . . told newsmen he wished the Alabama group had chosen 'a better symbol than the black panther.' He said he would have preferred 'an American eagle with black and white feathers.'"[23] A black-and-white American eagle was not destined to fly with the younger generation of Black radicals in the 1960s.

The Los Angeles FBI office filed a report in April 1965 about a meeting that Gil Green had recently held with local African-American Communists, revealing just how isolated the Party was from a vital constituency. There was an informer in the group, who reported to the FBI that Green said: "The party's strength among the Negro people is very weak. GREEN stated that there had been little if any recruiting of Negroes into the party, and that with the current upsurge in the Negro movement, the percentage of Negroes in the party is still only one to two percent of the total party membership."[24]

Assuming 5,000 dues-paying Communists nationwide in 1965 (a generous estimate), if 2 percent of them were African-American that meant there were only a hundred Black Communists in the entire country (or fifty, if they represented 1 percent). In contrast, in the late 1940s there had been close to 500 Black members of the CP in Los Angeles alone, roughly 10 percent of local Party membership.[25]

In June 1966, the Party held its first national convention since the one in 1959 when Gus Hall became general secretary. Hall declared to the assembled delegates that the Communist Party was "again the largest and most decisive influence on the left." If by "largest" he meant in terms of membership, that was assuredly not the case. He provided no actual numbers, although on other occasions in decades to come he would claim that the Party had grown to as many as 20,000 members.[26]

Undoubtedly Hall would have preferred to lead a bigger organization. But attracting recruits was never his top priority. Rather, first and foremost he sought to reap the benefits of loyal support of the Soviet Union. Denied a passport as long as he was under indictment for violating the McCarran Act, Hall could not visit Moscow in his first years in office, as former general secretaries in the 1920s and 1930s did on an annual basis. For the time being, he could only communicate with Soviet leaders through intermediaries, or through correspondence.

Hall's first years in office also coincided with the emergence of the Sino-Soviet split. American Communists had welcomed the triumph of the Chinese Communist revolution in 1949, but in 1960 Mao Zedong began attacking Soviet leaders as "revisionists" whose emphasis on "peaceful coexistence" represented capitulation to American imperialism. Hall made it clear to Soviet leaders, first Khrushchev and after 1964 Leonid Brezhnev, where his loyalties lay. In 1964, Hall proposed that the Soviet Communist Party establish a new Communist International, "to prevent the communist parties of the world, including the CPUSA, from 'drifting,'" and to counter the influence of the Chinese Communists. That proposal went nowhere.[27]

The following year, in November 1965, he wrote a letter to "Dear Comrade L. Brezhnev," to honor "the glorious stormers and builders of the first Socialist beachhead of world Communism" on the occasion of the forty-eighth anniversary of the Bolshevik Revolution. After several more paragraphs of praise for the Soviet Union and its current leaders, Hall turned to the current unpleasantness in Sino-Soviet relations:

> As you so well know, because you have carried the full weight of the attack, the damage caused by the political insanity expressed by the policies of the Communist Party of China is beyond the scope of estimation. That the peak of the tide of this, history's most serious wave of petty-bourgeois radicalism, has been passed is of the greatest importance. The latest, almost hysterical, proclamation by the leaders of the Communist Party of China is now a reflection of this turning point.[28]

With the restoration of his passport by the State Department in 1966, Hall finally got to meet Brezhnev in Moscow. In the years that followed, the Soviet leader extended repeated invitations to Hall to attend and sometimes address Party Congresses in Moscow. On such occasions Hall flew first class to Moscow, and on arrival was whisked off in a government limousine to comfortable lodgings. The opportunity to deliver an address to thousands of Communist delegates from around the world reinforced Hall's belief that he was a figure of genuine importance in international affairs. He began to look down on the rather better-known Fidel Castro as an immature and late-coming arriviste in the Communist movement.[29]

The price to be paid for these boosts to Hall's self-esteem was his absolute dependability defending Soviet interests, whatever the issue at hand. After his return from Moscow in 1966, at a time when there was growing concern in the United States over the treatment of Soviet Jews, he wrote that during his visit he found "no anti-Semitism in the Soviet Union," but instead met many Soviet Jews who were angry about a "campaign of falsehoods" alleging their beloved country was antisemitic.[30] Ten years later, Hall attended yet another Party Congress in Moscow, at a time when Western European Communists were embracing a new reform-minded "Eurocommunism." British CP leader Gordon McLennan told the gathering that British Communists were committed to constructing socialism on the basis of guarantees of "personal freedom, the plurality of political parties, the independence of trade unions, religious freedom." That received a tepid response from the assembly, few of whom represented countries where such freedoms were valued or practiced. In contrast, as reported by the *New York Times*, "The delegates warmly received Gus Hall [who] made it clear that his party would remain loyal to Moscow, and not follow some Western European Communists who have taken independent positions and even criticized the Soviet Union."[31]

Hall reaped other less visible rewards. In the first two decades of his reign, the American Communist Party received upward of $28 million in secret Soviet subsidies, with senior CP officials (and secret FBI informants) Jack and Morris Childs handling the transfer. Although the Childs brothers retired from both their roles as Communist couriers and FBI agents in the late 1970s, Soviet payments to the CPUSA continued by other means until the end of the 1980s. Some of the funds were invested in banks and businesses, generating additional income. As a result, the CP was able to relaunch a daily newspaper, the *Daily World*, in 1967, and purchase a new downtown Manhattan headquarters at 235 West Twenty-Third Street. Although the American CP was not the only foreign Communist Party subsidized by Moscow, in per capita terms it was almost certainly the most richly rewarded. The money it received in those years exceeded the funds provided the Italian Communist Party, with its 1.5 million members.[32]

With millions of dollars in cash coming in off the books, Hall could spend it as he chose with no accountability to either the Internal Revenue Service or to his own comrades. Party leaders and staff were not highly paid, but Hall awarded bonuses to loyal supporters in the form of envelopes stuffed with money, or all-expenses-paid junkets to the Soviet Union or to Soviet Bloc countries. Hall also skimmed funds for his own use, just as he had accused Eugene Dennis of doing back in 1959. Some of the money was used as a down payment on his Yonkers home, as well as to pay for homes, cars, and vacations for his children and other relatives. Hall vacationed in the Hamptons. When other Party leaders asked him about the source of this financial bounty, he replied that it came from "big donors" who preferred to remain anonymous.[33]

By 1968, the hopeful feelings shared earlier in the decade on both the liberal and radical Left that the United States stood on the brink of meaningful, redemptive reform were increasingly replaced by frustration and anger. Events seemed to be spinning out of control. Racial inequality was no longer regarded as a problem confined to the South, to be extirpated once and for all by the passage of civil rights legislation, but one far more deeply rooted in American society and institutions, affecting the entire country, and with no obvious solutions. Nonviolent protests in the Deep South had given way to urban rioting in northern cities in a succession of "long hot summers." Violence had taken the life of President John F. Kennedy in 1963, followed not five years later by the assassinations of his brother Robert and Dr. Martin Luther King Jr. Militant confrontations were increasingly common on university and college campuses, as student activists, radicalized by the Vietnam War, turned to the tactic of building occupations, most dramatically in the Columbia University strike of April–May 1968. The Democratic Party fell into disarray over issues of racial justice and the Vietnam War, culminating in the street disorders of August 1968 at the Chicago Democratic National Convention. "The Revolution Has Come / Time to Pick Up the Gun!" was a popular chant at rallies of the recently founded Black Panther Party. Meanwhile, Panther leaders like Chicago's Fred Hampton were being targeted and killed in police raids.[34]

Back in 1963 when he was elected president of Students for a Democratic Society (SDS), Todd Gitlin was confident that the New Left represented the advent of a movement capable of avoiding the sins of its Communist predecessor. SDS, Gitlin hoped, would share the values of Clancy Sigal's vision of the ideal radical group: a "small circle of friends, friends of grace and purpose," joined together "on a basis of mutual respect, work, and a kind of humorous, informal dignity." By 1968, SDS's small circle of friends had grown into a sprawling organization of roughly 100,000 adherents. And, in place of "mutual respect," and other virtues it may have possessed in its earlier incarnation, under new leaders SDS was rapidly transforming itself, at least at the national level, into a caricature of the Communist Party at its most extreme and sectarian. This was due in part to the influence of a cadre from the Maoist-oriented Progressive Labor Party (PLP), who moved into SDS en masse after 1965 and brought with them the well-honed factional skills of the Old Left. In response, other factions sprang up, preaching variations of the Maoist dogmas that the PLP imported into the student Left.[35]

In the spring of 1969 SDS dissolved into a morass of internecine ideological warfare, with some of its best-known leaders founding the soon-to-be notorious "Weatherman" faction, who by year's end devolved into an underground terrorist group of a few dozen cadres. Most of SDS's tens of thousands of members simply dispersed, but some thousands were drawn into one or another of the competing "New Communist" parties that sprang up in the early 1970s, including the Revolutionary Communist Party, the Communist Party (Marxist-Leninist), the Communist Workers' Party, and the Communist Labor Party of the United States of North America, groups whose internal organization and rhetorical style echoed the worst aspects of Third Period US Communism. While the "independent, unillusioned, rambunctious, joyful" movement that Todd Gitlin had envisioned when reading *Going Away* in the early 1960s survived in a few post-1969 corners of the New Left, especially in the localized "underground press" that carried on its legacy, its main national organizational presence, SDS, had been killed by the Leninist temptation.[36]

While the New Left splintered, the Communists once again were experiencing their own internal divisions, once again because of decisions taken in Moscow. In January 1968, a reform-minded Communist named Alexander Dubček replaced Stalinist hard-liner Antonín Novotný as first secretary of the Communist Party of Czechoslovakia. In what came to be known as Prague Spring, Dubček oversaw a program of political and cultural liberalization that he described as "Socialism with a Human Face," relaxing restrictions on the press, speech, and travel. There was even talk of a gradual return to the multiparty democracy the country had known before the Second World War. Reform-minded Communists in the United States looked at these developments as a model for democratizing their own movement, as did many Western European Communists.[37]

Prague Spring was brought to an abrupt end in the third week of August when the Red Army, along with troops from three other Soviet Bloc nations, invaded and occupied Czechoslovakia. Twelve years after the suppression of the Hungarian Revolution, Soviet leaders were no less determined to preserve their domination over Eastern Europe. There were nonviolent protests in the streets of Prague against the invaders, but to no avail. Dubček was removed from office and replaced by a Soviet-picked hard-liner.[38]

The Communist parties of Britain, France, and Italy, moving toward a political stance more independent of the Soviet Union, condemned the invasion. In the United States, the Southern California district of the Communist Party led by Dorothy Healey also denounced the attack on Czechoslovakia, as did the West Coast Communist newspaper, *People's World*, edited by Al Richmond. But on the East Coast, the *Daily World* applauded the Soviet Union's decision. Gus Hall declared flatly that "the need for military action by one's Socialist neighbors in defense of Socialism . . . is not going to destroy Czechoslovakia's sovereignty—it is going to strengthen it."[39]

At a meeting of the CP's National Committee over Labor Day weekend, Healey, Richmond, Gil Green, Bettina Aptheker, and a few others voted to condemn the invasion. (Bettina's historian father Herbert Aptheker was in the majority who endorsed the invasion, and quickly turned out a book for the Party's publishing house defending the suppression of Prague Spring.) Hall's own speech supporting the Soviet invasion was subsequently published in full in the official Soviet Communist Party newspaper *Pravda*. "Under Gus's leadership," Healey observed, "the American CP had picked up the dubious distinction of being the chief ideological sheepdog in the international Communist movement, barking on command when any of the other lambs threatened to stray from the fold."[40]

In her dismay over the Party's embrace of the Soviet invasion of Czechoslovakia, Healey resigned as leader of the Southern California district later that year, and quit the Party altogether in 1973. Before she stepped down, she signed off on one political innovation that would have a dramatic impact in the years to follow, and that was the creation of an all-Black Party unit in LA known as the Che-Lumumba Club. Its best-known member was Angela Davis.

Born in Birmingham, Alabama, in 1944, Angela Yvonne Davis was the daughter of two schoolteachers. Her father also owned a service station, which offered the family a measure of economic independence. Angela's mother, Sallye Bell Davis, was a respected political activist in Birmingham's Black community, her involvement stretching back to the Scottsboro Boys defense campaign in the 1930s. In the 1940s she was a leading figure in the CP-organized Southern Negro Youth Conference (SNYC), headquartered in Birmingham.[41]

As a child, Angela lived in a section of Birmingham where Black families were displacing white families. In the 1940s and 1950s, the Ku Klux Klan bombed Black homes so often in her neighborhood that it became informally known as "Dynamite Hill." Later, when she was a college student, Klan members set off a bomb in the Sixteenth Street Baptist Church in downtown Birmingham on September 15, 1963, killing four young girls and blinding another; Davis knew their older siblings.

Sallye Davis's political links to the circle of SNYC veterans who settled in Harlem in the 1940s and 1950s, including Esther and James Jackson, and Louis and Dorothy Burnham, provided her daughter with a glimpse of a life far removed from the limited opportunities afforded Black children in Birmingham. The summer before she began attending the city's segregated schools, she stayed with the Burnhams in Harlem, where she had white as well as Black playmates, sat where she wanted on the city's buses, and went to the same movie theaters as white children. At age fifteen she returned north to live in Brooklyn, thanks to an American Friends Service

Committee program placing African-American children from the South in integrated northern schools. She spent the last two years of high school at Elisabeth Irwin High School (a progressive private school in Greenwich Village nicknamed "the Little Red School House" for its employment of a number of Communist teachers blacklisted from the city's public schools). Her circle of friends in Brooklyn included Bettina Aptheker, Eugene Dennis Jr. (son of the late general secretary) and other teenaged Communists. They founded a youth group called Advance, which took part in peace and civil rights demonstrations, including picketing a Woolworth's store in downtown Brooklyn in solidarity with the southern sit-ins in the spring of 1960.[42]

After high school, Davis attended Brandeis University in Massachusetts, where she encountered the Marxist philosopher Herbert Marcuse. She went on to a graduate program in philosophy at the University of Frankfurt, returning to the United States in 1967 to study for her PhD with Marcuse, who had in the meantime accepted a position at the University of California, San Diego.

In Southern California, Davis was drawn to the militancy of the Black Panther Party and other Black-nationalist groups. She still retained the socialist sympathies of her high school days, but initially showed no interest in joining the Communist Party, viewing its members "as being too conservative, and behind the times in their uncritical attitude toward the working class," by which she meant white workers in the United States. But then she learned about the Che-Lumumba Club.[43]

Responding to the Black Power movement's emphasis on racial pride and self-determination, Charlene Mitchell, a veteran Black Communist in Los Angeles, oversaw the formation in 1967 of a local all-Black Party group named for the famous Latin American guerrilla leader Che Guevara and the Congolese independence leader Patrice Lumumba, both of whom died in the revolutionary struggle. Other local Black leaders involved in the club's creation included Mitchell's younger brother Franklin Alexander and sister-in-law Kendra Alexander. While the Communist Party was

an interracial organization, there was no reason, Mitchell and the Alex-
anders (and Healey) thought, why it could not make organizational concessions to the current go-it-alone mood among the angry and disaffected
young African-Americans on college campuses and in the urban ghetto.
As usual, Los Angeles remained an outlier in terms of political innovation
in the Communist movement. Facing official disapproval from Gus Hall
and others in Party leadership, the Che-Lumumba Club experiment did
not spread to other cities.[44]

Davis soon came in contact with Dorothy Healey. As Healey recalled
her initial impression,

> Angela was a young Black woman not yet twenty-four years old,
> strikingly beautiful, intelligent, articulate, and poised. She clearly
> had the potential to be anything she wanted. . . . But she was con-
> fronted with a dilemma: she had these genuine intellectual gifts,
> yet had to prove herself at a moment when anti-intellectualism
> was running rampant in the movement, when the only thing that
> seemed to count was proving yourself . . . able to stand up to the
> Man with a gun.[45]

In her autobiography, Davis described a series of personal meetings
with Healey, where they "had long, involved discussions—sometimes
arguments—about the Party, its role within the movement, its potential as
the vanguard party of the working class."[46] After six months of disheart-
ening involvement in the turbulent and sometimes-murderous factionalism of the late-sixties Black Power movement in Los Angeles, she changed
her mind about the Communists. The existence of the Che-Lumumba
Club proved the key element in her decision to join the Party in July 1968.
"I needed to become part of a serious revolutionary *party*," she recalled.
"I wanted an anchor, a base, a mooring. I needed comrades with whom I
could share a common ideology."[47]

Davis first attracted national attention in the fall of 1969. She had been hired as a visiting assistant professor of philosophy at the University of California, Los Angeles, when the University's Board of Regents, invoking McCarthy-era regulations against the employment of Communists, fired her. UCLA faculty voted overwhelmingly to condemn the regents. Davis was allowed to offer a noncredit course in the fall semester pending a final decision. Governor Ronald Reagan, coming up for reelection the following year, weighed in on the controversy, threatening to cut the UCLA budget if Davis continued to teach on its campus. Students rallied to her defense, with more than two thousand attending her opening lecture on the legacy of Frederick Douglass. A Los Angeles Superior Court judge ruled that Davis could not be fired simply for being a member of the Communist Party, and the university decided her course would count for credit after all. It was a singular victory for academic freedom, and the controversy transformed Angela Davis, at age twenty-five, into the most famous young radical in the country.[48]

In the meantime, Davis helped found a group known as the Soledad Brothers Defense Committee. Soledad Correctional Training Facility, located in the Salinas Valley in California, was a hotbed of Black-inmate political activism in the late 1960s. It was also an extremely violent place. In January 1970, in retaliation for the killing of three Black inmates by a white correctional officer a few days earlier, a different white guard, John Mills, was killed by unknown assailants. Three Black inmates, including twenty-eight-year-old George L. Jackson, were charged with his murder. Jackson had been sentenced to one year to life back in 1961, as a teenager, for taking part in a seventy-dollar robbery of a gas station. In the years since then he had become a committed revolutionary. At the initiative of the Che-Lumumba Club, Black activists in California rallied to the defense of the three accused men. As it turned out, Jackson would never come to trial. Following the publication of his book *Soledad Brother: The Prison Letters of George Jackson* in the fall of 1970, he became the country's

Angela Davis (right) and Jonathan Jackson (left) at Los Angeles march on behalf of the Soledad Brothers, June 19, 1970

(Photo by Bettmann Archive/ Getty Images)

best-known advocate for prisoner's rights, but less than a year later, in August 1971, he was killed in an escape attempt. In March 1972 the other two Soledad Brothers, Fleeta Drumgo and John Clutchette, were acquitted by a San Francisco jury of the charge of murdering the guard.[49]

Angela Davis's life would be profoundly altered by her involvement in the Soledad Brothers campaign in 1970. That spring and summer, she developed an intimate personal relationship with George Jackson, to the limited extent possible under the circumstances. She got to know Jackson's family, and Jonathan, Jackson's seventeen-year-old brother, began to serve as one of her bodyguards. Her impassioned public defense of the Soledad Brothers also resulted in her being dismissed for a second and final time by the University of California Regents, this time charged with giving "inflammatory speeches" off campus.[50]

"Self-defense" was becoming a watchword on the Left in the late 1960s, inspired by the Black Panthers, who became famous for carrying weapons as they monitored the conduct of police on the streets of Oakland, California. Younger Communists were not immune to the appeal of militant, sometimes threatening posturing. As Bettina Aptheker noted self-critically, some years later, "the revolutionary rhetoric of the times equated manhood with guns and armed struggle." Nor was that only true of men: "We women on the Left and in the Communist Party also equated our own liberation with armed insurrection."[51] Some Party members, including Angela Davis, began frequenting gun shops. Between January 1968 and August 1970, she purchased four guns, legally and under her own name: a pistol, two carbines, and a shotgun. This was a period when she was regularly receiving death threats. "For a black person growing up in the South," she later explained, "guns were a normal fact of life."[52]

Whatever reasons Davis had to purchase weapons, "self-defense" proved a dangerously slippery concept. Jonathan Jackson, Dorothy Healey remembered, "was a very young man who did not know the difference between what was said for atmospherics and what was really being advocated by the leaders he admired."[53] He had access to Angela's arsenal and put it to purposes of his own devising. On August 7, 1970, he smuggled the guns into a courtroom in Marin County, California, where a Black San Quentin prisoner, James McClain, was on trial for attempting to assault a guard. Two other San Quentin prisoners, Ruchell Magee and William Christmas, were also in the courtroom as defense witnesses. Jackson armed the three prisoners with Angela's guns, and took the judge, Harold Haley, a district attorney, and three jurors as captives. Jackson may have believed he could bargain for the freedom of his brother; he was said to have shouted "Free the Soledad Brothers!" as he exited the courtroom, although witness memories varied. The three armed men and their hostages made their way outside to Jackson's van. But they were stopped at a roadblock, and San Quentin prison guards opened fire, killing Jackson,

McClain, and Christmas. Judge Haley was killed by a blast from the shot-gun Angela Davis had purchased two days earlier.[54]

On hearing the news on television that evening, knowing it would not be long before police learned whose guns and ammunition Jonathan Jackson carried into the courtroom, Davis went underground. For two months she eluded her pursuers, during which time she was placed on the FBI's ten-most-wanted list. President Richard Nixon publicly denounced her as a "dangerous terrorist." Finally, on October 13 she was arrested in a New York City motel. Extradited to California in late December, she was charged with murder, kidnapping, and conspiracy, accused of being an accomplice in the plotting of the Marin County courtroom raid. She was held behind bars for sixteen months until granted bail in February 1972.[55]

Their most famous member now the country's most famous pris-oner, Communist leaders were at first reluctant to come to her defense. If Davis was found guilty, they feared, the Party would be linked in the public mind with revolutionary violence, sparking a return to McCarthy-ism. Some leading Communists, Bettina Aptheker recalled, "wanted the Party to separate itself entirely from Angela, and a few (privately) advo-cated her expulsion on the grounds that she was a terrorist."[56] The solu-tion the national leadership arrived at was to defend Angela but condemn Jonathan for adventurism, separating his actions from Davis's. Angela was livid, telling Aptheker, who became a crucial member of her defense team, that she wanted to quit the Party. She did not endorse Jackson's actions, but regarded them as an act of resistance to white supremacy, however misconceived. The tension between the views of older and young Commu-nists on this issue was covered over but never resolved.[57]

Regardless of what Communist leaders might think was the prudent line to take on the Angela Davis case, the African-American community across the country was rallying to her defense, including such prominent figures as Coretta Scott King, Aretha Franklin, and James Baldwin. They saw her not as a terrorist, but as a Black woman victimized by a racist justice system. When, after some hesitation, the Party decided to launch a defense campaign spearheaded by the newly created National United Committee to Free Angela Davis and All Political Prisoners (the "All Political Prisoners" added at Angela's insistence), it proved the most successful political effort led by Communists in decades. Under Charlene Mitchell's leadership, there were countless rallies on her behalf across the country. Support for the campaign was not confined to the African-American community. The international Communist movement, drawing on long experience in such campaigns, made her case a cause célèbre, inside and outside the Soviet Bloc. Angela's face and Afro hairstyle, featured on posters and magazine covers, turned her into an instantly recognizable worldwide pop icon. The Rolling Stones even recorded a song about her case, "Sweet Black Angel," with Mick Jagger employing a Caribbean patois to deliver lines like "She's a sweet black angel, not a gun toting teacher, not a Red lovin' school marm."[58]

In the end, after a thirteen-week trial in San Jose, California, a jury of eleven whites and one Mexican-American acquitted Davis on all three counts of kidnapping, murder, and conspiracy. Afterward, in a scene unimaginable in the era of the Smith Act trials, she held a joint press conference with the jurors and hugged each of them. This was undoubtedly the greatest victory in the long history of Communists in legal jeopardy in the United States. Following her acquittal, Davis went on a nationwide tour, culminating in a rally in Madison Square Garden on June 29, 1972, before an ecstatic crowd of 15,000 supporters.[59]

In another of those contradictory twists in the history of American Communism that prevent it, even in moments of triumph, from ever quite achieving feel-good status, Davis followed up her celebratory American tour with another that took her to the Soviet Union, Eastern Europe, and Cuba—all places with their own share of political prisoners. At least as quoted in the Soviet press, her public statements on tour sounded as though scripted for her by Gus Hall. Thus, in the Soviet Uzbek republic, she declared: "The possibility of seeing with my own eyes the practical realization of Lenin's ethnic policy will be of tremendous help in our own struggle of resolving the ethnic problem in the United States." In response, an unnamed Soviet dissident was quoted in the *New York Times* asking, "Is she a fool or is she dishonest? It seems to me she is doing a disservice to her own countrymen by her statements here."[60]

Her missteps abroad did not attract much attention in the United States, at least among youthful admirers. Victory in the Angela Davis case represented political gold for the Communists, bringing some new recruits to the Party and the Young Workers Liberation League (YWLL), the successor organization to the by-then-defunct Du Bois Clubs. If there was ever a moment when the Party seemed ready to move beyond its post-McCarthyism torpor, it was the early 1970s.

But that's not what happened. Gus Hall's refusal throughout his years as general secretary to reveal membership figures (unlike predecessors in the 1930s and 1940s) make it difficult to speak with certainty about the Party's actual size, but suggestive hints are preserved in its archives. Ten years after Davis's acquittal, in 1982, Gil Green wrote to Hall, despairing at the Communist Party's continued sectarian isolation:

> Our Party apparatuses are too cumbersome, too tied with explicitly "inner" affairs, leaders are too "exhausted" by meeting with other Party leaders, and too many have no time to meet with nonparty people, never speak at nonparty gatherings, and answer most questions in general clichés.[61]

That same year, the second of Ronald Reagan's presidency, Hall claimed in a speech to the delegates at the CP's national convention, "The tempo of people coming into the Communist Party now is the fastest and the biggest in 50 years," which if true would have meant the Party was gaining more members than at the height of the Popular Front.[62]

That does not seem to be the case. In 1991, "Larry M," who had served as organizational secretary of the New York district of the Party for the past five years, wrote to Hall to share his own concerns. The "Party's size is not qualitatively different now than it was in 1976," he noted. In the mid-1970s, following the Angela Davis case, "our 'older' comrades were 15 years younger and our youth organization was much bigger with large numbers of Afro-American and other nationally oppressed youth." What followed, he said, were fifteen years of "stagnation":

> The mix of present leadership lies too heavily among older comrades whose main mass and Party experiences are in the past. . . . Objectively this is a big factor in the inability of the cadre to implement policy. It is also a big factor in why leadership tends to [be] a laundry list leadership that is throwing out one project after another for clubs and districts without struggling with what is really possible for our Party to accomplish.[63]

Instead of experiencing growth through meaningful political engagement, the Communist Party in the later 1970s and throughout the 1980s settled into an elaborate multiyear liturgical cycle. There were annual celebrations of May Day and the anniversary of the Bolshevik Revolution. Every four years, from 1972 through 1984, Gus Hall would run for president of the United States. (In all that time, he never broke 60,000 votes and usually got half that—and in the first two rounds, suffered the humiliation of getting fewer votes than the candidates of the hated Trotskyist rival, the Socialist Workers Party.) Every five years delegates gathered for the CPUSA's national convention, where a "laundry list" of resolutions were proposed, debated, approved, and, soon after, forgotten. It seemed like it could go on like that forever, year after year, as American Communism approached the fourth decade of its Gus Hall era.[64]

And then the world began to change. In Moscow, of all places.

Soviet Communism had been undergoing its own Períod zastóya, or "Era of Stagnation," in the later years of the Brezhnev era (1964–1982), followed by the brief reigns as general secretary of seventy-year-olds Yuri Andropov (1982–1984) and Konstantin Chernenko (1984–1985). These were years when the Soviet economy saw declining industrial growth rates, and Soviet scientific progress, symbolized by its early lead in the space race in the late 1950s and early 1960s, fell steadily behind Western standards. The Soviet military establishment was lavishly funded, but following the Red Army's invasion of Afghanistan in 1979 was locked in a bloody stalemate with guerrilla insurgents backed by the United States. Soviet consumer goods were shoddy and scarce; Soviet teenagers hungered for Western jeans and Beatles albums. A folk saying popular in the Soviet Union in the 1970s summed up the mood of resigned cynicism that ordinary citizens felt about their supposed workers' state: "They pretend to pay us, and we pretend to work!"[65]

From the moment Mikhail Gorbachev took office as general secretary of the Soviet Communist Party in 1985, he embodied a challenge to the political, cultural, and economic stagnation of the old order. Gorbachev was just fifty-four years old that year, a youngster in comparison to his immediate predecessors. The new Soviet leader, soon known affectionately on both sides of the Iron Curtain as "Gorby," displayed an unusually popular and affable touch, given to plunging into crowds, smiling and shaking hands, sometimes accompanied by his stylish wife. And there was substance behind the surface changes. Gorbachev, his biographer William Taubman noted without hyperbole, "almost single-handedly changed his country and the world."[66]

Gorbachev promised he would overturn the stagnation plaguing the Soviet economy and society by embracing policies of *perestroika* (reform/

restructuring) combined with *glasnost* (openness/candor). What that meant in practice was unclear in the beginning, save that Gorbachev's intent was to strengthen and improve rather than to dismantle Communism. But he soon would be swept along by developments he did not originally intend. At first he believed that relatively minor economic reforms could create a more efficient version of a command economy; within a year he was talking about introducing more far-reaching changes, introducing elements of the free market. Restrictions on speech (particularly in discussing the past) were loosened, although again Gorbachev was not at first proposing to establish anything like a free multiparty democracy. Popular expectations overcame his inherent caution, not just in the Soviet Union, but even more so in an increasingly restive Eastern Europe.[67]

When Gorbachev announced his program for reform, Gus Hall initially expressed enthusiastic support for *perestroika* and *glasnost*. As the first anniversary of Gorbachev's accession to office approached in March 1986, Hall was in Moscow to attend the Twenty-Seventh Soviet Communist Party Congress. There he had a brief personal meeting with the new Soviet leader. Afterward Hall told reporters: "I have never been in a meeting where there has been such a total, critical examination of everything." He predicted that under Gorbachev, "the Soviet Union is in the midst of the greatest leap forward ever . . . in production, science, quality of life, culture, education." Hall's initial high regard for Gorbachev may also have been affected by the fact that for the moment, perhaps out of inertia, the new Soviet leader continued providing an annual cash subsidy to the CPUSA, which in 1987 alone totaled $2 million.[68]

By 1989 Hall had changed his mind. For one thing, that was the year that Gorbachev finally turned off the cash spigot. The American Communist Party could no longer expect a subsidy from its Soviet angel.

More importantly, in the autumn of 1989, the citizens of the so-called "People's Democracies" of Eastern Europe overwhelmingly demonstrated their desire to be free of any continued association with either Communism

or the Soviet Union. Gorbachev, who could have responded as Chinese
Communist leaders did earlier in the year with the armed repression of
protesters in Beijing's Tiananmen Square, instead let the largely peaceful
revolution in the Soviet Bloc proceed unhindered. When the Berlin Wall
fell on November 9, 1989, and jubilant East Berliners poured through the
gates into West Berlin while East German border guards stood aside, Gorbachev was sound asleep in his Moscow quarters, and his aides decided
not to wake him with the news. The next morning, he was briefed on the
situation in a telephone call from the Soviet ambassador in East Berlin,
and his response was simply that the border guards "did the right thing."
The nearly 400,000 Red Army troops stationed in East Germany stayed in
their barracks.[69]

Communist leaders who fell from power in the aftermath of the fall of
the Berlin Wall included East Germany's Erich Honecker, Hungary's János
József Kádár, Czechoslovakia's Miloš Jakeš, Bulgaria's Todor Zhivkov, and
Romania's Nicolae Ceaușescu (who along with his wife, Elena, was executed
by insurgents on Christmas Day). Hall knew the Eastern European Communist leaders, having visited them in their home fiefdoms, or encountered them at various Soviet Party Congresses in Moscow. They were all
men, like Hall, of roughly the same generation, products of the Stalinist
era, stolid, dutiful, autocratic. And although Hall did not hold state power
(and would not face the possibility of execution if overthrown), he did not
intend, in his own modest bailiwick, to share their fate.[70]

Some American Communists believed that their own movement would
benefit from a little *glasnost* and *perestroika*. Their number included leading African-American Communists who by the mid-1980s strongly disagreed with the direction Hall was taking the Party on racial issues.

When Henry Winston, the CP chairman, died in the Soviet Union
in 1986, age seventy-five, he was missed by many Party members, young

and old. He was a venerated figure, who had joined the Young Communist League in 1930, been one of the original Smith Act defendants, and gone blind while serving his sentence in federal prison. He did not advocate big changes in Party outlook or structure, but he was known as a sympathetic listener—certainly far more so than Hall. He also symbolized the Party's commitment to interracial leadership, and it was widely expected, at his death, that he would be replaced by another African-American, or some other minority candidate. Instead, Hall simply combined the positions of general secretary and chairman, with himself in sole command.[71]

More than a slight to Winston's memory was at issue. Beginning in the early 1980s, Hall had subtly downplayed the Party's long-standing commitment to the Black struggle, emphasizing class over race as its principal concern. In the midst of the Reagan presidency, the Party's ruling body declared optimistically that "most white people reject racism. . . . They reject the basic premise of white supremacy."[72] Arguing that a new progressive third party was in the offing, and himself wanting to keep running as an independent presidential candidate, Hall kept the CP from endorsing Jesse Jackson's bids for the Democratic presidential nomination in 1984 and 1988, despite the enthusiasm of younger and Black Communists for the civil rights veteran's candidacy. Hall's conception of the American working class, in line with Party traditions, emphasized the centrality of workers in mass-production industries such as steel (largely male, mainly white, if less so than in the 1930s), as if the US economy had remained unchanged since his long-ago days as a CIO organizer. Workers in other sectors of the economy, like the service industry in which Blacks, Hispanics, Asians, and other minorities, as well as women, were in the majority in the 1970s and 1980s, did not interest him as much. He was equally resistant to changing the CP's long-standing hostility to the gay rights movement, and indifferent to the women's movement when it addressed issues outside the workplace, opposing the passage of the Equal Rights Amendment. When some Communists challenged the narrowness of Hall's political vision, he treated their dissent as evidence of "petty-bourgeois radicalism" imported into the Party by younger members, or, worse, the machinations of "enemy" agents. He was getting old and cranky, and regarded his hostility to any new currents in left-wing thought as fidelity to revolutionary principle.[73]

The year 1989 saw the growing discomfort with Hall's leadership in the CPUSA's ranks begin to take organizational form. Charlene Mitchell invited like-minded comrades, white and Black, from around the country to an informal get-together at her New York City apartment following the April meeting of the Party's National Committee. The strong support she got from other African-Americans was an ominous sign for Gus Hall. Kendra and Franklin Alexander were at the first meeting, along with Maurice Jackson, a Black leader of the Party section in Washington, DC. So was Carl Bloice, another Black Californian, who had edited the West Coast *People's World* until it was merged with the East Coast *Daily World* in 1986, after which he spent three years as the new *People's Daily World* Moscow correspondent. Bloice was sympathetic to the changes Gorbachev was bringing to the Soviet Union and Eastern Bloc, and reported to the group on recent developments. At subsequent meetings of what evolved into an organized faction, longtime dissident Gil Green also came to play an influential role.[74]

When the CP National Committee met in late January 1990, Hall responded to the fall of Communism in Eastern Europe with a belligerent denialism, telling his comrades:

The ideological sections of the FBI and CIA and the propaganda departments of universities are in high gear spreading the new big lies about the death throes of communism. However, based on past experience people are not so ready to accept another big lie.[75]

At the same meeting, he attacked those American Communists who issued "sweeping broadsides about lack of inner-Party democracy" in the
CPUSA, an accusation he vehemently rejected.[76]

For the moment, there was stalemate between Hall and the reform-minded
Communists. The showdown would come in December 1991, when the
Party held its twenty-fifth national convention. What made this final struggle over the future of American Communism different from all those that
came before was that this time the Party establishment was simultaneously
at odds with both the dissidents pushing for meaningful reforms at home
and the leader of the Soviet Union. Hall, in the name of defending orthodoxy, had by now begun to link "right opportunism" in the American CP
with Gorbachev's policies in the Soviet Union. He regarded both as enemies of socialism.[77]

And then, as so many times in the past, unforeseen events in Moscow
changed the political calculations of American Communists. On August 18,
1991, hard-line leaders of the Soviet Communist Party, the so-called Gang of
Eight—backed by the KGB, embittered over the loss of Soviet control of Eastern Europe, and fearing the dissolution of the Soviet Union itself—launched
a coup attempt. They sent a military delegation to confine Gorbachev to his
dacha in Crimea where he had been on vacation since early August, declared
a state of emergency in Moscow, shut down independent newspapers, pro-
hibited demonstrations, and established a new governing committee that
promoted one of their own as the new Soviet president. But unlike the ten
days that shook the world seventy-four years earlier, this attempted seizure
of power fizzled in just three days. The president of the Russian Republic,
Boris Yeltsin, who for the moment supported Gorbachev, rallied opposition from the Soviet parliamentary building, known as the White House.
Moscow citizens turned out in thousands to surround the building and

block any attempt by the plotters to seize it by armed force. The military was divided in its loyalties, with some Red Army units refusing to be deployed against the protesters. By August 22 it was all over. The self-appointed Emergency Committee of hard-liners was arrested, Gorbachev returned to Moscow, and the Soviet Communist Party was banned.

But Gorbachev's power to influence events was over, as Yeltsin emerged as the hero of the affair. In the weeks that followed one Soviet republic after another seceded. At 7:00 p.m. Moscow time on December 25, 1991, Gorbachev delivered a televised farewell address, declaring, "I am ceasing my activities as president of the USSR." When he was done speaking, at 7:32 p.m., the familiar red flag with the hammer-and-sickle emblem was ceremoniously lowered over the Kremlin for the last time. Soviet Communism was relegated to the dustbin of history.[78]

Hall was vacationing in Minnesota when news of the attempted coup was broadcast, and he rushed back to New York City. At a meeting of the National Board on August 20, while the outcome of the events in Moscow was still uncertain, he stopped just short of openly endorsing the hard-liners' plot, his reaction recorded and sent out to Party clubs across the country as political guidance: "Well, the question of course emerges what specifically should we as the Party do? Well, I think obviously what we should not do is to join in the bring back Gorbachev campaign because that is the basis of the Cold War, that we would line up with them and I don't think that's necessary."[79]

Denunciations of Hall's evident sympathies for the plotters poured in to the national office, and at a subsequent emergency meeting of the Party's National Committee, for the first time ever, Hall lost a vote when committee members voted thirty-three to thirty to condemn the coup.[80]

In the days that followed, when it became clear that the attempt to restore the old order had failed in Moscow, Hall tried to walk back his August 20 remarks, telling reporters at a news conference at the end of August that the coup "was an attempt to deal with real problems, but in a wrong way."[81] But the more he talked, the more unhinged he sounded, to the unconcealed delight of the reporters gathered in his office. Alessandra Stanley's report for the *New York Times* mocked Hall's attempts to downplay the significance of recent events in Moscow:

> Looking hale and rested in a plaid sports shirt and powder-blue jacket, Mr. Hall said he was not depressed. He also insisted that Communism was still alive in the Soviet Union. "I think the mass media is going through one of its 'the Communist Party is dead periods.'" He paused, then added quietly, "Though I have to admit you have more material for such conclusions now than in past episodes."

Stanley ended her article with another, slightly loony observation from Hall (recycled in subsequent articles about him, including his *New York Times* obituary in 2000):

> Mr. Hall, who was last in Moscow three months ago, said he had no plans to visit the Soviet Union in the near future. Instead he offered fellow travelers a new model of the worker's paradise. "The world should see what North Korea has done," said Mr. Hall, who recently visited that country. "In some ways it is a miracle. The capital is one of the nicest, finest cities in the world.
>
> "If you want a nice vacation, take it in North Korea."[82]

In the months leading up to the CPUSA convention in December, 900 Communists, approximately a third of the Party's total membership, signed a manifesto entitled "An Initiative to Unite and Renew the Party." Their number included Angela Davis, Charlene Mitchell, Kendra Alexander, Herbert Aptheker, and many other veterans.[83] The statement, largely written by Carl Bloice, did not propose a split, as the "unite and renew" title suggested. It reaffirmed the signers' commitment to the fight for socialism. But, in an echo of 1956, it called upon the Party to undertake a searching analysis of the reasons for the collapse of the Soviet Union and Eastern European Communism. It also demanded that the Party restructure its internal organization on a democratic basis and renew its commitment to the struggle for racial justice. And, without mentioning Gus Hall's name, it condemned the current leadership of the Party for "cultism," and for failure over many years to provide "accurate information of membership, finances, personnel and the work of leading bodies."[84]

Six hundred Communists, one-fifth of the Party's remaining membership, arrived to take part in the CPUSA's twenty-fifth national convention, scheduled for December 6–8, 1991, in the Sheraton City Centre hotel in downtown Cleveland. Angela Davis was too ill to attend but sent a message to the delegates emphasizing what was at stake in the deliberations to come:

> I believe the Communist Party will become ever more rapidly obsolescent—mere fossilized evidence of past struggles won and lost . . . if it is afraid to engage in rigorous self-evaluation, radical restructuring and democratic renewal.

She reported feeling "a profound sense of sadness" when she found herself wondering "when was the last time I could in good faith invite a fervent and spirited young activist—as I was when I joined the party—to consider becoming a member?"[85]

Many of those who showed up in Cleveland from the centers of Party dissent were not seated on a variety of pretexts by the Hall loyalists in charge of credentialing delegates. Northern California, the second-largest district in the CP after New York, had its delegation cut from sixty-three to thirty-three.[86]

The convention took place on the sixth floor of the hotel. Only those who displayed delegate credentials were allowed access to the floor by armed off-duty Cleveland police officers, hired by the Party as security guards. The convention opened with a three-hour speech by Gus Hall, attacking the reformers as "the enemy within" the Party. According to the account in the *New York Times*: "The dissidents smiled sardonically about the irony: the leader of a party whose members were once persecuted by police, and whose ideas were once denounced as an 'alien ideology' issuing the same denunciations and calling on police to protect him."[87]

The Gus Hall loyalists outnumbered the opposition two to one. Few of the dissenters who made it into the convention were allowed to speak, and those who gained the floor were met with chants of "Gus, Gus, Gus!"[88] One of the dissident speakers was Herbert Aptheker, who ironically had for years been a Party hard-liner, the author of polemics defending the invasion of Hungary in 1956 and the invasion of Czechoslovakia in 1968. But in recent years, under the influence of his daughter Bettina, who had quit the CP in 1981 due to its hostility to feminism and gay rights, he had changed his mind about many things. He told the delegates, in his final speech to a Communist Party gathering, that past Soviet leaders had been guilty of "monstrous crimes . . . involving mass murder." And American Communists were not blameless, for "many of us were easily deceived; we were credulous because we felt we had to be."[89]

A majority of delegates voted for a slate of Gus Hall loyalists for the new National Committee. The opposition delegates, and their supporters, defeated at the Sheraton City Centre, met across the street in another hall to found a new organization, the Committees of Correspondence. The name was suggested by Aptheker, in tribute to the patriots who led an earlier American revolutionary movement. (The group later changed its name to the Committees of Correspondence for Democracy and Socialism.)[90]

With the departure of the reformers, the Communist Party USA lost a third of its strength. With the end of the Soviet Union, two and a half weeks later, it lost its reason to exist. At its founding in 1919, the American Communist movement drew inspiration from the revolution that Lenin and his followers had launched in the streets of Petrograd two years earlier. Communists in the United States, like their comrades around the world, regarded the Soviet Union as a model for the society they hoped to create in their own country. Defense of the Soviet Union, its leaders, its economic, political, and legal system, and its foreign policy, remained the one consistent and central element of the American Communist Party's beliefs and program from the 1920s through the 1980s. Those Communists who questioned any aspect of Soviet conduct and institutions were forced to depart the movement, or keep their concerns to themselves. And the result was that, for all their commitment, discipline, self-sacrifice, and organizational prowess, Communists in the United States were incapable of offering a meaningful vision of a good society, a "Soviet America," that could possibly be made to appeal to any but a tiny portion of their fellow Americans. Or, as Clancy Sigal has his disillusioned protagonist admit in *Going Away*, "We never touched that *source* of life which provides alternatives, meaningful, stark and immense."

For seven decades, the conflict between faith in and doubts about the Soviet experiment defined the history of American Communism. In the aftermath of the end of that experiment in 1991, a faithful few still clung to the Party, as always their church and citadel. But the church and the citadel stood for and guarded nothing, nothing but ashes.

CODA

The Communist Party USA continues to exist. After the end of the Soviet Union in 1991, it remained for another nine years under Gus Hall's leadership, until his death in 2000 at age ninety, and since then has had several other general secretaries. It retains its national headquarters in the building it owns at 235 West Twenty-Third Street in the rapidly gentrifying Chelsea district of Manhattan, with the building's market value as of 2023 some $8.6 million. The Party rents out most of the floors and is thus the beneficiary of a steady income stream. It no longer publishes a newspaper or theoretical journal but maintains a website. Its current membership is unknown.

ACKNOWLEDGMENTS

As always, the librarians are essential behind-the-scenes collaborators, and I am very grateful to Reid S. Larson, of the Hamilton College library, and Malia Guyer-Stevens and Shannon O'Neill, of the Tamiment Library at New York University, for all their help in steering me to the sources I needed. Bettina Aptheker, Max Elbaum, Harvey Klehr, and Sam Webb will all doubtless find a little or a lot to disagree with in these pages, but nonetheless made their own valuable contributions to my research and interpretation. Michael Kazin and Mark Erlich, with whom I have been discussing the history of the American Left for the past half century, deserve my thankful acknowledgment for shaping my historical perspective in ways beyond counting. Sandra Dijkstra, my agent of many years, went above and beyond her usual stellar representation of my interests by actually being the first to suggest to me that it was time I returned to a topic I had examined at some length early on in my scholarly career. And Michael Kaler, my editor at Basic Books, proved a skilled and patient artisan at his craft, as did copy editor Joseph Gunther.

Speaking to striking textile workers at the 1913 silk strike in Paterson, New Jersey, Big Bill Haywood of the Industrial Workers of the World (IWW) explained why it was that labor radicals saluted one another with a clenched fist. "Every finger by itself has no force," he said, showing his hand to the gathering, fingers spread. "Now look," he continued, making a fist. "See that, that's the IWW." As in the class struggle, so in writing a book. Thank you, comrades.

NOTES

Prologue

1. Will Lissner, "Moscow Assailed by Some US Reds," *New York Times*, August 23, 1968, https://www.nytimes.com/1968/08/23/archives/moscow-assailed-by-some-u-s-reds -state-leader-calls-invasion-a-very.html.

2. FBI Memorandum to J. Edgar Hoover, Subject Gil Green, October 28, 1968, TAM 95, box 5, Czechoslovakia folder, Gil Green Papers, Tamiment Library, New York University.

3. J. Edgar Hoover, *Masters of Deceit: The Story of Communism in America and How to Fight It* (New York: Henry Holt, 1958).

4. Irving Howe and Lewis Coser, *The American Communist Party: A Critical History* (Boston: Beacon Press, 1957), 95.

5. William Appleman Williams, *The Tragedy of American Diplomacy* (Cleveland: World Publishing Company, 1959), 19.

Introduction

1. Elizabeth Gurley Flynn, *The Rebel Girl: An Autobiography, My First Life (1906–1926)*, rev. ed. (New York: International Publishers, 1973), 62.

2. Helen Camp, *Iron in Her Soul: Elizabeth Gurley Flynn and the American Left* (Pullman: Washington State University Press, 1995), 2.

3. James Joll, *The Second International, 1889–1914* (New York: Praeger, 1956), 94–96, 130–131.

4. Melvyn Dubofsky, *We Shall Be All: A History of the Industrial Workers of the World* (Chicago: Quadrangle, 1969), 146–170; Ralph Darlington, *Radical Unionism: The Rise and Fall of Revolutionary Syndicalism* (Chicago: Haymarket Books, 2013).

5. Gary Dorrien, *American Democratic Socialism: History, Politics, Religion, and Theory* (New Haven, CT: Yale University Press, 2021), 52–53.

6. Ralph Chaplin, *Wobbly: The Rough-and-Tumble Story of an American Radical* (Chicago: University of Chicago Press, 1948), 167–168.

7. Bert Cochran, *Labor and Communism: The Conflict That Shaped American Unions* (Princeton, NJ: Princeton University Press, 1977), 7.

8. Mary Heaton Vorse, *A Footnote to Folly: Reminiscences of Mary Heaton Vorse* (New York: Farrar & Rinehart, 1935), 8–9. For Flynn's efforts in the Lawrence strike, see Camp, *Iron in Her Soul*, 26–37.

9. Dubofsky, *We Shall Be All*, 227–262.

10. "Joe Hill—The Rebel Girl Lyrics," Genius, https://genius.com/Joe-hill-the-rebel -girl-lyrics.

11. Theodore Draper, *The Roots of American Communism* (New York: Viking Press, 1957), 42.

12. Nick Salvatore, *Eugene V. Debs: Citizen and Socialist* (Urbana: University of Illinois Press, 1982), 9–22.

13. Salvatore, *Eugene V. Debs*, 22–25, 264–265.

14. Quoted in Salvatore, *Eugene V. Debs*, 229–230.

15. Salvatore, *Eugene V. Debs*, 171.

16. James Weinstein, *The Decline of Socialism in America, 1912–1925* (New York: Monthly Review Press, 1967), 84–118.

17. Maurice Isserman, "Inheritance Lost: Socialism in Rochester, 1917–1919," *Rochester History* 39, no. 4 (October 1977), 1–2, https://www.libraryweb.org/~rochhist /v39_1977/v39i4.pdf.

18. Weinstein, *Decline of Socialism*, 5–16; "The Socialist Party Platform of 1912," Teaching American History, https://teachingamericanhistory.org/document/the-socialist -party-platform-socialist-party-national-convention-indianapolis-indiana/.

19. Theodore Draper, *American Communism and Soviet Russia: The Formative Period* (New York: Viking Press, 1960), 154; Harvey Klehr, *Communist Cadre: The Social Background of the American Communist Party Elite* (Stanford, CA: Hoover Institution Press, 1978), 21.

20. Morris Hillquit, *Loose Leaves from a Busy Life* (New York: Macmillan, 1934), 145; Joll, *The Second International*, 158–183.

21. Michael Kazin, *War Against War: The American Fight for Peace, 1914–1918* (New York: Simon & Schuster, 2017), 133.

22. Kazin, *War Against War*, 212–213; "The Socialist Party and the War," Early American Marxism, http://www.marxisthistory.org/history/usa/parties/spusa/1917/0414-spa-stlouis resolution.pdf.

23. Draper, *Roots of American Communism*, 99–102.

24. Leopold H. Haimson, *The Russian Marxists and the Origins of Bolshevism* (Cambridge, MA: Harvard University Press, 1955), 133–139.

25. Quoted in Joshua Rubenstein, *Leon Trotsky: A Revolutionary Life* (New Haven, CT: Yale University Press, 2011), 38.

26. Eric Blanc, *Revolutionary Social Democracy: Working-Class Politics Across the Russian Empire (1882–1917)* (Leiden, Netherlands: Brill, 2021), 383.

27. Orlando Figes, *A People's Tragedy: The Russian Revolution, 1891–1924* (New York: Viking, 1997), 154.

28. André Liebich, *From the Other Shore: Russian Social Democracy After 1921* (Cambridge, MA: Harvard University Press, 1997), 36–42, 62–63; Vladimir N. Brovkin, *The Mensheviks After October: Socialist Opposition and the Rise of the Bolshevik Dictatorship* (Ithaca, NY: Cornell University Press, 1987), 1–11.

29. Isaac Deutscher, *The Prophet Armed: Trotsky, 1879–1921* (1954; reprint, New York: Vintage,1965), 242–243; Stephen F. Cohen, *Bukharin and the Bolshevik Revolution: A Political Biography, 1888–1938* (New York: Knopf, 1973), 43–44.

30. Deutscher, *Prophet Armed*, 247–248.

31. Quoted in Philip S. Foner, *The Bolshevik Revolution: Its Impact on American Radicals, Liberals, and Labor* (New York, International Publishers, 1967), 71, 154.

32. Robert A. Rosenstone, *Romantic Revolutionary: A Biography of John Reed* (New York: Vintage, 1981), 7–59.

33. Rosenstone, *Romantic Revolutionary*, 76–116.

34. Rosenstone, *Romantic Revolutionary*, 387.

35. John Reed, *Ten Days That Shook the World* (New York: Signet, 1967), 101; Rosenstone, *Romantic Revolutionary*, 296.

36. Reed, *Ten Days*, 114; Rosenstone, *Romantic Revolutionary*, 297.

37. Irving Howe, *World of Our Fathers: The Journey of the Eastern European Jews to America and the Life They Found and Made* (New York: Harcourt Brace Jovanovich, 1976), 325–326.

38. Quoted in Adam Hochschild, *American Midnight: The Great War, a Violent Peace, and Democracy's Forgotten Crisis* (New York: Mariner Books, 2022), 21.

39. Beverly Gage, *G-Man: J. Edgar Hoover and the Making of the American Century* (New York: Viking, 2022), 55.

40. Robert K. Murray, *Red Scare: A Study in National Hysteria, 1919–1920* (New York: McGraw-Hill, 1964), 13–14.

41. "E.V. Debs: The Canton, Ohio Speech, Anti-war Speech," Marxists Internet Archive, https://www.marxists.org/archive/debs/works/1918/canton.htm.

42. Salvatore, *Eugene V. Debs*, 291–294; "Speech by Eugene V. Debs, June 16, 1918," Documented Rights, National Archives, https://www.archives.gov/exhibits/documented -rights/exhibit/section3/detail/debs-speech-transcript.html.

43 Salvatore, *Eugene V. Debs*, 323.

44. Salvatore, *Eugene V. Debs*, 295.

45. Murray, *Red Scare*, 21–22.

46. Murray, *Red Scare*, 29–31.

47. Gage, *G-Man*, 61–62; Julia Rose Kraut, *Threat of Dissent: A History of Ideological Exclusion and Deportation in the United States* (Cambridge, MA: Harvard University Press, 2020), 71–73.

48. Draper, *Roots of American Communism*, 148–153.

49. Nelson Lichtenstein et al., eds., *Who Built America? Working People and the Nation's Economy, Politics, Culture, and Society*, vol. 2, *Since 1877*, 2nd ed. (New York: Worth Publishers, 2000), 301–305.

50. Dorrien, *American Democratic Socialism*, 220.

51. Draper, *Roots of American Communism*, 176–187.

52. Quoted in Salvatore, *Eugene V. Debs*, 315.

Chapter 1: The Flood or the Ebb?

1. "The Steel Strike," *The Communist*, October 4, 1919, https://archive.org/details/ TheCommunistVol.I2Oct41919; Irving Howe and Lewis Coser, *The American Communist Party: A Critical History* (Boston: Beacon Press, 1957), 73.

2. Theodore Draper, *The Roots of American Communism* (New York: Viking Press, 1957), 223.

3. E. P. Thompson, *The Making of the English Working Class* (New York: Vintage, 1966), 12.

4. Christian A. Smith, *Shakespeare's Influence on Karl Marx: The Shakespearean Roots of Marxism* (New York: Routledge, 2021), 248–250.

5. Townsend Ludington, *John Dos Passos: A Twentieth Century Odyssey* (New York: Dutton, 1980), 191; Carl E. Schorske, *German Social Democracy, 1905–1917: The Development of the Great Schism* (Cambridge, MA: Harvard University Press, 1955), 323–326.

6. Dorothy Ray Healey and Maurice Isserman, *California Red: A Life in the American Communist Party* (Urbana: University of Illinois Press, 1994), 15.

7. Draper, *Roots of American Communism*, 190; James Gregory, "Communist Party Membership by Districts 1922–1950," Mapping American Social Movements Project, University of Washington, https://depts.washington.edu/moves/CP_map-members.shtml.

8. Theodore Draper, *American Communism and Soviet Russia: The Formative Period* (New York: Viking Press, 1960), 20.

9. Benjamin Gitlow, *The Whole of Their Lives: Communism in America, A Personal History and Intimate Portrayal of Its Leaders* (Boston: Western Islands, 1968), 3–4.

10. Draper, *Roots of American Communism*, 190–192, 391–393; Harvey Klehr, *Communist Cadre: The Social Background of the American Communist Party Elite* (Stanford, CA: Hoover Institution Press, 1978), 20–22, 28–29, 33; Walter T. Howard, *Forgotten Radicals: Communists in the Pennsylvania Anthracite, 1919–1950* (Lanham, MD: University Press of America, 2005), 2–4; Steve Nelson, James R. Barrett, and Rob Ruck, *Steve Nelson: American Radical* (Pittsburgh: University of Pittsburgh Press, 1981), 299; Aaron Goings, Brian Barnes, and Roger Snider, *The Red Coast: Radicalism and Anti-radicalism in Southwest Washington* (Corvallis: Oregon State University Press, 2019), 75–76; Vernon L. Pedersen, *The Communist Party on the American Waterfront: Revolution, Reform, and the Quest for Power* (Lanham, MD: Lexington Books, 2020), 6; Mark Naison, *Communists in Harlem During the Depression* (Urbana: University of Illinois Press, 1983), 4–5; Mark Solomon, *The Cry Was Unity: Communist and African Americans, 1917–1936* (Jackson: University Press of Mississippi, 1998), 3, 10–15; Kate Weigand, *Red Feminism: American Communism and the Making of Women's Liberation* (Baltimore: Johns Hopkins University Press, 2001), 20; Lisa Rubens, "The Patrician Radical: Charlotte Anita Whitney," *California History* 65, no. 3 (September 1986), https://online.ucpress.edu/ch/article-abstract/65/3/158/32526/The-Patrician-Radical-Charlotte-Anita-Whitney.

11. Vladimir N. Brovkin, *The Mensheviks After October: Socialist Opposition and the Rise of the Bolshevik Dictatorship* (Ithaca, NY: Cornell University Press, 1987), 220–293; Vera Broido, *Lenin and the Mensheviks: The Persecution of Socialists Under Bolshevism* (Boulder, CO: Westview Press, 1987).

12. Joseph Stalin, *Foundations of Leninism* (New York: International Publishers, 1932), 107.

13. Vladimir Lenin, "The Urgent Tasks of Our Movement," *Iskra*, December 1900, https://www.marxists.org/archive/lenin/works/1900/nov/tasks.htm.

14. Quoted in Bryan D. Palmer, *James P. Cannon and the Origins of the American Revolutionary Left, 1890–1928* (Urbana: University of Illinois Press, 2007), 325.

15. James R. Cannon, *The History of American Trotskyism: From Its Origins (1928) to the Founding of the Socialist Workers Party (1938)* (New York: Pathfinder Press, 1972), 14.

16. Quoted in Jacob A. Zumoff, *The Communist International and US Communism* (Leiden, Netherlands: Brill, 2014), 71.

17. Joseph Freeman, *An American Testament: A Narrative of Rebels and Romantics* (New York: Farrar & Rinehart, 1936), 315–316.

18. James Oneal and Robert Minor, *"Resolved: That the Terms of the Third International Are Inacceptable to the Revolutionary Socialists of the World."; Being the Report of a Debate [. . .] Affirmative James Oneal [. . .] vs. [. . .] Negative Robert Minor [. . .]* (New York: Academy Press, 1921), 22.

19. Freeman, *American Testament*, 329.

20. Eugene V. Debs to David Karsner, April 30, 1920, in J. Robert Constantine, ed., *Letters of Eugene V. Debs*, vol. 3, *1919–1926* (Urbana: University of Illinois Press, 1990), 85.

21. Eugene V. Debs to W. S. Van Valkenburgh, January 15, 1926, in Constantine, *Letters of Debs*, 3:530–532.

22. Draper, *Roots of American Communism*, 205–209.

23. "Workers Don't Vote! Strike! Boycott This Election!" leaflet, Communist Party USA, Fond 515, microfilm, reel 1, Records of the CPUSA, Tamiment Library, New York University.

24. Draper, *Roots of American Communism*, 214–222.

25. Draper, *Roots of American Communism*, 388–391; Gregory, "Communist Party Membership"; Zumoff, *Communist International*, 168.

26. Draper, *Roots of American Communism*, 341, 353–390.

27. Draper, *American Communism and Russia*, 53–57, 244.

28. Draper, *Roots of American Communism*, 263–264.

29. Stephen Kotkin, *Stalin*, vol. 1, *Paradoxes of Power, 1878–1928* (New York: Penguin Press, 2014), 363, 442; Charles Shipman, *It Had to Be Revolution: Memoirs of an American Radical* (Ithaca, NY: Cornell University Press, 1993), 110.

30. Klehr, *Communist Cadre*, 96–97.

31. John Reed et al., Letter from American Delegation, United Communist Party, ca. July–August 1920, Fond 515, microfilm, reel 1, Records of the CPUSA, Tamiment Library, New York University; Harvey Klehr, John Earl Haynes, and Fridrikh Igorevich Firsov, *The Secret World of American Communism* (New Haven, CT: Yale University Press, 1995), 21–25. For continued infusions of "Moscow Gold" into the CP treasury in the 1920s and 1930s, see Harvey Klehr, John Earl Haynes, and Kyrill M. Anderson, *The Soviet World of American Communism* (New Haven, CT: Yale University Press, 1998), 107–147.

32. Branko Lazitch and Milorad M. Drachkovitch, *Lenin and the Comintern*, vol. 1 (Stanford, CA: Hoover Institution Press, 1972), 271; Draper, *Roots of American Communism*, 254.

33. Draper, *Roots of American Communism*, 264; Jonathan Haslam, *The Spectre of War: International Communism and the Origins of World War II* (Princeton, NJ: Princeton University Press, 2021), 23.

34. Draper, *Roots of American Communism*, 248–251.

35. Shipman, *It Had to Be Revolution*, 108.

36. Melvyn Dubofsky, *We Shall Be All: A History of the Industrial Workers of the World* (Chicago: Quadrangle, 1969), 445–468.

37. Draper, *Roots of American Communism*, 255–257, 283.

38. Robert A. Rosenstone, *Romantic Revolutionary: A Biography of John Reed* (New York: Vintage, 1981), 379–382.

39. Sheila Fitzpatrick, *The Russian Revolution*, 3rd ed. (Oxford: Oxford University Press, 2008), 94–102.

40. Kevin McDermott and Jeremy Agnew, *The Comintern: A History of International Communism from Lenin to Stalin* (Basingstoke, UK: Macmillan Press, 1996), 23–24.

41. Isaac Deutscher, *The Prophet Unarmed: Trotsky 1921–1929* (New York: Oxford University Press, 1959), 77–78.

42. Deutscher, *Prophet Unarmed*, 157–158.

43. Quoted in Deutscher, *Prophet Unarmed*, 139.

44. Zumoff, *Communist International*, 156–157.

45. Peggy Dennis, *The Autobiography of an American Communist: A Personal View of a Political Life, 1925–1975* (Westport, CT: Lawrence Hill, 1977), 19–23; George J. Sánchez, *Boyle Heights: How a Los Angeles Neighborhood Became the Future of American Democracy* (Oakland: University of California Press, 2021), 70, 81, 130–131.

46. Dennis, *Autobiography*, 58.

47. "Workers! Your Fatherland, the Socialist Fatherland of All Workers, Is in Danger!," *Daily Worker*, July 17, 1929, https://www.loc.gov/resource/sn84020097/1929-07-17/ed-1/?sp=1.

48. Tony Michels, "Socialism with a Jewish Face: The Origins of the Yiddish-Speaking Communist Movement in the United States, 1907–1923," in Gennady Estraikh and Mikhail Krutikov, eds., *Yiddish and the Left* (London: Routledge, 2017), 42–44.

49. Howe and Coser, *American Communist Party*, 104.

50. Ludington, *John Dos Passos*, 244; John Dos Passos, "The New Masses I'd Like," *New Masses*, June 1926, 20.

51. John Dos Passos, "America and the Pursuit of Happiness," *The Nation*, December 29, 1920, 778.

52. Patrick Chura, *Michael Gold: The People's Writer* (Albany: State University of New York Press, 2020), 123.

53. Marvin E. Gettleman, "The New York Workers School, 1923–1944: Communist Education in American Society," in Michael E. Brown et al., eds., *New Studies in the Politics and Culture of US Communism* (New York: Monthly Review Press, 1993), 261–280; Marvin E. Gettleman, "The Lost World of United States Labor Education: Curricula at East and West Coast Communist Schools, 1944–1957," in Robert W. Cherny, William Issel, and Kieran Walsh Taylor, eds., *American Labor and the Cold War: Grassroots Politics and Postwar Political Culture* (New Brunswick, NJ: Rutgers University Press, 2004), 205–215.

54. David A. Lincove, "Radical Publishing to 'Reach the Million Masses': Alexander L. Trachtenberg and International Publishers, 1906–1966," *Left History* 10, no. 1 (Winter 2004), 85–124.

55. Jennifer R. Uhlmann, "The Communist Civil Rights Movement: Legal Activism in the United States, 1919–1946" (PhD diss., University of California at Los Angeles, 2007), 97–100; Palmer, *James P. Cannon*, 262–284.

56. James R. Barrett, *William Z. Foster and the Tragedy of American Radicalism* (Urbana: University of Illinois Press, 1999), 10–11, 53, 76–103.

57. Draper, *American Communism and Russia*, 64–67.

58. Draper, *Roots of American Communism*, 315–322.

59. Nelson Lichtenstein et al., eds., *Who Built America? Working People and the Nation's Economy, Politics, Culture, and Society*, vol. 2, *Since 1877*, 2nd ed. (New York: Worth Publishers, 2000), 325–326.

60. Irving Bernstein, *The Lean Years: A History of the American Worker, 1920–1933* (Boston: Houghton Mifflin, 1972), 50.

61. Bernstein, *Lean Years*, 84–86.

62. Lichtenstein et al., *Who Built America?*, 2:325–326.

63. Bert Cochran, *Labor and Communism: The Conflict That Shaped American Unions* (Princeton, NJ: Princeton University Press, 1977), 39; Irving Howe, *World of Our Fathers: The Journey of the Eastern European Jews to America and the Life They Found and Made* (New York: Harcourt Brace Jovanovich, 1976), 331–332.

64. Robert D. Parmet, *The Master of Seventh Avenue: David Dubinsky and the American Labor Movement* (New York: New York University Press, 2005), 42–46.

65. Jacob A. Zumoff, *The Red Thread: The Passaic Textile Strike* (New Brunswick, NJ: Rutgers University Press, 2021), 36–37.

66. Zumoff, *Red Thread*, 23–24, 43–47; Martha Stone Asher, "Recollections of the Passaic Textile Strike of 1926," *Labor's Heritage* 2, no. 2 (1990), 17.

67. Quoted in Zumoff, *Red Thread*, 31.

68. Quoted in Dee Garrison, *Mary Heaton Vorse: The Life of an American Insurgent* (Philadelphia: Temple University Press, 1990), 239, emphasis in the original.

69. Mary Heaton Vorse, *The Passaic Textile Strike, 1926–1927* (Passaic, NJ: General Relief Committee of Textile Workers, 1927), 20.

70. Zumoff, *Red Thread*, 100–103.

71. Zumoff, *Red Thread*, 163–164; Cochran, *Labor and Communism*, 31–33.

72. Draper, *American Communism and Russia*, 32–38.

73. Draper, *American Communism and Russia*, 38–48, 75–77.

74. William Z. Foster, "The Federated Farmer-Labor Party," *Labor Herald*, August 1923, 3.

75. Draper, *American Communism and Russia*, 234–235.

76. Dennis, *Autobiography*, 32.

77. Draper, *American Communism and Russia*, 160–161.

78. Martin Abern, "Party Campaign: Thru Branch or Shop Nuclei?," *Daily Worker*, November 8, 1924, https://www.loc.gov/resource/sn84020097/1924-11-08/ed-1/?sp=7.

79. Draper, *American Communism and Russia*, 160–163.

80. Nelson, Barrett, and Ruck, *Steve Nelson*, 43.

81. Paul Mishler, "Red Finns, Red Jews: Ethnic Variation in Communist Political Culture During the 1920s and 1930s," in *Yivo Annual*, vol. 22 (Evanston, IL: Northwestern University Press, 1995), 134–135.

82. S. Ani Mukherji, "Reds Among the Sewer Socialists and McCarthyites: The Communist Party in Milwaukee," *American Communist History* 16, nos. 3–4 (2017): 117.

83. Zumoff, *Communist International*, 183; Gregory, "Communist Party Membership."

84. Arthur J. Sabin, *Red Scare in Court: New York Versus the International Workers Order* (Philadelphia: University of Pennsylvania Press, 1993); Paul C. Mishler, *Raising Reds: The Young Pioneers, Radical Summer Camps and Communist Political Culture in the United States* (New York: Columbia University Press, 1999), 64–75.

85. Harvey Klehr, *The Heyday of American Communism: The Depression Decade* (New York: Basic Books, 1984), 158–159.

86. Julia Rose Kraut, *Threat of Dissent: A History of Ideological Exclusion and Deportation in the United States* (Cambridge, MA: Harvard University Press, 2020), 83.

87. Errol Wayne Stevens, *In Pursuit of Utopia: Los Angeles in the Great Depression* (Norman: University of Oklahoma Press, 2021), 96.

88. Bruce Watson, *Sacco and Vanzetti: The Men, the Murders, and the Judgment of Mankind* (New York: Viking, 2007).

89. "German Protest for Sacco-Vanzetti: Big Demonstrations Held in Many Cities on News of the Decision Against Them," *New York Times*, August 20, 1927, https://www.nytimes.com/1927/08/20/archives/germans-protest-for-saccovanzetti-big-demonstrations-held-in-many.html; "The NY Sacco and Vanzetti Meeting," *Labor Defender*, August 1927, 115–117; Palmer, *James P. Cannon*, 274–278; Judy Kutulas, *The Long War: The Intellectual People's Front and Anti-Stalinism, 1930–1940* (Durham, NC: Duke University Press, 1995), 26–27.

90. John Dos Passos, "They Are Dead Now," *New Masses*, October 1927, 7; Robert C. Rosen, *John Dos Passos: Politics and the Writer* (Lincoln: University of Nebraska Press, 1981), 52–56.

91. "50,000 Demonstrate in New York," *Daily Worker*, August 23, 1927, https://www.loc.gov/resource/sn84020097/1927-08-23/ed-1/?sp=2.

92. John Dos Passos, *The Big Money* (New York: Harcourt, Brace, 1936), 462–463.

93. For the "subterranean" impact of the Sacco-Vanzetti case on American politics, see Malcolm Cowley, *Exile's Return: A Literary Odyssey of the 1920s* (New York: Penguin Books, 1976), 221, 223.

Chapter 2: "Toward Soviet America"

1. "The Wall Street Crash and the Working Class," *Daily Worker*, October 29, 1929, https://www.loc.gov/resource/sn84020097/1929-10-29/ed-1/?sp=1; "Mass Unemployment and Class Battles Grow in Crisis," *Daily Worker*, January 1, 1930, https://www.loc.gov/resource/sn84020097/1930-01-01/ed-1/?sp=1.

2. Nelson Lichtenstein et al., eds., *Who Built America? Working People and the Nation's Economy, Politics, Culture, and Society*, vol. 2, *Since 1877*, 2nd ed. (New York: Worth Publishers, 2000), 367–372, 382–383; US Bureau of the Census, *Historical Statistics of the United States: Colonial Times to 1970*, vol. 1, bicentennial ed. (Washington, DC: Government Printing Office, 1975), 70.

3. Harold Meyerson and Ernie Harburg, *Who Put the Rainbow in the Wizard of Oz? Yip Harburg, Lyricist* (Ann Arbor: University of Michigan Press, 1993), 46–52.

4. Francis MacDonnell, "If I Only Had a Brain: Yip Harburg, J. Edgar Hoover, and the Failures of FBI Intelligence Work," *Intelligence and National Security* 33, no. 1 (2018); Meyerson and Harburg, *Who Put the Rainbow*, 271–274.

5. Nick Salvatore, *Eugene V. Debs: Citizen and Socialist* (Urbana: University of Illinois Press, 1982), 341.

6. For Ruthenberg's descent into obscurity following his death, see Jack Stachel, "C. E. Ruthenberg and Problems of the Party Today," *Daily Worker*, March 7, 1933, https://www.loc.gov/resource/sn84020097/1933-03-07/ed-1/?sp=4.

7. Theodore Draper, *American Communism and Soviet Russia: The Formative Period* (New York: Viking Press, 1960), 243–244.

8. Ted Morgan, *A Covert Life: Jay Lovestone, Communist, Anti-Communist, and Spymaster* (New York: Random House, 1999), 5–18; Charles Shipman, *It Had to Be Revolution: Memoirs of an American Radical* (Ithaca, NY: Cornell University Press, 1993), 151.

9. Shipman, *It Had to Be Revolution*, 165–166; Maurice Isserman, "When New York City Was the Capital of American Communism," Opinion, *New York Times*, October 20, 2017, https://www.nytimes.com/2017/10/20/opinion/new-york-american-communism.html.

10. Benjamin Gitlow, *I Confess: The Truth About American Communism* (New York: E. P. Dutton, 1940), 430–431.

11. Bryan D. Palmer, *James P. Cannon and the Origins of the American Revolutionary Left, 1890–1928* (Urbana: University of Illinois Press, 2007), 300–301.

12. Quoted in Draper, *American Communism and Russia*, 272. On Bukharin's political evolution in the 1920s, see Stephen F. Cohen, *Bukharin and the Bolshevik Revolution: A Political Biography, 1888–1938* (New York: Oxford University Press, 1980), 123–159.

13. Quoted in Draper, *American Communism and Russia*, 278. On Bukharin's views about American capitalism, see Cohen, *Bukharin*, 43.

14. Leonard Schapiro, *The Communist Party of the Soviet Union*, 2nd ed. (New York: Vintage, 1971), 365–372.

15. Draper, *American Communism and Russia*, 301–305.

16. Leon Trotsky, "The Third International After Lenin," Marxists Internet Archive, https://www.marxists.org/archive/trotsky/1928/3rd/ti07.htm#p2–12.

17. Palmer, *James P. Cannon*, 326–334.

18. "NY Communists Hit Trotskyism," *Daily Worker*, November 21, 1928, https://www.loc.gov/resource/sn84020097/1928-11-21/ed-1/?sp=1; Palmer, *James P. Cannon*, 338–342.

19. Leon Trotsky, "On the Founding of the Fourth International," October 1938, Marxist Internet Archives, https://www.marxists.org/archive/trotsky/1938/10/foundfi.htm.

20. Draper, *American Communism and Russia*, 289–290.

21. Trade Union Unity League, *The Trade Union Unity League: Its Program, Structure, Methods and History* (New York: Trade Union Unity League, 1930), https://www.mltranslations.org/US/archive/tuul.htm; Irving Bernstein, *The Lean Years: A History of the American Worker, 1920–1933* (Boston: Houghton Mifflin, 1972), 140–141.

22. "The American Federation of Labor," *Fortune*, December 1933, 80; Bernstein, *Lean Years*, 506.

23. Edward P. Johanningsmeier, "The Trade Union Unity League: American Communists and the Transition to Industrial Unionism, 1928–1934," *Labor History* 42, no. 2 (Spring 2001), 160.

24. Bernstein, *Lean Years*, 41.

25. John A. Salmond, *Gastonia 1929: The Story of the Loray Mill Strike* (Chapel Hill: University of North Carolina Press, 1995), 8–10; Janet Irons, *Testing the New Deal: The General Strike of 1934 in the American South* (Urbana: University of Illinois Press, 2000), 29.

26. Bernstein, *Lean Years*, 20.

27. Irving Howe and Lewis Coser, *The American Communist Party: A Critical History* (Boston: Beacon Press, 1957), 176.

28. Glenda Elizabeth Gilmore, *Defying Dixie: The Radical Roots of Civil Rights, 1919–1950* (New York: Norton, 2008), 75.

29. Salmond, *Gastonia 1929*, 18; Gregory S. Taylor, *The History of the North Carolina Communist Party* (Columbia: University of South Carolina Press, 2009), 19–20.

30. Salmond, *Gastonia 1929*, 65–67; Gilmore, *Defying Dixie*, 80–81.

31. Fred W. Beal, *Proletarian Journey* (New York: Hillman-Curl, 1937), 159; Salmond, *Gastonia 1929*, 51–52, 61–63. On Wiggin's affiliation with the ILD, see Jennifer R. Uhlmann, "The Communist Civil Rights Movement: Legal Activism in the United States, 1919–1946" (PhD diss., University of California at Los Angeles, 2007), 159.

32. Salmond, *Gastonia 1929*, 46; Chuck McShane, "The Loray Mill Strike in Gastonia," *Our State*, https://www.ourstate.com/loray-mill-strike/.

33. Paul Blanshard, "Communism in Southern Cotton Mills," *The Nation*, April 24, 1929, 501.

34. William F. Dunne, *Gastonia: Citadel of the Class Struggle in the New South* (New York: Workers Library, 1929), https://mltranslations.org/US/archive/gastonia.htm#A_Living_Document.

35. Beal, *Proletarian Journey*, 129; Salmond, *Gastonia 1929*, 27–28.

36. Salmond, *Gastonia 1929*, 75–78.

37. Quoted in Dee Garrison, *Mary Heaton Vorse: The Life of an American Insurgent* (Philadelphia: Temple University Press, 1990), 226.

38. Garrison, *Mary Heaton Vorse*, 229; Taylor, *North Carolina Communist Party*, 47–48.

39. Taylor, *North Carolina Communist Party*, 49–51; Gilmore, *Defying Dixie*, 103–104.

40. Quoted in Bernstein, *Lean Years*, 28. Also see Beal, *Proletarian Journey*, 237–334.

41. William Z. Foster, *History of the Communist Party of the United States* (New York: International Publishers, 1952), 250–254.

42. Taylor, *North Carolina Communist Party*, 65–66; Michael Denning, *The Cultural Front: The Laboring of American Culture in the Twentieth Century* (New York: Verso, 2011), 262.

43. Joseph Stalin, "First Speech Delivered in the Presidium of the ECCI, on the American Question, May 14, 1929," Marxists Internet Archive, https://www.marxists.org/reference/archive/stalin/works/1929/cpusa.htm; Robert J. Alexander, *The Right Opposition: The Lovestoneites and the International Communist Opposition of the 1930s* (Westport, CT: Greenwood Press, 1979), 16–28.

44. "NY Functionaries for Comintern Address, Against Open and Concealed Opposition," *Daily Worker*, June 10, 1929, https://www.loc.gov/resource/sn84020097/1929-06-10/ed-1/?sp=1.

45. Morgan, *Covert Life*, ix–x, 84–104; Alexander, *Right Opposition*, 29–135; Landon R. Y. Storrs, *The Second Red Scare and the Unmaking of the New Deal Left* (Princeton: Princeton University Press, 2013), 112.

46. Al Richmond, *A Long View from the Left: Memoirs of an American Revolutionary* (Boston: Houghton Mifflin, 1973), 82–83.

47. David Shannon, *The Decline of American Communism: A History of the Communist Party of the United States Since 1945* (New York: Harcourt, Brace, 1959), 10.

48. Maurice Isserman, *Which Side Were You On? The American Communist Party During the Second World War* (Middletown, CT: Wesleyan University Press, 1982), 5.

49. James G. Ryan, *Earl Browder: The Failure of American Communism* (Tuscaloosa: University of Alabama Press, 1997), 8–27.

50. Ryan, *Earl Browder*, 34.

51. Peter Hartshorne, *I Have Seen the Future: A Life of Lincoln Steffens* (Berkeley, CA: Counterpoint, 2011), 315.

52. Peter Kuznick, *Beyond the Laboratory: Scientists as Political Activists in 1930s America* (Chicago: University of Chicago Press, 1987), 106.

53. Samantha A. Kravitz, "The Business of Selling the Soviet Union: Intourist and the Wooing of American Travelers, 1929–1939" (master's thesis, Concordia University, 2006), 40; Judy Kutulas, *The Long War: The Intellectual People's Front and Anti-Stalinism, 1930–1940* (Durham, NC: Duke University Press, 1995), 43.

54. John Dewey, "Impressions of Soviet Russia," *New Republic*, November 20, 1928, 343–344.

55. Jay Martin, *The Education of John Dewey: A Biography* (New York: Columbia University Press, 2002), 350–358; Kutulas, *Long War*, 46.

56. Richard Wright, "I Tried to Be a Communist," *Atlantic Monthly*, August 1944, 62. For the John Reed Clubs' growth and vitality in the early 1930s, see Kutulas, *Long War*, 39–40.

57. League of Professional Groups for Foster and Ford, *Culture and the Crisis: An Open Letter to the Writers, Artists, and Other Professional Workers of America* (New York: Workers Library, 1932); Alan Wald, *The New York Intellectuals: The Rise and Decline of the Anti-Stalinist Left From the 1930s to the 1980s* (Chapel Hill: University of North Carolina Press, 1987), 58–59.

58. Whittaker Chambers, "Can You Hear Their Voices?," *New Masses*, March 1931, 7–16; Sam Tanenhaus, *Whittaker Chambers: A Biography* (New York: Random House, 1997), 71–73.

59. For Soviet espionage efforts in the United States in the 1930s and 1940s, see Allen Weinstein and Alexander Vassiliev, *The Haunted Wood: Soviet Espionage in America—the Stalin Era* (New York: Random House, 1999), and John Earl Hayes, Harvey Klehr, and Alexander Vassiliev, *Spies: The Rise and Fall of the KGB in America* (New Haven, CT: Yale University Press, 2009).

60. "110,000 Demonstrate in New York for Jobless' Demands; Defy Police," *Daily Worker*, March 7, 1930, https://www.loc.gov/resource/sn84020097/1930-03-07/ed-1/?sp=1; "35,000 Jammed in Square: Views of the Red Rioting in Union Square Yesterday," *New York Times*, March 7, 1930, https://www.nytimes.com/1930/03/07/archives/35000-jammed-in -square-views-of-the-red-rioting-in-union-square.html.

61. "35,000 Jammed in Square," 1; Fraser Ottanelli, *The Communist Party of the United States: From the Depression to World War II* (New Brunswick, NJ: Rutgers University Press, 1991), 31–32.

62. Dorothy Ray Healey and Maurice Isserman, *California Red: A Life in the American Communist Party* (Urbana: University of Illinois Press, 1994), 32–33.

63. Steve Nelson, James R. Barrett, and Rob Ruck, *Steve Nelson: American Radical* (Pittsburgh: University of Pittsburgh Press, 1981), 76; Randi Storch, *Red Chicago: American Communism at Its Grassroots* (Urbana: University of Illinois Press, 2007), 74.

64. Rick Halpern, *Down on the Killing Floor: Black and White Workers in Chicago's Packinghouses, 1904–1954* (Urbana: University of Illinois Press, 1997), 110; Ottanelli, *The Communist Party of the United States*, 29.

65. James Gregory, "Communist Party Votes by State and County 1922–1946," Mapping American Social Movements Project, University of Washington, https://depts.washington .edu/moves/CP_map-votes.shtml.

66. "Roosevelt to Carry on the Hoover Hunger Rule," *Daily Worker*, November 9, 1932, https://www.loc.gov/resource/sn84020097/1932-11-09/ed-1/?sp=1; "Communist Vote in New York City," *Daily Worker*, November 10, 1932, https://www.loc.gov/resource /sn84020097/1932-11-10/ed-1/?sp=1; Michael Kazin, *What It Took to Win: A History of the Democratic Party* (New York: Farrar, Straus and Giroux, 2022), 165–168.

67. Ottanelli, *Communist Party*, 57.

68. Harvey Klehr, John Earl Haynes, and Kyrill M. Anderson, *The Soviet World of American Communism* (New Haven, CT: Yale University Press, 1998), 280–281; Ottanelli, *Communist Party*, 18–19, 55.

69. William Z. Foster, *Toward Soviet America* (New York: Coward McCann, 1932), 1–2, 268–275.

70. Quoted in Tony Michels, "The Abramovitch Campaign and What It Tells Us About American Communism," *American Communist History* 15, no. 3 (2016), 286.

71. Joseph Shaplen, "Mr. Foster's Vision of a Soviet United States of America," *New York Times Book Review*, June 19, 1932.

72. Theodore Draper, "Communists and Miners, 1928–1933," *Dissent*, April 1972, 380.

73. Healey and Isserman, *California Red*, 37.

74. Justin Akers Chácon, *Radicals in the Barrio: Magonistas, Socialists, Wobblies, and Communists in the Mexican-American Working Class* (Chicago: Haymarket Books, 2018), 402; Cletus Daniel, *Bitter Harvest: A History of California Farmworkers, 1870–1941* (Ithaca, NY: Cornell University Press, 1981), 142, 220.

75. Robert H. Zieger, *The CIO, 1935–1955* (Chapel Hill: University of North Carolina Press, 1995), 47–48.

76. "Thomas Joins Roosevelt in Fooling the Workers," *Daily Worker*, June 17, 1933, https://www.loc.gov/resource/sn84020097/1933-06-17/ed-1/?sp=1.

77. United States Senate, *To Create a National Labor Board: Hearings Before the Committee on Education and Labor, United States Senate, Seventy-Third Congress, Second Session* (Washington, DC: Government Printing Office, 1934), 990–991.

78. Quoted in David F. Selvin, *A Terrible Anger: The 1934 Waterfront and General Strikes in San Francisco* (Detroit: Wayne State University Press, 1996), 58.

79. Bruce Nelson, *Workers on the Waterfront: Seamen, Longshoremen, and Unionism in the 1930s* (Urbana: University of Illinois Press, 1988), 79–80, 88–90.

80. Selvin, *Terrible Anger*, 58.

81. Nelson, *Workers on the Waterfront*, 88–94, 104–105.

82. "Oh Mr. Dink," *Waterfront Worker*, March 1933, 8; Charles P. Larrowe, *Harry Bridges: The Rise and Fall of Radical Labor in the United States* (New York: Lawrence Hill, 1972), 13.

83. *Waterfront Worker*, February 1934, 3.

84. Robert W. Cherny, *Harry Bridges: Labor Radical, Labor Legend* (Urbana: University of Illinois Press, 2023), 12–26, 42–44; Selvin, *Terrible Anger*, 57–59.

85. Cherny, *Harry Bridges*, 59–106; Nelson, *Workers on the Waterfront*, 127–155.

86. Earl Browder, *Report of the Central Committee to the Eighth Convention of the Communist Party* (New York: Workers Library, 1934), 34.

87. Quoted in Vernon L. Pederson, *The Communist Party on the American Waterfront: Revolution, Reform, and the Quest for Power* (Lanham, MD: Lexington Books, 2019), 138.

88. Draper, *American Communism and Russia*, 315–316.

89. Robin D. G. Kelley, *Hammer and Hoe: Alabama Communists During the Great Depression* (Chapel Hill: University of North Carolina Press, 1990), 4–7.

90. Robin D. G. Kelley, "This Ain't Ethiopia, But It'll Do," in Danny Duncan Collum, ed., *African Americans in the Spanish Civil War: "This Ain't Ethiopia, But It'll Do"* (New York: G. K. Hall, 1992), 8.

91. Winston James, *Claude McKay: The Making of a Black Bolshevik* (New York: Columbia University Press, 2022), 347–348.

92. Gilmore, *Defying Dixie*, 33–43.

93. Mark Solomon, *The Cry Was Unity: Communists and African Americans, 1917–1936* (Jackson: University Press of Mississippi, 1998), 70.

94. Harry Haywood, *Black Bolshevik: Autobiography of an Afro-American Communist* (Chicago: Liberator Press, 1978), 148–175; Solomon, *Cry Was Unity*, 343–344.

95. Kelley, "This Ain't Ethiopia," 9; Gilmore, *Defying Dixie*, 51–56.

96. Gilmore, *Defying Dixie*, 96.

97. Nell Irvin Painter, *The Narrative of Hosea Hudson: His Life as a Negro Communist in the South* (Cambridge, MA: Harvard University Press, 1979), 139.

98. Angelo Herndon, *Let Me Live* (New York: Random House, 1937); Gilmore, *Defying Dixie*, 161–166; Gerald Horne, *Black Liberation/Red Scare: Ben Davis and the Communist Party* (Newark: University of Delaware Press, 1994), 35–40.

99. Kelley, *Hammer and Hoe*, 30.

100. Kelley, *Hammer and Hoe*, 33, 39–42, 61.

101. Gilmore, *Defying Dixie*, 118–121.

102. James S. Allen, *Organizing in the Depression South: A Communist's Memoir* (Minneapolis: MEP Publications, 2001), 21–22, 34–36; Gilmore, *Defying Dixie*, 118–119.

103. Dan T. Carter, *Scottsboro: A Tragedy of the American South* (New York: Oxford University Press, 1975), 51–52; Allen, *Organizing in Depression South*, 79–80.

104. Carter, *Scottsboro*, 51–61; Gilmore, *Defying Dixie*, 122.

105. Erik McDuffie, *Sojourning for Freedom: Black Women, American Communism, and the Making of Black Left Feminism* (Durham, NC: Duke University Press, 2011), 63; Erik McDuffie, "'For a New Antifascist, Anti-imperialist People's Coalition': Claudia Jones, Black Left Feminism, and the Politics of Possibility in the Era of Trump," in Vernon Pederson, James G. Ryan, and Katherine A. S. Sibley, eds., *Post-Cold War Revelations and the American Communist Party: Citizens, Revolutionaries, and Spies* (London: Bloomsbury Academic, 2021), 189.

106. W. E. B. Du Bois, "The Negro and Communism," *The Crisis*, September 1931, 315. Also see Patrick Anderson, "Pan-Africanism and Economic Nationalism: W. E. B. Du Bois's *Black Reconstruction* and the Failings of the 'Black Marxism' Thesis," *Journal of Black Studies* 48, no. 8 (November 2017), 742–743.

107. Haywood, *Black Bolshevik*, 443–444; Halpern, *Down on Killing Floor*, 108–109; Kelley, *Hammer and Hoe*, 21–23, 79–80, 108; Mark Naison, *Communists in Harlem During the Depression* (Urbana: University of Illinois Press, 1983), 57–71; Walter T. Howard, *Black Communists Speak on Scottsboro: A Documentary History* (Philadelphia: Temple University Press, 2008), 2–3.

108. "Why We Can't Hate Reds," *Chicago Defender*, January 14, 1933.

109. Harvey Klehr, *Communist Cadre: The Social Background of the American Communist Party Elite* (Stanford, CA: Hoover Institution Press, 1978), 57.

110. James Gregory, "Communist Party Membership by Districts 1922–1950," Mapping American Social Movements Project, University of Washington, https://depts.washington.edu/moves/CP_map-members.shtml.

111. George Charney, *A Long Journey* (Chicago: Quadrangle, 1968), 42–44.

Chapter 3: "Double-Check American"

1. Martin L. Duberman, *Paul Robeson* (New York: Knopf, 1988), 236–237.

2. Earl Robinson, *Ballad of an American: The Autobiography of Earl Robinson*, with Eric A. Gordon (Lanham, MD: Scarecrow Press, 1998), 28–29, 68–69; Lisa Barg, "Paul Robeson's Ballad for Americans: Race and the Cultural Politics of 'People's Music,'" *Journal of the Society for American Music* 2, no. 1 (2008), 34–35; Richard A. Reuss and JoAnne C. Reuss, *American Folk Music and Left-Wing Politics, 1927–1957* (Lanham, MD: Scarecrow Press, 2000), 49–53; Maria Cristina Fava, "The Composers' Collective of New York, 1932–1936: Bourgeois Modernism for the Proletariat," *American Music* 34, no. 3 (Fall 2016), 301–343.

3. Robinson, *Ballad of an American*, 51–54, 76–78.

4. Duberman, *Paul Robeson*, xii.

5. Whether or not Robeson was a card-carrying Communist was long a subject of debate. Biographer Martin Duberman concluded Robeson was not. Duberman, *Paul Robeson*, 418. But CPUSA general secretary Gus Hall published a pamphlet many years after Robeson's death entitled *Paul Robeson: American Communist* (New York: Communist Party USA, 1990).

6 Barg, "Paul Robeson's Ballad," 27, 58–59; "I Hear America Singing," *Time*, July 8, 1940; Robinson, *Ballad of an American*, 95–100.

7. Kevin Jack Hagopian, "'You Know Who I Am!' Paul Robeson's Ballad for Americans and the Paradox of the Double V in American Popular Front Culture," in Joseph Dorinson and William Pencak, eds., *Paul Robeson: Essays on His Life and Legacy* (Jefferson, NC: McFarland, 2002), 176.

8. Richard Hofstadter, *The Age of Reform: From Bryan to FDR* (New York: Knopf, 1955), 36; Susan Stout Baker, *Radical Beginnings: Richard Hofstadter and the 1930s* (Westport, CT: Greenwood Press, 1985), 89–90, 141–143.

9. Fernando Claudín, *The Communist Movement: From Comintern to Cominform*, vol. 1, *The Crisis of the Communist International* (New York: Monthly Review Press, 1975), 127.

10. "Support German Masses in Struggle Against Fascism!," *Daily Worker*, February 1, 1933, https://www.loc.gov/resource/sn84020097/1933-02-01/ed-1/?sp=1.

11. "Still Preparing to Repeat the Betrayal of 1914," *Daily Worker*, June 1, 1933, https://www.loc.gov/resource/sn84020097/1933-06-01/ed-1/?sp=4.

12. "Manifesto and Program of the American League Against War and Fascism," *Daily Worker*, June 30, 1934, 4; Judy Kutulas, *The Long War: The Intellectual People's Front and Anti-Stalinism, 1930–1940* (Durham, NC: Duke University Press, 1995), 76–77.

13. "Rally Today at Madison Square Garden," *Daily Worker*, February 16, 1934, https://www.loc.gov/resource/sn84020097/1934-02-16/ed-1/?sp=1; "Despite Provocations of SP Leaders, Workers Unite for Garden Meet," *Daily Worker*, February 17, 1934, https://www.loc.gov/resource/sn84020097/1934-02-17/ed-1/?sp=1.

14. Jonathan Haslam, *The Soviet Union and the Struggle for Collective Security in Europe, 1933–39* (New York: St. Martin's Press, 1984), 54–57, 184.

15. Marietta Stankova, *Georgi Dimitrov: A Biography* (London, I. B. Tauris, 2010), 103–111.

16. Georgi Dimitrov, *The United Front: The Struggle Against Fascism and War* (New York: International Publishers, 1938), 9–94.

17. Dimitrov, *The United Front*, 23.

18. Dimitrov, *The United Front*, 99–100.

19. Earl Browder, "The United Front—the Key to Our New Tactical Orientation," *The Communist*, December 1935, 1075–1076.

20. Dimitrov, *The United Front*, 106.

21. Quoted in Fraser Ottanelli, *The Communist Party of the United States: From the Depression to World War II* (New Brunswick, NJ: Rutgers University Press, 1991), 92.

22. Irving Howe and Lewis Coser, *The American Communist Party: A Critical History* (Boston: Beacon Press, 1957), 341.

23. George Charney, *A Long Journey* (Chicago: Quadrangle, 1968), 59. For Howe's rethinking of the meaning of the Popular Front see his *Socialism and America* (New York: Harcourt, Brace, 1985), 87–104.

24. Paula S. Fass, *The Beautiful and the Damned: American Youth in the 1920s* (New York: Oxford University Press, 1977).

25. For the impact of the Depression on college and university students in the early Depression years, see James Wechsler, *Revolt on the Campus* (New York: Covici, 1935), 49–59.

26. Robert Cohen, *When the Old Left Was Young: Student Radicals and America's First Mass Student Movement, 1929–1941* (New York: Oxford University Press, 1993), 24–30.

27. Cohen, *When the Old Left Was Young*, 38.

28. Cohen, *When the Old Left Was Young*, 92–95.

29. Cohen, *When the Old Left Was Young*, 54–97; Wechsler, *Revolt on the Campus*, 171–175.

30. Cohen, *When the Old Left Was Young*, 234–237.

31. Anders Stephenson, "Interview with Gil Green," in Michael E. Brown et al., eds., *New Studies in the Politics and Culture of US Communism* (New York: Monthly Review Press, 1993), 307–308.

32. Harvey Klehr, *Communist Cadre: The Social Background of the American Communist Party Elite* (Stanford, CA: Hoover Institution Press, 1978), 22–23.

33. Harvey Klehr, *The Heyday of American Communism: The Depression Decade* (New York: Basic Books, 1984), 217, 258–259.

34. Maurice Isserman, *Which Side Were You On? The American Communist Party During the Second World War* (Middletown, CT: Wesleyan University Press, 1982), 259, footnote. The author's full interview with George Watt is available in the Maurice Isserman Oral History Interviews collection at the Tamiment Library, New York University, http://dlib.nyu.edu/findingaids/html/tamwag/oh_036/dscaspace_ref48.html.

35. Howe and Coser, *American Communist Party*, 341; Ryan, *Earl Browder*, 104–105.

36. Isserman, *Which Side Were You On?*, 259, footnote.

37. "American Jews in the Spanish Civil War," Stroum Center for Jewish Studies, University of Washington, https://jewishstudies.washington.edu/american-jews-spanish-civil-war/george-watt/.

38. Isserman, *Which Side Were You On?*, 11.

39. Glenda Elizabeth Gilmore, *Defying Dixie: The Radical Roots of Civil Rights, 1919–1950* (New York: Norton, 2008), 308–309.

40. Quoted in Erik S. Gellman, *Death Blow to Jim Crow: The National Negro Congress and the Rise of Militant Civil Rights* (Chapel Hill: University of North Carolina Press, 2012), 28–29.

41. Lawrence S. Wittner, "The National Negro Congress: A Reassessment," *American Quarterly* 22, no. 4 (Winter 1970), 867.

42. Johnetta Richards, "Fundamentally Determined: James E. Jackson and Esther Cooper Jackson and the Southern Negro Youth Congress, 1937–1946," *American Communist History* 7, no. 2, 2008, 191–202.

43. Quoted in Henry Hart, ed., *The Writer in a Changing World* (London: Lawrence and Wishart, 1937), 56–62.

44. *Daily Worker*, June 7, 1939, 7.

45. Camille Yvette Welsh, "The Critical Reception of John Steinbeck's *Grapes of Wrath*," in Keith Newlin, ed., *Critical Insights: The Grapes of Wrath* (Pasadena, CA: Salem Press, 2011), 92.

46. Letter from John Steinbeck to Louis Paul, February 1936, in Elaine Steinbeck and Robert Wallsten, eds., *Steinbeck: A Life in Letters* (New York: Penguin Books, 1989), 120; Susan Shillinglaw, *Carol and John Steinbeck: Portrait of a Marriage* (Reno: University of Nevada Press, 2013), 140–145, 171–172, 192–193.

47. Steve Fraser and Gary Gerstle, eds., *The Rise and Fall of the New Deal Order, 1930–1980* (Princeton, NJ: Princeton University Press, 1990); David Plotke, "The Wagner Act, Again: Politics and Labor, 1935–37," *Studies in American Political Development* 3 (Spring 1989), 114–118.

48. Robert H. Zieger, *The CIO, 1935–1955* (Chapel Hill: University of North Carolina Press, 1995), 2.

49. Zieger, *The CIO*, 42–65; Judith Stepan-Norris and Maurice Zeitlin, *Left Out: Reds and American Industrial Unions* (Cambridge: Cambridge University Press, 2003), 39.

50. Dimitrov, *The United Front*, 63; Robert W. Cherny, "Prelude to the Popular Front: The Communist Party in California, 1931–1935," *American Communist History* 1, no. 1 (2002), 28–29.

51. Harvey Klehr, John Earl Haynes, and Fridrikh Igorevich Firsov, *The Secret World of American Communism* (New Haven, CT: Yale University Press, 1995), 55, 68.

52. Gilbert J. Gall, *Pursuing Justice: Lee Pressman, the New Deal, and the CIO* (Albany: State University of New York Press, 1999), 62.

53. Quoted in Ottanelli, *The Communist Party of the United States*, 139.

54. Quoted in Zieger, *The CIO*, 83.

55. Irving Bernstein, *The Turbulent Years: A History of the American Worker, 1933–1941* (Boston: Houghton Mifflin, 1970), 122–123, 782.

56. Rosemary Feurer, "William Sentner, the UE, and Civic Unionism in St. Louis," in Steve Rosswurm, ed., *The CIO's Left Led Unions* (New Brunswick, NJ: Rutgers University Press, 1992), 95–96; Ronald L. Filippelli and Mark D. McColloch, *Cold War in the Working Class: The Rise and Decline of the United Electrical Workers* (Albany: State University of New York Press, 1995), 6–7, 36–37.

57. Robert Cherny concluded that if Harry Bridges "was ever a formal party member, it was likely for only a brief period." See Robert W. Cherny, *Harry Bridges: Labor Radical, Labor Legend* (Urbana: University of Illinois Press, 2023), 166.

58. Quoted in Isserman, *Which Side Were You On?*, 14.

59. Ottanelli, *Communist Party of the United States*, 144–145.

60. Sidney Fine, *Sit-Down: The General Motors Strike of 1936–1937* (Ann Arbor: University of Michigan Press, 1969), 21–22.

61. Wyndham Mortimer, *Organize! My Life as a Union Man* (Boston: Beacon Press, 1971), 1–57.

62. Sidney Fine, *Frank Murphy: The New Deal Years* (Chicago: University of Chicago Press, 1979), 291–292.

63. Roger Keeran, *The Communist Party and the Auto Workers Unions* (Bloomington: Indiana University Press, 1980), 148–151.

64. Keeran, *Communist Party and Auto Workers*, 153.

65. Michael Torigian, "The Occupation of the Factories: Paris 1936, Flint 1937," *Comparative Studies in Society and History* 41, no. 2 (April 1999), 328, 341–342.

66. Torigian, "Occupation of the Factories," 325–329; Fine, *Frank Murphy*, 293–294.

67. Fine, *Frank Murphy*, 295–297; Gall, *Pursuing Justice*, pp 64–65.

68. Fine, *Sit-Down*, 156–167.

69. Carl Haessler, "The Auto Union Shifts into High," *New Masses*, January 19, 1937, 7; Torigian, "Occupation of the Factories," 342.

70. Nelson Lichtenstein, *The Most Dangerous Man in Detroit: Walter Reuther and the Fate of American Labor* (New York: Basic Books, 1995), 78–79.

71. Fine, *Sit-Down*, 327.

72. Mary Heaton Vorse, *Labor's New Millions* (New York: Modern Age, 1938), 90; Dee Garrison, *Mary Heaton Vorse: The Life of an American Insurgent* (Philadelphia: Temple University Press, 1990), 275–282; Henry Kraus, *The Many and the Few: A Chronicle of the Dynamic Auto Workers* (Urbana: University of Illinois Press, 1985), 289–291.

73. Zieger, *The CIO*, 71.

74. Lichtenstein, *The Most Dangerous Man in Detroit*, 126–127.

75. Klehr, *Heyday of American Communism*, 173–176.

76. Charney, *A Long Journey*, 95.

77. David Saposs, *Communism in American Politics* (New York: PublicAffairs Press, 1960), 33–34; Gerald Meyer, *Vito Marcantonio: Radical Politician, 1902–1954* (Albany: State University of New York Press, 1989), 53–86; Klehr, *Heyday of American Communism*, 291.

78 Earl Browder, *Fighting for Peace* (New York: International Publishers, 1939), 200; Dorothy Ray Healey and Maurice Isserman, *California Red: A Life in the American Communist Party* (Urbana: University of Illinois Press, 1994), 78–79.

79. Klehr, *Heyday of American Communism*, 205.

80. Charney, *A Long Journey*, 94; Klehr, *Heyday of American Communism*, 370.

81. *Daily Worker*, February 13, 1933, quoted in Howe and Coser, *American Communist Party*, 218.

82. Ottanelli, *Communist Party*, 127; Ed Cray, *Ramblin' Man: The Life and Times of Woody Guthrie* (New York: Norton, 2004), 152–153.

83. Mike Gold, "Change the World," *Daily Worker*, August 31, 1935, 7.

84. James Gregory, "Communist Party Membership by Districts 1922–1950," Mapping American Social Movements Project, University of Washington, https://depts.wash ington.edu/moves/CP_map-members.shtml.

85. Charney, *A Long Journey*, 6.

86. Hugh Thomas, *The Spanish Civil War* (New York: Harper and Row, 1961), 117–164.

87. Peter Carroll, *The Odyssey of the Abraham Lincoln Brigade: Americans in the Spanish Civil War* (Stanford, CA: Stanford University Press, 1994), 11–12.

88. Giles Tremlett, *The International Brigades: Fascism, Freedom, and the Spanish Civil War* (London: Bloomsbury Publishing, 2020), 231–233; Adam Hochschild, *Spain in Our Hearts: Americans in the Spanish Civil War, 1936–1939* (Boston: Houghton Mifflin, 2016), 99–103.

89. John Gates, *The Story of an American Communist* (New York: Thomas Nelson, 1958), 42–48; Bruce Lambert, "John Gates, 78, Former Editor of the Daily Worker, Is Dead," *New York Times*, May 24, 1992, https://www.nytimes.com/1992/05/25/nyregion/john-gates -78-former-editor-of-the-daily-worker-is-dead.html.

90. Carroll, *Odyssey of Lincoln Brigade*, 66–68.

91. Carroll, *Odyssey of Lincoln Brigade*, 94–95.

92. Hochschild, *Spain In Our Hearts*, 110–111.

93. Carroll, *Odyssey of Lincoln Brigade*, 97–102; Marion Merriman and Warren Lerude, *American Commander in Spain: Robert Hale Merriman and the Abraham Lincoln Brigade* (Reno: University of Nevada Press, 1986), 75–77.

94. Fred Klonsky, "My Father Chose to Be a Red," *Jacobin*, August 28, 2017, https://jacobin.com/2017/08/spanish-civil-war-international-brigades-communist-party; "Guide to the Robert Klonsky Papers," Tamiment Library, New York University, http://dlib.nyu.edu/findingaids/html/tamwag/alba_219/.

95. Charney, *A Long Journey*, 84.

96. Carroll, *Odyssey of Lincoln Brigade*, 77–79; Merriman and Lerude, *American Commander in Spain*, 134.

97. Ernest Hemingway, *For Whom the Bell Tolls* (New York: Charles Scribner, 1940), 163.

98. Ichiro Takayoshi, "The Wages of War: Liberal Gullibility, Soviet Intervention, and the End of the Popular Front," *Representations* 115, no. 1 (Summer 2011), 119.

99. Carlos Baker, *Ernest Hemingway: A Life Story* (New York: Charles Scribner, 1969), 330.

100. George Watt, *The Comet Connection: Escape from Hitler's Europe* (Lexington: University Press of Kentucky, 1990), 97, 108, 110; Gates, *Story of an American Communist*, 57–60; Merriman and Lerude, *American Commander in Spain*, 216–217; Hochschild, *Spain in Our Hearts*, xiv–xv, 305–308.

101. Quoted in Tremlett, *The International Brigades*, 512. Also see Gates, *Story of an American Communist*, 66–67; Hochschild, *Spain in Our Hearts*, 335–337.

102. Ernest Hemingway, "On the American Dead in Spain," *New Masses*, February 14, 1939, 3.

103. "Between Ourselves," *New Masses*, February 14, 1939, 2.

104. Alvah Bessie, "Hemingway's 'For Whom the Bell Tolls,'" *New Masses*, November 5, 1940, 29.

105. Gavin Bowd, "André Marty and Ernest Hemingway," *Forum for Modern Language Studies* 55, no. 1 (September 2018), 11–13.

106. Baker, *Ernest Hemingway*, 356–357; Patrick Chura, *Michael Gold: The People's Writer* (Albany: State University of New York Press, 2020), 206–207.

107. For the concept of the 1940s as the "harvest time" for Soviet espionage, see Allen Weinstein and Alexander Vassiliev, *The Haunted Wood: Soviet Espionage in America—the Stalin Era* (New York: Random House, 1999), 151–237.

108. Klehr, Haynes, and Firsov, *The Secret World of American Communism*, 42.

109. Klehr, *Heyday of American Communism*, 161.

110. Weinstein and Vassiliev, *The Haunted Wood*, 22–23.

111. Ronald Radosh and Joyce Milton, *The Rosenberg File*, 2nd ed. (New Haven: Yale University Press, 1997), 29; Maurice Isserman and Ellen Schrecker, "'Papers of a Dangerous Tendency': From Major Andre's Boot to the VENONA Files," in Ellen Schrecker, ed., *Cold War Triumphalism: The Misuse of History After the Fall of Communism* (New York: New Press, 2004), 167.

112. Weinstein and Vassiliev, *The Haunted Wood*, 162.

113. Weinstein and Vassiliev, *The Haunted Wood*, 75.

114. Anne Applebaum, *Gulag: A History* (New York: Doubleday, 2003), 578–586.

115. "'I Am at Home,' Says Robeson at Reception in Soviet Union," *Daily Worker*, January 15, 1935, https://www.loc.gov/resource/sn84020097/1935-01-15/ed-1/?sp=5.

116. "Review and Comment," *New Masses*, January 19, 1937, 23.

117. Quoted in Garrison, *Mary Heaton Vorse*, 239, emphasis in the original.

118. Earl Browder, *Traitors in American History: Lessons of the Moscow Trials* (New York: Workers Library, 1938), 27.

119. Dennis, *The Autobiography of an American Communist*, 117–118.

120. Malcolm Cowley, "Stalin or Satan," *New Republic*, January 20, 1937, 348–349.

121. "Letters to the Editor," *The Nation*, May 27, 1939, 626.

122. "Letters to the Editor," *The Nation*, August 26, 1939, 228.

Chapter 4: "Welcome Back to the Fight"

1. "Real Boy Meets Real Girl," *New Masses*, December 15, 1942, 29–30.

2. Aljean Harmetz, *Round Up the Usual Suspects: The Making of Casablanca—Bogart, Bergman, and World War II* (New York: Hyperion, 1992), 245; Howard Koch, *As Time Goes By* (New York: Harcourt Brace Jovanovich, 1979), 80, 164–165; "Howard Koch, a Screenwriter for 'Casablanca,' Dies at 93," *New York Times*, August 18, 1995, https://www.nytimes.com/1995/08/18/obituaries/howard-koch-a-screenwriter-for-casablanca-dies-at-93.html.

3. See, for example, "Roosevelt Budgets New Warships, Bans Bonus," *Daily Worker*, January 1, 1935, https://www.loc.gov/resource/sn84020097/1935-01-01/ed-1/?sp=1.

4. "Caballero Asks Americans Aid, Defend Spain," *Daily Worker*, October 27, 1936, 1.

5. Judy Kutulas, *The Long War: The Intellectual People's Front and Anti-Stalinism, 1930–1940* (Durham, NC: Duke University Press, 1995), 104.

6. Earl Browder, *Fighting for Peace* (New York: International Publishers, 1939), 206–214.

7. Joseph Stalin, *Report on the Work of the Central Committee* (Moscow: Foreign Languages Publishing House, 1939), 8–17; "Bid to Germany Seen," *New York Times*, March 12, 1939, 1; Stephen Kotkin, *Stalin: Waiting for Hitler, 1929–1941* (New York: Penguin Press, 2017), 608–609.

8. George Charney, *A Long Journey* (Chicago: Quadrangle, 1968), 124.

9. *Daily Worker*, July 6, 1939, 1.

10. Jonathan Haslam, *The Soviet Union and the Struggle for Collective Security in Europe, 1933–39* (New York: St. Martin's Press, 1984), 317–323.

11. Melech Epstein, *The Jew and Communism, 1919–1941* (New York: Trade Union Sponsoring Committee, 1959), 350; Kotkin, *Stalin: Waiting for Hitler*, 659–667.

12. "Pacts Hurt Axis, Browder Asserts," *New York Times*, August 24, 1939, https://www.nytimes.com/1939/08/24/archives/pacts-hurt-axis-browdbr-asserts-he-sees-fascist-powers-not-the.html.

13. Granville Hicks, "On Leaving the Communist Party," *New Republic*, October 4, 1939, 244–245.

14. Charney, *A Long Journey*, 125; Epstein, *The Jew and Communism*, 351; The *Nation*, September 30, 1939, 344.

15. *New Republic*, September 6, 1939, 114.

16. Auden to League of American Writers, typescript, August 11, 1939, League of American Writers Collection, Bancroft Library, University of California at Berkeley. (Auden's letter was obviously misdated, and was probably written in early September 1939.)

17. Henry F. Srebrnik, "'The Jews Do Not Want War!': American-Jewish Communists Defend the Hitler-Stalin Pact, 1939–1941," *American Communist History* 8, no. 1 (2009), 60.

18. Thomas R. Maddux, "Red Fascism, Brown Bolshevism: The American Image of Totalitarianism in the 1930s," *The Historian* 40, no. 1 (November 1977), 99–100.

19. "Discussion by CP National Committee on International Situation," typescript, September 14–16, 1939, Phillip Jaffe private collection.

20. Fraser Ottanelli, *The Communist Party of the United States: From the Depression to World War II* (New Brunswick, NJ: Rutgers University Press, 1991), 185.

21. Harvey Klehr, John Earl Haynes, and Fridrikh Igorevich Firsov, *The Secret World of American Communism* (New Haven, CT: Yale University Press, 1995), 74, 81.

22. Maurice Isserman, *Which Side Were You On? The American Communist Party During the Second World War* (Middletown, CT: Wesleyan University Press, 1982), 41.

23. *Daily Worker*, November 23, 1939, 6.

24. The *Communist*, November 1939, 995; Philip Jaffe, *The Rise and Fall of American Communism* (New York: Horizon Press, 1975), 40–47.

25. Michael Gold, *The Hollow Men* (New York: International Publishers, 1941), 125.

26. Michael R. Belknap, *Cold War Political Justice: The Smith Act, the Communist Party, and American Civil Liberties* (Westport, CT: Greenwood Press, 1977), 22–27; M. J. Heale, *American Anticommunism: Combating the Enemy Within 1830–1970* (Baltimore: Johns Hopkins University Press, 1990), 126; John E. Haynes, *Red Scare or Red Menace? American Communism and Anticommunism in the Cold War Era* (Chicago: Ivan R. Dee, 1996), 33–34.

27. Harold Ickes, *The Secret Diary of Harold L. Ickes: The Lowering Clouds, 1939–1941* (New York: Simon and Schuster, 1954), 97.

28. Isserman, *Which Side Were You On?*, 85–87, 122–123.

29. Andrew Feffer, *Bad Faith: Teachers, Liberalism, and the Origins of McCarthyism* (New York: Fordham University Press, 2019), 56, 216; Marjorie Heins, *Priests of Our Democracy: The Supreme Court, Academic Freedom, and the Anti-Communist Purge* (New York: New York University Press, 2013), 51–66.

30. "TRB" [Kenneth Crawford], "Case History of a Red Hunt," *New Republic*, December 6, 1939, 189.

31. Corliss Lamont, ed., *The Trial of Elizabeth Gurley Flynn by the American Civil Liberties Union* (New York: Horizon Press, 1968); "ACLU Reverses Ouster of Elizabeth Gurley Flynn," *New York Times*, June 22, 1976, https://www.nytimes.com/1976/06/22/archives/aclu-reverses-ouster-of-elizabeth-gurley-flynn.html.

32. Peggy Dennis, *The Autobiography of an American Communist: A Personal View of a Political Life, 1925–1975* (Berkeley, CA: Lawrence Hill, 1977), 138–139, 144–146.

33. Dennis's figures for the remaining 1941 membership may have been inflated—at a meeting of the CP National Committee a year later in April 1942, total membership was reported as under 44,000, even though recruits had begun to trickle back into the Party by then. John Earl Haynes and Harvey Klehr, "The CPUSA Reports to the Comintern," *American Communist History* 4, no. 1 (2005), 26, 34; "National Committee Meeting Minutes," typescript, April 1942, Phillip Jaffe private collection.

34. Isserman, *Which Side Were You On?*, 84–85.

35. Isserman, *Which Side Were You On?*, 61, 78.

36. Isserman, *Which Side Were You On?*, 78–79.

37. Mortimer quoted in *Daily Worker*, November 24, 1940, 1. Also see "Agreement Ends the Vultee Strike," *New York Times*, November 27, 1940, https://www.nytimes.com/1940/11/27/archives/agreement-ends-the-vultee-strike-airplane-workers-return-to-plant.html.

38. *Daily Worker*, December 25, 1940, 5; Isserman, *Which Side Were You On?*, 81–82.

39. FDR to Henry Stimson and Frank Knox, typescript, June 4, 1941, OF: 263, FDR Library; Isserman, *Which Side Were You On?*, 89–90.

40. *The Communist*, January 1941, 93; Isserman, *Which Side Were You On?*, 90–100.

41. Martin Halpern, *UAW Politics in the Cold War Era* (Albany: State University of New York Press, 1988), 38; James Matles and James Higgins, *Them and Us: Struggles of a Rank-and-File Union* (Englewood Cliffs, NJ: Prentice-Hall, 1974), 53; Ronald L. Filippelli and Mark D. McColloch, *Cold War in the Working Class: The Rise and Decline of the United Electrical Workers* (Albany: State University of New York Press, 1995), 2, 80.

42. *Daily Worker*, June 12, 1940, 6.

43. *New Masses*, April 15, 1941, 5–6; *The Communist*, May 1941, 424.

44. *Daily Worker*, June 20, 1941, 6.

45. *Daily Worker*, June 25, 1941, 6.

46. Dimitrov quoted in Haynes and Klehr, "CPUSA Reports to Comintern," 59.

47. *The Communist*, August 1941, 707–708.

48. Isserman, *Which Side Were You On?*, 104.

49. John Gates, *The Story of an American Communist* (New York: Thomas Nelson, 1958), 81.

50. *Weekly Review*, December 9, 1941, 14.

51. *New Republic*, June 30, 1941, 877.

52. Will Kaufman, *Woody Guthrie: American Radical* (Urbana: University of Illinois Press. 2011), xxi.

53. "The Ballad of October 16," Almanac Singers, https://www.youtube.com/watch?v=2GtBV3uTfpI; Jon Pareles, "Millard Lampell, Writer and Supporter of Causes, Dies," *New York Times*, October 11, 1997, https://www.nytimes.com/1997/10/11/arts/millard-lampell-78-writer-and-supporter-of-causes-dies.html.

54. Woody Guthrie quoted in Allen M. Winkler, *"To Everything There Is a Season": Pete Seeger and the Power of Song* (New York: Oxford University Press, 2011), 30. Also see Robert Cantwell, *When We Were Good: The Folk Revival* (Cambridge, MA: Harvard University Press, 1996), 117–122; Robbie Lieberman, *"My Song Is My Weapon": People's Songs, American Communism, and the Politics of Culture* (Urbana, IL: University of Illinois Press, 1989) 56.

55. Lieberman, *"My Song Is My Weapon,"* 52–57; Jesse Jarnow, *Wasn't That a Time: The Weavers, the Blacklist, and the Battle for the Soul of America* (New York: Da Capo Press, 2018), 14–23.

56. Ed Cray, *Ramblin' Man: The Life and Times of Woody Guthrie* (New York: Norton, 2004), 280–281.

57. Cantwell, *When We Were Good*, 129–130.

58. *The Communist*, December 1941, 1045.

59. *Clarity*, Summer 1941, 67; Charney, *A Long Journey*, 126.

60. Author's interview with Max Gordon, February 15, 1977.

61. Earl Browder, *Victory and After* (New York: International Publishers, 1942), 132.

62. Author's interview with Ben Dvosin, January 8, 1978; Simon W. Gerson, *Pete: The Story of Peter V. Cacchione, New York's First Communist Councilman* (New York: International Publishers, 1976).

63. Mark Naison, *Communists in Harlem During the Depression* (Urbana: University of Illinois Press, 1983), 296–297, 310–311.

64. *The Communist*, October 1941, 894–895.

65. Irving Howe and Lewis Coser, *The American Communist Party: A Critical History* (Boston: Beacon Press, 1957), 416.

66. *Sunday Worker*, January 4, 1942, 1.

67. "Negro to Command Ship," *New York Times*, September 23, 1942, https://www.nytimes.com/1942/09/23/archives/negro-to-command-ship-mulzac-gets-the-booker-t-washington-ready.html; Hugh Mulzac, *A Star to Steer By* (New York: International Publishers, 1963), 130–151.

68. Isserman, *Which Side Were You On?*, 143.

69. Quoted in Edwin R. Lewinson, *Black Politics in New York City* (New York: Twayne Publishers, 1974), 78.

70. Joseph Starobin, *American Communism in Crisis, 1943–1957* (Cambridge, MA: Harvard University Press, 1972), 24.

71. Naison, *Communists in Harlem*, 314.

72. Guy Endore, *The Sleepy Lagoon Mystery* (Los Angeles: Sleepy Lagoon Defense Committee, 1944), 3.

73. Edward J. Escobar, *Race, Police, and the Making of a Political Identity: Mexican Americans and the Los Angeles Police Department, 1900–1945* (Berkeley: University of California Press, 1999), 275–288. Also see Justin Akers Chácon, *Radicals in the Barrio: Magonistas, Socialists, Wobblies, and Communists in the Mexican-American Working Class* (Chicago: Haymarket Books, 2018), 555–569.

74. *Daily Worker*, January 8, 1942, 7.

75. *CIO News*, May 1942, 2; Karl Yoneda, *A Brief History of US Asian Labor* (New York: Political Affairs Reprint, 1976), 11–15; Steve Nelson, James R. Barrett, and Rob Ruck, *Steve Nelson: American Radical* (Pittsburgh: University of Pittsburgh Press, 1981), 244.

76. David Corn, "Pete Seeger's FBI File," *Mother Jones*, December 18, 2015, https://www.motherjones.com/politics/2015/12/pete-seeger-fbi-file/; David King Dunaway, *How Can I Keep from Singing? Pete Seeger* (New York: McGraw-Hill, 1981), 96–97.

77. Quoted in Aaron J. Leonard, *The Folk Singers and the Bureau: The FBI, the Folk Artists, and the Suppression of the Communist Party USA, 1939–1956* (London: Repeater Books, 2020), 73.

78. Isserman, *Which Side Were You On?*, 132.

79. Richard Layman, *Shadow Man: The Life of Dashiell Hammett* (New York: Harcourt Brace Jovanovich, 1981), 186–191; Joan Mellen, *Hellman and Hammett: The Legendary Passion of Lillian Hellman and Dashiell Hammett* (New York: Harper Collins, 1996), 190–225.

80. Isserman, *Which Side Were You On?*, 182–183; Collum, in Danny Duncan Collum, ed., *African Americans in the Spanish Civil War: "This Ain't Ethiopia, But It'll Do"* (New York: G. K. Hall, 1992), 88.

81. *The Communist*, October 1942, 832–833; Kate Weigand, *Red Feminism: American Communism and the Making of Women's Liberation* (Baltimore: Johns Hopkins University Press, 2001), 26.

82. "Die, But Do Not Retreat," *Time*, January 4, 1943, 22–24; "The Peoples of the USSR," *Life*, March 29, 1943, 23–26.

83. Quoted in J. Samuel Walker, *Henry A. Wallace and American Foreign Policy* (Westport, CT: Greenwood Press, 1976), 89.

84. Charney, *A Long Journey*, 129; "George Charney, Who Resigned as Top State Communist, Dead," *New York Times*, December 14, 1975, https://www.nytimes.com/1975/12/14/archives/george-charney-who-resigned-as-top-state-communist-dead.html.

85. Kevin J. Smant, *Principles and Heresies: Frank S. Meyer and the Shaping of the Modern Conservative Movement* (Wilmington, DE: Intercollegiate Studies Institute, 2002), 1–18.

86. Smant, *Principles and Heresies*, 12.

87. Frank S. Meyer to Browder, typescript, November 29, 1943, II-157, Earl Browder Papers, Syracuse University; "Frank S. Meyer, Political Writer," *New York Times*, April 3, 1972, https://www.nytimes.com/1972/04/03/archives/frank-s-meyer-political-writer-national-review-editor-and-ex.html; Isserman, *Which Side Were You On?*, 152–156. Meyer remained in the CP for another two years, encouraged by Browder's decision to dissolve the Party in 1944. In the fall of 1945 he quit, becoming a leading conservative activist and intellectual, and a cofounder of *National Review* magazine. He was the author of an early study of the CPUSA, *The Moulding of Communists: The Training of Communist Cadre* (New York: Harcourt, Brace, 1961).

88. *Daily Worker*, December 20, 1942, 5; *The Communist*, January 1943, 36.

89. Isserman, *Which Side Were You On?*, 184.

90. Isserman, *Which Side Were You On?*, 184–186.

91. Isserman, *Which Side Were You On?*, 189–190.

92. "Statement of the Presidum of the ECCI on the Dissolution of the Communist International, June 8, 1943," in Jane Degras, *The Communist International, 1919–1943*, vol. 3, *Documents* (Hoboken, NJ: Taylor and Francis, 2014), 480, https://www.marxists.org/history/international/comintern/documents/volume3-1929-1943.pdf.

93. Earl Browder, *Teheran and America* (New York: Workers Library, 1944), 29, 40; Harvey Klehr, John Earl Haynes, and Kyrill M. Anderson, *The Soviet World of American Communism* (New Haven, CT: Yale University Press, 1998), 92–93.

94. Allen Weinstein and Alexander Vassiliev, *The Haunted Wood: Soviet Espionage in America—the Stalin Era* (New York: Random House, 1999), 84–103, 158; Kathryn S. Olmsted,

Red Spy Queen: A Biography of Elizabeth Bentley (Chapel Hill: University of North Carolina Press, 2002), 20–23, 62–65; James G. Ryan, "Socialist Triumph as a Family Value: Earl Browder and Soviet Espionage," *American Communist History* 1, no. 2 (2002), 125–142; John Earl Haynes and Harvey Klehr, *Venona: Decoding Soviet Espionage in America* (New Haven, CT: Yale University Press, 1999), 210–212; Maurice Isserman and Ellen Schrecker, "'Papers of a Dangerous Tendency': From Major Andre's Boot to the VENONA Files," in Ellen Schrecker, ed., *Cold War Triumphalism: The Misuse of History After the Fall of Communism* (New York: New Press, 2004), 164.

95. Isserman, *Which Side Were You On?*, 193–197.

96. John Earl Haynes and Harvey Klehr, "The 'Mental Comintern' and the Self-Destructive Tactics of the CPUSA, 1944–1948," in Vernon Pederson, James G. Ryan, and Katherine A. S. Sibley, eds., *Post-Cold War Revelations and the American Communist Party: Citizens, Revolutionaries, and Spies* (London: Bloomsbury, 2021), 26.

97. Quoted in Dorothy Ray Healey and Maurice Isserman, *California Red: A Life in the American Communist Party* (Urbana: University of Illinois Press, 1994), 93.

98. Author's interview with Steve Nelson, October 13, 1977.

99. "Communism, 1944 Model," Editorial, *New York Times*, January 11, 1944, https://www.nytimes.com/1944/01/11/archives/communism-1944-model.html.

100. Isserman, *Which Side Were You On?*, 203–205.

101. *The Communist*, March 1944, 199.

102. David Shannon, *The Decline of American Communism: A History of the Communist Party of the United States Since 1945* (New York: Harcourt, Brace, 1959), 7.

103. Isserman, *Which Side Were You On?*, 211.

104. *Daily Worker*, November 9, 1944, 2.

105. The Duclos article can be found in English translation in *Political Affairs*, July 1945, 656–672.

106. For a knowledgeable discussion of the "Duclos Letter" drawing on Soviet sources that only became available in the 1990s, see Klehr, Haynes, and Anderson, *Soviet World of American Communism*, 90–106.

107. "Minutes of the National Board Meeting," typescript, May 22–23, 1945, Phillip Jaffe private collection, shared with the author 1977.

108. *Daily Worker*, June 21, 1945, 7; *Daily Worker*, June 14, 1945, 7.

109. *Daily Worker*, February 7, 1946, 2; *Daily Worker*, February 14, 1946, 2.

Chapter 5: Speaking Their Own Sins

1. Brooks Atkinson, "At the Theatre," Amusements, *New York Times*, January 23, 1953, https://www.nytimes.com/1953/01/23/archives/at-the-theatre.html; John Lahr, *Arthur Miller: American Witness* (New Haven, CT: Yale University Press, 2022), 98–99.

2. Lahr, *Arthur Miller*, 135.

3. Brooks Atkinson, "The Crucible," *New York Times*, February 1, 1953, https://www.nytimes.com/1953/02/01/archivesthe-crucible-arthur-millers-dramatization-of-the-salem-witch-trial.html.

4. Richard F. Shepard, "Brooks Atkinson, 89, Dead; Times Drama Critic 31 Years," *New York Times*, January 14, 1984, https://www.nytimes.com/1984/01/14/obituaries/brooks-atkinson-89-dead-times-drama-critic-31-years.html.

5. Christopher Bigsby, *Arthur Miller: 1915–1962* (Cambridge, MA: Harvard University Press, 2009), 454. For the poll results, see Survey by Gallup Organization, February 22–27, 1953, available at iPOLL Databank, http://www.ropercenter.uconn.edu/data-access/ipoll/ipoll.html.

6. John Gates, *The Story of an American Communist* (New York: Thomas Nelson, 1958), 5. Gates's comment about mastering the art of persuasion, "deceptively or otherwise," was a reference to J. Edgar Hoover's best-selling anti-Communist polemic *Masters of Deceit*, published the same year as his own memoir.

7. Lahr, *Arthur Miller*, 30–32, 40–41.

8. Bigsby, *Arthur Miller*, 123.

9. Bigsby, *Arthur Miller*, 128–129, 144; "Neafus, Ralf Lawrence," Abraham Lincoln Brigade Archives, https://alba-valb.org/volunteers/ralf-lawrence-neafus/.

10. Bigsby, *Arthur Miller*, 144, 290–297, 346–360; "Chronology," in Arthur Miller, *Collected Plays, 1944–1961* (New York: Library of America, 2006), 753–770.

11. Lahr, *Arthur Miller*, 117.

12. Bigsby, *Arthur Miller*, 423; Lahr, *Arthur Miller*, 116–119.

13. Stephen J. Whitfield, *The Culture of the Cold War*, 2nd ed. (Baltimore, MD: Johns Hopkins University Press, 1996), 111–113.

14. Quoted in John Lahr, *Arthur Miller*, 154.

15. Lahr, *Arthur Miller*, 129–130.

16. Lahr, *Arthur Miller*, 130.

17. Miller, *The Crucible*, 141; Bigsby, *Arthur Miller*, 364–365.

18. Joseph Starobin, *American Communism in Crisis, 1943–1957* (Cambridge, MA: Harvard University Press, 1972), 108–111.

19. George Charney, *A Long Journey* (Chicago: Quadrangle, 1968), 154.

20. Starobin, *American Communism in Crisis*, 113; Dorothy Ray Healey and Maurice Isserman, *California Red: A Life in the American Communist Party* (Urbana: University of Illinois Press, 1994), 104–105.

21. Robert Korstad, *Civil Rights Unionism: Tobacco Workers and the Struggle for Democracy in the Mid-Twentieth-Century South* (Chapel Hill: University of North Carolina Press, 2003), 268, 272. Also see Rick Halpern, *Down on the Killing Floor: Black and White Workers in Chicago's Packinghouses, 1904–1954* (Urbana: University of Illinois Press, 1997); Moon Kie-Jung, *Reworking Race: The Making of Hawaii's Interracial Labor Movement* (New York: Columbia University Press, 2010); and Justin Akers Chácon, *Radicals in the Barrio: Magonistas, Socialists, Wobblies, and Communists in the Mexican-American Working Class* (Chicago: Haymarket Books, 2018), 578–580.

22. Starobin, *American Communism in Crisis*, 35, 113.

23. Maurice Isserman, *Which Side Were You On? The American Communist Party During the Second World War* (Middletown, CT: Wesleyan University Press, 1982), 254–255. There is no exact count of just how many Communists in the later 1940s fit the "YCL generation" profile. But in 1950, when the FBI assembled a "Security Index" of Communists to be rounded up in event of national emergency, there were twelve thousand names on the list, which seems like a good approximation in determining the number of seasoned, trained cadre in the Party. See Ellen Schrecker, *Many Are the Crimes: McCarthyism in America* (Princeton, NJ: Princeton University Press, 1999), 208.

24. Gerald Horne, *Black Liberation/Red Scare: Ben Davis and the Communist Party* (Newark, DE: University of Delaware Press, 1994), 164–164; Joshua B. Freeman, *Working-Class New York: Life and Labor Since World War II* (New York: New Press, 2000), 56–57; Gerald Meyer, *Vito Marcantonio: Radical Politician, 1902–1954* (Albany: State University of New York Press, 1989), 66.

25. Nelson Lichtenstein et al., eds., *Who Built America? Working People and the Nation's Economy, Politics, Culture, and Society*, vol. 2, *Since 1877*, 2nd ed. (New York: Worth Publishers, 2000), 530–532; Starobin, *American Communism in Crisis*, 108–110, 142; Freeman, *Working-Class New York*, 61.

26. William Z. Foster, *The Twilight of World Capitalism* (New York: International Publishers, 1949), 24.

27. Charney, *A Long Journey*, 163.

28. Alexander Bittelman, "How Shall We Fight for Full Employment," *Political Affairs*, January 1946, 58.

29. Lichtenstein et al., *Who Built America?*, 2:570–575.

30. Lichtenstein et al., *Who Built America?*, 2:575–578.

31. M. J. Heale, *American Anticommunism: Combatting the Enemy Within, 1830–1970* (Baltimore: Johns Hopkins University Press, 1990), 132–137.

32. James Patterson, *Grand Expectations: The United States, 1945–1974* (New York: Oxford University Press, 1997), 88.

33. Whitfield, *Culture of Cold War*, 9.

34. Kathryn S. Olmsted, *Red Spy Queen: A Biography of Elizabeth Bentley* (Chapel Hill: University of North Carolina Press, 2002); Allen Weinstein, *Perjury: The Hiss-Chambers Case* (New York: Random House, 1978).

35. Allen Weinstein and Alexander Vassiliev, *The Haunted Wood: Soviet Espionage in America—the Stalin Era* (New York: Random House, 1999), 104–109; Olmsted, *Red Spy Queen*, 105–106, 125–136. For the impact of the Rosenberg case on the children of Communists in the 1950s, see Bettina Aptheker, *Intimate Politics: How I Grew Up Red, Fought for Free Speech, and Became a Feminist Rebel* (Emeryville, CA: Seal Press, 2006), 20–23.

36. William Z. Foster, "Leninism and Some Practical Problems of the Postwar Period," *Political Affairs*, February 1946, 102.

37. Eugene Dennis, "Defeat the Imperialist Drive Toward Fascism and War," *Political Affairs*, September 1946, 797; Starobin, *American Communism in Crisis*, 123, 139.

38. William Z. Foster, "American Imperialism, Leader of World Reaction," *Political Affairs*, August 1946, 691.

39. Starobin, *American Communism in Crisis*, 125–126, 148–149; Maurice Isserman, *If I Had a Hammer: The Death of the Old Left and the Birth of the New Left* (New York: Basic Books, 1987), 6.

40. Mary Sperling McAuliffe, *Crisis on the Left: Cold War Politics and American Liberals, 1947–1954* (Amherst: University of Massachusetts Press, 1978), 3–5.

41. Arthur M. Schlesinger Jr., "Not Left, Not Right, but a Vital Center," *New York Times Magazine*, April 4, 1948, https://www.nytimes.com/1948/04/04/archives/not-left-not-right-but-a-vital-center-the-hope-of-the-future-lies.html; Arthur M. Schlesinger, *The Vital Center: The Politics of Freedom* (Boston: Houghton Mifflin, 1949).

42. Starobin, *American Communism in Crisis*, 157–158.

43. Landon R. Y. Storrs, *The Second Red Scare and the Unmaking of the New Deal Left* (Princeton: Princeton University Press, 2013), 2.

44. Garry Wills, "Introduction," in Lillian Hellman, *Scoundrel Time* (Boston: Back Bay Books, 2000), 10–11.

45. Starobin, *American Communism in Crisis*, 159–162: Gates, *Story of an American Communist*, 115–116.

46. Quoted in Starobin, *American Communism in Crisis*, 165.

47. According to Harvey Klehr and John Haynes, who in their accounts of the Party's history nearly always emphasize Soviet control over the decisions of American Communists, "The Progressive Party disaster was not the result of the CPUSA blindly following orders from Moscow. Moscow had issued no orders." See John Earl Haynes and Harvey Klehr, "The 'Mental Comintern' and the Self-Destructive Tactics of the CPUSA, 1944–1948," in Vernon Pederson, James G. Ryan, and Katherine A. S. Sibley, eds., *Post-Cold War Revelations and the American Communist Party: Citizens, Revolutionaries, and Spies* (London: Bloomsbury, 2021), 17–40.

48. Willie Thompson, *The Communist Movement Since 1945* (Oxford, UK: Blackwell, 1998), 34–38; Starobin, *American Communism in Crisis*, 170–171.

49. Starobin, *American Communism in Crisis*, 170–172.

50. Healey and Isserman, *California Red*, 110.

51. Platform for the Progressive Party, July 1948, MS 312, W. E. B. Du Bois Papers, Special Collections and University Archives, University of Massachusetts Amherst, https://credo.library.umass.edu/view/full/mums312-b121-i298.

52. Joshua Freeman, *In Transit: The Transport Workers Union in New York City, 1933–1966* (New York: Oxford University Press, 1989), 137.

53. Ronald L. Filippelli and Mark D. McColloch, *Cold War in the Working Class: The Rise and Decline of the United Electrical Workers* (Albany: State University of New York Press, 1995), 114.

54. Filippelli and McColloch, *Cold War in the Working Class*, 115–116; Robert W. Cherny, *Harry Bridges: Labor Radical, Labor Legend* (Urbana: University of Illinois Press, 2023), 230–231.

55. Quoted in John C. Culver and John Hyde, *American Dreamer: The Life and Times of Henry A. Wallace* (New York: Norton, 2000), 464.

56. Quoted in Karl M. Schmidt, *Henry A. Wallace: Quixotic Crusade 1948* (Syracuse, NY: Syracuse University Press, 1960), 93.

57. David Shannon, *The Decline of American Communism: A History of the Communist Party of the United States Since 1945* (New York: Harcourt, Brace, 1959), 148.

58. Michael Kazin, *What It Took to Win: A History of the Democratic Party* (New York: Farrar, Straus and Giroux, 2022), 200; Ted Morgan, *Reds: McCarthyism in Twentieth-Century America* (New York: Random House, 2003), 308; Thomas W. Devine, *Henry Wallace's 1948 Presidential Campaign and the Future of Postwar Liberalism* (Chapel Hill: University of North Carolina Press, 2013), 18.

59. Quoted in Morgan, *Reds*, 311.

60. Starobin, *American Communism in Crisis*, 192, 298n.

61. Quoted in Kazin, *What It Took to Win*, 201.

62. Filippelli and McColloch, *Cold War in the Working Class*, 155–159; Laurie Mercier, "'Instead of Fighting the Common Enemy': Mine Mill Versus the Steelworkers in Montana, 1950–1967," *Labor History*, 40 (1999), 459–480.

63. Scott Martell, *The Fear Within: Spies, Commies, and American Democracy on Trial* (New Brunswick, NJ: Rutgers University Press, 2011), 32–55; Michael R. Belknap, *Cold War Political Justice: The Smith Act, the Communist Party, and American Civil Liberties* (Westport, CT: Greenwood Press, 1977), 52–53, 65–66; Tuomas Savonen, *Minnesota, Moscow, Manhattan: Gus Hall's Life and Political Line Until the Late 1960s* (Helsinki: Finnish Society of Sciences and Letters, 2020), 148–149.

64. Isserman, *Which Side Were You On?*, 123–124.

65. I. F. Stone, "The G-String Conspiracy," *The Nation*, July 26, 1941, 66–67.

66. I. F. Stone, "The Shadow Cast at Foley Square," *Daily Compass*, October 14, 1949, reprinted in I. F. Stone, *The Truman Era: 1945–1952* (Boston: Little Brown, 1972), 93–95.

67. Gates, *Story of An American Communist*, 127.

68. Gates, *Story of an American Communist*, 126–127; Belknap, *Cold War Political Justice*, 106.

69. Quoted in Shannon, *Decline of American Communism*, 200.

70. Jerold S. Auerbach, *Unequal Justice: Lawyers and Social Change in Modern America* (New York: Oxford University Press, 1976), 234–235. The lawyers who went to jail and were disbarred, full disclosure, included the author's uncle, Abraham Isserman.

71. "Korea Army Frees Seoul," *Daily Worker*, June 29, 1950, 3.

72. Belknap, *Cold War Political Justice*, 157–158.

73. Walter Bernstein, *Inside Out: A Memoir of the Blacklist* (New York: Knopf, 1996), 197.

74. Julia Rose Kraut, *Threat of Dissent: A History of Ideological Exclusion and Deportation in the United States* (Cambridge, MA: Harvard University Press, 2020), 122–124; Erik McDuffie, "'For a New Antifascist, Anti-imperialist People's Coalition': Claudia Jones, Black Left Feminism, and the Politics of Possibility in the Era of Trump," in Vernon Pederson, James G. Ryan, and Katherine A. S. Sibley, eds., *Post-Cold War Revelations and the American Communist Party: Citizens, Revolutionaries, and Spies* (London: Bloomsbury Academic, 2021), 191.

75. Schrecker, *Many are the Crimes*, 126–127.

76. David Caute, *The Great Fear: The Anti-Communist Purge Under Truman and Eisenhower* (New York: Simon and Schuster, 1978), 344; Freeman, *Working-Class New York*, 86–87.

77. "Hundreds Greet Gil Green as He Enters Courthouse," *Daily Worker*, February 28, 1956, 1. Also see Gil Green, *Cold War Fugitive: A Personal Story of the McCarthy Years* (New York: International Publishers, 1984).

78. Healey and Isserman, *California Red*, 123, 125.

79. Starobin, *American Communism in Crisis*, 220–221; Healey and Isserman, *California Red*, 130. The Party's campaign against the supposed "white chauvinism" of many of its members, actually made it less attractive to black members, and reduced their numbers drastically. See David Shannon, *Decline of American Communism*, 247; and Healey and

Isserman, *California Red*, 128. Harry Hay, expelled by the Los Angeles CP in 1951, went on to found the Mattachine Society, the first gay rights group in the United States. He is profiled in Bettina Aptheker, *Communists in Closets: Queering the History, 1930s–1990s* (New York: Routledge, 2023), 81–103.

80. Gerald Horne, *Communist Front? The Civil Rights Congress, 1946–1956* (New York: International Publishers, 2021); Arthur J. Sabin, *Red Scare in Court: New York Versus the International Workers Order* (Philadelphia: University of Pennsylvania Press, 1993).

81. "Best Loved Man on Earth," *Daily Worker*, March 9, 1953, 2.

82. John Gates, *On Guard Against Browderism, Titoism, Trotskyism* (New York: New Century Publishers, 1951). The pamphlet was a reprint of Gates's report to the Fifteenth National Convention of the Communist Party, December 28–30, 1950.

83. Healey and Isserman, *California Red*, 138.

84. Charney, *A Long Journey*, 215.

85. Healey and Isserman, *California Red*, 146.

86. Quoted in Healey and Isserman, *California Red*, 146.

87. Belknap, *Cold War Political Justice*, 244.

88. Charney, *A Long Journey*, 226; Starobin, *American Communism in Crisis*, 222.

89. Joseph R. Starobin, *Paris to Peking* (New York: Cameron, 1955), 269.

90. Joseph Starobin, "1956—A Memoir," *Problems of Communism* 15, no. 6 (November–December 1966), 65; "Joseph Starobin Dies; Ex-editor at Worker," *New York Times*, November 7, 1976, 42.

91. Gates, *Story of an American Communist*, 154.

92. Gates, *Story of an American Communist*, 156.

93. Robert Cohen, *When the Old Left Was Young: Student Radicals and America's First Mass Student Movement, 1929–1941* (New York: Oxford University Press, 1993), 25–26.

94. Joseph Clark, *The Real Russia* (New York: International Publishers, 1954), 19–20.

95. Joseph Clark, "Joseph Stalin, Three Years Later," *Daily Worker*, March 12, 1956, 5.

96. Alan Max, "US Marxists and Soviet Self-Criticism," *Daily Worker*, March 13, 1956, 4.

97. *Daily Worker*, "Letters to the Editor," March 29, 1956.

98. *Dally Worker*, "Letters to the Editor," June 27, 1956, 4.

99. *Daily Worker*, "Letters to the Editor," May 3, 1956, 4.

100. Healey and Isserman, *California Red*, 153.

101. Healey and Isserman, *California Red*, 154–155.

102. Author's interview with Steve Nelson, October 13, 1977; Steve Nelson, James R. Barrett, and Rob Ruck, *Steve Nelson: American Radical* (Pittsburgh: University of Pittsburgh Press, 1981), 386–387.

103. Starobin, *American Communism in Crisis*, 4, 14–18.

104. "Stalin's Repressions Spelled Out in Khrushchev Speech Made Public Here," *Daily Worker*, June 5, 1956, 2; "Khrushchev Speech Now Made Public," *Sunday Worker*, June 10, 1956, sec. 2, 1.

105. Isserman, *If I Had a Hammer*, 24; Morris Schappes, "The Martyred Soviet Yiddish Writers," *Jewish Currents*, May 1980, 12–16.

106. Author's interview with Max Gordon, October 10, 1980.

107. Author's interview with Dorothy Healey, May 30, 1984.

108. Starobin, *American Communism in Crisis*, 227.

109. Peter Unwin, *Voice in the Wilderness: Imre Nagy and the Hungarian Revolution* (London: Macdonald, 1991).

110. "Letter to the Editor," *Daily Worker*, November 12, 1956, 4.

111. Isserman, *If I Had a Hammer*, 29–30.

112. Charney, *A Long Journey*, 296; Karl P. Benziger, *Imry Nagy, Martyr of the Nation: Contested History, Legitimacy, and Popular Memory in Hungary* (Lanham, MD: Lexington Books, 2008), 59–80.

113. "Letter to the Editor," *Daily Worker*, November 14, 1956, 4.

114. Charney, *A Long Journey*, 300.

115. Charney, *A Long Journey*, 298.

116. Starobin, *American Communism in Crisis*, 227.

117. Healey and Isserman, *California Red*, 163–164. For Lenin's "Better Fewer, But Better" principle, see his 1923 essay by the same name, https://www.marxists.org/archive/lenin/works/1923/mar/02.htm.

118. Shannon, *Decline of American Communism*, 360.

119. Author's interview with Dorothy Healey, May 30, 1984; Healey and Isserman, *California Red*, 164; Al Richmond, *A Long View from the Left: Memoirs of an American Revolutionary* (Boston: Houghton Mifflin, 1973), 381.

120. John Gates, *Evolution of an American Communist: Why I Quit After 27 Years, Where I Stand Now* (self-published pamphlet, 1958); "John Gates Replies to Clark," *Daily Worker*, September 10, 1957, 2.

121. Gates, *Story of an American Communist*, 189–191.

122. Quoted in Irving Howe and Lewis Coser, *The American Communist Party: A Critical History* (Boston: Beacon Press, 1957), 416, 560.

123. Quoted in Schrecker, *Many Are the Crimes*, 144.

124. Irving Howe, "New Styles in Leftism," *Dissent*, Summer 1965, 300–301. Emphasis in the original.

Chapter 6: Ashes to Ashes

1. Clancy Sigal, *Going Away: A Report, a Memoir* (Boston: Houghton Mifflin, 1961), 369.

2. Todd Gitlin, "In Pursuit of Clancy Sigal: A Writer's Radical Life," *Yale Review* 109, no. 3 (Fall 2021), https://yalereview.org/article/in-pursuit-of-clancy-sigal; Katharine Q. Seelye, "Todd Gitlin, 79, Activist Who Was Both Voice and Critic of the New Left, Dies," *New York Times*, February 7, 2022, https://www.nytimes.com/2022/02/05/us/todd-gitlin-dead.html. For the passage cited by Gitlin, see Sigal, *Going Away*, 187–188.

3. Gus Hall, "Some Thoughts on Returning," *Political Affairs*, June 1959, 23.

4. Sam Tanenhaus, "Gus Hall, Unreconstructed American Communist of 7 Decades, Dies at 90," *New York Times*, October 17, 2000, https://www.nytimes.com/2000/10/17/us/gus-hall-unreconstructed-american-communist-of-7-decades-dies-at-90.html; "Top US Communist: Gus Hall," *New York Times*, June 27, 1966, https://www.nytimes.com/1966/06/27/archives/top-us-communist-gus-hall.html. A detailed account of Hall's life is found in Tuomas Savonen, *Minnesota, Moscow, Manhattan: Gus Hall's Life and Political Line Until the Late 1960s* (Helsinki: The Finnish Society of Sciences and Letters, 2020).

5. Savonen, *Minneapolis, Moscow, Manhattan*, 167, 171, 193.

6. Dorothy Ray Healey and Maurice Isserman, *California Red: A Life in the American Communist Party* (Urbana: University of Illinois Press, 1994), 172.

7. Harry Schwartz, "US Reds Name Hall as Leader," *New York Times*, December 14, 1959, https://www.nytimes.com/1959/12/14/archives/u-s-reds-name-hall-as-leader-midwest -chief-in-top-post-after.html.

8. "Eugene Dennis, 56, Red Leader Dies," *New York Times*, February 1, 1961, https:// www.nytimes.com/1961/02/01/archives/eugene-dennis-56-red-leader-dies-communist -chairman-in-the-u-s.html; "William Z. Foster is Dead at 80; Ex-head of Communists in US," *New York Times*, September 2, 1961, https://www.nytimes.com/1961/09/02/archives/william -z-foster-is-dead-at-80-exhead-ot-communists-in-us-illness.html; "Elizabeth Gurley Flynn Is Dead; Head of US Communist Party," *New York Times*, September 6, 1964, https://www .nytimes.com/1964/09/06/archives/elizabeth-gurley-flynn-is-dead-head-of-us-communist -party-chairman.html.

9. Schwartz, "US Reds Name Hall as Leader," 19.

10. "US Reds Oust Theoretician As an 'Anti-party Revisionist,'" *New York Times*, November 24, 1960, https://www.nytimes.com/1960/11/24/archives/us-reds-oust-theoretician -as-an-antiparty-revisionist-bittelman.html; "Comrade Milton Rosen, 1926–2011," https://www .marxists.org/history/erol/1960-1970/rosen.htm.

11. David Garrow, *The FBI and Martin Luther King, Jr.* (New Haven: Yale University Press, 2006), 53, 84, 182–183.

12. "US Drops Charges Against Gus Hall over Listing Party," *New York Times*, May 5, 1966, https://www.nytimes.com/1966/05/05/archives/us-drops-charge-against-gus-hall-over -listing-party.html; Healey and Isserman, *California Red*, 188–189.

13. Maurice Isserman and Michael Kazin, *America Divided: The Civil War of the 1960s*, 6th ed. (New York: Oxford University Press, 2021), 34–35.

14. Maurice Isserman, *If I Had a Hammer: The Death of the Old Left and the Birth of the New Left* (New York: Basic Books, 1987), 202–208.

15. Peter Yarrow, Noel Paul Stookey, and Mary Travers, *Peter Paul and Mary: Fifty Years in Music and Life* (Watertown, MA: Charlesbridge, 2015), 24; Ronald Radosh, "The Communist Party's Role in the Folk Revival: From Woody Guthrie to Bob Dylan," *American Communist History* 14, no. 1, 2015, 12.

16. Eric Burner, *And Gently He Shall Lead Them: Robert Parris Moses and Civil Rights in Mississippi* (New York: New York University Press, 1994), 25, 139.

17. David Levering Lewis, *W. E .B. Du Bois: The Fight for Equality and the American Century, 1919–1963* (New York: Henry Holt, 2000), 567; Peter Kihss, "Dr. W. E. B. DuBois Joins Communist Party at 93," *New York Times*, November 23, 1961, https://www.nytimes .com/1961/11/23/archives/dr-web-dubois-joins-communist-party-at-93-noted-negro -sociologist.html; Healey and Isserman, *California Red*, 186.

18. "Bettina Aptheker Identified as Figure in Berkeley Riot," *New York Times*, June 2, 1965, https://www.nytimes.com/1965/06/02/archives/bettina-aptheker-identified-as-figure -in-berkeley-riot.html; John Corry, "California Coed, 21, Is the American Communist Party's Foremost Ingenue," *New York Times*, November 21, 1965, https://www.nytimes.com /1965/11/21/archives/california-coed-21-is-the-american-communist-partys-foremost

.html; "Berkeley Students Elect a Communist," *New York Times*, November 25, 1965, https://www.nytimes.com/1965/11/25/archives/berkeley-students-elect-a-communist.html; Bettina F. Aptheker, *Intimate Politics: How I Grew Up Red, Fought for Free Speech, and Became a Feminist Rebel* (Emeryville, CA: Seal Press, 2006), 93–94, 129–139, 217.

19. Brian Purnell, *Fighting Jim Crow in the County of Kings: The Congress of Racial Equality in Brooklyn* (Lexington: University of Kentucky Press, 2013), 48–55; "Oliver Leeds, 68, Ex-head of CORE Chapter," *New York Times*, February 23, 1989, https://www.nytimes.com/1989/02/23/obituaries/oliver-leeds-68-ex-head-of-core-chapter.html; Diane Esses, oral history interview with Oliver Leeds, December 15, 1988, 3–5, copy provided to the author by Brian Purnell.

20. C. Wright Mills, "Letter to the New Left," *New Left Review* 5 (September–October 1960), https://www.marxists.org/subject/humanism/mills-c-wright/letter-new-left.htm.

21. Potter quoted in Kirkpatrick Sale, *SDS: The Rise and Development of Students for a Democratic Society* (New York: Random House, 1973), 188.

22. Gus Hall, "Crisis of Petty-Bourgeois Radicalism," *Political Affairs*, https://www.marxists.org/archive/hall/1970/crisis-petty-bourgeois-radicalism.htm.

23. Peter Kihss, "Leaders Urge US Communists to Work 'In and Around the Orbit of the Democratic Party,'" *New York Times*, June 26, 1966, https://www.nytimes.com/1966/06/26/archives/leaders-urge-us-communists-to-work-in-and-around-the-orbit-of-the.html.

24. FBI Report from Los Angeles FBI Officer, April 20, 1965, 44–45, TAM 95, box 12, "CPUSA Communist Literature and Party Activities in California" folder, Gilbert Green Papers, Tamiment Library, New York University.

25. Healey and Isserman, *California Red*, 125.

26. Quoted in Savonen, *Minnesota, Moscow, Manhattan*, 330. For Hall's claim that the CPUSA had 20,000 members, see, for example, Anthony Austin, "Gus Hall, the Bit Player, Is Star at Moscow Parley," *New York Times*, February 27, 1981, https://www.nytimes.com/1981/02/27/world/gus-hall-the-bit-player-is-star-at-moscow-parley.html.

27. Savonen, *Minnesota, Moscow, Manhattan*, 259–261. On the open rupture between Mao and Khrushchev in 1960, see Lorenz M. Lüthi, *The Sino-Soviet Split: Cold War in the Communist World* (Princeton, NJ: Princeton University Press, 2008), 163.

28. Letter from Gus Hall to Leonid Brezhnev, November 3, 1965, TAM 132, box 195, folder 7, CPUSA Papers, Tamiment Library, New York University.

29. Email to the author from Samuel Webb, April 19, 2022; "Gus Hall Urges End of US Raids," *New York Times*, October 27, 1966, https://www.nytimes.com/1966/10/27/archives/gus-hall-urges-end-of-us-raids-back-from-77day-trip-he-gives-plan.html; Christopher S. Wren, "Guests from 96 Lands at Moscow Parley," *New York Times*, February 26, 1976, https://www.nytimes.com/1976/02/26/archives/guests-from-96-lands-at-moscow-parley.html; Austin, "Gus Hall, Bit Player."

30. Peter Kihss, "US Reds Shelve Appeal on Jews," *New York Times*, January 22, 1967, https://www.nytimes.com/1967/01/22/archives/us-reds-shelve-appeal-on-jews-party-leaders-now-denying.html. Also see Herbert Aptheker, *The Fraud of Soviet Anti-Semitism* (New York: New Century Publishers, 1962) and Hyman Lumer, *Soviet Anti-Semitism: A Cold War Myth* (New York: Political Affairs, 1964).

31. David K. Shipler, "Kosygin Says Soviets Top Western Economic Rivals," *New York Times*, March 2, 1976, https://www.nytimes.com/1976/03/02/archives/new-jersey-pages-kosygin-says-soviet-tops-western-economic-rivals.html.

32. Garrow, *FBI and Martin Luther King, Jr.*, 34–40; Harvey Klehr, John Earl Haynes, and Kyrill M. Anderson, *The Soviet World of American Communism* (New Haven, CT: Yale University Press, 1998), 149–151.

33. Harvey Klehr and John Haynes, "The American Communist Con Man," *Commentary*, October 2020, 42–46; Francis X. Clines, "Kremlin Reportedly Gave $2 Million a Year to US Communist Party," *New York Times*, December 1, 1991, https://www.nytimes.com/1991/12/01/world/kremlin-reportedly-gave-2-million-a-year-to-us-communist-party.html; Gary Murrell, *"The Most Dangerous Communist in the United States": A Biography of Herbert Aptheker* (Amherst: University of Massachusetts Press, 2015), 326.

34. Isserman and Kazin, *America Divided*, 187–202.

35. Sale, *SDS*, 470–471.

36. Max Elbaum, *Revolution in the Air: Sixties Radicals Turn to Lenin, Mao and Che* (New York: Verso, 2002), 4, 339–342; Isserman and Kazin, *America Divided*, 287–288.

37. Z.A.B. Zeman, *Prague Spring* (New York: Hill and Wang, 1969), 115–128.

38. Mark Kurlansky, *1968: The Year That Rocked the World* (New York: Ballantine Books, 2004), 287–305.

39. Healey and Isserman, *California Red*, 222, 230–232; Will Lissner, "Moscow Assailed by Some US Reds," *New York Times*, August 23, 1968, https://www.nytimes.com/1968/08/23/archives/moscow-assailed-by-some-u-s-reds-state-leader-calls-invasion-a-very.html; Reuben Falber, "The 1968 Czechoslovak Crisis: Inside the British Communist Party," Socialist History Society, http://www.socialisthistorysociety.co.uk/?page_id=176.

40. Murrell, *"Most Dangerous Communist,"* 261–264; Healey and Isserman, *California Red*, 233; Aptheker, *Intimate Politics*, 210–211. Herbert Aptheker's book about the events in Czechoslovakia was Herbert Aptheker, *Czechoslovakia and Counter-Revolution: Why the Socialist Countries Intervened* (New York: New Outlook, 1969).

41. Angela Davis, *Angela Davis: An Autobiography* (New York: International Publishers, 1974), 77–89; Erik McDuffie, *Sojourning for Freedom: Black Women, American Communism, and the Making of Black Left Feminism* (Durham, NC: Duke University Press, 2011), 196–197.

42. Davis, *Angela Davis*, 105–113; Aptheker, *Intimate Politics*, 67–68.

43. Davis, *Angela Davis*, 162–163, 189.

44. Healey and Isserman, *California Red*, 208–209.

45. Healey and Isserman, *California Red*, 214.

46. Davis, *Angela Davis*, 189.

47. Davis, *Angela Davis*, 187–189; Aptheker, *Intimate Politics*, 220–221.

48. Mike Davis and Jon Wiener, *Set the Night on Fire: LA in the Sixties* (New York: Verso, 2020), 472–476; Lawrence E. Davies, "UCLA Teacher Is Ousted as Red," *New York Times*, September 20, 1969, https://www.nytimes.com/1969/09/20/archives/ucla-teacher-is-ousted-as-red-a-battle-in-court-predicted-on-action.html; Steven V. Roberts, "UCLA Students Are Urged to Resist Regents," *New York Times*, October 7, 1969, https://www.nytimes.com/1969/10/07/archives/ucla-students-are-urged-to-resist-regents-ousted

-instructor.html; Steven V. Roberts, "Battle Over Academic Freedom at UCLA," *New York Times*, October 12, 1969, https://www.nytimes.com/1969/10/12/archives/battle-over-academic-freedom-at-ucla.html.

49.   George L. Jackson, *Soledad Brother: The Prison Letters of George Jackson* (New York: Coward, McCann, 1970). For a skeptical reading of George Jackson's role as a revolutionary hero, see Eric Cummins, *The Rise and Fall of California's Radical Prison Movement* (Stanford, CA: Stanford University Press, 1994), 151–186. For Jackson's relationship with Angela Davis, and for his death, see Paul Liberatore, *The Road to Hell: The True Story of George Jackson, Stephen Bingham, and the San Quentin Massacre* (New York: Atlantic Monthly, 1996).

50.   Davis, *Angela Davis*, 266–269; "Ousted Red Teacher Sues UCLA for Job," *New York Times*, July 2, 1970, https://www.nytimes.com/1970/07/02/archives/ousted-red-teacher-sues-ucla-for-job.html.

51.   Bettina Aptheker, *The Morning Breaks: The Trial of Angela Davis* (Ithaca, NY: Cornell University Press, 1999), xvii. This was a reprint of the original 1975 International Publishers edition, with a new introduction by Aptheker reflecting her changing views since quitting the Communist Party.

52.   Steven R. Weisman, "Scholarly Activist: Angela Yvonne Davis," *New York Times*, June 5, 1972, https://www.nytimes.com/1972/06/05/archives/scholarly-activist-angela-yvonne-davis.html; Healey and Isserman, *California Red*, 212.

53.   Healey and Isserman, *California Red*, 217.

54.   Aptheker, *Intimate Politics*, 239–240.

55.   Aptheker, *The Morning Breaks*, 27–156.

56.   Aptheker, *Intimate Politics*, 245, 254.

57.   Aptheker, *Intimate Politics*, 247; Healey and Isserman, *California Red*, 218–219.

58.   Aptheker, *Intimate Politics*, 249–251; Matt Wake, "The Story Behind the Rolling Stones' Angela Davis Song," Associated Press, February 15, 2019, https://apnews.com article /f3e0dc25ebb840e98d752fe4803689f4.

59.   Aptheker, *The Morning Breaks*, 157–275; Earl Caldwell, "Angela Davis Acquitted on All Charges," *New York Times*, June 5, 1972, https://www.nytimes.com/1972/06/05 /archivers/angela-davis-acquitted-on-all-charges.html; Les Ledbetter, "15,000 Exhorted by Angela Davis," *New York Times*, June 30, 1972, https://www.nytimes.com/1972/06/30 /archives/5000-exhorted-by-angela-davis-garden-crowd-hears-plea-for-socialist.html.

60.   James F. Clarity, "Angela Davis Warmly Welcomed in Moscow," Notes on People, *New York Times*, August 29, 1972, https://www.nytimes.com/1972/08/29/archives/angela-davis-warmly-welcomed-in-moscow.html; "Miss Davis Hails Soviet's Policies," *New York Times*, September 10, 1972, https://www.nytimes.com/1972/09/10/archives/miss-davis-hails-soviets-policies-but-the-comments-on-tour-arouse.html.

61.   Gil Green to Gus Hall, April 1, 1982, TAM 132, box 195, folder 24, CPUSA Papers, Tamiment Library, New York University.

62.   Laurie Goodstein, "Letter from Communist Headquarters," *Washington Post*, August 31, 1991, https://www.washingtonpost.com/archive/politics/1991/08/31/letter-from-communist-headquarters/dc225dba-0947–4bf9–83e4–6b67555303c7/.

63.   Memo from "Larry M" to Gus Hall, ca. 1991, TAM 132, box 195, folder 10, CPUSA Papers, Tamiment Library, New York University.

64. Associated Press, "Final 1972 Presidential Returns Show 17.9-Million Nixon Margin," *New York Times*, December 22, 1972, https://www.nytimes.com/1972/12/22/archives /final-1972-presidential-returns-show-179million-nixon-margin.html; United Press International, "Official Tabulation Shows Carter Defeated Ford by 1,681,477 Votes," *New York Times*, December 11, 1976, https://www.nytimes.com/1976/12/11/archives/official -tabulation-shows-carter-defeated-ford-by-1681417-votes.html; Walter Goodman, "Hall, at 74, Still Seeks Presidency," *New York Times*, November 2, 1984, https://www.nytimes .com/1984/11/02/us/hall-at-74-still-seeks-presidency.html; Alice V. McGillivray et al., eds., *America at the Polls, From Kennedy to Clinton, A Handbook of American Presidential Election Statistics* (Washington, DC: Congressional Quarterly, 1998), 8, 10, 12, 14.

65. Steven Kotkin, *Armageddon Averted: The Soviet Collapse, 1970–2000* (New York: Oxford University Press, 2008), 39–57; Robert Service, *A History of Modern Russia: From Tsarism to the Twenty-First Century*, 3rd ed. (Cambridge, MA: Harvard University Press, 2009), 397–411.

66. William Taubman, *Gorbachev: His Life and Times* (New York: Norton, 2017), 1; Serge Schmemann, "Gorbachev Freed the Soviet Union but Could Not Save It," Opinion, *New York Times*, August 31, 2022, https://www.nytimes.com/2022/08/31/opinion/gorbachev -death-soviet-union.html.

67. Stephen Kotkin, *Uncivil Society: 1989 and the Implosion of the Communist Establishment* (New York: Modern Library, 2009), 142.

68. William J. Eaton, "Gus Hall Startled by Gorbachev Congress," *Los Angeles Times*, March 2, 1986, https://www.latimes.com/archives/la-xpm–1986-03-02-mn–1650 -story.html; Michael Dobbs, "Panhandling the Kremlin: How Gus Hall Got Millions," *Washington Post*, March 1, 1992, https://www.washingtonpost.com/archive/politics/1992/03/01 /panhandling-the-kremlin-how-gus-hall-got-millions/c7442bd5-871f-42c7-9295 -2b8f0574c025/.

69. Taubman, *Gorbachev*, 463–464.

70. Taubman, *Gorbachev*, 465–466.

71. James Barron, "Henry Winston Dead in Moscow; Top Leader of Communists in US," *New York Times*, December 16, 1986, Section B, https://www.nytimes.com/1986/12/16 /obituaries/henry-winston-dead-in-moscow-top-leader-of-communists-in-us.html; Murrell, *"Most Dangerous Communist,"* 322, 327.

72. Central Committee, CPUSA, "Political Resolution," *Political Affairs*, April 1987, 15.

73. Daniel Rosenberg, "From Crisis to Split: The Communist Party USA, 1989–1991," *American Communist History* 18, no. 1–2 (2019), 3–7, 16–17; "Crisis in the CPUSA: Interview with Charlene Mitchell," Heart of Hope, https://omalley.nelsonmandela.org/index .php/site/q/03lv02424/04lv02730/05lv03005/06lv03006/07lv03075/08lv03082.htm; Murrell, *"Most Dangerous Communist,"* 324–328; Aptheker, *Intimate Politics*, 406.

74. Rosenberg, "From Crisis to Split," 28; Jaiveer Kohli, "The Last American Communists: The Story of the Fall of the Communist Party," The Journalist as Historian, May 22, 2019, http://www.journalist-historian.com/?p=501.

75. Gus Hall, "Developments in the Socialist Countries," *People's Daily World*, February 7, 1990, 3.

76. "Club Discussion Outline on 'Socialism and Capitalism in a Changing World" [based on Hall's report to the January 1990 National Committee meeting], TAM 657, box 40, Daniel Rubin Papers, Tamiment Library, New York University.

77. Rosenberg, "From Crisis to Split," 35; Beth Slutsky, "American Communism in a Time of Détente," in Vernon Pederson, James G. Ryan, and Katherine A. S. Sibley, eds., *Post-Cold War Revelations and the American Communist Party: Citizens, Revolutionaries, and Spies* (London: Bloomsbury, 2021) 220–226.

78. Taubman, *Gorbachev*, 602–619, 645–647.

79. Rosenberg, "From Crisis to Split," 39.

80. Rosenberg, "From Crisis to Split," 40–41.

81. Michael Riley, "Last of the Red Hot Believers: Gus Hall," *Time*, September 9, 1991, https://content.time.com/time/subscriber/article/0,33009,973782-1,00.html.

82. Alessandra Stanley, "A Lament by America's Top Communist," *New York Times*, August 31, 1991, https://www.nytimes.com/1991/08/31/us/a-lament-by-americas-top -communist.html; Sam Tanenhaus, "Gus Hall, Unreconstructed American Communist of 7 Decades, Dies at 90," *New York Times*, October 17, 2000, https://www.nytimes.com/2000 /10/17/us/gus-hall-unreconstructed-american-communist-of-7-decades-dies-at-90 .html.

83 Max Elbaum, "DeStalinizing the Old Guard," *The Nation*, February 10, 1992, 159.

84. "An Initiative to Unite and Renew the Party," *Crossroads*, January 1992, 5–7.

85. Elbaum, "DeStalinizing the Old Guard," 158; Murrell, *"The Most Dangerous Communist in the United States,"* 336.

86. Elbaum, "DeStalinizing the Old Guard," 159; Rosenberg, "From Crisis to Split," 49–50.

87. Felicity Barringer, "US Communists' Meeting Has Its Own Fractionalism," *New York Times*, December 9, 1991, https://www.nytimes.com/1991/12/09/us/us-communists -meeting-has-its-own-fractionalism.html; Murrell, *"Most Dangerous Communist,"* 330–331.

88. Elbaum, "DeStalinizing the Old Guard," 159.

89. Elbaum, "DeStalinizing the Old Guard," 160; Murrell, *"Most Dangerous Communist,"* 332–333.

90. Murrell, *"Most Dangerous Communist,"* 336.

INDEX

Browder's push to dissolve the Party,
213–216
clandestine operations and espionage,
163–166
CPA cutting ties with, 216–218
effect of the Hungarian Revolution,
266–267
effect on Wallace's presidential
campaign, 245–246
end of the Stalin era, 254–255
espionage activities, 235–236
Moscow trials of 1936-1938, 167–169
Soviet Era of Stagnation, 302–303
Stalin's purges, 166
superpower status of the Soviet Union,
231
Teheran Declaration, 210

vanguard role of the Communist Party,
20, 120, 152–156, 264–265, 294
Vanzetti, Bartolomeo, 72–75,
72(fig.), 127
Vermont resolution, 245–246
Vietnam conflicts, 231, 284, 289
Vital Center, 239
Voorhis, Jerry, 181
Voorhis Act (1940), 181
Vorse, Mary Heaton
"Bread and Roses" strike, 13–14
on the kulaks, 168
textile workers strike, 64, 93
UAW strike, 123, 150–151
Vultee Aircraft plant strike, 185–186

Wagner, Robert F., 108
Wagner Act (1935), 108–109, 142
Wallace, Henry, 206, 238, 241, 243–244
Walter, Francis, 269
Ward, Harry F., 129
Warsaw Pact, 231, 265–266
waterfront workers, 109–112
Watt, George
Germany's invasion of the USSR, 190
military service, 204

questioning the "Five Minutes to
Midnight" line, 257
Spanish Civil War, 161–162
youth movement, 137–138
Weatherman faction, 290
Weisbord, Albert, 63–65, 87, 93–94
Wiggins, Ella May, 90, 92–93
Williams, William Appleman, 6–7
Williamson, John, 205, 208–209, 218–219,
247–248, 247(fig.)
Wills, Gary, 240
Wilson, Woodrow, 19–20, 26–27
Winston, Henry, 247–248, 247(fig.), 252,
284, 304–305
Winter, Carl, 247–248
Wise, Stephen S., 63
Wobblies, 12–13, 28, 73. *See also*
Industrial Workers of the World
women
first-generation Communists, 40
International Unemployment Day
demonstrations, 101
Passaic textile workers strike, 63–65
replacing Communists serving in the
military, 205
women's movement, Hall's lack of
sympathy for, 305–306
Woolworth's sit-in, 279–280, 283
Workers (Communist) Party, 46–47,
59–60, 66–67, 69–71, 94
Workers School, New York, 57
World Tourists travel agency, 98
World War I
drop in SP membership, 19–20
Foster's AFL organizing, 59
international Party disunity, 49–50
segregation of troops, 115
World War II
attack on Pearl Harbor, 194–195
Casablanca, 171–173
CP position, 179–184
German invasion of the USSR, 189–191
German-Soviet Nonaggression Pact,
175–178

Hamilton College

MAURICE ISSERMAN is the Publius Virgilius Rogers Professor of American History at Hamilton College. A former Fulbright visiting professor in Moscow, he is the author of award-winning books on the history of the Left and other topics. His writing has appeared in the *New York Times, Washington Post*, and *Los Angeles Times.* He lives in Clinton, New York.